The Quality of Life

RICHARD KRAUT was educated at the University of Michigan and Princeton University. He has taught in the Philosophy Departments at the University of Illinois at Chicago, and Northwestern University, where he is Charles E. and Emma H. Morrison Professor in the Humanities. His recent books in value theory are *Against Absolute Goodness* (Oxford, 2011) and *What is Good and Why* (Harvard, 2007).

Also published by
OXFORD UNIVERSITY PRESS

Against Absolute Goodness
Richard Kraut

Aristotle: Political Philosophy
Richard Kraut

Reasons and the Good
Roger Crisp

Pleasure and the Good Life
Fred Feldman

Well-Being
Neera Badhwar

The Quality of Life

Aristotle Revised

Richard Kraut

OXFORD
UNIVERSITY PRESS

UNIVERSITY PRESS

Great Clarendon Street, Oxford, OX2 6DP,
United Kingdom

Oxford University Press is a department of the University of Oxford.
It furthers the University's objective of excellence in research, scholarship,
and education by publishing worldwide. Oxford is a registered trade mark of
Oxford University Press in the UK and in certain other countries

Published in the United States of America by Oxford University Press
198 Madison Avenue, New York, NY 10016, United States of America

British Library Cataloguing in Publication Data
Data available

Library of Congress Cataloging in Publication Data
Data available

ISBN 978-0-19-882884-6 (Hbk.)
ISBN 978-0-19-886872-9 (Pbk.)

Links to third party websites are provided by Oxford in good faith and
for information only. Oxford disclaims any responsibility for the materials
contained in any third party website referenced in this work.

To
David Copp, Doug MacLean, Jeff McMahan, and Susan Wolf

Contents

Acknowledgments

I first presented some of the ideas in this book—concerning the experience machine and McTaggart's "oyster-like" existence—at several conferences in 2013. I am grateful to my audiences for giving me encouragement and much to think about. At one of them, organized in Copenhagen by Douglas MacLean and Toni Rønnow-Rasmussen, I benefited enormously not only from my discussion with the other participants but also from the written critique I received from Susan Wolf. I kept revising and enlarging that draft as I received more comments over the years from colleagues and audiences.

In the 2016–17 academic year, I was able to devote myself fully to the issues of well-being, time, virtue, experience, and reality, when I received a year of sabbatical leave, which I spent as a Visiting Fellow of Corpus Christi College, Oxford. I also had the good fortune that year of receiving a fellowship from the Guggenheim Foundation. I am most grateful to these institutions for their support, and to Northwestern University for giving me the opportunity to pursue my research. Throughout the year, Jeff McMahan helped make my stay at Corpus one of the most pleasant and stimulating experiences of my academic career. I am grateful to him not only for that but for the questions he raised about my project at a meeting of the Moral Philosophy Seminar that he ran.

My work took on greater scope, and led me back to Aristotle, as a result of the invitation I received from Stanford University to present the Tanner Lectures on Human Values in April of 2017.[1] I am indebted to Stanford, to Josh Ober, and to many others who helped with the arrangements for that visit. The penetrating and thoughtful comments I received on that occasion—from Rachel Barney, Steve Darwall, Rebecca Newberger Goldstein, and Tom Hurka—led to many improvements. In these and other venues, I profited from the excellent questions, challenges, and suggestions of my audiences. I regret that I have not been able to compile a list of everyone who deserves acknowledgment. Fortunately, I can single out and give my thanks to some of them for invitations, encouragement, and comments: Richard Bett, Gwen Bradford, Bruce Brower, Giuseppe Cumella, Christian Coons, Ursula Coope, Roger Crisp, Carl Genet, Terry Irwin, Dhananjay Jagannathan, Rachana Kamtekar, Antti Kauppinen, David Killoren, Josh Ober, Debra Satz, Chris Shields, Tom Sinclair, Richard Sorabji, Nick Sturgeon, Nandi Theunissen, Ralph Wedgwood, Michael Williams, and Paul Woodruff.

[1] The two lectures I gave were called 'Prospects for a Neo-Aristotelian Ethics.' They will appear in a condensed form in 'Oysters and Experience Machines: Two Puzzles in Value Theory,' *The Tanner Lectures on Human Values*, Vol. 37, forthcoming, 2019. Some key points defended in the present work will also be found there.

The penultimate draft of my manuscript was read by Roger Crisp and an anonymous referee for Oxford University Press. I am grateful to them for their penetrating criticism and friendly advice. Thanks as well to Peter Momtchiloff of Oxford University Press for his encouragement and counsel.

This book is dedicated to four marvelous friends and philosophers, with heartfelt appreciation and admiration.

1

The Oyster and the Experience Machine

Two Puzzles in Value Theory

1. Aristotle, the oyster, and the experience machine

Our topic is "the quality of life"—what it is for a human life to be of *high* quality, a life that is good for the person whose life it is. "Well-being" is another term I will often use to designate our subject. As my subtitle indicates, I will draw on some themes in Aristotle to shed light on this issue. I do not claim that my thoughts agree fully with his. Aristotle is here "revised" in that I allow myself to depart to some degree from what he may have had in mind.

One of my Aristotelian themes is that "goods of the soul" are of far greater value than "goods of the body" and "external goods." A second is that human well-being has a *quantitative* and *temporal* dimension: as he says, one swallow does not make a summer, and similarly we seek the good not just for a while, but over the course of a "complete life."[1] A third is that a good life for a human being is (or can be) an *ethical* life, one devoted to the exercise of such virtues as justice and courage. A fourth is that ethical life is not all there is to human well-being: there are non-ethical activities of the soul that also make human life good (which is not to say that they are *un*ethical). Aristotle, in other words, is a pluralist about human well-being: it is composed of goods of several different kinds. (Good philosophical thinking, in which one activates one's understanding of the nature of the universe, is one such good—in fact, he thinks, the very highest.) But his pluralism has limits: all components of well-being are psychological goods (goods of the soul). Or, as I will put it, they are experiential in nature. They are features of conscious life whose qualitative nature we are aware of through introspection. Pleasure is one such component—here is a fifth Aristotelian theme—but it is only part of a complex array of experiences that make human life good.[2]

---

[1] Some translations have "spring" rather than "summer." Here and throughout, the translation of the *Nicomachean Ethics* I use is that of Roger Crisp.

[2] These doctrines of Aristotle are put forward in the following passages of the *Nicomachean Ethics*: I.8 1098b13–14 (goods of the soul, goods of the body, external goods); I.7 1098a18–19 (a complete life); Books II, IV, V (ethical life); X.7–8 (philosophical contemplation); X.1–5 (pleasure is a good).

Two thought experiments devised by twentieth-century philosophers will also occupy us. One was the invention of the British idealist, J. M. E. McTaggart, in *The Nature of Existence*.[3] He asks us to compare two lives: the first he calls "oyster-like" because it has "very little consciousness and...a very little excess of pleasure over pain"; the second is that of a human being. His striking thesis is that a sufficiently longer oyster-like life is better than any shorter human life, no matter how wonderful the goods in the human life are. Let it be full of knowledge, virtue, love, pleasure, and whatever else makes for a good human life. McTaggart holds that the oyster-like creature would more than compensate for the hour-by-hour poverty of its simple life by the greater quantity of time during which it possessed the simple, faint pleasures it enjoys—so long as its greater longevity is great enough.[4]

The germ of the idea that McTaggart is working with goes back to Plato's *Symposium*, where *erôs* is treated as a desire to have the good *forever* (205a, 206a).[5] (How odd it would be to want the good for only a month but no longer. Recognizing that, we then see that the same oddity attaches to any finite duration. That, I assume, is Plato's tacit argument.) McTaggart takes Plato's idea and turns it against him by positing a wonderful human life of a great but finite duration—he suggests one million years—and then setting against it the yet longer life of a simple "oyster-like" creature.[6] At some point or other, well beyond one million years, that creature will have had more value in its existence than the human being. In fact, McTaggart adds, at some later point, it will have had a life *one million* times better than that of a human being!

I will keep his example closer to our familiar world by assuming instead that the marvelous human life is about eighty-five or ninety years long, not a million. I will refer to the other creature in this comparison as "McTaggart's oyster" (not just oyster-like). To simplify matters further, I will assume that this oyster feels no pain and only the mildest of pleasures as it takes in nourishment. The term "McTaggart's thesis" will refer

---

[3] Volume 2, book 7, chapter 7, sections 868–70, pages 452–3.

[4] McTaggart writes: "The value of states in time vary, *caeteris paribus*, with the time they occupy. From this principle it follows that any value, which has only a finite intensity, and which only lasts a finite time, may be surpassed by a value of much less intensity which lasts for a longer time." (This is cited by Larry S. Temkin, *Rethinking the Good*, 119, where I first encountered it.) Roger Crisp has also used a comparison between long-lasting, oyster-like, simple pleasures and human life in his discussion of hedonism. See his *Routledge Philosophy Guidebook to Mill on Utilitarianism*, 24, 28, 31; also his encyclopedia entry, 'Well-Being'; and his 'Hedonism Reconsidered,' 619–45.

[5] Another relevant dialogue is the *Philebus*: at one point, Socrates asks us to consider someone who feels much lifelong pleasure but lacks any form of thought. He would "not live a human life but the life of a mollusk (*pleumôn*) or of one of those creatures in shells that live in the sea" (21c–d, translated by Dorothea Frede). (Unless noted otherwise, translations of Plato are found in *Plato Complete Works*, edited by John M. Cooper.) An alternative translation is "oyster." Another simple form of marine life—the jellyfish—is also of interest here: it might be said (depending on one's metaphysics) to have achieved immortality. At any rate, when a member of one species of jellyfish—the Turritopsis dohrnii—"dies," its cells reassemble within five days. See Lisa-ann Gershwin, *Stung! On Jellyfish Blooms and the Future of the Ocean*, 91–2.

[6] See the preceding footnote. I conjecture that McTaggart has that passage of the *Philebus* in mind when he speaks of an "oyster-like" life. He accepts Plato's assumption that the longer one has a good the better off one is, and uses it to undermine Plato's further assumption that the best human life of normal length is far superior to that of any oyster.

to the claim that this oyster eventually has more well-being than even the best of human lives of normal length.[7]

Our second thought experiment was devised by Robert Nozick.[8] He asks us to imagine an "experience machine"—a device that induces in a detached brain any illusory experience that the subject chooses.[9] The principal claim of Nozick's remarkably brief (only four paragraphs long) discussion of this device is that we would not (and *should not*) choose to live in such a machine, whatever its surface or initial attractions. Inside the machine we would be merely passive consumers of experience, cut off from the real world. It is better for us to *live* our lives—something no machine can do for us—and to be in contact with a reality beyond our own brains.[10]

Nozick's thought experiment confronts us with a trade-off: we have at least some initial attraction to the prospect of entering the experience machine (we can have any kind of life we want!), but at the same time we naturally recoil because of our radical severance, inside the machine, from our bodies, immediate surroundings, and all of social and physical reality. If Nozick is right, the trade-off is not worth it—it is not even

---

[7] The comparison I make here and throughout between the best life of a human being and that of McTaggart's oyster presupposes that such inter-species comparisons are meaningful. That assumption can be challenged: it might be thought that although we can make sense of such sentences as "human being A is better off than human being B," such sentences as "human being A is better off than oyster B" have no meaning. Human well-being, according to this line of thought, can be neither greater than, less than, nor equal to the well-being of any other type of species. A human being might have an oyster-like life, and such an individual would be worse off than many other humans; but an actual oyster cannot be worse off than a human being. This strikes me as an implausible doctrine. If a human being living an oyster-like existence has a lower quality of life than many fellow humans, because the only good he enjoys is no better than one any oyster has, then surely, for the same reason, an oyster has a lower quality of life than do many human beings. In Keats's 'Ode to a Nightingale,' human anxiety about death is seen as a respect in which the nightingale is better off ("no hungry generations tread thee down"). It is easy for us to grasp Keats's point and even to accept it as true, but whether true or false, his thought has meaningful content.

[8] *Anarchy, State, and Utopia*, 42–5. He returns to this thought experiment in *The Examined Life: Philosophical Meditations*, 104–7. Its influence on the study of well-being has been enormous. Many leading authors accept without hesitation its attack on "mental state" accounts of well-being. See, for example, Griffin, *Well-Being*, 9; Neera K. Badhwar, *Well-Being*, index s.v. *experience machine*; and Thomas Hurka, *The Best Things in Life*, index s.v. *experience machine*. There are important dissenting voices, however. Hedonism is defended against Nozick's critique by Fred Feldman, 'What We Learn from the Experience Machine'; and Roger Crisp, 'Hedonism Reconsidered'. For a full defense of hedonism, see Fred Feldman, *Pleasure and the Good Life*.

[9] Nozick does not himself specify that the brain that is manipulated by the experience machine is detached from the body. For now, this is a detail that can be set aside. In this chapter and the next, I will make no use of my description of the brain of someone in the experience machine as "detached." But I will explain in Chapter 3 (section 5) why it is best to carry out Nozick's thought experiment in this way.

[10] *Anarchy, State, and Utopia* is of course a treatise on political philosophy, so it might be wondered what contribution, if any, the experience machine makes to the work's political theory. One possible answer is this: "…the lesson we are supposed to draw from Nozick's Experience Machine parable…is that most of us want to *accomplish* something, not just *experience* something. Nozick might have complained that Rawls's original position is, in a way, an 'experience machine,' because it suggests the following: It does not matter what we accomplish before arriving at the table to choose principles of justice.…In essence, we choose principles that respect our separateness as consumers." Thus David Schmidtz and Christopher Freiman, 'Nozick,' in David Estlund (ed.), *The Oxford Handbook of Political Philosophy*, 416.

a close call. Life outside the machine, in favorable circumstances, is much, much better than life inside it ever could be.

It may seem odd to bring Aristotle together with these two episodes in twentieth-century value theory. What have they to do with each other? My reply is this: If we reject McTaggart's thesis, we must say what assumption leads him astray, or what he fails to recognize. My diagnosis is that he fails to apply to his thought experiment the idea that a sufficient supply of peculiarly human goods is superior to any amount of the lower goods available to the oyster. That goods belong to different orders of value (and are in that sense "incommensurable") is a thesis that fits comfortably within Aristotle's framework (as well as that of Plato and the Stoics). He would say that a good that resides in the rational soul—the conscious emotional and intelligent activities of a human being—belongs to a higher order than the good of the pleasurable nourishment available to an oyster. He assumes that to give a convincing account of where the value of ethical virtue lies, one must depict the inner life of a good person—what it is about such a person's thoughts, feelings, aspirations, pleasures, memories, and so on that makes that individual's life appealing. He might therefore accept what I will call an "experientialist conception of well-being" ("experientialism," for short). But whether he would accept that doctrine or not, the more important point is that he would be right to do so—or so I will argue. That is why I discuss Nozick's experience machine. He takes it to reveal that much matters to us beyond "how our lives feel from the inside," as he puts it.[11] And he has convinced many that he is right.

Experientialism, as I define it, holds that: (A) well-being is composed of many goods; (B) all of them are experiential; but (C) pleasure is only one element of good experience.[12] Those are some of my Aristotelian themes. McTaggart seeks to show that (C) leads inexorably to an astounding conclusion (when we make common assumptions about well-being and time). Nozick seeks to show that there is a deep error lurking in (B).[13]

Well-being has an opposite, and although English lacks a common expression for it, "ill-being" would be apt. It is not the absence from one's life of the good things that

---

[11] *Anarchy, State, and Utopia*, 43.

[12] I will use "good experience" to refer to experiences that are good for someone to have (that is, good for the individual having those experiences). They are good as experiences because of that feature. I do not mean that they are experiences that have the property of goodness. For reasons against interpreting "good experience" in that way, see my *Against Absolute Goodness*.

[13] This definition will be refined in Chapter 3, section 1, where we will distinguish a strong and a weak form of experientialism. The compositional nature of well-being is explained below in section 4. Notice that Henry Sidgwick is in partial agreement with experientialism as I define it. He holds that well-being consists entirely in experiential states: "...if a certain quality of human Life is that which is ultimately desirable, it must belong to human Life regarded on its psychical side, or briefly, Consciousness." See *The Methods of Ethics*, 396. He accepts both parts of this conditional, as I do. But he rejects two parts of my definition of experientialism: for him, well-being consists in just one good, namely, pleasure. I believe that he has a faulty conception of what pleasure is, and that when it is replaced by a better account, we see that it has less value than he supposes. Those differences between us are important, but so too is the thesis about which we agree—that the elements of well-being "belong to human Life regarded on its psychical side." I will discuss his conception of pleasure in section 8 below.

make up well-being; rather, it is the possession of bad things—to such an extent that on balance one's life is bad for one. Expanding on the above definition of experientialism, we can say that ill-being is composed of many bad things, that all of them are experiential and that pain is only one of them. For a life to be bad is for it to be filled with suffering. (I return to this idea below in section 8.)

If McTaggart is right, the acceptance of (C)—not the hedonist's bold claim that pleasure is the only good, but merely that it is one good among others—suffices to show that there is far less value in human life than we thought, if we also suppose that well-being increases over time. (That assumption does seem reasonable: it is better for a constituent of well-being to last a longer time than a shorter time.) Attached as we are to the full range of human experiences, we should trade them away for a simple pleasure that is sufficiently long-lasting.

I expect that many readers will agree with me that McTaggart can arrive at his conclusion only by making some assumption that can reasonably be rejected. But which assumption? It will be salutary to explore several ways of resisting him. The relationship between well-being and time, we will see, is filled with intriguing philosophical puzzles.

If Nozick is right, (B) misses something that matters deeply to us, even if we tend to overlook it: either there are non-experiential components of well-being, or the value of good experiences greatly diminishes, perhaps disappearing altogether, if they do not bring us into contact with the reality that lies behind those experiences. Two lives might feel exactly the same "from the inside," but if one of them is lived inside the experience machine and the other outside it, that creates a vast difference in their value. Nozick's thought experiment downgrades the value not only of pleasure but experience in general. It is meant to bring out the importance of living in the real world, having a correct conception of reality and one's place in it—facts about oneself that are not a matter of the quality of one's consciousness.

I am sure that many of my readers will come to this book already convinced that Nozick is right. Philosophers often cite his thought experiment as having settled the matter.[14] I hope to change their minds, but failing that, I would like to show that something very close to experientialism is true: even if some components of well-being are non-experiential, they are of far less value than the ones that are. That claim will be made more precise as we proceed. (I return to it in section 6 below.)

Throughout our examination of the experience machine, we must remember that it can serve its intended purpose only if the many kinds of experiences available to us in the real world are no less available, without detectable differences, within the machine. If we decide, upon reflection, that we should not plug into it because there is a sphere of experiential life that no manipulation of the brain by a neuroscientist could simulate,

---

[14] Katarzyna De Lazari-Radek and Peter Singer write: "Many philosophers consider the experience machine thought experiment a knock-down objection to hedonism. (Dan Weijers gives 'just a sample' of authors who have stated or implied this, and then lists 28 references.)" See *The Point of View of the Universe*, 254. The essay they refer to is 'Nozick's Experience Machine is Dead, Long Live the Experience Machine!'

the thought experiment would lose its power to demonstrate the limited value of experience. It would instead reveal how important experience is, in that it serves as our basis for deciding whether to enter the machine.

One question we will need to explore is whether the experience machine deserves as much attention as it has received. It is, after all, a piece of science fiction. Fanciful thought experiments, as a general rule, have less evidential force than examples drawn from common occurrences with which we are familiar. Could we not more easily recognize the limited place of experience in the quality of life by means of examples that draw on everyday cases? One standard objection to the thesis that only what is experienced has value alleges that if your friends betray you behind your back, that by itself is bad for you—even if you forever remain unaware of their betrayal and it has no bad consequences for you.[15] A second standard objection is that we can be benefited or harmed posthumously. I will not neglect these sorts of objections to experientialism. But I will also argue that the experience machine is full of philosophical interest, and has much to teach us about the quality of life.

We will encounter, in our discussion of well-being and time, yet another problem for experientialism: some philosophers hold that the upward or downward direction of well-being over a life partly constitutes its overall quality, even apart from its psychological effect. Of two lives that have identical experiences but in a different order, it is better for their quality to ascend steadily than decline steadily. As it were, a whole life gets "extra points" when and just because its phases keep getting better.

These, then, will be our Aristotelian themes: well-being (the quality of life) and its relationship to conscious experience, ethical virtue, and time. I believe that experientialism and the doctrine of higher goods found in ancient ethics captures a deep insight about how we should live our lives. It is expressed somewhat misleadingly by Goethe's Faust, in dialogue with Helen of Troy, when they say that we must learn from the ancient thinkers to live fully in our present consciousness of the world—"only the present is our happiness."[16] We can arrive at a greater appreciation of what to value by seeing that our well-being, the quality of our lives, lies entirely in what is here before us, in our appreciative attentiveness to conscious experience—if we develop our natural powers so that they give us experiences of the highest order.

2. Plato, Aristotle, and the value of virtue

In Plato's *Republic*, Adeimantus challenges Socrates to set aside the extrinsic rewards of justice, and to focus entirely on the effect it has on the just person's soul. He wants an

---

[15] See Thomas Nagel, 'Death', in *Mortal Questions*, 4.

[16] Johann Wolfgang Goethe, *Faust*, Part II, Act Three, lines 9382–3. More fully: "Faust: Nun schaut der Geist nicht vorwärts nicht zuruck, / Die Gegenwart allein— / Helena: Ist unser Glück." Goethe's endorsement of this sentiment is the subject of Pierre Hadot, "'Only the Present is Our Happiness': The Value of the Present Instant in Goethe and in Ancient Philosophy', in *Philosophy As A Way of Life*, edited with an introduction by Arnold I. Davidson, 217–37. See esp. 217. We will return to and expand on this idea in Chapter 4, sections 15 and 16.

account of what justice "does itself, through its own power, by its presence in the soul of the person who possesses it, even if it remains hidden from gods and humans" (366e). Several lines later, he adds: "Do not merely demonstrate to us by argument (*logos*) that justice is stronger than injustice, but tell us what each one itself does, because of itself, to someone who possesses it, that makes the one bad and the other good" (367b; cf. 367e).[17]

It might at first strike us as puzzling that Adeimantus is asking for something that is not *just* an *argument*, but here is a way to understand what he is seeking. A just person has a certain kind of inner life, something he is acquainted with "from the inside," even when it cannot be detected by outside observers. Socrates is being asked to give a description of what that inner life is. For him to succeed, we must have some idea of what he is talking about. The effect justice has on the soul ought to be recognizable to us because we ourselves have had some experience of it, however intermittently and faintly. A defense of justice that bypassed this depiction of the conscious life of a just person would not be fully convincing to us; it would be mere argument, because it would not be grounded in anything inside ourselves with which we are familiar.

What is most important for my purposes here is not fidelity to Plato's exact meaning, but the idea (whether Plato has it or not) that there is such a thing as *what it is like* to be a good person. The phrase "what it is like" acquired wide circulation in philosophical circles because of Thomas Nagel's classic essay, 'What is it like to be a bat?' which emphasized that some states of mind have a phenomenological quality, something we can become directly acquainted with only through introspection.[18] Forms of experience quite alien to ours must therefore elude our grasp, Nagel argued. It may or may not be anachronistic to read Plato as seeking a phenomenological depiction of the mind of a good person, but in any case, I hope to show that this is a project worth pursuing.

It is a project conspicuously absent from much twentieth-century and recent moral philosophy. W. D. Ross, for example, argues for the goodness of virtue by asserting that when we compare two worlds containing equal amounts of pleasure, but differing in that one contains virtuous people and the other contains people who are not virtuous, we see that the world of virtue and pleasure is better than the world of mere pleasure.[19] Plato's question, "Is justice good not only for others but for the individual who is just?" is thus bypassed. A phenomenologically detailed depiction of the inner life of a virtuous person is of no interest to Ross, presumably because he thinks it has no place in moral philosophy. Plato, he assumes, does not explain why we ought to be virtuous by calling our attention to the inner life of the virtuous person. Evading Plato's question in

---

[17] Here and throughout, translations of the *Republic* are those of C. D. C. Reeve.

[18] Reprinted in *Mortal Questions*, 165–80.

[19] *The Right and the Good*, 134–5. An approach similar to Ross's in this respect is defended in Thomas Hurka, *Virtue, Vice, and Value*. For the reaction to Plato and Aristotle of British moral philosophers near the beginning of the twentieth century, see Hurka, *British Ethical Theorists from Sidgwick to Ewing*, 259–67.

this way is, I believe, a mistake. It is the evasion of a legitimate question that deserves our attention. (I return to this issue in Chapter 2, sections 7–9.)

A further historical question concerns *Aristotle's* conception of a human well-being. In one intriguing passage (*NE* I.5 1095b31–1096a1, reaffirmed at I.8 1098b33–1099a2), he takes up and rejects the suggestion that the ultimate end of human life consists in *virtue*. That cannot be right, he says, as we can see by recognizing that a virtuous person might be asleep for the whole duration of his life.[20] Someone in this condition, Aristotle claims, would not be entirely enviable; he would not possess the highest good of human life, for he would not be *active*. So, he concludes, it is more plausible to say that the ultimate end consists not in virtue but in virtuous *activity*.

It sounds like a good point, but exactly what is the idea? I suspect that many of us tacitly read into Aristotle's words the obvious point that sleep contains little in the way of conscious experience—only the brief periods during which one dreams. For the most part, there is nothing it is like to be asleep; and so a virtuous person who slept away his life would have little in the way of conscious experience. How could that possibly be a good life?[21]

This is not a point that Aristotle makes in so many words—in fact, it might be a way of reading him that distorts his thinking.[22] But if we become more cautious about how we read the passage, and take him simply to be saying that a good life must to a large extent be active—whether or not there is an experiential component to it—his claim becomes more difficult to assess and less obvious than we had at first taken it to be. When we deliberately activate our psychological skills and powers, we are aware that we are doing so, and so the prudential value of activating them may derive from the conscious experiences that are thereby brought about.[23] Set aside the phenomenology,

---

[20] The passage I am referring to does not say exactly this. It reads: "But even virtue, in itself, seems to be lacking something, since apparently one can possess virtue even when one is asleep or inactive throughout one's life" (1095b31–1096a1). Here "throughout one's life" is attached to "inactive," but does it apply as well to "asleep"? I am assuming, for my own philosophical purposes, that it does, whether or not this is exegetically defensible. Further, I am imagining a virtuous person who falls asleep and remains asleep for the remainder of his life, and assuming this to form a large portion of his adult years, not a brief sleep before death.

[21] The Socrates of Plato's *Apology* may seem to disagree. He argues that death cannot be bad for us, as we can see when we realize that our best moments are nights of dreamless sleep. But, tellingly, he describes such nights as pleasant (40c–d). Apparently he assumes that one is aware of that pleasure as one sleeps. Diogenes Laertius says that Epimenides was held to be blessed by the gods because he took a nap that lasted fifty-seven years. See *Lives of Eminent Philosophers* I.10 109–10. I am grateful to Rachel Barney for this reference.

[22] One point to keep in mind is that Aristotle believes that all living things—including plants—have a soul (the "nutritive" soul). So, his category of ensouled things does not coincide with our category of creatures that have psychological properties. It is the Stoics who first put together human beings and animals in one category (all such creatures represent the world by means of *phantasiai*), and plants in another (none of them do so). See Victor Caston, *The Stoics on Content and Mental Representation*. Nonetheless, Aristotle holds that the proper functioning of our nutritive soul is no part of *eudaimonia* (*NE* I.7 1097b33–1098a1). That self-awareness plays a role in his conception of human well-being is perhaps most evident in his discussion of the value of friendship (*NE* X.9 1170a29–b14).

[23] I use "prudential value" as one of several phrases that express the concept of well-being. It appears throughout James Griffin, *Well-Being* (see the index s.v. *value, prudential*). It is similarly found throughout L. W. Sumner, *Welfare, Happiness, and Ethics* (see the index s.v. *prudential value*).

and it is less clear whether and why a portion of someone's life is made better by its being active rather than passive. It is no doubt better for *other* people, when someone is not only a good person but also treats them as a good person ought to; but why is it better *for him*, simply in virtue of his movement from having an excellent quality of mind to his exercising that quality, setting aside what he experiences when he acts?

Our mental powers can move from dormancy to activity even while we sleep. We sometimes become aware of this because upon wakening we have ready to hand an answer to a question that we struggled with but could not answer the evening before. Now, if the mind is active during sleep and makes cognitive progress without our being conscious of its doing so at the time, then it does not matter whether we retrieve the results when we are awake—the mental processing has occurred even if we never have access to it during our waking hours. A talented mathematician might solve problems in her sleep but the further mental processing needed to make her aware of her progress might not occur. Is it good for her that her mind is active in this way? If there were a drug that frees the mind to solve problems in this inaccessible way, should she pay even a low price for it? I would not. When mental activity is so completely walled off from consciousness, it has by itself no prudential value. If the mind of one mathematician finds a genuine proof of a theorem in her sleep, and a second mathematician unconsciously goes through a train of thinking that is flawed and therefore not a genuine proof, that difference does not make for a difference in the quality of their lives, if there is no effect in either case on their conscious experiences. The standard of success in logic and mathematics lies outside the mind, but the prudential value of being a logician or mathematician resides in the rich experience of intellectual exploration.[24]

These brief encounters with Plato and Aristotle (and this further thought experiment) suggest to me that we ought to regard with skepticism any attempt to show that it is non-instrumentally good for someone to be a good human being that ignores the question what it is *like* to be a good human being—what the life of a good person feels like from the inside.

Here is one such argument, based loosely on Aristotle's practice of moving from claims about craft-skills to analogous points about ethical virtue. It begins by asking such questions as these: "What constitutes the good of a cook?" "What constitutes the good of a sculptor?" "What constitutes the good of a doctor?" These are not questions about the equipment or resources it would be good for someone to have in order to *become* a cook or sculptor or doctor. Rather, they ask: "Insofar as someone is a cook (sculptor, doctor), what is good for him? What, in other words, does being beneficial for a cook (sculptor, doctor) consist in?" Once we understand how these questions are to be understood, it is tempting to reply that what is good *for* anyone occupying these

---

[24] Here I depart from F. M. Kamm, who is persuaded by Nozick's thought experiment and therefore writes: "We are harmed if our inner life has all the qualities of someone who is being loved, or someone who is proving a theory, but in fact, we are not really being loved or proving a theory." See *Morality, Mortality*, vol. 1, 17. I will discuss the phenomenon of feeling but not being loved in Chapter 3, section 20.

roles is to be good *at* them. At bottom, what is good for a cook (sculptor or doctor) is to cook (sculpt, doctor) well—and so the things that are *instrumentally* good for a cook are the ones that help him perform as an excellent cook.

Once these points are taken on board, the next step is to infer, by induction, that the things in which prudential value consists are *always* perfectionist values. That is, the things that count as non-instrumental benefits for something of a certain kind are the ones that make it good of its kind. Accordingly, when we ask, not what is non-instrumentally good for a cook (sculptor, doctor), but what is non-instrumentally good for *a human being*, the answer must be: having and exercising the qualities that make one a good human being.

My reaction to this argument is that it is too abstract—too removed from human experience—to be fully convincing. Arguments from analogy are inherently vulnerable to the objection that a string of similarities is compatible with the presence of dissimilarities as well. So, even if being a good person may in some ways be like possessing and exercising craft-skills, it could also be, in other ways, unlike them. What makes something non-instrumentally beneficial for someone insofar as he is a cook is not its place within the cook's conscious mental life, but its contribution to his success with respect to the standards of his vocation—his success in creating a product that meets legitimate social expectations. By contrast, the quality of life that a human being has (how good a life it is *for him*) is at least partially constituted by its experiential component. That is why, if you have said nothing about what a human being's life is like phenomenologically, you cannot draw any firm, all-things-considered conclusion about how good a life it is for him.

The analogical argument just rehearsed, which bears some similarities to Aristotle's "function argument" in the *Nicomachean Ethics* Book I, chapter 7, has precisely this limitation. Little wonder, then, that few (if any) contemporary students of his work are convinced by it. He seems to say little or nothing, in this well-known passage, to satisfy the demand that Adeimantus makes of Socrates: "Do not merely demonstrate to us by argument that justice is stronger than injustice, but tell us what each one itself does, because of itself, to someone who possesses it, that makes the one of them bad and the other good." Of course, *later* in the *Ethics*, Aristotle does have much to say about the inner life of a good human being. But if the function argument is construed as a self-contained proof that virtuous activity is beneficial to the virtuous agent, it is unpersuasive.

Aristotle, as I read him, accepts this point. Like Adeimantus and Socrates in the *Republic*, he holds that arguments or theories about how we should live our lives must not only be acceptable to rational appraisal but must pass a further test. They must in some way register with the way things seem to us as we live our lives—as we might put it, their truth must correspond to our experience of life. That is what I believe he is getting at when he says, near the end of the *Ethics*, that "the truth in practical issues is judged from the facts (*erga*) of our life.... We must therefore examine what has been said in the light of the facts of our life, and if it agrees with the facts, then we should accept it, while if it conflicts, we must assume it to be no more than theory" (X.8 1179a17–22).[25] Just as a theory about how physical objects move should be abandoned, even if it seems rationally cogent, if it is contradicted by what our eyes plainly and regularly tell us, so a theory about practical matters must face what I would call an "experiential" test. If, for example, a Stoic philosopher claims that pain is not bad for us, our introspective sense of what pain is like gives us good reason to believe that something has gone wrong with the arguments used to arrive at this conclusion. Similarly, if a philosophical theory purports to show that ethically virtuous activity is a great good, we should ask ourselves, before we fully accept that theory: does this harmonize with "the facts of our life"? If we think we know something about what it is like to be a good person "from the inside," that introspective awareness can be used to confirm or disconfirm what philosophy tells us.[26]

3. Rational egoism rejected

My framework for thinking about the quality of human life is Aristotelian in many ways, but it is important to emphasize from the start one respect in which I depart from him. In his discussion of friendship, he asks whether one should love oneself more than one loves others, and replies that one should—but only if one's self-love is the sort that is expressed in virtuous activities of great value to others. In defense of his answer, he says:

It is true also of the good person that he does a great deal for his friends and his country, and will die for them if he must; he will sacrifice money, honours, and in general the things for which people compete, procuring for himself what is noble (*kalon*). He would prefer a short period of intense pleasure to a long period of mild pleasure, a year of living nobly to many indifferent years, and a single noble and great action to many trivial ones. Presumably, this is what happens with those who die for others; it is indeed a great and noble thing that they choose for themselves. They will also sacrifice money on the condition that their friends gain more; while the friend gets money, he gets what is noble, and therefore assigns himself the greater good.... In all praiseworthy actions, then, the good person is seen to assign himself the larger share of what is noble.   (IX.8 1169a18–1169b1)

---

[25] See too *NE* IX.8 1168a35 and X.1 1172a35. For discussion, see my 'Aristotle's Method of Ethics,' 90–1; and my comments in *Aristotle Politics Books VII and VIII*, 54–5. I take Aristotle to be presupposing this methodology when he says of a virtuous person who experiences agonizing pain and suffering: "no one would call a person living this kind of life happy, unless he were closely defending a thesis" (I.5 1095b33–1096a2). This is what we would call "defending a thesis at all costs" or "biting the bullet."

[26] The kind of Aristotelianism I favor is, in this respect, rather different from the one advocated by Michael Thompson, insofar as his theory is silent about the quality of the introspectable and experiential life of a good human being. For Thompson, judgments of value are ultimately grounded in generalizations (dubbed "Aristotelian categoricals") such as "the yellow finch breeds in spring." A defect in a human being, like any deficiency in an animal's or plant's life, counts as a defect because it is a departure from the norm embodied in general "natural-historical" truths. See *Life and Action*, esp. 64–5 and 80–2.

I take this to mean that, all things considered, the virtuous person never sacrifices his well-being to any extent. He is prepared to make sacrifices of a certain sort for others—transferring to them some property or money or other resources, so that he has less of these things than he had before. But on balance he gains more than he loses, because he has done the virtuous, noble thing—and that brings him a benefit that more than compensates for his losses.

This entails that a virtuous person can and should adopt the following policy: "I will never do anything for others that makes me the slightest bit worse off, on balance, than I would otherwise be." That strikes me as a deeply problematic thesis. It is certainly far removed from our common sense conception of what an ethically virtuous person is like. If you were introduced to someone who told you that he has this policy of no self-sacrifice, you would certainly not seek him out as a friend or a colleague. You would think that such a person could not be a good parent.

A defender of Aristotle on this score might remind us that this policy of no self-sacrifice is quite different from the mundane egoism that common sense rightly condemns. The Aristotelian agent, unlike the ordinary egoist, can be relied upon always to give to others whatever a good person ought to give, because his pursuit of well-being calls upon him to do so. How then can there be any complaint about him?

But there is a fatal defect in this way of defending Aristotle: yes, such an agent can be counted on to treat others well, but he does so for the wrong reason. His *ultimate* goal is no one's well-being but his own. His relationship to others is always mediated and indirect: it takes a route through his conception of what makes his life go well, and arrives at service to them only because such service is what he takes *his* well-being to consist in.

My complaint is not that the Aristotelian agent fails to care about others "for their sake." Aristotle makes it abundantly clear in his discussion of friendship that we *are* to love others in this way. But since he is committed to the doctrine of no self-sacrifice, the love of others that he sanctions comes with a condition: giving up certain goods for them is justified only on condition that one is on balance better off for having done so. Aristotle offers no reason for imposing that condition on the policy of acting for the sake of others. Against him, we can say that if it should ever happen that a *small* sacrifice in one's well-being would lead to *great* improvements in the quality of life of other people dear to one, it should be accepted. It is part of many people's conception of moral virtue that one ought to make sacrifices of this sort, and Aristotle offers no reason to think that this common conception is in error.

There is nothing inherently defective about being motivated by self-love. In many circumstances reasons of self-interest stand on their own as sufficient and decisive reasons to act. They do not have force only on condition that by doing what is in one's interest one achieves some further goal. "Why should I care about myself?" is not a question to which we need an answer, if self-regard is to be warranted. But once we see that reasons of self-interest can have this "rock bottom" character, we should recognize as well that in certain circumstances reasons that advert to someone else's interests can also stand on their own as sufficient and decisive reasons to act. The fact that someone is not you does not by itself make it impossible that facts about that individual (for example, his well-being) by themselves give you reason to care about him and act for his sake. Suppose someone is your friend, has always treated you well, and is in great need of your assistance; you could easily help him at little cost to yourself. In these circumstances, the fact that he is not you does not undermine or even weaken the case that you ought to help him. You do not need to find some self-interested reason for coming to his aid, without which the case for helping him collapses.[27]

For all that, we should recognize a kernel of insight in the passage we have been discussing. What Aristotle says here can be scaled back so that we recognize in it a familiar and plausible idea—namely, that sacrifices in one kind of good may bring with them gains in some other kind. That often happens when one accepts rewarding but burdensome responsibilities. Being a good parent or friend, for example, requires a willingness to make sacrifices, sometimes large ones, for one's child or one's companion. But there are at the same time certain goods that one acquires by taking on and playing these roles; something is gained as well as lost. An altruist who failed to recognize that one can benefit to some extent even while making sacrifices—benefit not at some later time, but because being the kind of person who is devoted in this way to others is by itself a great good—would be seriously defective. He would be ignoring some of the reasons he has for serving others, and underestimating the value of what he does. I will elaborate on these ideas in Chapter 2, section 7. And we will then see (Chapter 2, section 8) that Aristotle's doctrine of no-sacrifice, though false, is not as distant from the truth as it now appears.

We should also recognize some ways in which self-concern rightly plays a greater role in our practical thinking than do altruistic reasons. Without knowing anything about you, I can name one person whose well-being you should care about: yourself. I cannot say that you should care about your children—you may have none. Similarly,

---

[27] For a defense of Aristotle against this criticism, see Julia Annas, 'Virtue Ethics and the Charge of Egoism,' in Paul Bloomfield (ed.), *Morality and Self Interest*, 205–21. She is responding to Thomas Hurka, *Virtue, Vice and Value*, 234–43. I have no quarrel with her when she formulates her defense of Aristotle as follows: "The formal point, that I am aiming at my flourishing, just comes down to the point that I am trying to live my life virtuously. If you point out that I am doing this as *my* way of flourishing not yours, the retort is that I am trying to be virtuous in living *my* life, not yours, because my life is the only life I can live" (220). But this "formal point" is weaker than the one she calls "eudaimonism, the kind of theory in which the agent's flourishing is *basic*" (213, my emphasis). Eudaimonism, so defined, holds that *only* one's own well-being is basic: the well-being of others has no independent value; I have reason to care about them only if my well-being justifies doing so. Annas acknowledges this, when she says: "what ethically justifies what I do, and the way I am, is my own good, where that is distinct from, and potentially in conflict with, the good of others" (205). Here my own good alone is "what ethically justifies what I do." Even if (as Annas holds) "... my flourishing will be constituted by my virtuous activity, which is focused on others as much as on myself" (214), I have no reason, according to this theory, to care about their well-being except insofar as this benefits me. Hurka returns to these issues in 'Aristotle on Virtue: Wrong, Wrong, and Wrong,' in Julia Peters (ed.), *Aristotelian Ethics in Contemporary Perspective*. For a non-egocentric interpretation of Aristotle's conception of friendship, see Jennifer Whiting, 'Impersonal Friends,' in *First, Second, and Other Selves: Essays on Friendship and Personal Identity*.

you may have no friends. Your parents and the rest of your family may have died long ago. Admittedly, depending on your circumstances, it could be the case that there are other people you should care more about than yourself, and you might be morally required to make great sacrifices for them. But that would not make it the case that you should have no degree of self-concern for your own sake. You should take good care of yourself in order to be an effective servant of others, but not only for that reason.

A utilitarian might say that you should care about everyone who exists, no matter who they are, whatever their circumstances, and *that* is why you should care about yourself. But although it is true that anyone might, in the right circumstances, *become* a proper object of your concern, it is implausible to suppose that each of us ought *actually* to care for the good of every other human being. No one could meet that demand. And no one needs the help of every other human being.

A second difference between the force of self-interest and of other-regarding considerations emerges when we remind ourselves that, according to common sense morality, individuals may refrain from helping others when doing so would require too great a sacrifice. Suppose two strangers are in great danger, and unless I help them, each will lose an arm.[28] I am nearby and can save them, but to do so, I must lose an arm. A certain kind of utilitarian will say that I must make this sacrifice, because that is the least bad outcome, impersonally considered. But this is a departure from the widely held assumption that I am not required to suffer so great a loss to serve these others. It is not as though my arm has more value than two arms of others, or my well-being makes a greater contribution to the amount of good in the universe than does the well-being of others. Even so, I am permitted to protect the well-being of a certain individual in that situation, even at the cost of the well-being of two others, because that individual is me. In these sorts of circumstances, we rightly give individuals leeway to protect their well-being and to refrain from helping others. (If the good I would have to sacrifice, in order to help others, is very far in my future, its temporal distance from the present does not by itself lessen its weight. I will address this issue in Chapter 4.)

4. Well-being and the quality of life

It is a truism that lives differ not only quantitatively but qualitatively—not only in how many years they contain but in how good those years are for those who live through them. We want our lives to be high in quality, and we want this not only for ourselves but also for others we care about—but what precisely is such a life?

Before we try to answer that question, it will be useful to take note of several other phrases that can be used to pose it. As I noted in section 1, "well-being" is another term often used to designate our subject. But it sounds stilted to say: "he has well-being." A better way to express the same idea is to say: "his life is going well for him," or "he is

---

[28] This sort of example is used often by Derek Parfit. See, for example, *On What Matters*, vol. 1, 139–40; and *On What Matters*, vol. 3, 340.

faring well" or "he has a good life," or "he is well off," or "he is flourishing."[29] Another phrase, one that only recently entered the philosophical lexicon, is "prudential value": for X to be of prudential value is for it to be a component of well-being or to make a causal contribution to attaining or sustaining it.[30] Things that have prudential value are benefits or advantages. They are good for the individual who has them.[31] (They might be called "personal" goods. They do not just make the universe a better place—they make someone better off.) The opposites of these things are spoken of as "harms" or "evils."

There is disagreement, of course, about what well-being is, but it is uncontroversial that a distinction must be drawn between (A) what constitutes well-being and (B) what is a necessary means towards or a pre-condition of well-being. This *kind* of distinction is familiar, and is applicable in all sorts of cases. For example, we distinguish between what a breakfast consists in (cereal, juice, coffee) and the things one needs in order to eat breakfast (spoons, bowls, mugs). There is no such thing as eating breakfast but not eating anything that breakfast consists in. In the same way, well-being must be sought and fostered by seeking and fostering the good or goods in which well-being consists. Rival theories of well-being are competing ways of answering the question: what are its constituents? Of particular interest to us is the doctrine, favored by Aristotle and other philosophers of antiquity, that ethical virtue (or actualizing it) is a major component of well-being, if not its only component. (The Epicureans are here the outliers among Greek and Roman philosophers: for them pleasure is the sole element of well-being; what makes virtue special, they think, is that it is the only secure path to a good life.)

Philosophers sometimes speak of "perfectionist value," as distinct from "prudential value." In plain English, this is the sort of distinction we make by using the terms "good for" and "good at." When one tries to become good at something—playing a musical instrument, tennis, mathematics—one hopes to move at least somewhat closer to the ideal of perfection, or at any rate to perform less badly. The fact that perfectionist and prudential value differ is obvious (once one understands how these

---

[29] These terms are often used interchangeably, but it has been argued that there are two subjects here, not one: (A) what is good for an *individual*, and (B) what is good for an individual's *life*. So argues Shelly Kagan, 'Me and My Life,' 309–24. Someone who is disliked or betrayed without realizing it is not harmed, but his life is worsened, according to this view. I discuss these sorts of examples in Chapter 3, sections 19–20. "The story of a life" will be discussed in Chapter 3, sections 20–1; and Chapter 4, sections 11–13. Yet another proposed bifurcation of well-being into two is based on the distinction between well-being at a time and well-being over time. I discuss that view in Chapter 4, section 11. The possibility that there is no single property designated by ordinary or philosophical discourse about well-being is sympathetically explored in Stephen M. Campbell, 'The Concept of Well-Being,' in Guy Fletcher (ed.), *The Routledge Handbook of Philosophy of Well-Being*, pp. 402–13.

[30] See note 23.

[31] "Welfare" is another term often used to designate well-being or prudential value. It is, for example, the word that L. W. Sumner and Stephen Darwall use in the titles of their important studies (Sumner, *Welfare, Happiness, and Ethics*; Darwall, *Welfare and Rational Care*). Darwall writes: "This book concerns what we variously call a person's good, interest, well-being, or welfare: the good of a person in the sense of what benefits *her*" (his emphasis, 1). He proposes that "what it is for something to be good for someone *just is* for it to be something one should desire for him for his sake, that is, insofar as one cares for him" (his emphasis, 8). I am doubtful about the value of this definition for reasons I will give later (Chapter 3, note 49).

terms are used). "He is good at detective work" says one thing; "detective work is good for him" another. If detective work is extremely stressful, or extremely boring, it might not be a line of work that is good for anyone. But it could still be true of someone that he is good *at* it (he is a good detective)—for this would not entail that such work is good for him.

It might be said: just as a good cook is good at something, and a good mathematician is good at something, so too a good human being is good at something. That is not controversial. Good human beings, when placed in situations that call for moral thinking, are good at recognizing what the right thing to do is. But is it good *for* them to be good at this? The fact that they are good human beings does not by itself settle that question.

Why is it so easy to see that being good at detective work might not be good for the individual who does it? When I offered this example, I said that such work might be stressful or boring. Notice how natural it is to accept the idea that if an activity has bad psychological effects on those who engage in it—effects that cannot but be felt and recognized as bad "from the inside"—then it detracts from their well-being.

This suggests that Plato was looking in the right place when he put into the mouth of Adeimantus the demand that Socrates describe what justice "does itself, through its own power, by its presence in the soul of the person who possesses it." Admittedly, Plato would be open to criticism if we understood his demand in a certain way. We might take him to mean that if you have justice in your soul, then that will inevitably bring about something else in your psyche; and that the value of justice derives from the fact that it produces this further mental condition. For example, he could be saying that if you are unjust, you will feel a great deal of stress (just as detective work might have this effect); whereas if you are just, that will produce in you a sense of being at peace with yourself.

I don't think that this is the right way to read Plato, but the point I would like to make now is that when I raise the question, "Is it good for someone to be a good person?" I am not calling for an inquiry into the psychological effects that accrue to someone as a causal consequence of his having the moral virtues. Rather, my idea is this: A good person is not simply someone who behaves in a certain way, but is also someone who has certain desires, feelings, and thoughts—particularly as regards other people and his relationship to them. Are those mental items among the constituents of well-being? One might similarly ask whether being a good parent is a role that is good for someone to play—whether the intimacy, patience, and insight that constitute being good at this role can plausibly be regarded as components of a good life. In fact, for parents in the midst of bringing up children, being a good person partly consists in being a good parent, and so if it is good for someone to be a good parent, it is also good to be a good person in that respect.

Several further linguistic remarks will round out our discussion. The first is that we might hesitate or refuse to say of a thoroughly immoral or amoral person—someone who defies or is indifferent to legitimate moral norms—that he is living well. The way he treats others by itself shows that this is not how a person should live. How, then, could we call that a good life or a life well lived? But even though this reflects a natural way to apply or refuse to apply these phrases ("a good life," "a life well lived"), that linguistic point would not be a good reason to dismiss the question addressed in Plato's *Republic*. One would be an obtuse reader of this work if one thought that nothing of philosophical or practical import is taking place when Thrasymachus and Socrates argue about whether justice is not only of value to those who are treated justly (they agree that it obviously is) but also of value to the individual who treats others justly. Is it in that person's interest to be just? Is the possession of that quality good *for him*, and not good only for others? We can agree that, in a way, the unjust person does not have a good life. What we would mean by speaking this way is that his is not a morally good life. It is not good for others that he lives as he does. But we should not pretend that we would thereby have addressed the question, Is it good *for him* that he lives as he does?[32]

Just as we rightly balk at saying that an immoral or unjust person has a good life (when this would mean that it is a life one should live), we might say that when someone performs a morally good act and does so from the best of moral motives, that is quite simply "a good thing." (And in opposite cases, that is "a bad thing.") These phrases—"a good thing," "a bad thing"—can be applied to anything that we think is as it ought to be, or as it ought not to be. An act might in this sense be a good thing, but not good for the agent.

One further linguistic observation: although I have said that several phrases can be used to designate our topic ("the quality of life," "well-being," "prudential value," "flourishing," what is "good for" someone, what is in his "interest" or to his "advantage"), there are some subtle differences between them. Here is one: it would sound odd to say that after someone dies the quality of his life can increase or decrease (assuming that there is no posthumous existence), but that does not settle the question whether anything good or bad for an individual can occur when he is no longer alive. Suppose someone maligns you when you are dead. Although you do not exist, that does not stop it being the case that you are the subject of someone's hateful speech, which has treated you unfairly. Some philosophers would go further: they would say that the way you have been treated is bad for you; it takes something away from the total amount of well-being you had while you were alive. Admittedly, it would be implausible to say that the quality of your life has diminished—after all, your life is over. But that indicates that these phrases—"that is bad for you" and "the quality of your life diminishes"— have somewhat different connotations.

---

[32] It is a further question whether Aristotle's *Nicomachean Ethics*, like Plato's *Republic*, aims to persuade its audience that ethically virtuous activity is good for the agent. Aristotle's treatise opens with a statement about what is good: it is sought in all that we do. Is that equivalent to the proposition that one seeks what is good for oneself, or good for someone, in all that one does? I discuss this issue in 'Aristotle on Well-Being,' in Guy Fletcher (ed.), *The Routledge Handbook of Philosophy of Well-Being*, 20–9. For doubts about the importance of Plato's question about justice, see H. A. Prichard, 'Does Moral Philosophy Rest on a Mistake?' 21–37; reprinted in *Moral Writings*, 7–20.

I have chosen *The Quality of Life* as the title of this work partly because that phrase is a rough equivalent of "well-being," which is increasingly used as the principal name for our topic, and will appear often in what follows. But I have also selected it because its connotation is one that I find salutary. It pulls us in the right direction by suggesting that what is of prudential value in a life (aside from its length) is something that has an experiential quality. The quality of a life, if I am right, is like the quality of a sound (its tone, color, and pitch)—it is a matter of what it is like, as it is experienced. It is life as it is lived—as we know it from the inside. ("Qualia" is the philosophical term of art that is sometimes used to designate the felt quality of our sensory world.[33]) When life is over, there remains no quality of life, whether good or bad.[34] Someone who thinks that there are posthumous goods and harms—that our overall well-being is affected by what happens to us after we die—will reject my experientialism, and will regard "the quality of life" as a misleading name for prudential value. I, however, embrace the term.

The point just made is merely linguistic and I do not offer it as a significant argument in favor of experientialism. Its evidential force is zero or close to zero. The anti-experientialist will correctly point out that even if the quality of life is not altered by posthumous events, that is no reason to hold that nothing bad can happen to us after we die. From the point of view of that anti-experientialist, "the quality of life" is not the best term to designate our subject. He thinks that bad things and good things can happen to us after we die, and so if we keep a running total of all that is good or bad for us, the tally must continue after our lives are over. That is the substantive issue that must be addressed, and it is not affected by my point that "the quality of life" is an experientialist way of designating our topic.

5. Inferior responses to McTaggart

One might believe that McTaggart's thesis is correct, and so the problem of explaining where he goes wrong does not arise. But even if one had this conviction, there would still be some value in noticing what assumptions he needs to make or reject to arrive at his conclusion. I assume that you, like me, reject his thesis; but that is not what matters most here. The more important task is to take apart his reasoning, and *if* we reject it, to identify what the best alternative is.

One possibility is this: Although we might attribute to an oyster the desire to eat now, it does not have a desire to eat tomorrow. Its mental life does not include a conception of itself as something that endures. It cannot matter *to it* whether its life

---

[33] Notice that "quality" in "quality of experience" can be used to pick out both an empirical property (its phenomenology) and an evaluative property (how good it is). In the phrase "quality of life," "quality" is most often understood as an evaluation. That is how I will understand "quality of life" throughout this work.

[34] The point is trivial, on the assumption that a dead person has neither good nor bad experiences. There is, however, a further question: after someone has died, does he have a "welfare-level" of zero, or rather is there no longer any such thing as his "welfare-level" (is it, in other words, undefined)? See Ben Bradley, *Well-Being and Death*, 98–111.

continues beyond its present experience. McTaggart can reach his conclusion only if he keeps adding one day's pleasures to the next day's, and the next day's, and so on. But that aggregation is not something the oyster can perform or care about. It has a good now, and another good later, but not more good over time. Since well-being is an assessment of how well a life is going from the perspective of the individual whose life it is, and McTaggart's oyster has no perspective on its long-term future, its moment-by-moment well-being does not accumulate over time, as it does for human beings.

I will argue that this strategy for undermining McTaggart's thesis does not work (Chapter 4, section 14). But even if it did, his thesis could be modified in a way that leaves the essential challenge it poses undiminished. Instead of comparing a human life (of normal length, and however rich in prudential value) to that of a single long-lived oyster, as McTaggart does, we could posit a very large number of oysters (one million, let's suppose) each of which exists for only a day. Our question would then become this: which world is better, the one that contains these one million oysters of a day, or one populated by a much smaller number of human beings (suppose they are only one thousand), each of whom lives a wonderful life of normal length?[35]

The alternative to McTaggart's thesis (concerning one oyster and one human being) that I will defend is applicable to this further question about *collective* well-being. If all members of the small human community have lives of sufficient length and prudential value, so that each such life is incommensurably better than that of any oyster, no matter how long that oyster lives, then it is better that the small human community exist than that the much larger oyster population exist. But because I believe that McTaggart is right—his single oyster keeps accumulating more good, each day bringing as much good as the previous one, for an enormous period of time—I will set aside this modification of his challenge, and address the question he raises in more or less its original form (by comparing one very long-lived oyster-like life to one human life of normal length).

Here is a second possible strategy for rejecting McTaggart's thesis: The oyster's life does keep getting better for a while. But, at a certain point, the good in its life has reached a limit. It continues to experience pleasure for however long it lives—let it be thousands or millions of years—but pleasure is no longer good for it after a few days, or months, or years, for by then it has reached the limit of its goodness. But the peculiarly human goods, which are unavailable to an oyster, retain their goodness for the full length of a normal human lifespan.

A third possibility is a variation on the second. It holds that the value of an oyster's pleasure is always such that *some* further increase in well-being is available to it without end. But the amount by which it can be increased keeps diminishing; it approaches but never reaches a limit, and therefore it can never exceed that limit. With human

---

[35] So transformed, McTaggart's thesis becomes a version of what Derek Parfit calls "the repugnant conclusion." See *Reasons and Persons*, 388. McTaggart uses this term as well: "this conclusion would, I believe, be repugnant to certain moralists" (*The Nature of Existence*, vol. 2, 453).

beings, it is different. If the marginal value of human goods diminishes, the rate or onset of diminution is such that a normal human life filled with the elements of well-being is better than the life of McTaggart's oyster.

Like the first strategy described earlier, these second and third ways of resisting McTaggart's thesis are, I will argue, problematic and inferior to the one I favor. A fourth way to block that thesis will prove to be best. It is the one I briefly mentioned in section 1: we must recognize that goods belong to different orders of value (and are in that sense "incommensurable"). A sufficient supply of peculiarly human goods, in other words, is superior to any amount of the lower goods available to the oyster. We will see, in fact, that McTaggart himself accepts this claim—he puts love into the superior category (Chapter 4, section 4). It is remarkable and disappointing that he does not put this part of his philosophy to work when he discusses the "oyster-like" life that he holds is superior (if sufficiently long) to human life. Of course, the fact that McTaggart believes that some human goods belong to a higher level or order is not evidence that this belief is true. The existence of incommensurably superior goods is a thesis that needs to be assessed on its merits.

6. Incommensurable superiority

Goods are not all at the same level. What this talk of "levels" or "orders" amounts to is this: for a good to belong to a higher order is for it to be the case that a sufficient amount of it is better than any amount of a good of a lower order. They are "incommensurable" in that there is no common coin or measure applicable to the two orders that would tell us how many more goods belonging to the lower order are needed for them, taken together, to be superior to a smaller quantity of goods of the higher order.

Human life at its best involves a richness of experience that is "incommensurably" better than anything available to the meager form of consciousness an oyster has. To use the terms that John Stuart Mill employed in *Utilitarianism*: choices are not always to be made by finding the greatest quantity of something; the qualitative differences between experiences matters as well as their duration, so much so that in some cases no quantity of the inferior kind of experience can compensate for its qualitative inferiority. In particular, the quality of human consciousness, its amazing richness, variety, complexity, and depth, is so good (provided that it endures over a sufficient period of time) that no amount of simple oyster pleasure, however long-lasting, will give it a better life. This conception of the richness of human life will be an important component of my argument that it is good to be a good person, for I believe that the experiences that come with the ethical virtues add significantly to the depth, variety, and complexity of our consciousness. (Although I have invoked Mill's distinction between the quantity and the quality of pleasures, we will soon see what is misleading about these terms.)

The term "incommensurable" is sometimes applied to values to mean that there is no such thing as one being better than, worse than, or equal (whether roughly or exactly) to the other. Incommensurable values, so construed, are "apples and oranges"—not capable of fitting together into any attempt to compare their value. ("Incomparable" would in this case be a more accurate term than "incommensurable."[36]) But when I say that human life is *incommensurably* better than oyster life, I am of course using that term in a different way. I mean that the quality of life of an oyster, no matter how much life it has, is definitely comparable to the quality of a good human life: it is inferior. So inferior, in fact, that it can never *measure up* to the quality of a sufficiently long human life at its best. There is no number of years of life McTaggart's oyster could have so as to make it better than a normal human life rich in experience. Its life belongs to a different and lower order of value that renders any such numerical equation inapplicable.

There is nothing mysterious or suspect about the concept of incommensurable superiority (or "immeasurable" superiority, as I will sometimes call it). We are familiar with the possibility, for example, that a student who writes a long series of mediocre papers may be inferior as a scholar to a second student who writes fewer papers that are all excellent. No matter how many weak papers the first student writes, his performance in the course will never outstrip that of his highly talented but less prolific counterpart.[37]

Here is a different sort of example: An author who is eager to have his recent publication enjoy a wide readership is offered an opportunity to increase sales. The only drawback is that this would require him to do some traveling, which would put his young child at some risk of serious injury. (There is a small chance that he will need to be taken to the hospital.) Suppose the risk is very small, and the jump in sales enormous. Even so, he ought to refuse to increase his child's exposure to danger, even to the slightest degree, for the sake of a boost in readership, however large. The two values in question need to be ranked in a way that blocks their assessment along a single common dimension. Safety is not to be sacrificed even slightly in exchange for some amount, however large, of popularity.

In this example, no amount of popularity is better than even the smallest amount of safety. That is one way in which a higher-order value can be superior to one that is lower. But the thesis I will defend is that certain human experiences, when they are of *sufficient* length (not any length, however small), are greater in prudential value than are the combined lifetime pleasures felt by McTaggart's oyster, however long it lives. That is still incommensurable superiority, but it holds only when the higher value is above a designated threshold.[38] I will therefore need to discuss this matter of "sufficient length." How much time is that? (See Chapter 4, section 17.)

---

[36] See Ruth Chang, 'Value Incomparability and Incommensurability,' in Iwao Hirose and Jonas Olson (eds.), *The Oxford Handbook of Value Theory*, 205–24. She uses "incommensurability" in the strict sense: "there is no cardinal unit of measure that can represent the value of both terms" (205).

[37] The example comes from Larry Temkin, *Rethinking the Good*, 56. A work that has played a major role in shaping recent discussion of incommensurable value is James Griffin, *Well-Being*. See 75–92.

[38] These stronger and weaker forms of incommensurability are distinguished by Griffin, *Well-Being*, 83–5 (where the stronger is called "trumping," the weaker "discontinuity"). Roger Crisp invokes the notion of

Several philosophers of the modern period and most especially of the later decades of the twentieth century have noticed that value superiority might take this form, and my thinking is indebted to them.[39] But we can find at least an adumbration of this idea in the statement of Aristotle cited in section 3 above. One portion of that passage reads: "He would prefer a short period of intense pleasure to a long period of mild pleasure, a year of living nobly to many indifferent years, and a single noble and great action to many trivial ones." What if "the long period of mild pleasure" were a thousand years, ten thousand years, or however long you like? Would the virtuous person prefer a pleasure that long to a short period of intense pleasure? On a charitable reading of Aristotle, the great duration of an ignoble pleasure can never make it superior to what is felt by a virtuous person performing a single noble and great action. Implicit in this passage, then, is the notion of two orders of value, one of them unsurpassably above the other.

A major theme of Stoic ethics is that there are two incommensurable orders of value. Within one of them, the order of genuine goodness, there is just one item: virtue; in the other, the order of what-is-to-be-chosen, there are many items—health, physical pleasure, beauty, reputation, and the ordinary things that nature inclines us to prefer.[40] If you ask a Stoic whether a very long period of health, pleasure, and so on could be long enough to be more desirable than a brief life of virtue, the answer will be no.[41]

Turning back to Aristotle, we should note that his theory of well-being, at least on one interpretation of it, also makes a distinction, like the one observed by the Stoics, between two orders of value. According to this interpretation, although many items are desirable in themselves and not as mere means, *eudaimonia* consists not in the aggregation of these several goods, but in just one of them, namely, virtuous activity of the rational soul.[42] *Eudaimonia*—that is, the good in which *eudaimonia* consists—is superior to other goods in a special way: by itself it makes life better than any good that is not a component of *eudaimonia*, or any combination of such goods. Virtuous activity, in other words, is incommensurably better than other goods.

Incommensurable value, then, is an idea with a long history. Because it has appealed to philosophers of different schools and eras, and because we use it, at times, in ordinary

---

discontinuity in his discussion of Mill. See *Routledge Philosophy Guidebook to Mill on Utilitarianism*, 24–5, 31.

[39] Parfit's "repugnant conclusion" (see note 35) has been a major source of interest in incommensurable value superiority. For references, see Gustaf Arrhenius, Jesper Ryberg, and Torbjörn Tännsjö, 'The Repugnant Conclusion,' *The Stanford Encyclopedia of Philosophy*, section 2.2. For further references, see Gustaf Arrhenius and Wlodek Rabinowicz, 'Value Superiority,' in Iwao Hirose and Jonas Olson (eds.), *The Oxford Handbook of Value Theory*, 225 and 243–4 notes 4 and 5.

[40] For some of the basic texts that expound this theory of value, see A. A. Long and D. N. Sedley, *The Hellenistic Philosophers*, vol. 1, 354–7.

[41] The Stoic thesis that well-being is no greater for lasting longer will be discussed in Chapter 4, section 15.

[42] I defend this reading in *Aristotle on the Human Good*, 197–311. For a different interpretation, see Terence Irwin, 'Conceptions of Happiness in the *Nicomachean Ethics*,' in Christopher Shields (ed.), *The Oxford Handbook of Aristotle*.

practical thinking, we have good reason to give it a serious hearing in our investigation of well-being.

I will appeal to it not only because it is my favored tool for dissenting from McTaggart's thesis, but also because it will help us explore competing conceptions of the relative value of inner life and non-experiential goods. Nozick's experience machine is often thought to reveal the great prudential significance of what lies beyond our awareness. One option to be explored, in our discussion of his thought experiment, is that although non-experiential goods are indeed components of well-being, they have far less value than its experiential elements. How much less value? One possibility is that experiential goods are immeasurably superior to non-experiential goods. (This is a more precise formulation of a statement made in section 1: "even if some components of well-being are non-experiential, they are of far less value than the ones that are.")

We can return now to McTaggart's oyster. You might say: "I don't claim that your comparison between the lives of human beings and oysters is meaningless or incoherent. But it is mere assertion. Do you have any *argument* for your thesis?" My reply is that we sometimes acquire knowledge through observation rather than argument. I know that there is a table in front of me because I see it. I know that orange and red are closer in color than either is to blue because I have experienced all three, and I have the ability to compare their phenomenological likeness. Turning back to the oyster, we can have some notion of its inner life: it takes in nourishment and (we are assuming) it seeks more of the same because it has a pleasant sensation when it eats. We know through introspection what it is like to get pleasure from the taste of something. We can imagine what it is like to have nothing but that as one's form of consciousness, and can compare that kind of life to the much larger form of consciousness we are lucky enough to have, with respect to how good they are.[43]

If someone were to say that when he makes this comparison, he judges the life of the oyster to be superior, my reaction would be that either he is upholding a thesis at all costs for the sake of argument, or he has not come to appreciate what is valuable in human life. In either case, there would be no basis for arguing with him. As for McTaggart, we will see (Chapter 4, section 4) that the proper diagnosis of his error is far from simple. He is aware, as I noted in section 5, that goods can belong to higher or lower orders, in that a sufficient amount of a higher good is better than any amount of one that is lower. (He puts love into the higher category.) He is also aware that the prudential value of a state of mind might diminish over time and therefore never exceed a fixed amount of goodness. Apparently, in his opinion, the diminution of the value of his oyster's pleasures will begin only in the *very* far future—or, at any rate, we must put it in the very far future if we believe (mistakenly) in the reality of time.

[43] A similar style of argument is used by Plato in the *Republic* (580d–583a) to show that the pleasures of learning are superior to those of making money and receiving honors: the experiences of a philosopher put him in a position to compare all three, whereas those who do not enjoy learning have no basis for evaluating its pleasures. Mill likewise appeals to this basis for comparing the value of different kinds of pleasure in *Utilitarianism*, chapter 2.

I have said that human life, when it is rich in experiential goods, is superior in prudential value to the life of McTaggart's simple long-lived oyster—provided that the human life endures over a sufficient period of time. A full elaboration and defense of that idea will be presented in Chapter 4. One question we will have to address is this: what counts as a "sufficient period of time"? It might be thought that any answer will be arbitrary—and furthermore that my theory is committed to a puzzling "tipping point" of value. Too short a human life will be inferior to that of the oyster, but then it seems that—suddenly and mysteriously—with just a bit more time, it becomes incommensurably superior. How can that happen? True, we observe such tipping points in nature: water gradually cools and then almost instantly becomes ice. But can time bring about this sort of transformation of prudential value? We will see that no instantaneous radical change need be posited. Just as a man with a full head of hair may gradually become bald, so brief periods of human consciousness can ascend to a higher order of value when they endure and are enriched.

7. The richness of human experience

Let me elaborate now on my statement that there is, or can be (in favorable circumstances), a wonderful richness in the consciousness of a human being. To begin with, there is perceptual and sensory awareness: we are open to a world of colors, sounds, smells, tastes, and sensations of pleasure and pain. There is also a phenomenal quality to our active cognitive life: we are conscious of making judgments and conjectures, entertaining possibilities, searching through our memory, venturing predictions, encountering intellectual surprises, and the like. Conative phenomenology is no less varied, including our awareness of wanting, choosing, planning, wishing, hoping, and so on. A further phenomenological category includes the emotions: being happy, glad, proud, excited; feeling affection, love, admiration, respect, lust, sadness, shame, frustration, disappointment, anger, fear, jealousy, humiliation, guilt, indignation, boredom.[44] Typically, several of these modalities are experienced together as an integrated whole, and they are deepened by our remarkable sense of the past and our anticipations of the future. The present moment can include within it an awareness of its deep significance for our lives.[45]

As the items near the end of my list indicate, experiences can be bad as well as good. Inner life can be hellish, and when it is, someone might reasonably wish that he could be transformed into McTaggart's oyster. ("I should have been a pair of ragged claws / Scuttling across the floors of silent seas."[46]) But McTaggart's thesis, we should recall, is that human life *even at its best* is inferior in prudential value to that of a sufficiently

[44] The scope and structure of human consciousness is a controversial matter. I have been helped by Uriah Kriegel, *The Varieties of Consciousness.*

[45] On the complexity of our experience of time, see section 9 below and note 56; see too Chapter 4, section 17. The importance of a "narrative sense of self" is the theme of Peter Goldie, *The Mess Inside: Narrative, Emotion, and the Mind.*

[46] T. S. Eliot, 'The Love Song of J. Alfred Prufrock.'

long-lived oyster. I have included some negative emotions on my list because when they do not dominate our experience, they can make a contribution to the overall goodness of our lives. Someone who never felt frustration, anger, fear, sadness, or jealousy would be radically alienated from his social world. When these negative emotions are seen not in isolation but as components of our entire experience of the world, they make an ineliminable contribution to the goodness of our lives. "Sweet are the uses of adversity."[47]

It should be emphasized that pleasure is only one part of our conscious internal lives, and is not the only kind of phenomenal quality it is good for someone to experience. In saying this, I am not merely making the familiar (but still contested) claim that there are other goods besides pleasure. Rather, I hold, in addition, that *within the realm of experience*—the aspect of life that is available in the experience machine—pleasure is only one small part of a proper inventory of what is good for us. This is one component of my account of where McTaggart's thesis goes wrong: when we compare the rich experiences of human life with the thin pleasure of the oyster, the former has incommensurably greater value.

Here are some examples to illustrate and support the point I am making. Imagine someone standing in front of a painting that he finds visually stunning. All sorts of *thoughts* are going through his mind; he is *intrigued* by what the figures in the painting are doing; many subtle *emotions* are called forth by the narrative significance of the painting's subject; he *decides* to linger and to look at it from different angles; his eyes take in the contrast of *colors and shapes*; he is *uncertain* whether he fully *understands* what the artist intended, and continues to *explore* the painting's meaning and the reason for its emotional impact. This is a good experience for anyone to have—not because of something it later brings about, but simply in virtue of what occurs while it is going on. Pleasure may be part of what our viewer experiences, but he is of course also aware of the painting in front of him and his variegated internal responses to it. The goodness of this experience for him supervenes on *all* of the many aspects of his consciousness—not simply on the fact that he is feeling pleasure. Suppose the pleasure he is feeling could somehow be pried apart from the rest of his mental state, and experienced in isolation from his perception of colors and shapes, his thoughts, and his feelings. The value of the resulting mental state would be greatly diminished. His experience would have been flattened out into something thin, one-dimensional, and uninteresting.[48]

---

[47] Shakespeare, *As You Like It*, Act 2, scene 1, line 12. It does not follow that, as the Duke supposes, there is "good in everything" (line 18).

[48] What is in play in this example is the mutual causal interaction of various components of one's experience, not the idea, brought to the attention of moral philosophers by G. E. Moore in *Principia Ethica* (chapter 1, sections 18–20), that the value of a whole need not be the sum of the value of its parts (in which case he calls it an "organic whole"). There are two ways to interpret this principle, but neither is what I have in mind. See Thomas Hurka, 'Two Kinds of Organic Unity,' in *Drawing Morals: Essays in Ethical Theory*; and Erik Carlson, 'Organic Unities,' in Iwao Hirose and Jonas Olson (eds.), *The Oxford Handbook of Value Theory*, 285–99.

Even when we do not expect to get pleasure from an experience, we can be warranted in seeking it, because we know that there will be other phenomenological qualities that make it a good experience to have. We might wonder how something (a root, a leaf, the bark of a tree) tastes and might decide to sample it, even though we assume that it will give us no pleasure (we might even expect it to be unpleasant). Doing so would enlarge our sensory exposure to the world, and that kind of experiential knowledge can be sought for itself. The same point applies to intellectual and emotional experiences. We might see many performances of "King Lear" or "Othello" over the course of our lives, because we know that this will be a profound, disturbing, experience. Do we necessarily think that pleasure will be part of what we feel when we are there in the theater? I doubt it. We go because we believe that our lives are enhanced by experiencing great drama and great acting, even when (or perhaps because) it presents a side of life that we hope never to see outside the theater. (In the same way we might sometimes revisit a taste sensation, knowing that it will again be unpleasant, because we find it unique, complex, and interesting.) If, to make up our minds whether to attend a particular piece of tragic theater, we asked ourselves whether it would be fun, amusing, or entertaining, we would be asking the wrong question, and should certainly stay home. It would be dogmatic to insist that nonetheless there must be, somewhere in our aesthetic experience, *some* sort of pleasure felt in our reaction to a tragedy, if it is to be worth our time.[49]

Why would or should one read a biography of Hitler, to take another example? This might of course be a mere means to a further end—to pass an exam on twentieth-century European history. But there are other sorts of reasons as well. One's grandparents might have left Germany because of Hitler; knowledge of their situation would give one a stronger sense of connection to one's past. One would then experience one's life differently, bringing to bear on it a deeper historical understanding. Even if one has no personal connection to that time and place, one might read about Hitler or more generally about the Third Reich because of something one values in that intellectual and emotional experience. Evil not only distresses us but draws us towards it as an object of fascination. Some sort of pleasure *might* be one element of this experience, but, again, it would be dogmatic to insist that it cannot be valuable unless this is the

---

[49] Aristotle himself overestimates the degree to which pleasure figures in what we are drawn to. He holds that whenever we choose an act because it is advantageous or *kalon* (noble, fine, beautiful), we are pleased that it has these features (II.3 1104b30–1105a1). That overlooks those occasions when we act for a non-hedonic reason but take no pleasure in the mere fact that we have such a reason. But notice as well the implication, in this passage, that we make many decisions without grounding them in pleasure. Pleasure supplements our other reasons and does not stand on its own as a basis for its choice. Aristotle says in the *Poetics*, chapter 14 (1453b10–13) that there is a kind of pleasure proper to tragedy, but that does not commit him to the thesis that for the experience of tragedy to be choiceworthy for itself, it must have pleasure in it. It can be choiceworthy because it has one or both of the other good-making features (advantageousness and beauty); its desirability would be the greater because we are pleased that it is advantageous and beautiful. Aristotle's conception of the pleasure that properly accompanies tragedy is the subject of scholarly debate. For a recent contribution and guide, see Pierre Destrée, 'Aristotle on The Paradox of Tragic Pleasure,' in Jerrold Levinson (ed.), *Suffering Art Gladly*.

case. Yet another reason to read about historical periods filled with suffering and turmoil is to enhance one's understanding of the politics of one's own time. One's engagement with current events would then become multi-dimensional; it would be deeper than the experience of someone who lives through present times with no sense of the past. That is worth having even if it does not make one's life more pleasant.

No light would be shed on this question if one merely said: "it is a good thing to read about Hitler." That would be tantamount to asserting merely that one ought to do so. We would be right to respond that if one ought to do so, there must be a reason why. What is that reason? The answers offered in the preceding paragraph respond to that question by noting the ways in which we might benefit from such reading.

I have used the words "richness" and "complexity" several times in my portrait of human experience at its best, and have contrasted it with the impoverished consciousness of a simple creature like an oyster. Can these terms be given a more precise definition? Can we capture with greater exactitude the quality of our conscious lives by counting how many different kinds of experiences we have? It is not clear how to carry out such a project, but in any case it is doubtful that it would bring any gain in our understanding of what makes our inner lives so worthwhile. Certainly an experience can be quite complex and yet worthless. Think of a composer who writes a symphony scored for a large orchestra and two choruses, and fills it with lengthy musical complexities lacking coherent organization or auditory appeal. Now think of a song for voice and flute of heart-piercing beauty—a simple lament, repeated several times. The first has greater complexity, but it is meaningless, containing no depth of feeling. The second is simpler, but touches us to the core. The latter is the richer experience—and that comparison can be made only by listening and making a qualitative evaluation. Part of what makes our experiences valuable to us is that the elements they contain, even when small in number, are integrated into a meaningful whole. The flute accompaniment, for example, is just the right match for the voice and words. The feeling expressed is poignant and resonates with us, and the song has some variation—it is not a single note like a dial tone. There is enough complexity to make it appealing to us. An orchestration of that simple song might ruin it with heavy-handed pomposity.

The richness of human consciousness, then, rests partly on its having some degree of complexity—but a complexity of manageable size, one we can integrate into a significant whole, to which we are drawn because of what it is like. Our facility with language, our temporal sophistication (drawing on memory and blending the present with the anticipated future), our visual and auditory powers, and our sociability each makes a contribution to the remarkable quality of our conscious lives. But if these powers lie dormant and unused, they do us no good.

That human experience is deep, rich, meaningful, complex, and cohesively organized is a fact that will play a central role in both our discussion of McTaggart's oyster and of Nozick's experience machine. This is what his oyster lacks, and this is why human life is superior. Similarly, for the experience machine to be a true test of the value of experience, it must give us everything that our normal encounter with the external world provides by way of experience, without any differences detectable to the individual inside it. Experience within the machine must be phenomenologically indistinguishable from experience outside it, not a faint, pallid, dreamlike simulacrum of it. The colors and sounds we see and hear must be no less vivid and varied. Similarly, every other aspect of experience—emotional, cognitive, conative, hedonic—must be reproducible within the machine. Our conscious existence in the machine must be just as it would be if we were having the full range of experiences given to us in the real world. Would the quality of our lives nonetheless sink to zero, or perhaps just barely above zero? Would it not diminish at all, or only slightly? Or would it fall somewhere between these extremes—substantially reduced, but still of significant value?

8. Sidgwick and the definition of pleasure

Another point I have made requires elucidation: I said that pleasure is not the only kind of phenomenal quality it is good for someone to experience.[50] Some readers may object to this on the grounds that it presupposes that pleasure is a single kind of experience. Against this, they will claim that pleasures have nothing in common as phenomenal qualities. They will point out, correctly, that there is a great heterogeneity in the experience of pleasure. The pleasures of having a back rub, of listening to a sweet melody, of rejoicing in the home town team's victory, and of engaging in a lively philosophical discussion do not feel the same. Introspection does not detect one and the same experience in each case, as it does whenever we drink a cup of black Italian roast coffee or smell smoke.

We should accept this point, but we should also be careful not to infer from it that the only thing pleasures have in common is something that lies outside experience. That is a mistake Sidgwick makes, and we should not fall into the same trap.[51] He asks whether pleasure is some undefinable "quality of feeling" like the sweetness of a taste (his example), and replies that it is too heterogeneous to be so characterized. He adds:

When I reflect on the notion of pleasure,—using the term in the comprehensive sense I have adopted, to include the most refined and subtle intellectual gratifications, no less than the coarser and more definite sensual enjoyments,—the only common quality that I can find in the feelings so designated seems to be that relation to desire and volition expressed by the general term "desirable".... I propose therefore to define Pleasure ... as a feeling which, when experienced by intellectual beings, is at least implicitly apprehended as desirable or—in cases of comparisons—preferable.[52]

---

[50] Is pleasure *always* good to some degree, no matter what one takes pleasure in? I will address that question in Chapter 2, section 10.

[51] For my understanding of Sidgwick's account of pleasure, I am indebted to Roger Crisp, 'Pleasure and Hedonism in Sidgwick,' in Thomas Hurka, *Underivative Duty: British Moral Philosophers from Sidgwick to Ewing*, 26–44; Thomas Hurka, *British Ethical Theorists from Sidgwick to Ewing*, 194–8; and Roger Crisp, *The Cosmos of Duty: Henry Sidgwick's Methods of Ethics*, 57–96.

[52] *The Methods of Ethics*, 127. See also 93, 131, 402. The principal sections in which Sidgwick discusses pleasure and its value are Book I, chapters 4, 7, and 9; Book II, chapters 1–4 and 6; and Book III, chapter 14.

Sidgwick here uses the word "feeling" to define pleasure, but his point is that what unifies pleasures is not something felt to be the same in kind. Pleasure, as he here conceives it, is a feature of our lives that is experienced, but what brings all such experiences together into a single category is not what they are like, but the fact that they are "apprehended" or judged, at the time they are felt, to be good.[53]

Presumably he would add that they are not apprehended as good merely because they are taken to be means to something else that we desire. Suppose I am teaching myself to recognize the sound of someone's voice because that will enable me to identify him on some future occasion. That is an experience that I might, as I undergo it, judge to be good (that is, useful); but if there is nothing I find acoustically appealing about his voice, then I am not feeling pleasure in listening to him. Sidgwick is none-theless committing to saying that if I judge it to be good *in itself* to listen to the sound of his voice, then what I am experiencing, as I make this judgment, is pleasure. The pleasure is not the same thing as the judgment; rather, it is its object. Pleasure is any experience judged (apprehended) by the experiencing subject to be good in itself. Accordingly, the question to be asked, when one decides whether what one is feeling should be called a pleasure, is not how it feels, but whether one judges it to be good in itself.

One problem with this view is that hardly anyone has the intellectual sophistication needed to judge, at the very time of having an experience, that it is desirable or good in itself and not merely as a means. Fortunately, we do not need such sophistication to feel pleasure. When we listen to someone's voice and ask whether we find it pleasant, we do not consider whether our experience is in itself desirable for us. It is a far simpler matter: we look within and either we find or fail to find that our experience has not only an auditory aspect but also involves what we recognize as a hedonic aspect.

We should remind ourselves that although certain kinds of animals surely feel pleasure, it would be odd to suppose that they "at least implicitly" apprehend their experience as desirable. They feel pleasure without being in the business of evaluating the way they feel.

A further example will reveal what is mistaken in Sidgwick's conception of the human experience of pleasure. Suppose a doctor injects himself with a drug simply out of curiosity about its effects on his consciousness. He discovers that it gives him a strange and complex sensation unlike any he has felt before. Among its features are a

---

[53] At times, Sidgwick characterizes pleasure quite simply as "desirable consciousness." See *The Methods of Ethics*, 397, 398, 402, 404. These passages omit any reference to the apprehension of the individual whose pleasure it is. If we take him to be offering here a second definition of pleasure, one that drops any reference to the apprehension of the individual whose pleasure it is, it is worse than the first. Now the subject's apprehension of his feeling as desirable no longer matters—what counts instead is whether it really is desirable. But whether someone is experiencing pleasure is an empirical rather than an evaluative question, and has something to do with how it affects him rather than others. Aristotle makes a distinction between a pleasure (period) and what is a pleasure *to* someone. Just as sweet food might not taste sweet to a sick person, so what feels pleasant to a bad person might not be, quite simply, a pleasure (X.3 1173b20–5). What is pleasant to someone is an empirical question; what is pleasant (period) is an evaluative question. Plato prepares the ground for this distinction in the *Philebus*, which explores the ways in which pleasures can be false.

peculiar combination of heat and cold, blue and circular images floating in his visual field, the sound of a siren, and the smell of tobacco. Other aspects of the experience may be so unfamiliar that he lacks words to describe them. His desire for a new experience has been fulfilled. He now has the knowledge he sought. But did the experience he observed in himself include any pleasure? Nothing I have said entails that it did.

Our doctor of course might be pleased that he carried out this experiment. After all, he now knows what the effects of the drug on his consciousness are. But that is a pleasure felt *about* the experience he had, not a pleasure *in* the experience as it occurred. The experience itself may have lacked any hedonic aspect, and may have consisted entirely of other sensory qualities. (In fact, he may have predicted that the experience induced by the drug would be neither pleasant nor unpleasant—and then be pleased to find that he was right about that.) In Sidgwick's terms, he "apprehends" his experience as "desirable," even though pleasure was not one of the qualities that appeared in the experience itself. His definition of pleasure goes astray because it fails to acknowledge what introspection plainly reveals to us: when we feel pleasure, there is some detectable quality of our experience that grounds that classification of it.

We can do better than Sidgwick by taking pleasure to be an introspectable and indefinable aspect of our experience—one such aspect among many others. He is of course right when he calls our attention to the differences exhibited by pleasures, ranging, as he says, from "the most refined and subtle intellectual gratifications" to the "coarser and more definite sensual enjoyments." But pleasures can differ among themselves, forming different species of experience, while at the same time retaining enough of a resemblance to each other to justify our linguistic habit of grouping them into the same broad genus called "pleasure."

The general idea is familiar: many species can belong to a single genus even though they differ greatly one from another. For their differences from items outside of that genus may be far greater. For example, there are many shades of yellow and many shades of blue. Even so, the yellows are close enough to be properly classified together as a single color, and so too the blues. Furthermore, yellow and blue, different as they are, have something experiential in common in that they are colors. Our experience of a color is quite different from our experience of a sound or an odor. For all the difference between the way yellow looks and the way blue looks, they have more in common as experiences than either does to the smell of smoke.

In the same way, we should say that even though different types of pleasures have a very different feel to them, there is enough of a resemblance in their experiential quality to make it the case that they are closer to each other than they are to pains, or sounds, or colors, or tastes, or thoughts.[54] The pleasure taken in today's back rub is no different from the pleasure felt in yesterday's back rub, and is quite different from other

---

[54] C. D. Broad "thought there might be different determinate forms of pleasure, as there are different shades of a colour...." See Hurka, *British Ethical Theorists from Sidgwick to Ewing*, 197. He refers to *Five Types of Ethical Theory*, 232.

sorts of pleasures, but in calling each kind a pleasure we bring them together into a broad relation of felt resemblance. It need only be the case that they resemble each other more than they resemble non-pleasures to justify the thesis that pleasure is an introspectable feature of our experiences.[55]

I conclude that nothing is amiss in the thesis that pleasure is one kind of phenomenal quality, marked off from other kinds by its distinctive introspectable character, a kind that is often (perhaps not always) good for someone to experience, but far from the only valuable feature of consciousness. In spite of the manifest heterogeneity of the various species of pleasure, they are members of a single experiential genus because there is more similarity among them, in what they are like, than there is between them and the other varieties of experience.

I noted earlier (section 1) that well-being has an opposite, which might be called "ill-being." According to experientialism, it is composed of many bad things, all of them experiential. Pain is one of them, but there are many others. Here is a partial list: nausea, dizziness, itchiness, soreness, discomfort, disgust, boredom, anxiety, stress, worry, loneliness, frustration, alienation, anguish, sorrow, despair, irritation, annoyance, anger, hatred, fear, shame, guilt, embarrassment, humiliation, depression, weariness, disorientation.

There is, I think, no single phenomenological aspect that is identical in all these states—as there is whenever we have the sensation of a throbbing pain. But it might nonetheless be true that there is *some* similarity in the way they feel. Certainly, there is more similarity among them than between them and the very different sorts of experiences that are the components of well-being. The similarities run deeper than that. Phenomenologically, shame, guilt, embarrassment, and humiliation are not far apart. Nor are annoyance, anger, and hatred; anxiety, stress, and worry; disgust and nausea; boredom and depression. If there is some remote phenomenological kinship among all these components of ill-being, we could appropriate the term "suffering" as a name for that generic commonality. That would deviate somewhat from the normal use of

---

[55] Here I am in agreement with Roger Crisp, who uses "determinable" and "determinate" in place of my "genus" and "species" to express the idea that pleasure is a distinctive "feeling tone" in spite of its heterogeneity. See *Reasons and the Good*, 109–10. My theory recognizes more phenomenological variety among pleasures than is suggested by the analogy proposed by Shelly Kagan, which compares the hedonic aspect of experiences to the volume of sounds. See 'The Limits of Well-Being,' *Social Philosophy and Policy*, 172. A symphony and falling rain (his examples) are acoustically heterogeneous, but nonetheless each has a certain volume, which might be the same or different. His point, an important insight, is that pleasures can differ markedly yet still admit quantitative comparison, just as sounds can be compared with respect to volume despite their qualitative differences. Even so, there is also an important disanalogy between volume and pleasure. All loud sounds have a phenomenological sameness when each is just as loud as the other. Their equal volume is not just a physical feature of each but also something that the ear detects and reports as the same. By contrast, when we isolate the pleasantness of a back rub from non-hedonic features of that experience, and isolate the pleasantness of playing chess from the rest of that experience, we notice qualitative differences between these pleasures. They do not feel exactly the same (as loud sounds can sound exactly as loud). But when we compare the hedonic aspects of our experience of back rubs and playing chess to radically different experiences (pain, suffering, dizziness, the color red, the smell of turpentine), we see their similarities to each other as well as their differences.

this word—we would not normally count, for example, a short, mild pain or a mild feeling of embarrassment as suffering. But in any case, the important point is that pain is a small part of ill-being. Just as pleasures, for all their great phenomenological variety, are just one of the many experiential components of well-being, so too pain is only one of the experiential components that detracts from the quality of life. Using "suffering" in a broader way than usual, we can say that for life to be bad is for it to be filled with much suffering, with too little good to compensate for it. It is too much suffering that makes a life bad, not just pain.

Experientialism does not hold that there is a phenomenological kinship among all elements of well-being. On the contrary, it says that although all such elements have an experiential nature, they are evidently very different kinds of experiences. What unifies experience of pleasures, and good experiences of colors, sounds, tastes, cognitions, volitions, and emotions is not some generic introspectable similarity between them, but simply the fact that they have basic prudential value. I do not claim that the components of ill-being have a degree of phenomenological heterogeneity among themselves equal to the heterogeneity of good experiences. It *may* be that they belong together in a single genus because of a similarity in the way they feel (just as pleasures do); but perhaps they do not—perhaps what they have in common is simply the fact that in themselves they are bad experiences. Even so, extending the word "suffering" beyond its normal usage and applying it to all experiences that are in themselves bad for someone to have (however little they have in common in their felt quality), we could say that for life to be bad is for it to be filled with too much suffering.

9. Mill and the quality of pleasure

I referred briefly (section 6) to Mill's familiar doctrine that pleasures differ not only in quantity (intensity and duration) but also in quality, but I must add now that this way of speaking carries with it the risk of leading us to overestimate the value of pleasure. Here is what I have in mind: suppose I enjoy two kinds of auditory experience—violin music and piano music. Obviously what one of them sounds like is different from what the other sounds like. Here we have a qualitative difference in my two experiences, something I easily and immediately detect through introspection. Both experiences are suffused with pleasure and not merely with auditory qualities. Now, suppose I attend just to my enjoyment in the one case and my enjoyment in the other, and ask myself whether, leaving aside the auditory differences in my two experiences, I detect a further phenomenological difference in the pleasure each gives me. Are there four things I am aware of—two different sounds, and two different feelings of pleasure? The answer is no—and not because I am being inattentive, but because there *is* no difference. I am aware of enjoying each, but there is no difference in the very enjoyment. So, a difference between the phenomenological quality of what we take pleasure *in* does not by itself require the pleasure *itself* to have a different phenomenological character.

That does not entail that there are *never* differences among pleasures. What it is like to scratch an itch and thereby get a feeling of relief is rather different from what enjoyment feels like when we listen to music. (Similarly, a throbbing dull pain feels different from a sharp piercing pain.) The error we must be careful to avoid is that of thinking that the enormous variety in our consciousness has to do only with the differences between the way different sorts of pains feel and pleasures feel. That would be to overlook the different way things sound, look, and smell; the differences among conative states, cognitive states, emotional states, and so on. And it might tempt us to think that the only valuable aspect of our consciousness is its pleasantness. "Of course," we would say, "there is greater richness in the experience of a human being than in that of an oyster—that is because we have pleasures of higher quality." In so saying, we would be accounting for the superiority of our lives solely in terms of one good—pleasure.

It is a mistake to think that pleasure (its quantity or quality) is the only aspect of experience that can account for its value. We can see that this is wrong every time we listen to an orchestra or have any other complex sensory experience: it is to a large extent the quality of the *sound*, not the alleged qualitative aspect of the *pleasure*— that makes us count this as a good experience.

Even if we supposed that pleasure must be an ingredient of any experience that is good for us to have (a supposition I have questioned), it would not follow that it is the only or most important ingredient that makes it good. That would be like saying that because the main item on one's dinner menu should always contain one or more spices, it is those spices alone that make one's meal good to taste. *All* of the different taste sensations we experience simultaneously join together in making a good-tasting dinner. In the same way, it is the complexity of the experiential life of a human being—its containing so many phenomenological components besides pleasure, blending together and modifying each other—that makes it better than an oyster's simple consciousness. Adding depth to our experience of life is our sense of the present as just one temporal portion of an experience that extends backward to the past and forward to the future. At each brief moment spent listening to music, for example, we bring to bear on our present experience our memory of what preceded it and an anticipation of what is to come. The same point applies outside the aesthetic realm: memories and expectations color our encounter with what we experience in the now.[56]

But perhaps Mill was not talking about the differences in the way certain pleasures feel (phenomenological differences beyond the differences in the way things taste, sound, look, and so on). We could instead take him to mean that for one pleasure to be different in quality from another—and of a higher quality—is simply for it to be better

---

[56] For discussion of the way in which our experience of time expands our consciousness, see Jenann Ismael, 'Temporal Experience,' in Craig Callender (ed.), *The Oxford Handbook of Philosophy of Time*. Speaking of autobiographical memory, she writes: "No other animal so far as we know has the cognitive infrastructure to support a reflexive conception of its autobiographical history with anything that approaches human complexity. And no animal so far as we know engages in this complex process of reflexive self-definition" (471).

to have the first than the second. In that case, his idea would be that sometimes we ought to choose the smaller of two pleasures, not because of any phenomenological differences between the pleasures themselves, but because it would be better to take the smaller pleasure. So read, Mill would be giving us no reason to choose the smaller pleasure. But there must be some such reason! If one pleasure is greater than another (by being more intense or lasting longer), that is surely *some* reason for choosing it over the second. If we should nonetheless choose the second, there must be some account of what makes the second more choiceworthy. Mill would have given no such answer—he would simply be saying that the second pleasure is better.

There is yet another problem for Mill's attempt to rescue hedonism by positing some other good-making feature of pleasure besides its quantity. He regards physical or sensory pleasure as inherently second-rate, and pleasures of the mind as inherently superior. To see the implausibility of this view, we need only alter McTaggart's thought experiment as follows: Instead of an oyster enjoying its food, we can imagine a human being whose mind has been so damaged that he can feel only a single, ongoing intellectual pleasure. He lies in bed and hears a voice repeating a funny joke several times an hour, day in and day out. The poor man is amused each time the joke is told, for his memory has been destroyed, and so each repetition of the joke comes as a fresh and pleasant surprise. Clearly, this kind of life is as impoverished as that of McTaggart's oyster. If they are of equal length, there is nothing to choose between them. The oyster's pleasure is sensory, whereas the man's pleasure engages his linguistic and mental competence—but these differences do not make a difference in the quality of their lives.

One lesson we can learn from McTaggart is that Mill's appeal to differences in the quality of pleasures will not by itself take him all the way to the conclusion that human life is superior in value to other forms of existence. If intellectual pleasures are awarded "extra points" for being intellectual, the oyster's life will still win out against a human life if the oyster's life is long enough. For Mill's quality–quantity distinction to do the work he wants it to do, he must say that "higher" pleasures are incommensurably better than "lower pleasures." But clearly a single ongoing intellectual pleasure is not incommensurably superior to a single ongoing physical pleasure—it is not even better when the quantities of each are the same.

Value theory does need the notions of incommensurable superiority and inferiority, as I have argued. But the items to which these relations apply are not two kinds of pleasure; they are a single, uniform pleasure on the one hand and a vastly more complex experience on the other. What makes the latter incommensurably superior is the presence of items that are in many other phenomenological categories besides pleasure.

The lesson to be learned from Mill would not be well expressed by the crude and simplistic formula, "higher quality trumps greater quantity." For whenever one alternative is superior in prudential value to another, that is partly because the better alternative has more (a greater quantity) of *something* than the other. The life of Socrates (to take Mill's example) contains a greater quantity of intellectual curiosity than does the life of McTaggart's oyster—for Socrates has much, and the oyster none.

True, the oyster has more of something else than Socrates has—it has many more years of the pleasures of the stomach. So, here we are making *two* quantitative comparisons: Socrates has more of one kind of good, the oyster more of another. The kernel of truth contained in Mill's use of the quantity–quality distinction is that one quantitative difference may be of greater significance than another. The kinds of experiences human beings can have and the oyster cannot are such that, when we have enough of them, our lives are made better than the oyster's, however long its simple pleasures last. We cannot make an all-things-considered assessment of the difference in the prudential value of the two kinds of life by finding some single dimension of comparison, and awarding the first prize to the kind of life that has a greater quantity along that dimension. There is no "exchange rate" that would allow us to say how much of one type of good is equal in value to another. This is why we can be helped by speaking of the quality of goods as well as their quantity. (I will return to this point in Chapter 4, section 4.)

10. Why grow up?

At one point in his discussion of pleasure, Aristotle says: "No one would choose to live the whole of his life with the mind of a child, even if he were to take the utmost pleasure in what pleases children" (X.3 1174a1–3).

Here he is conducting a thought experiment akin, in one respect, to McTaggart's. He is imagining a situation in which the temporal extent of a kind of life (that of a child rather than an oyster) is much larger than it ever really is, and then asking whether that transformation would make it worth choosing over some rather different form of life (one that proceeds as usual from childhood to adulthood). He assumes that childhood is not as good a time of life as adulthood—at any rate, when circumstances are favorable. (So too, McTaggart assumes that at any single time an oyster's life is inferior to a human being's.) That is because "the mind of a child" is not fully developed. Unlike McTaggart, Aristotle is not asking whether the vastly greater duration of one of two lives more than compensates for its moment-by-moment inferiority.

Even so, there is a conflict between Aristotle and McTaggart on the value of pleasure. Aristotle imagines a child whose childish pleasures are as great as you like. McTaggart would say that if that sort of childhood could be extended for a sufficiently long period of time, that would be better than normal human life, no matter what a child would be missing by not becoming an adult. Aristotle does not explicitly address himself to that question, but obviously he would deny what McTaggart affirms. Aristotle's thesis here is that no matter how much childish pleasure a life has, if it has *only* childish pleasures, it will be worse for an individual than the life he could have by moving on from these immature pleasures to the full range of goods (including adult pleasures) that he (Aristotle) takes well-being to consist in.

He might have added that it would be undesirable if *all of us together* remained children for the entire duration of our lives. A world that consisted solely of children and no adults would quickly sink into social chaos. But that point by itself does not secure Aristotle's conclusion that it would be worse for *a* child (any child you choose) to continue to have the mind and body of a child throughout a life of normal duration than to proceed from childhood to adulthood in the usual manner. Against him, it can be said that when childhood goes well, that is very good for the child—it can be a time filled with joy; and adulthood inevitably brings with it responsibilities and burdens that children are free of. So, it is a fair question whether Aristotle is right: for an individual's sake, would it not be best for him to continue to have the mind of a child throughout the whole of his life?

One way to answer this question would be to say that there are non-experiential goods that only an adult can have, and that we should leave the mentality of a child behind in order to attain them. What are these goods? I will address that question when I turn to the experience machine in Chapter 3. (They are things you cannot get when you are in the machine.) In the meantime, I suggest that if we think in terms of psychological phenomena that I mentioned earlier under the heading of the richness of human experience, we can give a satisfactory explanation of why it is best for an individual not to continue to have the mind of a child throughout the whole of life. Experience becomes increasingly rich as our cognitive, affective, and social powers develop.[57]

Think, for example, of the difference between the aesthetic experiences available to children and to adults. A child who read *War and Peace* would get nothing out of it. An adult can have a far fuller emotional response to a painting of da Vinci or Vermeer than any child. Bach's "Mass in B Minor" can be appreciated only by a musical sensibility more sophisticated than that of any child. Even simple folk melodies do not resonate in a child the way they do in an adult. Similarly, a child's limited cognitive skills restrict his ability to experience the joys of philosophy, science, and mathematics. A child cannot have a deep knowledge of history. The beauty of the natural world begins to strike us with full force only when we reach a certain age. A child cannot become excited about political events in the way an adult can, for he has no understanding of the forces and institutions of political life. A child's love of other people—his parents, for example—deepens as he becomes increasingly appreciative of their good qualities. A child cannot have a sense of being at peace with the world and with his fellow human beings, because he lacks the breadth of experience that make this sensibility possible. These remarks about a child's social, emotional, and cognitive limitations anticipate what I will say more fully when I turn, in Chapter 2, to the question of whether it is good to be a good human being.

11. The lives of plants and the value of pleasure

We should extend our discussion of well-being from the realm of simple conscious creatures like oysters to non-conscious living things. I assume that plants do not

---

[57] A child, Philippa Foot points out, cannot experience "deep" happiness. See *Natural Goodness*, 86.

experience phenomenal qualities. Instead, they have exquisite systems for taking in information about their immediate environment—light, odor, surface contact, gravity, and so on. (Roots grow downward because they respond to gravity. Trees growing on mountain ridges and thus exposed to high winds develop thick trunks. Plants "know" when it is spring or autumn by responding to variations in daylight hours.)[58] But they do not have auditory experiences, visual experiences, and so on; they feel no pleasure or pain; and in general they are devoid of any kind of phenomenal awareness. Even so, plants have needs. They fare well in certain environments and poorly in others. They can be harmed. They are teleological systems, and their *telos* is survival and reproduction.

In certain circumstances, a plant's needs serve as reasons for conclusions about how they should be treated. Suppose you are walking through a forest and notice a large group of plants that are "suffering" from dehydration; you also see a large pool of water just above the plants, and you realize that by removing an obstacle impeding the flow of the water, the plants will receive a good, long drink, and will survive and flourish. Should you remove the obstacle? It will just take an effortless movement of your arm; the cost to you would be nothing. Or should you walk on by without lifting a finger? The question is not whether indifference to the survival of the plants is morally permissible. It is: what should you do? Surely there is a reason to give the plants water: they need it. And there is no reason not to do so. So, you ought to remove the obstacle that is keeping water from flowing towards the plants. It does not matter that the plants are not *suffering* from their lack of water. They need it. It will be good for them to have it. It does not matter that plants lack consciousness; that does not weaken or undermine the case for giving them what they need.

So, there are non-experiential goods. The well-being of plants is constituted only by such goods. But that does not show that *human* well-being consists partly in non-experiential goods. When a human being suffers a terrible misfortune, irretrievably loses all consciousness, and becomes merely a locus for biological processes, he has been robbed of all the distinctively human goods he once had. Is what remains still him—the same individual, but one with a much lower level of well-being? Or has the individual that was present in that body ceased to exist? That of course is one of the great metaphysical debates of our time and earlier philosophical eras. Fortunately, for present purposes, it can be set aside. The point that should be recognized is that although there are non-experiential goods for certain forms of life, it does not follow that their counterparts in human life are part of what makes life good for you or me.

I now must address an apparent difficulty in my position. I have agreed with McTaggart that the longer an oyster lives, the better off it is, provided that it continues to experience pleasure as it takes in nourishment. The value of each new day's pleasure remains the

---

[58] For accessible overviews, see Daniel Chamovitz, *What a Plant Knows*. The elaborate and cooperative social network of trees in a forest is celebrated in Peter Wohlleben, *The Hidden Life of Trees*. The first part of that book's subtitle points to its great weakness: *What They Feel, How They Communicate*. See too Chauncey Maher, *Plant Minds: A Philosophical Defense*.

same. Now, suppose McTaggart had used a plant rather than an oyster in his thought experiment. That plant attains its *telos* day after day, and the value of its doing so remains undiminished over the length of its great life. Surely no one would be tempted to accept his conclusion that the life of a plant will eventually be better than a human life of normal duration, no matter how good that human life is. That conclusion is patently absurd—whereas many of us have at least some inclination to wonder whether his point about the oyster might be true.

What explains this difference? We might account for it by saying that pleasure really is good for creatures that can feel it—McTaggart got that right—whereas remaining alive is not good for any creature. But we should reject this suggestion. Remaining alive is one of the goals around which biological systems are organized. In certain circumstances, we should let water flow to the flora in a forest simply because that would be good for them.

Another diagnosis would be this: when we change McTaggart's thought experiment so that it concerns a plant rather than an oyster, it becomes immediately evident that there is no value in an individual's living beyond the amount of time allotted to it by its nature as a member of this or that species. It is not bad for a plant to die at the end of its normal life cycle, because that is what plants naturally do. We can see that point clearly, but (so the argument goes) we become less clear-headed when the same idea is extended to other creatures—oysters and human beings, for example. If we accept this diagnosis, we are back to the notion (mentioned briefly in section 5) that the pleasure experienced by the oyster is good for only a limited period of time—namely, for as much time as oysters normally live. But now that idea is presented not as a pure thesis about what time does to value, but as a conceptual connection between *nature*, value, and time.

We should reject this diagnosis because it is simply not so that if something interferes with a thing's nature, it cannot be good for it. When we can improve on nature in ways that involve no down-side, we have good reason to do so. If elderly people can see much better by wearing glasses or undergoing eye surgery, they should welcome these interventions, even though that interferes with the natural deterioration of their eyesight. So, I think we have no good reason to reject McTaggart's assumption that it would be best for an oyster to go on and on feeling pleasure far beyond the normal lifespan of oysters.

This commits me to saying that if the life of a plant could be extended far beyond what nature "intends," that would be good for the plant. But I see no reason not to embrace that commitment. A tree that lived several thousand years would be a marvel of evolutionary fitness; it would have succeeded in achieving its *telos* far beyond what is done by other living things. Flourishing over a long period of time is better than that same level of flourishing for a short while. Evolutionary forces have produced lives that have some value, but those forces have had limited success, because decay, deterioration, and destruction lie in wait for all of earth's creatures. Ours is not a perfect world.

I will make one further observation regarding the extension of McTaggart's thought experiment from oysters to plants. He compares human life at its best with the life of an extraordinarily long-lived simple creature that regularly experiences pleasure. Now we have added a third kind of living thing to the mix: plants, creatures whose lives contain no experiential goods whatsoever. Let us ask how to arrange these three kinds of lives on a scale from better to worse. For these purposes, we can set aside differences in longevity: let the three lives be of the same duration. The plant has only non-experiential goods; the oyster has those sorts of goods, and in addition it feels pleasure; and human beings at their best have a far richer range of experiential goods. What I find striking is that not only is there an obvious ordering—human life first, oyster life second, plant life third—but that two of these lives are much closer to each other in value than either is to the third. The oyster has a better life than a plant, but the gap between them is small in comparison with the distance of both from human life. Only a small leap in value took place on Planet Earth when creatures emerged that not only took in nourishment but did so because that produced a sensation of pleasure. By comparison, what is on offer for human beings at their best is far greater.

If these comparisons are correct, a striking conclusion follows: the value of pleasure in human life, considered on its own, is very small in comparison to the value of other aspects of our experience.[59] The fact that an oyster feels pleasure makes its life only a bit better than that of a plant (when we compare both to human life at its best). That is a point about the value of pleasure, considered on its own; and so it applies to pleasure on its own wherever it is found—whether in the life of an oyster or a human being. It cannot be the case that if a living thing is feeling pleasure (of no matter what sort) and that living thing is human, then that is very good for him or her, whereas if something non-human is feeling pleasure, its value is far smaller, simply because it is felt by a non-human. Pleasure on its own cannot vary in value simply in virtue of what sort of creature feels it.

So, we have found another way of supporting an observation that I made earlier (section 7): our phenomenological world is a highly variegated matter, and pleasure is only one small aspect of it. If we consider it in isolation from the riches of the other components of our experience, it remains something to which we are attracted, but we are (and ought to be) far more attracted to the complex phenomenological array of which it is often a part. It is only a small part of a full account of what is good for us. (So too is happiness, when it is understood as a state of mind different from pleasure—an emotion akin to contentment, delight, rapture, but differing in intensity. Oysters

---

[59] A similar point is made by Hurka: "Imagine a world containing only intense mindless pleasures, such as those of eating chocolate. (I make them mindless so there won't be anything else such as knowledge that could give this world value.) If we ask whether this is a good world...the answer is surely yes. But if we ask whether it's a very good world or only somewhat good, it seems to me that it's only somewhat good." See *The Best Things in Life*, 55. (He adds: a world that contains only intense mindless pain is a very bad world, and therefore "pleasure is a lesser good than pain is an evil.") My claim is that pleasure is a small component of well-being; his is that pleasure makes the universe a slightly better place. They are similar points but not the same.

cannot be happy. That we can be happy is an enrichment of our lives, but even so, like pleasure, it is only one small part of what is good for us.[60])

This point about pleasure remains true whether it is applied to very mild pleasures (such as the ones I imagine are available to an oyster) or those that are quite intense. Suppose McTaggart had asked us to assume not only that an oyster feels pleasure but that it feels a great deal of it at each moment of its extremely long existence. That would not have altered the force of his thought experiment one bit; it would have raised exactly the same issues. We would still be right to conclude that human life at its best is superior to that of any oyster, however long-lived, and however intense the pleasures of an oyster, because it would remain the case that the rich complexity of the phenomenal world of human experience is superior to the uni-dimensional life of even that kind of high-octane oyster.[61] That does not mean that intensity of pleasure can make no difference to the value of experience. Other things being equal, an experience that includes more pleasure is the better experience. But intensity of pleasure typically does not leave the rest of what we simultaneously experience the same: when it wipes out everything else in our experiential repertoire, it greatly reduces the quality of our lives.

We could also alter McTaggart's thought experiment by adding this feature: the oyster does not get pleasure from just one kind of food, but from many. The way things taste to it is not uniform, but varies according to the chemical composition of what it ingests. So its pleasurable experiences vary quite a bit over time (though, we are assuming, it does not remember what its earlier pleasures were like). But giving the oyster this kind of variability in its conscious existence does not and should not undermine our confidence that human life (of a normal length) can be incommensurably superior. It does not matter if the oyster is getting pleasure from a taste experience different from

---

[60] Nozick makes this point in *The Examined Life*, 99. It should also be recognized that "happiness" names not only an emotion like joy (which involves some excitation) but also a calm approval (the attitude of being glad that). Happiness in this sense has little value of its own. I might be glad to hear that Senator X has been re-elected, not recognizing how much his power will be used to harm me. In such cases as these, for my own good, I ought not to be glad or happy. Just as "unhappiness" is sometimes used to cover all bad experience ("suffering" in the broadest sense), so happiness frequently designates the paradigm of good experience (joy), and even refers to all that is good in experience. In this common but inflated sense, it can serve as a more-or-less apt stand-in for Aristotle's use of *eudaimonia*. For a philosophical theory of happiness that views it as a major component of well-being, see Daniel M. Haybron, *The Pursuit of Unhappiness*.

[61] I do not assume that the pleasures enjoyed by all animals are as simple and mild as those experienced by oysters. Consider the following depiction of bovine pleasure by Philip Roth: "... slow moving, strife-free cows, each a fifteen-hundred-pound industry of its own gratification, big-eyed beasts for whom chomping at one extremity from a fodder-filled trough while being sucked dry at the other by not one or two or three but by four pulsating, untiring mechanical mouths—for whom sensual stimulus simultaneously at both ends were their voluptuous due. Each of them deep into a bestial existence blissfully lacking in spiritual depth: to squirt and to chew, to crap and to piss, to graze and to sleep—that was their whole raison d'être.... The best of carnal everything, including savoring at their leisure mushy, dripping mouthfuls of their own stringy cud. Few courtesans have lived as well, let alone workaday women." *The Human Stain*, 47–8. One may wonder how Roth knows that cows can be "deep" into anything (especially if they lack depth), whether the word "blissfully" is applicable to anything they do, whether they do have "the best of carnal everything," and whether the life of a courtesan can be no more enjoyable than that of a cow. Even so, I find it plausible that a cow's pleasures can be greater than an oyster's.

those it had before—it has no sense of that difference. From the outside, we can see that its experience changes, but from the inside it makes no difference whether its food tastes the same or different from one day to another.

Aristotle had within his reach the point that pleasure's value to us derives from the way it combines with and enhances other parts of our mental life rather than from what it is on its own. He does not say: think of pleasure in isolation from all else, and you will then come to see that it is good. Rather, he agrees with Eudoxus that when it is added to something that is good, the result is better; and that could not be the case, if pleasure is not itself good (X.2 1172b23–25). *How* good it is to feel a certain kind of pleasure, I would say, depends not on any feature of that phenomenon itself but on the goodness of the rest of the total experience of which it forms a part. That is not far from Aristotle's claim that whether a pleasure is choiceworthy depends not on the pleasure assessed in isolation but on what it is a pleasure in (X.5 1175b24–28).

12. *The truth in hedonism: experientialism*

Some of the great philosophers—Epicurus, Lucretius, Mill, Sidgwick—have been drawn to hedonism; and yet what has emerged from my reflections on McTaggart's thought experiment is not only that there are other goods besides pleasure, but that it is in itself a small good. So small that no matter how intense it is and how long it lasts, some other bundle of goods (one that includes pleasure but much else) is superior, even when vastly shorter in duration.[62]

What then accounts for the appeal of the idea that only pleasure is good? My conjectural reply is that there is a kernel of truth in this doctrine: this is the thesis that what is good in human life is the quality of our conscious existence. It is what goes on in our minds, what constitutes the self, that accounts for the goodness and badness of our lives—not something external to us, or something we can have without being aware that we have it, or something that remains true of us even when we no longer exist. (Of course, according to this picture, the external world is important too: derivatively so, because it affects our internal world.) It is this idea, I have suggested, that makes readers of Plato, Aristotle, and the Stoics think there is something to what they say about the human good. If justice and the other features that characterize a good human being are good qualities for us to have (and not merely dispositions to deliver goods to others), that must be because of what the soul of a just person is like—something about

---

[62] Crisp's assessment of hedonism in 'Hedonism Reconsidered' is almost the opposite of mine. He argues that pleasure and pleasure alone can explain why something is good for us. Admittedly, he says, "the value of an experience might depend partly on the phenomenological quality of that experience, that is, on what the subject is taking enjoyment in" (634). So, for him, other things besides enjoyment itself matter for prudential value, but they matter derivatively. On my view, the value of an experience that includes pleasure not only depends on the other phenomenological features of that experience besides pleasure; what is valuable in the experience is the whole phenomenological array, only one aspect of which is hedonic. For example, part of what makes the experience of listening to music good is how the music sounds to us, how it makes us feel, and how we think as we listen. What we rightly value is the totality of our experience of music, not just the pleasure we feel as we listen.

the thoughts, desires, and feelings of such a person. Aristotle adds: true, but he had better not fall asleep for the rest of his life. Aristotle's point is compelling. It is not when we are unconscious that our lives are good. We feel that the goodness of our lives lies in what is closest to home: it is what life is like for us.

The ancient philosophers were right, then, to focus their attention on the inner life of a good person, and to ask what it is. In what follows, I leave aside their ways of answering that question. Drawing instead on our common sense assumptions about virtue, I will ask: what, in the experiential component of being a good person, is good for that person? Then I must confront a formidable challenge to the assumption that our introspectable world is what matters or should matter to us. Nozick's thought experiment is often thought to show that what is available to introspection is far from being the whole of human well-being. You can have whatever experiences you like in the experience machine, but even so your life would have meager value, for you would be nothing but a blob cut off from reality. Nozick, I will argue, was wrong. What is ultimately good or bad in human life resides entirely within the way we experience it. If two lives are introspectively indistinguishable, they cannot differ in quality.

2

Well-Being and Ethical Virtue

1. Well-being and lists

What is well-being? Philosophers (and not only they) disagree. But, as I noted (Chapter 1, section 4), it is part of the concept that it consists in something (or some things). The quality of your life cannot change on its own, without any other change (inside or outside you) occurring. For well-being to increase or diminish, something else must increase or diminish as well—namely, that in which it consists. So, it is important to distinguish the questions, (A) What is well-being—what does it consist in?, and (B) What are the things that we need in order to acquire the goods in which well-being consists?

Well-being must have at least one constituent. It might have just one. Or more than one but just a few. Or a great many. But in any case, every statement of what well-being is—what its constituent is or its constituents are—could be called a list. A list can have just one item on it, or be short, or very long. So, when philosophy tries to answer the question, "What is well-being?" it is, in a sense, proposing an "objective list" in response to that question. It purports to be objective, in that it offers what it takes to be the correct answer to that question.[1] (If our answer just gives a list, it might seem that we are evading a deeper issue: on what basis does an item go on the list? I return to that issue later in this chapter, section 3.)

Lists can be surprising and illuminating, especially when they are short. If someone announces, "there are just three things worth pursuing in life," and proceeds to list them, that should be of great interest to us, because he is proposing that beneath the variety and complexity of human existence something quite simple should guide

---

[1] In recent literature on well-being, the term "objective list" is often used differently: it designates one particular kind of theory of well-being, according to which its components (or at least some of them) are good for individuals regardless of whether those individuals have positive experiences of, or positive attitudes towards, those items. For example, an objective list theory might say that excellence in playing the piano has prudential value even if the individual who excels at this activity thoroughly dislikes it, sees no value in it, and it is altogether a bad experience for him. In that sense, the theory of well-being proposed here does not offer an "objective list" account. The term, with more or less this meaning, came into circulation due to the influence of Derek Parfit, *Reasons and Persons*, Appendix I. On the difficulties involved in defining or characterizing an "objective list theory" in the narrow sense, see Guy Fletcher, 'Objective List Theories,' in Guy Fletcher (ed.), *The Routledge Handbook of the Philosophy of Well-Being*; and two essays in Ben Eggleston and Dale E. Miller (eds.), *The Cambridge Companion to Utilitarianism*: Ben Bradley, 'Objective Theories of Well-Being'; and Chris Heathwood, 'Subjective Theories of Well-Being.'

us. If the three items on the list are not species belonging to a more general kind of good, there will be no answer to the question, "What do these items share that makes it the case that they ought to be on the list?" But that would not count against the claim that there are just these three goods. Nor would it diminish the great interest of such a claim.

According to the doctrine I am calling "experientialism," all components of well-being have a phenomenological aspect (Chapter 1, section 1). There is something it is like to be in that state. (Similarly for all that by itself diminishes well-being.) Of course, not every type of experience is a part of well-being. Which are? It is important to see that a theory of well-being need not be defective simply because it gives us a list without claiming that it is complete. In fact, leaving the list open might be exactly the right idea. Suppose someone said: "well-being consists only in reading good novels." Obviously, that won't do—it is too narrow. But it is not a further defect that we have not been given a definitive and closed list of which novels are the good ones. (After all, they keep on being written.) What we would need is some rough and ready standard for making aesthetic judgments, and sufficient exposure to novels to evaluate their quality. Similarly, experientialism needs to say *something* about good experience. That is not a task that is neglected here. It will be argued in this chapter that it is good to be a good person. The thesis of Chapter 1 that some human goods are incommensurably superior to those available to other forms of life relies for its plausibility on specific examples. It should be emphasized that this task need not take the form of a complete list of the experiences that are good. I will not propose an exact number of the higher-order goods of human life. That open-endedness might be a feature that a theory of well-being ought to have.

Just as the absurd theory that well-being consists only in reading good novels would be not only absurd but useless, if we had no way of distinguishing good ones from bad ones, so experientialism must address the question of how we can tell which are the good experiences. I turn to that question in sections 2–6 below.

In Chapter 1, I distanced myself from the hedonistic conception of well-being. I will assume, as well, that well-being does not consist in the satisfaction of one's desires.[2] Just as someone's belief that X is a component of his well-being can be mistaken, so someone's desire to possess some apparent good can be misguided, because it is not in fact good for him. Some people, for example, have a strong desire to be famous—regardless of what they are famous for. But you can achieve great fame and then fall asleep for the rest of your life. (Your perpetual state of sleep might in fact contribute to your fame.) Aristotle's point (Chapter 1, section 2) that we should seek not simply the state of having the virtues, but the far better state of activating them in our wakeful hours, applies here as well.

---

[2] My reasons for rejecting this approach are more fully presented in *What Is Good and Why*, 94–120. I will return to the desire-satisfaction account of well-being in Chapter 3, section 18.

The conception of well-being I advance and defend here might be called "experiential developmentalism" or "experiential eudaimonism," because it combines experientialism with Aristotelian ideas about the value of developing our natural powers.[3] I will not need a name for my theory in what follows, but if the reader wants to call my theory something, these would be apt descriptions. It is, in a way, a pluralistic conception of well-being, because there is considerable heterogeneity in the sorts of things it takes to be its basic elements. In particular, pleasure is only one aspect of good experiences, and they may be good for us even in its absence. But there is of course something that I believe they have in common, in addition to the fact that they constitute the quality of a life: their experiential nature.

I take it to be a strength of experientialism that it is pluralistic—it holds that well-being consists not just in some single good (such as pleasure) but in a variety, although they are alike in having an experiential nature. But some philosophers claim that, on the contrary, it counts *against* a conception of value that it recognizes an irreducible variety of heterogeneous goods. Sidgwick, for example, argues that although "Virtue, Truth, Freedom, Beauty, etc."[4] are treated by common sense as ultimate ends in themselves, there must be some single standard—pleasure (which he sometimes calls "happiness")—that resolves conflicts between them. "If we ask for a final criterion of the comparative value of the different objects of men's enthusiastic pursuit, and of the limits within which each may legitimately engross the attention of mankind, we shall…conceive it to depend on the degree to which they respectively conduce to Happiness."[5] "We have a practical need" he adds, of deciding between these values when one is incompatible with another, or more of one requires less of another.[6] His tacit assumption is that we can make such judgments only if there is one value that is the "criterion of the comparative value" of the others. The best candidate for that role is what he calls happiness or pleasure.

---

[3] It might be suggested that it also be called "experiential *perfectionism*," but that would not be an apt label, because of the way "perfectionism" is commonly used by moral philosophers. Perfectionism, construed as a theory of human well-being, holds that its sole constituent is the excellent development of the capacities we have because of our human nature. For example, according to such a theory, if you have written a novel of great literary merit, you have excelled as a wordsmith and story-teller, and so, to that extent, you have increased your level of well-being. What the experience of writing was like for you, according to such a theory, is neither here nor there—it might have been hell. By contrast, the quality of that experience (not the quality of the novel or one's excellence as a novelist) is what matters, according to the conception of well-being I endorse. A related point is that perfectionism cannot account for the prudential value of simple pleasant experiences like basking in the sun or eating a piece of chocolate. On my account, these experiences *are* good for us—although they are not what I am calling "higher order" goods (the kind that make human life of ordinary duration better than the life of any oyster, however long-lived). For a sympathetic treatment of this theory, see Gwen Bradford, 'Perfectionism', in Guy Fletcher (ed.), *The Routledge Handbook of Philosophy of Well-Being*. As she notes, a theory of value might be called "perfectionist" without being a theory of well-being. She rightly cites Thomas Hurka as "one of the central contemporary proponents of this view" (125). See his *Perfectionism*. For J. S. Mill's way of combining hedonism and perfectionism, see David Brink, *Mill's Progressive Principles*, 46–78.

[4] *The Methods of Ethics*, 405.   [5] Ibid., 406.   [6] Ibid., 406.

Sidgwick here overlooks the fact that even hedonism posits heterogeneous values: it holds not only that pleasure (enjoyment) is good but also that pain (suffering) is bad. When we decide whether it is worth it to experience certain pleasures (rich food) that will cause some suffering (indigestion), we are weighing two different values against each other, each with its own phenomenology. One way to answer that comparative question would be to say that pleasure in itself is just as good for us as pain is bad for us—they have equal (but opposite) values. We must then simply attend to the intensity and duration of these experiences, and let those differences decide between them. In doing so, we would be comparing a certain experience of pain with a certain experience of pleasure with respect to their prudential value. Our test would be: how good or bad for us is each of these two items? No third component of well-being need be posited to decide this question.[7] Nor would a third component be needed if we held instead that pain is in itself more bad for us than pleasure is good for us; or vice versa. In either case, we would not only attend to the intensity and duration of pain and pleasure, but would also put a thumb on the scale of comparison, in recognition of the greater place one or the other has in well-being and its opposite. We would have a dualism of ultimate values, with nothing but our judgment to resolve conflicts between them.

It therefore must not be counted against a conception of well-being that it takes there to be several different kinds of prudential value (at least one good thing and one bad thing). All theories of well-being have this feature. What makes it a strength of experientialism that it posits a variety of experiences (not just pleasure) as components of well-being is that this variety is precisely what our experience of life reveals to us. Our most treasured experiences are the ones that have more in them than a hedonic component, and we treasure them not only for that one feature but also because of their emotional, cognitive, conative, visual, auditory, and gustatory content.

We can get by, as we always have, with rough and ready ways of choosing between different types of experiences—by judging, for example, that standing outside for twelve hours in the cold and rain is not an excessive price to pay for a chance to hear the remarkable jazz band we have read about. We take into account what it is like to feel cold, wet, and tired; and what it will be like to hear those sounds and be moved by those songs. Similarly, it is possible to resolve a conflict between some of the values Sidgwick mentions, and we can do so without invoking some third value (pleasure) as the scale on which they must be measured. Just having a bit more beauty in one's life (an afternoon in the museum) would be too high a price to pay if it meant that over the course of a long existence one would never again have what is valuable in the inner life of a good person. There are, of course, many cases in which it is not easy to know what one should do for the sake of one's well-being. No theory of well-being can be expected to make that problem go away. Hedonism does not do so. And it gives the wrong explanation of what makes these hard choices.

---

[7] Here I follow James Griffin, *Well-Being*, 90.

I turn next to another feature that I believe is shared by the elements of well-being, in addition to the fact that we can introspect their quality: they arise in us in part because, being human, we possess certain natural powers. That is what I mean to suggest by the terms "experiential *developmentalism*" and "experiential *eudaimonism*."

2. *Methodology, philosophy, and flourishing*

One aspect of Aristotle's ethics to which I am attracted is his picture of human beings as creatures who (like others) go through a process of development and maturation. A background assumption that shapes his thinking contains a "should": we should grow up. Why should we? Because when we do so properly, better things are in store for us as grown-ups (Chapter 1, section 10). That being so (and here I draw a conclusion that puts me at odds with Aristotle), we adults must know something about what makes for a good childhood—what is good for an individual *when* he is a child (and not good only because it is preparation for later life).[8] We must also implicitly know what makes adulthood a potentially better period. We compare that early time of life with what comes after it, and we see that opportunities for well-being increase. A theory of well-being would be ignoring valuable data if it did not build on this common knowledge.

So, when life is good for us, that is because the potentialities that gradually are realized through education and training—our cognitive, emotional, and social powers— are regularly exercised over the many years of adulthood, as we engage in ethical activity (and other sorts of activity as well). The activities that express these powers are not to be valued only because they are productive of some further good; rather they constitute *eudaimonia* or well-being. As I read Aristotle, well-being is not composed of all the goods of human life—honor, for example, is not one of its constituents—but only those that are "internal" to us—what he calls the goods of the soul rather than external or bodily goods.[9] We do not benefit (or not very much) merely from *having* these goods—after all, someone who sleeps away his life still has them, but that is not a good life. I have adapted his idea and defended the thesis that well-being consists in a particular variety of ongoing and highly variegated forms of consciousness, one element of which is pleasure.

---

[8] Children ought to be nurtured and educated with a view to their overall lifetime well-being, not solely to their well-being as children. Even so, lifetime well-being is to be assessed by adding together the well-being of smaller temporal parts of life, one of which is childhood. That last clause—"one of which is childhood"—is anti-Aristotelian. He does not acknowledge childhood as a portion of lifetime well-being (chapter 4, sections 8, 9, and 20).

[9] Honor, he says, is often the ultimate goal pursued by those who devote themselves to politics, but they are misguided. "Honour, however seems too shallow to be an object of our inquiry, since honour seems to depend more on those who honour than on the person honoured, whereas we surmise the good to be something of one's own that cannot easily be taken away" (*NE* I.5 1095b23–6). "Goods have been classified into three groups: those called external goods, goods of the soul, and goods of the body. Goods of the soul are the ones we call most strictly and especially good" (I.8 1098b12–15). I will discuss these passages in Chapter 3, section 23.

Here is the methodology that should be employed when one is looking for an answer to the question, "What is well-being?"[10] (I return to this topic in section 4 below.) Start with some concrete activity that you are confident is good for you, not because it is a means to something further, but in itself. Ask whether there is some general feature of that activity that accounts for its goodness—a feature that is present in the lives of other human beings whom you take to be living good lives. Be careful to avoid the dangers of parochialism—of thinking that only you, or only those you associate with, have any of the elements of well-being. Ask yourself what it would take to make *any* human life a good one—or rather the life of anyone who lives in circumstances sufficiently similar to ours. (Not *homo habilis*, but *homo sapiens*; and particularly those of us who have adequate food, shelter, physical safety, literacy, political organizations, the arts and sciences, and so on.) If you can find a short enough answer to the question, "What makes a human life a good one for the individual living it?" then you are proposing that beneath the variety and complexity of human existence there is something quite simple that makes human life good. If the constituents of well-being that you propose strike us as obviously good, if no doubts about their goodness are found reasonable, and if they genuinely explain the goodness of everything else that we take to be good, you have found the right theory of well-being.

To speak of my own case: I believe my life is going well, and to a large extent that is because I spend much of my time doing what I love. Philosophy fascinates me, and I count my engagement with it as a component of my well-being. In addition, when I ask myself whether in presenting this subject to my students I am trying to benefit them, I reply that I am. It would be rather cynical of me to expose them to philosophy if I thought this could only be a waste of their time. (I believe as well that it would be good for many students who have not yet studied philosophy to be introduced to this subject.) And although philosophy may in some cases have instrumental value (for example, it trains people to "think outside the box," and as a result they become more creative entrepreneurs and business professionals), that is not the only sort of reason to value it. By itself, it adds to the quality of one's life.

Some readers may resist the suggestion that philosophy is non-instrumentally good *for* anyone, not because they dislike the subject or do not value it for itself, but because they would rather describe it as "worthwhile" than as "good for" anyone. To their ears, to say of something that it is good *for* you can only mean that it is good as a means to something else. But we should not be distracted by merely verbal questions. The important issue is whether a certain kind of engagement with this subject is itself an enhancement of the quality of one's life—whether it is a component of one's well-being, and not at best a mere means to well-being.

I don't need to assume that it would be in *everyone's* interest to study philosophy. There is such a thing as a philosophical temperament; perhaps there is also such a thing

---

[10] Here I draw upon some material in my 'Human Diversity and the Nature of Well-Being: Reflections on Sumner's Methodology.'

as philosophical talent. It could be that some people are totally lacking in these qual-ities or have so little of them that it would be a waste of their time to study philosophy. But in the same way it would be a waste of time for someone who is permanently blind to study art history. An inability to engage in abstract thought, or an unalterable lack of interest in speculative questions, is one kind of cognitive limitation or deficiency.

There are of course many other sorts of cognitive deficits besides these, and nearly all of us are intellectually deficient or weaker in certain areas, stronger in others. Some people are bad with numbers. Others lack the linguistic creativity needed for writing poetry. I do not claim that the absence of a philosophical temperament or philosophical skills is a worse cognitive debility than many other kinds. My thesis that philosophy is good for many students should be taken to mean that this is one component of their well-being.

It might be said that if one approaches philosophy in the right way, one becomes a deeper, more thoughtful person. It is mind-expanding, a form of mental enrichment. I agree, but we should once more apply the point Aristotle makes when he observes that a virtuous person would continue to possess the virtues even if he fell asleep for the rest of his life. Similarly, the non-instrumental value of philosophy does not lie in the mental condition of having a mind that has been expanded by the study of philoso-phy, but in the conscious activity of philosophizing. It is the experience one has when one is engaged with philosophical topics that is a component of one's well-being. Someone who once studied philosophy with the right attitude and then fell asleep for the rest of his life would have enhanced the quality of his life—but only at that earlier time, not for the remainder of his days.

Aristotle says that philosophy begins in "wonder" and refers to "puzzlement" as part of the process of philosophizing (*Metaphysics* I.2 982b12–18). These states of mind are also mentioned by Bertrand Russell, when he describes the value of philosophy in the following terms:

It is...to be sought largely in its very *uncertainty*. The man who has no tincture of philosophy goes through life imprisoned in the prejudices derived from common sense....To such a man the world tends to become definite, finite, obvious; common objects rouse no questions, and unfamiliar possibilities are contemptuously rejected. As soon as we begin to philosophize...we find...that even the most everyday things lead to *problems* to which only very incomplete answers can be given. Philosophy...is able to suggest many possibilities which enlarge our thoughts and free them from the tyranny of custom....It greatly increases our knowledge as to what [things] may be; it removes the somewhat arrogant dogmatism of those who have never travelled into the region of *liberating doubt*, and it keeps alive our sense of *wonder* by showing familiar things in an *unfamiliar aspect*.[11]

There is, in other words, something it is like to philosophize; and Russell is asserting that this is in itself a good experience—good *for* someone. Admittedly, part of his defense of philosophy in this passage might be seen as a reference to its instrumental

---

[11] *The Problems of Philosophy*, chapter XV, 'The Value of Philosophy,' 156–7, emphasis added.

value. For example, by ridding us of common prejudices, it prepares the way for better states of mind. But he also implies that being uncertain, recognizing problems, having a sense of intellectual enlargement, liberation, and wonder are in themselves good states to be in.

Although the "wonder" that both Aristotle and Russell refer to sounds like a desirable experience to have, one might balk at the idea that it is also good for someone to experience the uncertainty and puzzlement that they also mention. But there is no real difficulty here: in many circumstances we love puzzles for themselves, and a sense of uncertainty can be an essential ingredient of a positive experience (detective stories). At the same time, we should avoid falling into the trap of supposing that the valuable aspect of philosophical activity lies *only* in the emotions or feelings (wonder, puzzlement, and so on) that accompany its cogitations. It is the entire experience that must be considered; this will be partly a matter of feeling and emotion, but to a very large extent it will contain the philosophical thinking that one does when one philosophizes. One cannot have a good sense of what this experience is like unless one grapples with the subject matter—the problems of philosophy (metaphysics, epistemology, ethics, and all the rest). To come to know what makes philosophizing an experience that enhances the quality of one's life, one must be exposed to and gripped by such problems as free will, skepticism, realism and nominalism, causation, the existence of God, utilitarianism, and so on. Simply to be told that it is good because it expands one's mind ("enlarges one's thoughts," as Russell says) is to remain on the outside of philosophical experience. Only a first-hand engagement with its intellectual content will give one an appreciation for its far-reaching profundity. Without this, one would be in the same situation as someone who is told about music but lacks any experience of it. We know best why music enhances the quality of our lives by being thrilled as we listen to it, and similarly we know best why philosophy can also play this role by being fascinated by philosophical ideas, problems, and theories. Puzzlement and uncertainty are appropriate parts of that complex experience.

We can now generalize from this one intellectual activity—philosophy—and apply what we have said to many other subjects of intense and systematic study. Some of what has been said here about philosophy applies no less to the study of history, literature, the arts, the sciences, mathematics, and so on. True, they have emotional profiles that differ, to some extent, from that of philosophy (less puzzlement, more certainty), but they too are comprised of a process of intellectual investigation. The point of being a historian or a mathematician, for example, is not to store knowledge in one's mind—knowledge that would remain stored there even if one slept away the rest of one's life. It is to explore historical or mathematical questions. It is that experience that enhances the quality of life of a historian or mathematician.

But our list of the components of well-being, even in this expanded form, is quite one-sided, because it focuses on the *intellectual* growth of human beings—and surely this is not the only dimension in which people develop. We should not ignore the many other ways, less intellectual or non-intellectual, in which human beings can develop, grow, or flourish. The remedy for that, accordingly, will be to look at those other areas of human life, calling to mind what we already know about what it is for human beings to develop well in those spheres. We should round out our list of things that are good for us by adding to it the development of the affects and passions, the growth of the senses and imagination, and the enhancement of our skills as embodied creatures in such arenas as dance and athletics. This gives us a broader picture of the many kinds of human flourishing.

This is why, when we ask about what, if anything, would be lost by plugging into the experience machine, it is important to clarify what sorts of experiences it would enable us to have—whether it would allow us to carry on with philosophy, music, art, and literature; whether it could give us all the conation, imagination, and emotion of normal ethical life; and so on. If it left all this intact, we could exercise the full range of our powers when plugged in; that we wrongly assume, when inside the machine, that we are fully embodied, experiencing distal objects, located not in a laboratory but elsewhere, would not by itself make our lives worse for us. (These points will be more fully developed in Chapter 3.)

I pointed out earlier (Chapter 1, section 6) that some things are known by internal observation: this is how we know what pleasure and pain are like, what it is like to desire something, entertain doubts about something, find something intriguing, feel sadness, remorse, guilt, and so on. So, when we judge that an experience we are having or have had is immeasurably rich and worth having for itself—as when we are absorbed in a great work of art, or surrounded by great natural beauty—we have some basis for valuing this experience precisely because it is our experience and we know it from the inside. Similarly, if we judge that our relationship with our children is one of the best things in our lives, we are basing that assessment on what we have lived through. When we "do philosophy," it is *these* particular issues (pointing to the thoughts that comprise the problems of philosophy) and our sense of fascination, wonder, puzzlement, and depth, that convince us that philosophy is worthwhile. The *goodness* of these activities is not experienced (it is not an observational property), but our judgment that it is good is based on experience.[12]

It would nonetheless be misleading or worse to say that the test of a theory of well-being is *simply* experience. That would be a distortion because it would fail to acknowledge the role of theory-construction and philosophical argument in finding and testing a theory of well-being.[13] The power of a theory of well-being, to the extent that it

---

[12] Cicero reports in *De Finibus* I.30 that according to Epicurus we know that pleasure is to be pursued and pain avoided by sensing that this is so, just as we sense that fire is hot, snow is white, and honey is sweet. But there is no organ that delivers to us sensory appearances of what we ought to do, or what is good, or right, or obligatory.

[13] Here again I am in agreement with Plato's methodology in the *Republic*. He appeals at one point to the test of experience (which of two experiences is hedonically better, according to those who have been exposed to both?); but that test, he adds, must be accompanied by reasoned argument (582d). See too Chapter 1, note 43. By contrast, the methodology J. S. Mill presupposes in *Utilitarianism* is constrained by his commitment to a strict form of empiricism.

has any, derives from its ability to explain what is good in a wide range of human lives by appealing to a small number of good-making features. Hedonism would be just such a theory, if pleasure could satisfactorily explain, all by itself, what is valuable in art, child-rearing, philosophy, and so on. But, as I have said, a better explanation is available to us when we recognize that what we value in the experiences we take to be good for us extends beyond pleasure and sometimes omits pleasure.

A human infant is not born with an unlimited potential to develop in any direction whatsoever; it will never be able to fly by its own efforts, or swim like a fish, or hunt like a wolf. Its powers are a small portion of what nature provides to species. Further, when we train children, we do not (or should not) treat them as mere instruments to be used for communal purposes, or our own needs; we want, or ought to want, to educate them so that life will be good for them as they develop, and will remain good throughout adulthood. We make use of the potential they have and build from there. It is a speculative but not implausible hypothesis that *all* of the good we can experience as adults is the fruit of this developmental process—that moral life, aesthetic experience, philosophy and the sciences, and so on, are the expression of natural powers. This is by no means an empty hypothesis. Being famous, being honored, being loved: these things are often sought as though in themselves they are good for us. If such a theory does better than any other in accounting for the great variety of ways in which human beings can have good lives, finding beneath that variety the multi-faceted development of a small number of powers that form our nature, it will have passed the proper test for assessing a theory of well-being.[14]

There are several other reasons to reject the simplistic idea that one's own experience provides the only test of a theory of well-being: First, it requires philosophical insight, not merely experience, to understand the concept of well-being. Prudential value, for example, is not perfectionist value. A constituent of well-being, to take another example, is different from a means to well-being. Second, some philosophers hold that well-being has non-experiential components. Their views deserve a hearing; so it cannot be assumed from the start that experience alone gives us access to our good. That methodology is itself one philosophical thesis among many. Third, it is sound philosophical practice to assess the strength of reasoned arguments offered by other philosophers, and hence to consult something more capacious than one's own experience before arriving at one's philosophical conclusions.

When, upon careful reflection, we find that a particular conception of well-being is supported by better arguments than its alternatives, and that theory is also endorsed by the experiences we have when we live in accordance with its practical implications, we are fully justified in accepting it. As I noted earlier (Chapter 1, section 2), that is Aristotle's methodology. "The truth in practical issues is judged from the facts (*erga*) of

---

[14] I elaborate on the idea put forward here, that well-being consists in the flowering (flourishing) of natural powers, in *What Is Good and Why*. See 3–8 and the index s.v. *flourishing*. It also plays a central role in Alasdair MacIntyre, *Ethics in the Conflicts of Modernity*. See his index s.v. *human flourishing*.

our life.... We must therefore examine what has been said in the light of the facts of our life, and if it agrees with the facts, then we should accept it, while if it conflicts, we must assume it to be no more than theory" (X.8 1179a17–22).

Theory and experience often work together as complementary tests of value. Nothing can count as good music, for example, unless it sounds good to the ear—but the best ears for making this judgment are those that know how to listen and what to listen for. The study of music can greatly enhance musical appreciation. Philosophy and experience similarly must be enlisted in any sound judgment about the components of well-being.

3. Lists, good-making, and the nature of well-being

I said earlier in this chapter (section 1) that every philosophical theory of well-being offers a list (an "objective list"), in response to the question, "What is well-being?" But more needs to be said about that, because some philosophers say that theories of well-being must be in the business of proposing something more interesting and deeper than a "mere" list.

Roger Crisp, for example, distinguishes between what he calls "enumerative" and "explanatory" theories of well-being.[15] The former kind of theory proposes an answer to the question, "Which things make an individual's life go better for that individual?" It is here that we will find a list. Crisp illustrates his point by supposing that enjoyable experiences, achievement, and knowledge might appear in a catalogue of prudential goods. But when we are presented with this enumeration, Crisp adds, a further question naturally arises. As he puts it: "But what is it about these things that makes them good for people?"

He further illustrates his distinction by adding: if accomplishment appears on a philosopher's list of components of well-being, that philosopher might go on to say: "what makes accomplishment good for someone is its perfecting her nature." According to this theory, accomplishment is on the list of elements of well-being, but the perfection of one's nature (rather than accomplishment) is a "good-(for)-making" property (to use his phrase). It might be the only good-making property, or it might be one of several. But whether there is one good-making property or several, it might be assumed that a theory of well-being that tells us what the elements of well-being are, but says nothing about what makes those elements good—what entitles them to be on the list—is but half a theory. It faces the accusation that it is far from having fully done the job we properly expect of it. (One is naturally reminded here of a question raised by Socrates in some of Plato's early dialogues. In the *Meno*, for example, he is not satisfied with a list of virtues. He wants to know: What makes them virtues? Surely Meno needs an answer to that question.)

---

[15] 'Hedonism Reconsidered.' In his entry on 'Well-Being' in the *Stanford Encyclopedia of Philosophy*, Crisp alters his terms, now using "substantive" in place of "enumerative." The distinction between substantive and explanatory theories is made in section 4.1 and employed again in sections 4.2 and 4.3 of that entry.

Crisp goes on to say that hedonism is best thought of both as an enumerative and an explanatory theory of well-being. It says that pleasure alone is on the list of elements of well-being. And it denies that there is something other than pleasure that is good-making. For it would "not capture the spirit of the hedonist tradition" (he adds) to say that pleasure is to be pursued because it is made good by something else—for example, the fact that in experiencing pleasure we are perfecting our nature.[16] The hedonist means to say that pleasure is a "rock bottom" or underived value—its goodness is not the result of its having some feature other than its being pleasure.

Crisp is no doubt right that hedonism and all other theories of well-being seek to ground our everyday judgments about prudential value in certain goods whose goodness is basic and not derived. But that does not mean (and he should not be taken to mean) that there is something *inherently* defective in a philosophical theory of well-being that takes this form: "The elements of well-being are X, Y, and Z. You might ask me: what makes these good for us? My answer would be: nothing. They are good for us, and it is *you* who are in error, if you think that there must be something that they have in common, in virtue of which they are good-making. These items on my list are the things that make everything else in our lives good for us. But it would be absurd to suppose that whatever good thing makes other things good must in turn be made good by something else. And the notion of a thing making itself good is nonsense. So, it must be accepted that some things just are good, without being made good, by themselves or anything else. And that, I say, holds true of X, Y, and Z—the items I have put in my catalogue of goods."

I said in the previous paragraph that there is nothing "inherently" defective in a theory that takes that form, and I must explain what I have in mind when I use the word "inherently." But first I would like to elaborate on the claim, which I contest, that when a theory of well-being takes the form of a shortlist of the several different components of well-being, without offering an answer to the question of what puts them on the list (what "makes them good"), it has evaded an important task—that of *explaining* what is good—that is in principle achievable.

The first point to be noted is that a "mere" list of the several goods that comprise well-being can play an explanatory role even if there is no common feature that these items have in virtue of which they are made good. To see that this is so, consider a theory of well-being that holds that it has just these three basic components: knowledge, pleasure, and virtue. (This is not my theory, but it serves my purpose here.) Many things, seemingly important, are not on this list—for example friendship and the production of art. But that does not entail that these omitted items are irrelevant to human well-being—it does not even entail that they are at most of instrumental value. Rather, friendship and the production of art might be valuable because they are forms of

---

[16] 'Hedonism Reconsidered,' 623. Note, however, that in *De Finibus*, Cicero takes Epicurus to hold that pleasure is good because everyone (including children and animals) desires it, and because it is in accordance with nature (I.30). Does that mean that according to this school pleasure is not the most basic good, but is made good by being the object of desire and by according with nature? It is difficult to say.

knowledge, or kinds of pleasure, or are constituted by intellectual and moral virtues. They would in that case be derivatively good for us. Their goodness for us would not be basic, but *explained* in terms of the way they are constituted by the three basic goods. Similarly, by taking knowledge to be a basic good, the theory in question not only entails that such activities as learning mathematics, physics, and chemistry are good— it *explains why*, by saying that they are forms of knowledge.

It should be clear, then, that a theory of well-being that offers a list of goods but does not find any common element among them can be explanatory. In fact, not only can it be such—it *almost certainly* will be. For in the world as we know it, it is highly likely that those basic goods—knowledge, pleasure, and virtue—will be achievable only if we take measures to acquire them. The value of pursuing these means will be *explained by* the fact that they help us achieve what is prudentially valuable in itself.

Not only is it the case that a basic element of well-being is not made good by anything else; it is also the case (and here is my second point) that it need not make anything else good. It is a conceptual possibility that, in a very different world from ours, prudential goods come to its inhabitants without those individuals ever having to take any measures to acquire them. In such a world, all such benefits would accrue to individuals entirely through their good fortune, without any need for planning or effort on their part. Pleasures of a certain sort would be visited upon some of them as they passively sat back and enjoyed them. Nothing would be instrumentally valuable: there would be no means that are made good by their causal connection to good ends.

In such a world, the only correct response to the question "What makes things prudentially good?" would be: nothing. There would be no good-makers and no thing-made-good. For in this world, pleasure is the sole good, and nothing is made good by virtue of its leading to pleasure. Pleasure is good, but it is not made good; nor is anything else made good. This world would not be as rich in value as the one we inhabit, but it is worthwhile to keep it in mind as a conceptual possibility, for it shows us that the central question for any theory of well-being is: "What good or goods, the goodness of which is not derived from other goods, is well-being composed of?" The further question, "What makes certain good things (the ones that are not basic elements of well-being) good?" arises only when in fact there are, in addition to these basic elements of well-being, others whose goodness is derived from them.

Nonetheless, to repeat the first point made above, in our world and others like it, any theory of well-being that has said what its basic components are will thereby not merely be an enumeration but an explanation as well. It will tell us how to answer the question, "What is it that makes (certain) things good for us?" There will be no possible answer to the question, "What makes it good?" when that question is asked about any of the basic good-makers. But we will have an answer to that question, when it is asked of many other things.

I said earlier in this section: there is nothing "inherently" defective in a philosophical theory of well-being that takes the form of a list and asserts that the items on the list are valuable independently of each other, and do not derive their value from anything more basic. What work is the word "inherently" doing here? It leaves open the possibility that when such a theory is scrutinized with care and thoroughness, it will be seen to contain errors of omission or commission. The items on its list may not be good. Or it may omit one or more basic goods. Or the items on its list might have something in common in virtue of which they are good: they may be species of a higher-order good, the goodness of which explains the goodness of its sub-kinds. Only philosophical inquiry into a proposed theory of well-being will tell us whether it contains any such error. We have no basis for assuming, in advance of such an inquiry, that there must be one and only one basic good whose goodness explains the goodness of everything else.

I turn now to two objections that could be made against what I have said in this section. First, someone might insist, against me, that we can always answer the question, "What makes that good thing good?" even when the good in question is a basic (underived) component of well-being. Consider pleasure and pain, for example. Should we not say that the pleasantness of pleasure is what makes pleasure good, and the painfulness of pain is what makes it bad?[17]

We can say that. At any rate, we can find a way to read that sentence that allows us to understand the claim it makes. But the point does not generalize to other goods that are often taken to be basic elements of well-being. We would be mystified if someone said: "the fact that knowledge is knowledgeable is what makes it good"; "the fact that virtue is virtuous is what makes it good"; "the fact that friendship is friendly is what makes it good."[18]

Why does the corresponding statement, "that pleasure is pleasant is what makes it good?" seem acceptable, whereas these others do not? I suggest that when we hear someone say, "the pleasantness of pleasure is what makes it good," we take that to mean: "there is a certain way pleasures feel, and it is that indescribable experiential quality, known only through introspection, that grounds its claim to goodness." In any case, that is how *I* can make sense of the statement, "the pleasantness of pleasure is what makes it good." And there is no similar interpretation that can be put on such absurd statements as "the fact that knowledge is knowledgeable is what makes it good."

If my suggestion about how to make sense of "the pleasantness of pleasure makes it good" is right, then the hedonist who utters that sentence is putting pleasure into the general psychological category of good feeling, or feeling good, and is claiming that *this* (good feeling, feeling good) is the most basic and sole element of well-being. Many other things, of course, go into the category of feelings—feelings of warmth,

---

[17] Thus Crisp in 'Well-Being,' section 4.1.

[18] We can, however, understand such sentences as these: "what makes a bit of knowledge good for someone to have is just the fact that it is knowledge." That would be a way of indicating that although instances of knowledge are made good by virtue of the kind of thing they are (knowledge), knowledge itself is good without being made good by something else. Similarly for "what makes a virtue good for someone to have is just the fact that it is a virtue; what makes a friendship good for someone is just the fact that it is a friendship." I do not myself accept these statements as adequate explanations of the prudential value of knowledge, virtue, and friendship, but I have some idea of what they mean. I am grateful to Roger Crisp for discussion.

cold, pressure, pain, dizziness, etc. But only one kind of feeling, according to such a hedonist, is good to feel: pleasure. So construed, hedonism does not have an answer to the question, "What makes something's being a good feeling a prudential good?" It cannot answer that question and does not need to, just as every theory of well-being posits a good (or goods) not made good by anything else. Hedonism, so construed, would not take pleasure to be the most basic good; good feeling would play that role, and the goodness of pleasure would be explained by its being something good to feel.

I turn now to a second objection that could be made against my thesis that there is nothing *inherently* defective in a philosophical theory of well-being that offers a list of its basic elements but offers no answer to the question: What makes these good for us? Against this, it might be said that philosophy must find an answer to the even deeper Socratic question: "What is it for something to be good for someone?" We can imagine Socrates complaining: "You say that pleasure is the sole constituent of well-being, and that everything else is made good by the extent to which it is pleasant or leads to pleasure. But you haven't yet told us what well-being is. You've left unanswered the question of what it is for something to be of prudential value."[19]

The reply to this objection is that it dogmatically assumes that the property of prudential value (more strictly: the relation of X being good for Y) is best understood as a construction out of other and more basic properties. That could be so—but it need not be. What G. E. Moore said in *Principia Ethica* about the property of goodness *simpliciter*—that it cannot be defined in terms of pleasure or any other natural or metaphysical property—might be true of the relation of X being good for Y. We use several interchangeable expressions (as I noted earlier) to get across the idea of well-being. ("His life is going well for him." "He is faring well." "He has a good life." "He is well off." "He is flourishing.") But these words are normally treated as merely so many ways of conveying the same idea. The fact that we have several different words and phrases that we treat interchangeably in ordinary discourse is no evidence that the property of prudential value is a composite that is made out of more basic properties. If a philosopher thinks that it is such a composite, that must be shown—it cannot simply be assumed.

In *What is Good and Why*, I argued that our ordinary word "flourishing," properly understood, provides us with a way of seeing a certain kind of unity in the many different ways in which lives go well for those living them. As I said earlier (section 2), the main idea, drawn from Aristotle, is that life is made good for human beings by the maturation and successful exercise of our inherent biological powers. Speaking more generally,

---

[19] That question is one that L. W. Sumner seeks to answer in *Welfare, Happiness, and Ethics*. This work is an attempt to say what "the nature of welfare" is (his words)—just as a philosophical theory of causality must explain what it is for something to be a cause. (This is his analogy. See page 16.) I discuss this aspect of his theory in 'Human Diversity and the Nature of Well-Being: Reflections on Sumner's Methodology.' I myself have proposed, in *What Is Good and Why*, an account of what it is for something to have prudential value. My point here is that in searching for such an account, we should acknowledge the possibility that none can be given, and that none is needed. We could discover that there is no such thing as the nature of well-being.

what is good for *any* living thing is the successful unfolding or flowering (flourishing) of what nature has given it. Nourishment, growth, long life: that is how a plant flourishes. Non-human and human animals flourish in more complex ways, but we can recognize in all these cases so many different pathways along which an organism's potentiality for its good are actualized. When we listen with understanding and pleasure to music, or look with appreciation at the beauty of the natural world, or take pride in the ethical accomplishments of our children or fellow human beings, we are making good use of our natural and inherent human powers, just as hawks flourish when they soar, or sequoia flourish when they grow to immense heights in the forest.

If that way of looking at well-being sheds some light on the topic, then it could be said that there is such a thing as the nature of well-being after all. As it turns out, there *is* a correct answer to the question, "What is it for something to be of prudential value?" as well as an answer to the question, "What does human well-being consist in?" What I have added here is that it is not *necessary* that prudential value have a nature. It would not be a defective concept (one that we ought to stop deploying) if it were the case that the components of well-being have nothing in common, and the best we could do were "merely" to list them.

In the next section, I offer a further way in which we can, as it turns out, go beyond saying: "the elements of well-being are X, Y, and Z," adding nothing further about the common feature that makes them elements of well-being.

A final point about what we should look for in a philosophical account of well-being: if a theory holds that it has irreducibly diverse basic components, it ought not evade the further question of how those components compare with each other in their degree of goodness. If some parts of well-being have much more prudential value than others—and especially if some of them are incommensurably better for us than others—then we ought to be dissatisfied with a theory that does not go beyond listing them. It would have failed to acknowledge a fact of the greatest importance to the conduct of our lives. As I have proposed and will argue, if non-experiential goods are among the elements of well-being (I think their claim to be such is doubtful), they are immeasurably inferior to its experiential components (Chapter 1, section 6; Chapter 2, section 5; Chapter 3, sections 22 and 23).

4. Experientialism

On my conception of human well-being, its components are all experiences. That is one part of the thesis I am calling "experientialism about human well-being," or "experientialism" for short (Chapter 1, section 1). It is not a thesis about all that is good for living things, since not all of them are conscious (Chapter 1, section 11). Needless to say, I do not claim that *all* experiences, whatever their quality, constitute well-being. Only the good ones do so. If this thesis is correct, there is a second hidden unity underlying all that is good in human life, besides the unification provided by the concept of flourishing. When we list the good things of which good human lives are composed, we see that they have an experiential nature. They have a phenomeno-logical aspect; there is something it is like to have them.[20]

If this unifying thesis is correct, might that be a mere "accident"? In other words, should we say that the various elements of well-being (gaining philosophical insight, having dinner with a good friend, taking pride in one's civic institutions) are good for us *because* they are good experiences, or does it just happen to be the case that all of them have an experiential nature? Should we reject a proposed candidate for our list of prudential goods *simply because* it is not something we experience? Is it an a priori truth about human well-being that it can be composed only of experiences?

The answer I propose to these questions begins with the point that it is part of sound philosophical methodology to look for answers to philosophical questions by begin-ning with what we are most confident about and remain confident about as we con-tinue to explore our topic. We should not initiate philosophical theory-construction by suspending judgment about everything, no matter how simple and obvious, and trying to make progress while entertaining no working hypotheses or provisionally making assumptions that seem plausible and unobjectionable. We should not take ourselves to have no knowledge or reasonable opinions that we can draw upon.

Now, when it comes to the topic of well-being, we are not at a complete loss to say which elements of our lives (and the lives of others) seem prudentially valuable. And the things that strike us most forcefully as good (or bad) are experiential in nature, and typically include pleasure (or pain). Would we like to eat this food and avoid that one, not as a means to something else, but for itself? Our evening is well spent if we enjoy the dinner we eat, and poorly spent if we feel dizzy, nauseous, achy. As we continue to explore the range of items we confidently put on our lists of things that are good for us and things that are bad for us, we notice that a common theme emerges: these are good experiences or bad experiences. At that point, we would have good reason to adopt, as a working hypothesis, the thesis that an element of well-being *must* be a good experi-ence—that it belongs on our list *because* it is a good experience. That, at any rate, is the status I propose for experientialism: it deserves to be made a working hypothesis because it is supported by many instances of good things, and further examination of it reveals that the seeming exceptions to it only seem to be exceptions.

Furthermore, it is inherently plausible that for creatures that can have an inner life, the quality of that inner life should matter—should constitute (entirely or largely)

[20] A clarification of the term "experientialism" is needed, for it may bring to mind a similar phrase used in the literature on well-being: "the Experience Requirement." This is the term James Griffin uses to discuss a thesis he rejects. He says that in rejecting it he "allows my utility to be determined … by things that I am not aware of"—and this, he adds, "seems right: if you cheat me out of an inheritance that I never expected, I might not know but be worse off for it …" (*Well-Being*, 16–17, which refer back to 13). This "Experience Requirement" is not just a thesis about what the *components* of well-being are but also about what has some effect on it ("*determines*" is the word Griffin uses). I agree that I might be made worse off by someone cheating me out of an inheritance I never expected—but that is true, I hold, only if, as a result, my experi-ence is worse or not as good as it otherwise would have been. Griffin's Experience Requirement is discussed by Sumner in *Welfare, Happiness, and Ethics*. " … a state of affairs can make me better off only if, in one way or another, it enters or affects my experience" (127).

the quality of their existence. If something is not part of their lived experience, but is external to their existence as they feel it to be—if it is not part of what it is *like* (introspectively) to be who they are—it might have an important effect on their well-being, but, being external to them, its eligibility as a constituent of well-being is open to reasonable doubt.

Note how odd it would be to ask someone, "What is the quality of your life during those periods when you are asleep but not dreaming?" How is one to answer that question—to what should one look? Our bafflement can only be explained by saying that, during these periods, there is no awareness, no inner life, and so there is nothing whose quality is to be assessed, as there is during the conscious portions of our existence. Of course, while we dreamlessly sleep, there is much that is going on in the brain and the rest of the body. These processes certainly have a causal effect on the quality of the remaining parts of our lives, when we are awake, and so they can *influence* our well-being. But they are not themselves components of well-being. Further, it would be a mistake to say that our question—"What is the quality of your life during those periods when you are asleep but not dreaming?"—is odd because "quality of life" can sensibly be applied only to the whole of life, or large stretches of it, but not to any small portion of it. It makes perfect sense to say, "when I spend my summers in Italy, the quality of my life increases significantly, but then declines the rest of the year." Similarly, we can ask about the quality of our lives while we are dreaming. Do we have good dreams or bad? That question is not met with the response: "How can you ask such a question?—dreams are so brief!" It is not the brevity of the period of dreamless sleep that disqualifies it from being a component of well-being, but the fact that there is nothing it is like to be in that state. (Temporal aspects of well-being will occupy us in Chapter 4.)

So, it is not an a priori truth about human well-being that it can be composed only of experiences. Experientialism is not a thesis we impose on any conception of well-being in advance of our ideas about what its elements are. On the other hand, it is no mere accident that it is true (if we decide, in the end, that it survives critical scrutiny). That is because we will have gained justified confidence, over the course of our inquiry into well-being, that purported goods are elements of well-being *because* they are good experiences, and other purported goods are not elements because either they are not experiential at all or because they are bad experiences. It is at that point that we can react to someone's suggestion that what other people privately think about you is a component of your well-being by saying: "It can't be, because it is external to me, and my well-being is something that arises from what things are like for me from the inside." (That is not the only appropriate reaction. Other considerations will be presented in Chapter 3, sections 19–21.)

If experientialism is accepted, then it turns out that there would, after all, be a defect in our theory of well-being if we merely said: "the elements of well-being are X, Y, and Z" and said nothing further about what they have in common that makes them elements of well-being. We would have missed a good-making feature of those elements—the fact that they are good experiences. We had no guarantee, in advance of our inquiry, that there would be any such good-making features. But we have discovered that there are.

Experientialism proposes an explanation of why being rich, or famous, or influential are not elements of well-being: it is because they are not inherently components of our inner life. Admittedly, these are states of affairs that many people seek not only as means to further ends but because they assume that even by themselves they would be good to have. Their assumption is mistaken, but if philosophy rejects common beliefs and pursuits, it needs strong reasons to do so, for common sense is often an indispensable asset for philosophical inquiry. We will not have done our job well, as philosophers, if we merely say: "People seek fame as though it were good in itself, but they are wrong." We need some reason for rejecting this widely held belief. Experientialism, if it is true, gives us what we need. Popular opinion is mistaken about this because our best theory of well-being tells us not only which things are good, but tells us why they are good: because they are good experiences.

There are, then, two highly general categories into which the goods that comprise well-being fall. There is the one mentioned in the preceding two sections: human lives, like all lives, go well when certain natural biological powers are actualized—when organisms flourish. (Here "flourishing" is meant to retain its biological connotation, and is not a mere equivalent of "doing well.") And the second is the category of good experience, available to all and only those organisms that are conscious. Something is good for an individual if, in virtue of having it, that individual flourishes (or comes closer to flourishing): and also if, in virtue of having it, the conscious life of that individual is on the whole a good one (or comes closer to being such).

Notice that there is no conceptual connection between these two categories; they are independent concepts. Yet, with the exception of plants (assumed to lack consciousness), what falls under them coincides: the human lives that can plausibly be said to be *flourishing* lives (where this word retains its biological flavor) are also lives that are filled with *good experiences*, and when someone definitely is not flourishing, it is also the case that his existence is filled with bad experiences, or his experiences are only slightly good, or he is devoid of experience. One can have a flourishing mental life within the experience machine, because many of the good kinds of conscious existence available there make use of one's natural powers. A human life is not made to flourish in virtue of what is external to the mind (such as the attitudes others have towards that individual), because those external things do not make use of human powers. And although the dead can be honored or dishonored, as they can be the objects of just or unjust treatment, they cannot flourish, because they lack any form of consciousness and therefore their deployment of mental human powers is at an end. The things that we confidently believe are elements of a life rich in prudential value (engagement with the arts, intellectual exploration, satisfying personal relationships) pass two tests each of which seems appropriate for evaluating lives. Their doing so should increase our confidence that these items really are good, and that these tests are the appropriate ones to use.

5. Hell and experience

One way to see how great a role experience plays in our well-being is to remind our-selves of the picture painted by certain Christian thinkers of what life will be like for sinners when they die unrepentant and are sent to Hell. It is a place filled for an eternity with the most horrible experiences. No Christian theologian, to my knowledge, says anything about there being non-experiential aspects of Hell; they talk only about the evils that will be visited upon our consciousness. When we bring the details of their picture of Hell to mind, we should be struck by the fact that in their efforts to dissuade us from sin by giving us a sense of the punishments in store for us, the bad things they depict so vividly are entirely experiential in nature. That, of course, is not a proof of experientialism. To give a full defense of that thesis, I must rebut the arguments philo-sophers have used to show that well-being has non-experiential components. At this point in my defense of experientialism, I am merely trying to show how plausible a doctrine it is. One way to do that is to remind ourselves of a common picture of what life would be like at its worst—life in Hell.

In Section Three of *The Portrait of the Artist as a Young Man*, Stephen Dedalus listens to a sermon, delivered by Father Arnall, that describes in long and vivid detail (it goes on for nearly six pages) the torments that await him if he does not renounce his life of sin. Joyce's source is a work of Giovani Pietro Pinamonti, *Hell Opened to Christians, to Caution Them From Entering It* (1688), which follows the counsel of Ignatius Loyola, in *The Spiritual Exercises* (1548), that Christians meditate on the torments of Hell in order to steer themselves away from sin.[21]

Here is what is in store for some of us, according to Father Arnall (phrases in quota-tion marks are Joyce's):

It is "dark and foul-smelling," allowing no "liberty of movement." One is "not even able to remove from the eye a worm that gnaws at it." There is intense heat and the "torment of fire," which burns not only our skin but our "vitals." "The blood seethes and boils in the veins, the brains are boiling in the skull, the heart in the breast glowing and bursting, the bowels a redhot mass of burning pulp, the tender eyes flaming like molten balls." "The eyes [are tortured] with impenetrable utter darkness, the nose with noisome odours, the ears with yells and howls and execrations, the taste with foul matter, leprous corruption, and nameless suffo-cating filth, the touch with redhot goads and spikes, with cruel tongues of flame." "The damned howl and scream at one another, their torture and rage intensified by the presence of beings tortured and raging like themselves. All sense of humanity is forgotten. The yells of the suffering sinners fill the remotest corners of the vast abyss. The mouths of the damned are full of blasphemies against God and of hatred for their fellow sufferers and of curses against those souls which were their accomplices in sin." There are devils in Hell, and they "have become as hideous and ugly as they once were beautiful. They mock and jeer at the

---

[21] This information comes from the Penguin edition, 256 (note 42). This portion of the sermon runs from 109 to 114. The quotations that follow are drawn from several of these pages.

lost souls whom they dragged down to ruin. It is they, the foul demons, who are made in hell the voices of conscience. Why did you sin? . . . . God spoke to you in so many voices but you would not hear."

The evils of Hell fall into several different categories, all of them experiential. Many of them are sensory harms: the feeling of physical constraint, the heat, the burning sensations on the surface and the interior of the body, the stench, the foul tastes, the hideous "yells, howls, execrations." But there are cognitive evils as well: it is constantly brought to one's attention that one could have avoided all of this, had one repented one's sins. The sounds one hears are the voices of fellow sufferers, of tormenting devils—all bringing to mind oppressive thoughts. There is also a horrible emotional aspect to life in Hell: the guilt created by the voices of conscience, the hatred one feels towards others, the sense of shame aroused by mockery.

Now, suppose someone had tried to convince Stephen Dedalus that although Hell was indeed a bad place, containing all the evils described by Father Arnall, its badness could nonetheless be outweighed by good things available to those who have died. The argument would take this form: First, it could be claimed that Hell is not eternal; there is a fixed limit to the duration of its torments. Second, it could be claimed that there are non-experiential goods that the dead can have. Suppose a sinner has fooled people into thinking he is a great man, and he is honored and admired long after his death. Those honors and admiring thoughts can continue for centuries and centuries. Third, it could then be pointed out that if those posthumous goods continue for a long enough time, the total good that accrues to the sinner will be greater by far than the harms visited upon him in Hell. Sinning will eventually lead to more future good than harm.

If there are such non-experiential goods as these, then it is important for the success of Father Arnall's sermon that the evils of Hell be infinite in duration. But I suggest that his sermon would lose little of its persuasive force if he had said that the torments of Hell go on only for a few thousand years. It is not essential to the success of his argument that they be without end. If that is correct, the conclusion to be drawn is that either there are no elements of well-being beyond those that can be experienced; or, if there are, they are of an inferior sort, so that no matter how long they endure, their goodness can never be great enough to outweigh the badness of Hell's torments.

What about Heaven? What might it be like? The obvious answer is that it would be filled with experiential goods of many different kinds. Think of life as you sometimes experience it, and imagine that it might contain that and much more of the same sort. Only experienced goods will meet our hopes of what life at its best could be. If you were told that your heavenly reward will consist in an enduring good reputation, but that your experience will be at an end, that would be a most disappointing revelation. Heaven would not be heavenly unless it gave you an experiential afterlife of such a high quality that your posthumous future is guaranteed to be wonderful, even if your earthly reputation suffers, and future generations, fed misinformation about you, dishonor your name.

These reflections on Heaven and Hell do not depend for their force on the assumption that there actually is a life after death, and that we go to one of these places or the other. We can ask what they would be like without believing they are possible. We can therefore use these posthumous locations as devices for clarifying to ourselves the assumptions we make about the components of well-being. They reveal how large a role experienced goods and evils play in our thinking about what it is for a life to go well for the one who is living it.

6. Experience as a dependent good

I noted earlier (section 3) that if a theory of well-being holds that its components are irreducibly diverse, it ought not evade the question of their relative value. One way for it to meet that demand would be to say that a certain component has *no* value unless it is combined in some way with one or more others. That is the kind of view that Socrates seems to accept in several of Plato's dialogues (*Gorgias, Euthydemus, Meno,* and *Republic*). Whether that is really the best interpretation is an issue I set aside. What is undisputed is that for him wisdom (more generally: virtue) is a special sort of good, in that the other things we seek—health, wealth, and honor—become bad in its absence. If, in other words, one has those other goods (health, wealth, honor) without also having an understanding of how to use them well, they are goods in name only. Furthermore, he might also be understood to mean that it is better to have *all* these goods (both the virtues and the others) than to have just the virtues.

Such a theory addresses the question of the relative value of the ingredients of well-being not by ranking them or assigning each a numerical weight, but by recognizing that one of them has independent value whereas the others are dependent on its presence. Wisdom is good in all circumstances, the others only when directed by wisdom. A theory of this sort has greater practical value than one that merely proposes a list of goods but has nothing to say about whether some are better than others. The Socratic sort of theory directs us not to omit from our lives the good that is always good and the condition of the goodness of all others. Lacking one or more of the dependent goods is not nearly so grave a deficiency. (Kant's conception of the value of a good will also has this structure.)

That idea could be applied to the question we are concerned with here: what is the prudential value of the experiential aspect of our lives? One possible answer would be that it has no value on its own; it has value only when connected to the real world in the usual way, and not induced in the brain by a laboratory technician. That might be the lesson we learn from Nozick's thought experiment. It could be supported by the further general reflection that we don't want to live in a "fool's paradise." We do want to be happy, of course, but not if this means having only a feeling of happiness produced by ignorance of what is truly valuable and of our social circumstances. The title of a recent book by Neera Badhwar succinctly expresses this thought: *Well-Being: Happiness in a Worthwhile Life.*[22] Well-being, she says, has two components, one of

---

[22] See especially 45–8.

them experiential (happiness) and the other (worthwhileness) not. What we are happy with must be truly worthwhile; and what is truly worthwhile must make us happy. Either component without the other lacks prudential value.[23]

If this theory is correct, then two lives that are indistinguishable as judged from the inside—as judged by introspection of their experiential content—can be radically different in their prudential value. That is what many philosophers (including Badhwar) infer from Nozick's thought experiment.[24] According to this conception of well-being, when you look within, no matter how carefully, no matter what your training, no matter how wide your experience, what you find might be worthless without your realizing it. It can seem a paradise but be only a fool's paradise, appealing merely at the experiential level and entirely lacking in worth. Within the experience machine, you are completely taken in by the illusion of reality because your inner life is phenomenologically indistinguishable from its counterpart in the real world. Your paradise is that of a fool, worth nothing. And even though you and I are not within the machine (or so we assume), the same point applies: our acts of introspection by themselves give us no evidence that our lives have even the slightest prudential value. We have no basis for believing that our lives are worth living, unless we can justify our assumption that we are not brains in a vat. If we have no reason to suppose we are not inside the experience machine, we cannot justifiably assume that anything in our lives is good for us.

The implausibility of this view can be recognized if we think about our engagement with music, painting, literature, and other aesthetic productions. The careful introspection of a trained eye or ear is precisely what is needed—and it is all that is needed— to discover whether one's time is being well spent. If the music heard by an experienced listener meets every standard by which the phenomenological quality of the sound is appropriately judged, no further question remains about its worthwhileness. The value of time spent listening lies precisely in what is detectable in the experience. It does not rest on some further thing, worthwhileness, that lies hidden behind the experience, as reality lies hidden from the subject in the experience machine.

Another sort of example leads to the same conclusion.[25] A plumber fixes leaky pipes and installs sinks, toilets, boilers, and so on. What if the house in which these repairs are made sits forever unoccupied and unused (an outcome she did not foresee when she did her job)? Obviously her work has no value to anyone else, but is it possible that her time was not entirely wasted, because her activity had some value to her? That depends on the experiences she has as she performs her work. Suppose she regards each new task as an intellectual and physical challenge; she has a co-worker whose company she enjoys; and she appreciates the virtues of old houses, however much they need repair. In that case, there was something she did get from her work, even though

---

[23] As Badhwar points out (*Well-Being*, 45), a similar feature is present in the theory of meaningfulness proposed by Susan Wolf in *Meaning in Life and Why It Matters*. Some of what we are attracted to lacks objective worth, and such experiences give no meaning to our lives.

[24] *Well-Being*, 41–2.   [25] I use this example in my review of Badhwar in *The Philosophical Review*.

she benefited no one else.[26] But the features of her work that gave it some value are all experiential. According to the theory we are examining, experience is prudentially worthless unless there is something that lies behind it that is worthwhile—just as the experience machine offers nothing of value because it is not experience of the real world.

These examples show that something in the felt quality of certain experiences by itself makes them good to have, but they do not show that good experience is the only component of well-being. That further thesis requires other arguments.

7. The good in being a good human being

The remainder of this chapter will address the question whether there is a close connection—as ancient philosophers thought—between being a good person and having a good life.[27] I will set aside two ways of linking them: that of Epicurus, and that of Kant.

Epicurus holds that one's ultimate goal should be one's own pleasure, and that being a good human being is the best means to that end. But we should reject both his rational egoism and his hedonism.

Kant holds that we should not strive to be happy but to be *deserving* of happiness, and that we can reasonably hope to attain, in a future existence, as much of it as would reward our moral record. Implicit in Kant's treatment of this question is the assumption that we should discharge our moral duties because the dutifulness of an action (its conformity to the moral law) is so strong a reason in its favor that we should need no other. But I will try to show that it is misguided to downgrade self-interested motivation in this way. To treat other people as morality demands, we often must reflect not only on what is good for them, but also on what is good for ourselves.

In what follows, I will not claim that being a morally good human being is a necessary component of well-being. Nor a sufficient component. The Stoics uphold and defend both of these propositions. The weaker thesis I will defend is that the inner life

---

[26] In Wolf's terms (see note 23), the work she performed lacked meaning. If she is right about that, the conclusion we should draw is that certain meaningless portions of our lives are nonetheless time well spent, because they have prudential value. That in turn puts in doubt their designation as meaningless.

[27] I am happy to say that I am not alone as a defender of the thesis of antiquity that ethically virtuous activity is a great prudential good. See, for example, Stephen Darwall, *Welfare and Rational Care*, 73–104. He calls this "the Aristotelian thesis," and his presentation of it contains an experiential component. He speaks, for example, of a "direct experience" (89) of what has value (e.g. a child)—a "distinctive mode of awareness of merit and worth, namely appreciation... [This] involves feelings, experiences, and attitudes toward the meritorious or worthy thing *itself*" (90, his emphasis). Is it because of what those "feelings, experiences, and attitudes" *are like* that this awareness of merit has prudential value? Or is it rather the fact those are the *right* feelings to have, insofar as they are responses to what has value? If the former, our views are close; if the latter, not so close. For other treatments of this topic, see Rosalind Hursthouse, *On Virtue Ethics*, 163–91; Philippa Foot, *Natural Goodness*, 81–98; Joseph Raz, 'The Central Conflict: Morality and Self-Interest,' in Roger Crisp and Brad Hooker (eds.), *Well-Being and Morality*; David O. Brink, 'Self-Love and Altruism'; Daniel C. Russell, *Happiness for Humans*; Mark LeBar, *The Value of Living Well*; and Paul Bloomfield, *The Virtues of Happiness*. I have learned much from Nicolas Bommarito, *Inner Virtue*, which explores the interior aspects of moral goodness but does not treat them as components of well-being.

of a morally good human being is a component of well-being whose possession by an individual is by itself sufficient to constitute a very high quality of life for him, provided that he does not undergo a great deal of suffering. The Stoics would say that this conditional clause—"provided that he does not undergo a great deal of suffering"—should be dropped. In this respect, I am closer to Aristotle than to Stoicism.

It should also be kept in mind that, according to Aristotle, well-being (*eudaimonia*) is most fully available to an individual who has no ethical virtues (or ethical vices): the divine first mover of the universe has no need of such qualities as justice and courage, and in fact leads the best possible life without possessing them. I depart from him to some extent because, unlike him, I do not claim that ethically virtuous activity is a necessary component of *human* well-being. But we are in agreement that such activity is not a necessary component of *every* well-lived life.

The key idea I will put to use is that the phenomenological life of a human being, in favorable circumstances, is superior to that of a simple creature like an oyster, no matter how long the latter lives. I proposed in Chapter 1 that this is because a human being can have a richer experience, and I illustrated what I had in mind, in speaking of the richness of experience, by depicting the inner life of someone standing in front of a great painting (section 7). What I want to add now—in order to show a connection between being a good person and having a good life—is that, just as a connoisseur of the arts takes a deep interest in the worlds of music, painting, or literature, and thereby enriches his life, so a good person takes a deep interest in his social world and thereby enriches *his* experience of life. The arts enlarge our inner lives with their enormous variety and inexhaustible richness, engaging our senses, emotions, thoughts, desires, and imagination, and bringing us long-lasting pleasure. But our moral relationships with other human beings are no less complex and rewarding. Responding to the norms, opportunities, and challenges of our social world engages all aspects of our consciousness—one element of which is the pleasure we take in our relationship with others. Nothing like this is available to an oyster, and that is one respect in which there is less good in its life.

It might be objected that I have far too rosy a picture of moral experience, and am overlooking the misery, injustice, and cruelty that ought to be on the mind of anyone who has a conscience and an awareness of the human situation. My response is that one of the virtues that constitute being a good person is the ability not to be crushed by one's knowledge of the evils and misfortunes of the social world; to do one's part in making some portion of it a better place, while finding and appreciating the goodness there is. Rehearsing to oneself all the sufferings of the world would by itself be good for no one; it would be self-destructive, and of no use to others. It is a moral and a prudential failure to let oneself sink into misanthropy, cynicism, or despair. It is also an error to see one's moral relations to others solely in terms of burdensome debts, obligations, and duties—a realm that is supposedly by its nature at odds with self-interest, happiness, and pleasure. True, in some circumstances moral demands *are* burdensome; at an extreme, they can require tragic sacrifices. But to think of morality solely in these terms would be to oversimplify a highly variegated realm of our sociability.

One might resist my conception of the prudential value of moral experience by saying that the superiority of human to oyster life lies solely in the aesthetic realm—in the beauties of music, art, literature, and the natural world.[28] Or perhaps our superiority results from the joys of intellectual discovery; or the delicious and subtle flavors of what we eat and drink; or the thrills of athletic exuberance and grace. Anything *but* our moral relations with other human beings, according to this outlook. But anyone who insists that *only* aesthetic experience makes life worth living will have a hard time defending so narrow an outlook. So too will anyone who insists that only intellectual activity can redeem our lives, or only sports, or only food and drink. It would be no less implausible to say that *all* of these spheres, singly or combined, make human life better than oyster life—but that our moral engagement with other human beings (however pleasant and rich an experience it might be) does not. After all, eating and drinking are immeasurably enriched as experiences when they are embedded in good social relations—when we enjoy the company and conversation of other people. The same applies to athletics, intellectual endeavors, and the aesthetic realm.

The moral experience of a good person is, as I have admitted, not uniformly agreeable. It is rather a complex interplay of positive and negative experiences—and the positive ones may be available only if they are related in complex ways to the negative ones. The idea can be illustrated by thinking of what someone is typically looking for when he undertakes a difficult physical task—say, climbing Annapurna (in Nepal) or K2 (Pakistan and China). One knows in advance that this is going to be arduous and in many ways unpleasant—there will be pain, fatigue, cold, anxiety, and danger. But there will be no sense of accomplishment unless one's overall experience includes these "negative" elements as well. The goal is not simply to be at the top of the mountain, but to have a full mountain-climbing experience that results in reaching the top and then safely returning. (What if you had these experiences but were a brain in a vat? We will come to that question later.) Similarly, what enables moral experience to have its emotional and intellectual depth is the fact that it is not a simple, unvariegated, and effortless pleasure. Moral growth is not a smooth, easy, uncomplicated path; it cannot take place unless one makes serious mistakes, for which one feels a complex array of such emotions as remorse, guilt, and shame. Even when one reaches the stage at which one is more or less a good person, and is rather skillful in one's responses to moral cues, one will sometimes be perplexed, disturbed, frustrated, and so on. But there will be deep satisfactions as well, and they would not be available were morality as simple a task as winning a game of checkers or solving an easy crossword puzzle.

Another way to convey the point I am making is provided by our love of literature. Reading a novel—a certain kind of novel—can be a rich experience because it

---

[28] Nietzsche writes: "…only as an aesthetic phenomenon are existence and the world eternally justified…" See *The Birth of Tragedy*, section 5. Also: "Life without music would be an error." See *Twilight of the Idols*, 'Maxims and Arrows,' 33. Not only must there be art in our lives, it also provides a model of how to live. For discussion, see Aaron Ridley, 'Nietzsche and the Arts of Life,' in Ken Gemes and John Richardson (eds.), *The Oxford Handbook of Nietzsche*. Oscar Wilde's *The Picture of Dorian Gray* serves as a warning here.

requires us to enter the lives of fictional characters, and to pose questions to ourselves about their motives, their good and bad traits, their successes and blunders. When we enter these fictional worlds, we have an experience similar in important respects to the complex array of feelings that we would have were we to encounter the real-life counterparts of the characters. And lovers of literature believe that their emotional worlds would be diminished in the absence of these novel-reading experiences. If some damage were done to their brains that made them incapable of appreciating literature any longer, that would be a serious loss. So, it is not far-fetched to say that similarly if some damage were done to us that robbed us of the ability to experience the complex form of consciousness of a moral person, that too would be a loss in the quality of our lives.

A further point about ethical life that should be kept in mind is that it does not inherently make other sorts of valuable activities inaccessible. Being a good person is not inevitably so demanding of one's time that in developing such skills one must forego developing any others—as if a good person could not also be a good musician or a good athlete or a good cook. It is not an inherent cost of a moral life that this will be the only good thing in it. Of course, that leaves open the possibility that in certain circumstances a moral person *will* have to forego opportunities to engage in other valuable projects. I am not claiming that the advantages of having the consciousness of a moral person are inevitably so great that they will always outweigh whatever losses one must incur as a result of one's commitment to acting morally. Conversely, dishonesty and other moral failings can have consequences that make one's life better, all things considered. It can happen, for example, that by cheating on an exam, a student is admitted to music school, displacing a student who did not cheat, and as a result that dishonest student is able to live a rich and varied life full of musical accomplishment. That sort of example poses a problem for any attempt to ground ethical virtue entirely in self-interest, but that is not my goal.

Whether a disposition counts as a virtue of character is partly a matter of how someone who has that trait interacts with other people, but it is also partly a matter of its effects on the person who has it. For example, the best kind of disposition to have with respect to anger is one that will bring anger to an end at an appropriate time—and this is true partly because the quality of one's experience of life typically diminishes when one is experiencing this emotion. To be justified in one's anger is to be justified in feeling the right amount of it for the right amount of time; how angry, and for how long, is partly (but *only partly*) explained by facts that justify one's anger. In many cases anger should end even though the facts that justified the anger to begin with remain facts. Your father thoughtlessly said something that hurt your feelings, and you were right to be angry—but only for a time. Why not go on being angry, since it will always be true that he treated you that way? It would be implausible to answer this question without acknowledging that it will be better *for you*, if you do not remain angry forever. Emotions take up space in the psyche; never letting go of your anger leaves less room for you to move on to other and better things.

I take this to be a point that is applicable to many other ethical virtues. It is a virtue, for example, to find in other people the possibility for better relations (or continued good relations) with them—not only because this is more likely to lead to the proper treatment of other people, but also because that is a good state of mind from a self-interested point of view. Self-interest is a good reason to be the kind of person who is typically forgiving, hopeful, and charitable; to be aware of the faults of others, but without always dwelling on them; to take pleasure in the good one sees in them and in their good fortune; not to be filled with resentment and jealousy; to be patient in one's social interactions, for one's own peace of mind. These traits are rightly valued not only as expressions of kindness to others, but for their enhancement of the quality of one's own life.[29]

One reason why the phenomenology of moral life is so variegated is that no two human beings are exactly alike, so interacting with others as one should requires one to be attentive to their differences. A good person cares about and is interested in other people for their sake, and as one modulates one's response to them in accordance with their personality and character, the relationship one has with each takes on a different phenomenological character. The *kinds* of relationship we have are also quite varied: think of the different ways in which we interact with fathers, mothers, sisters, brothers, sons, daughters, friends, neighbors, colleagues, teammates, classmates, roommates, officemates, and so on. The phenomenology of our experience with individuals who occupy these roles is colored by our conception of what is appropriate for each station.

One of the most important experiences in the lives of many human beings is that of conceiving, giving birth to, nurturing, raising, and loving a child. We want to engage in these activities partly for their experiential aspect—because of what it will be like for us to enter into this kind of relationship with another individual. Part of what we seek is the intense emotional intimacy of the parent–child bond—it adds immeasurably to the richness of one's experience. Of course, it would be deeply wrong to have and raise a child *only* because of the kinds of experiences one expects to have. That would be pure selfishness. To act from this motive alone would mean ignoring questions about the quality of life of the child that one contemplates bringing into existence. At the same time, it would be a grave error if one decided to have and raise a child without giving any thought to one's own interest—that is, without considering whether it would be good for one to go through the experiences that come with raising a child from birth to maturity. A good person facing this decision must give great weight both

---

[29] My insistence on the great prudential value of ethical virtue is consistent with Hurka's thesis that a virtuous mental act has less value than what it concerns. See *The Best Things in Life*, 133–9; and *Virtue, Vice, and Value*, chapter 5. (To illustrate his idea: compassion for someone's pain is not as good as that person's suffering is bad.) My view is that a virtue is a higher-order *prudential* good, in that a sufficient amount of it is better for someone than any amount of a lower-order good like pleasure. (What is a sufficient amount? See Chapter 4, section 17.) Hurka's thesis is not about the *prudential* value of a virtuous person's inner life; rather, it attributes to each virtuous attitude or act some other sort of value, and holds that it has less of that value than what it concerns or aims at. Although I am not contradicting his thesis, we are nonetheless at odds in this respect: I believe he is not occupying the standpoint from which virtue must be viewed if its full worth is to be appreciated.

to self-interest and the interest of others—neglecting either component would be a serious mistake. In fact, if one neglected the question whether having a child would be in one's own interest, one would simultaneously be guilty of having insufficient concern for the well-being of one's child. One can be a good parent only if one sees that there is a great deal of good for oneself in being a parent, only if one recognizes and deeply appreciates the contribution loving a child makes to one's own well-being.

A related point can be made about most kinds of friendship. Of course, it would be unusual and odd to enter a friendship in the deliberate way in which people ought to become parents: first by deciding whether or not to have a friend, and then, having decided affirmatively, proceeding to befriend someone. Friendships develop in more roundabout, unforeseeable ways than that. But it can easily happen that we must decide whether to keep a friendship from lapsing or dissolving; and when we do that, it is appropriate to ask whether it would be in our interest to keep our relationship alive. It is incumbent on a friend to care about and be interested in the other person for that person's sake, so in deciding whether to continue investing in this kind of relationship, one must ask whether it is good for one to be in a relationship that can require one to make sacrifices for the sake of someone else. Just as a parent must give up some things that would benefit him, for the sake of his child, but is rewarded by the experiential riches of the relationship he has with his child, so too in a friendship we must be willing to inconvenience ourselves for the good of our friend, but are rewarded by the experiences we have when we interact with those who are dear to us. Neither parenthood nor friendship are or ought to be purely selfless undertakings.

When we ask whether to bring a new human being into existence, and thus are led to the question whether she would have good prospects for faring well, surely we must consider not only her likely external circumstances but also the quality of her internal life. We are in no position to know whether she will develop musical interests, or intellectual interests, or athletic interests—but one thing we do know is that she will enter a complex social world that will shape her inner life, and she will be subject to the norms, rules, and demands of morality. Will it be good for her to be trained in ways that will make her a good person? If the answer is no, human beings have good reason to stop having children (or they should make sure their children become immoralists). They should not bring a child into a world of moral demands that will chronically undermine her well-being.[30]

8. Being virtuous for the wrong reason: Kantian concerns

Because of what it is like to be a good person, it is advantageous, to some extent, to be such a person—not because it is a means to some further goal, but because moral experience is by itself a component of well-being. But so what? "Your conclusion," someone might say, "is insignificant. Even if everything you say is true, you have not even tried to cast doubt on the idea that, *all things considered*, virtue is *dis*advantageous.

---

[30] For a general discussion of such issues, see Rivka Weinberg, *The Risk of a Lifetime.*

Being a good person, you have admitted, involves a willingness to make sacrifices. Those sacrifices can be greater than whatever good accrues to someone by being good. What is the point, then, of trying to support the thesis that virtue is good *to some extent*? That is too weak a claim to be of real interest."

"Further," the objection continues, "your conclusion is insignificant because a virtuous person does what is morally right because it is morally right. It does not matter to him whether there is something good *for him* in being a virtuous person. Even if virtue were the *only* good, that would not be his reason for being virtuous."

To address the first of these objections, it is enough to point out that for most people the moral aspect of experiential life could hardly be a small portion of the whole. We are social creatures; our conscious lives are suffused with the thoughts, desires, plans, feelings, and pleasures that we experience as we respond, sometimes well, sometimes poorly, to the norms of the many overlapping communities to which we belong. The qualities of mind that we bring to bear on our day-to-day social intercourse form an enormous portion of our conscious lives. Furthermore, it should be kept in mind, as I noted in the previous section, that being a good person is not by its very nature an all-consuming job, leaving no room for non-moral activities—playing an instrument, reading philosophy, rock climbing, writing fiction, playing chess, acting, dancing, cooking, and so on. One does not in the very nature of things have to choose between these things and being a good person. So, a rich and varied life can be combined with moral goodness. Admittedly, being moral can require sacrifices in other components of one's well-being; these might be grave and long-lasting. But that does not show that being moral is at best a minor good. It only means that one's own good might sometimes have to be sacrificed for the good of others, and that it is not the only important element of well-being.

If *one* large component of a good life is determined by how good a person one is, then something not very distant from what Aristotle says about sacrifice turns out to be correct. Recall the passage I cited in Chapter 1, section 3. Good people, he says:

> will also sacrifice money on the condition that their friends gain more; while the friend gets money, he gets what is noble, and therefore assigns himself the greater good. ... In all praiseworthy actions, then, the good person is seen to assign himself the larger share of what is noble.
> (1169a26–b1)

He ought to have said instead that although a virtuous person will sometimes need to sacrifice certain goods (money, a good night's sleep, comfort) in order to act well towards others, the result will never be that his life is devoid of significant goods. Even if, in extreme circumstances, he must die, he will have been active as an ethical agent over a considerable period of time, and so there will have been much in his life that was good for him.

Furthermore, he could have added that a precise measure of how much good there is in someone's life is not possible. Well-being is not like money: it is not composed of things that have an exact quantity, allowing us to say how much more of it we have than someone else, or what the exchange rate is between one of its components and another. (There are many such realms of imprecision. No novel, for example, is 2.35 times better than another.) Accordingly, we cannot, in any exact way, compare the goodness of being virtuous with the value of what we give up because we are virtuous. So, something like what Aristotle claims in the above passage turns out to be right: although a virtuous person is certainly willing to have, for a certain period of time, a smaller quantity of this or that component of his well-being, the inherent imprecision of prudential value makes it impossible to know whether, all things considered, his life would have been better had he not been a virtuous person.

We can turn now to the other part of the objection under consideration: a virtuous person does what is morally right because it is morally right, not because being virtuous is good for him. So, it is charged, my thesis that it is good to be virtuous has no *moral* significance.

There is a short answer to this charge: whether or not it has moral significance, my thesis (or rather the thesis of Plato, Aristotle, and the Stoics) surely has *prudential* significance. What is good for oneself is a subject that one ought not forever put out of one's mind; what is good for human beings *in general* is one among several subjects that practical philosophy legitimately explores.

This answer can be supplemented by the point that part of being a good person is caring about the good of others. We can go badly astray, as individuals striving to do what is right by them, if we work with a misconception of what their well-being consists in. If you thought that your proper goal as a parent devoted to the well-being of your children is to insure their worldly success (high status, wealth, power), your efforts to be a good parent (a good person with respect to your children) would go for naught—assuming that well-being is what I claim it to be. And, as I noted earlier in this chapter (section 7), prospective parents also need to make correct assumptions about whether their child, if they have one, will have a good life. The question whether it is good to be a good person bears on this issue.

Although these responses to the "so what?" question are, I believe, sufficient to disarm it, I would like to address an issue that lingers beneath the suggestion that a good person does not care about the goodness-*for-him* of being morally good. What I have in mind is the Kantian theme that a sense of duty is the chief characteristic of moral life. Morality so conceived is all about acting from a recognition of one's obligations. Phenomenologically, these are felt as constraints, limitations, impingements on our desires; and moral virtue consists in willing ourselves to abide by these impingements against the biddings of pleasure and convenience. So, if you are acting from the best kind of motive, you should feel yourself going against the grain: you should recognize the rightness of your act, because of its conformity to the moral law, but you must will yourself to overcome the internal obstacles to doing so—otherwise what you do, however praiseworthy, has no moral worth.

This outlook is utterly at odds with the one we find in ancient ethics. The ancient philosophers of Greece and Rome depict the life of a good person as devoid of internal conflict; for Kant, the conflict between inclination and duty is the arena in which the moral worth of human beings (no angels they) shines like a jewel. Let us spell out his position more fully.[31]

Recall one well-known passage in the *Groundwork of the Metaphysics of Morals* in which he develops this theme. "Many souls are so compassionately disposed that, without any further motive of vanity or self-interest, they find an inner pleasure in spreading joy around them" (4:398).[32] He is by no means contemptuous of them—on the contrary, he says that they "deserve praise and encouragement" (4:398). But not the highest praise or the strongest encouragement. They do not deserve our esteem, because their motivation "has no genuinely moral worth." That is because the "maxim" of what they do "lacks the moral merit of such actions done not out of inclination but out of duty" (4:398).

If Kant is imagining the compassionate souls in his example to be people who help others only because this gives them a warm internal glow, he is surely right that they do not deserve our fullest admiration. We might be glad that it is spreading joy to others that gives them a kick rather than spreading sorrow; but ultimately they make others happy only because of the effect this has on themselves. They are self-interested hedonists who happen to feel good when they make others feel good. They fail a counterfactual test: when circumstances are such that they are obligated to help others, and doing so brings them no joy, would they do their duty? Whether or not this is an idea that Kant is trying to convey in this passage, it is a good one. To qualify fully as a good person, one must pass this test.

Later in this passage, Kant elaborates on his claim by imagining a transformation in one of these sympathetic and compassionate people: suppose someone's misfortunes have brought him sorrows that extinguish his feeling for others. He retains his power to "assist others in distress" but now "their adversity no longer stir[s] him." He feels no "inclination" to help them, but does so nonetheless, simply because he believes he has a moral duty to do so. Kant says that when this happens, this man's character and his action have "*moral* worth"—whereas they had none before. His motive is now "incomparably the highest" (4:399).

Let us embellish Kant's point by imagining this individual to be strongly *dis*inclined to assist a neighbor in distress—a neighbor whom our unfortunate but moral man has a duty to aid. His sense of duty now faces internal opposition, and it requires a real effort of will to make himself aid his neighbor. Compare his experience of struggle with the experience of someone who regards helping a neighbor as both the right thing to do and a great pleasure. Which is the greater accomplishment? Surely that of the Kantian agent. Granted, both helpers achieve the same result. But greater praise is due the Kantian agent than the one admired in ancient ethics, because the first had to fight

---

[31] In what follows, I draw on some material in my entry, 'Altruism,' in the *Stanford Encyclopedia of Philosophy*.

[32] Here and elsewhere, I use the edition edited by Thomas Hill and translated by Arnulf Zweig.

against the grain to help his neighbor and the other did not. Speaking more generally, the greater the difficulty felt in overcoming an obstacle, the more praise due. If, for example, one post office employee delivers the mail in the face of extreme weather conditions, and another does so in perfect weather, the accomplishment of the first is greater and more praiseworthy. Someone deserves our moral esteem, we might say, only if he faces heavy *internal* weather and nonetheless does his duty.

We should accept this point about degrees of achievement and praiseworthiness. But it does not follow that we should live our lives with a view to making our achievements greater, whenever we can. Imagine yourself going for a stroll when suddenly a great gulf in the earth opens before you, and you fall to its floor, sustaining serious injuries. To get out will require great strength, ingenuity, and courage. How much more you will have accomplished, how much more praise you will deserve, than would have been the case had you simply strolled along the surface of the earth as usual. All that is true, but it does not follow that when we go for a walk, we should arrange or hope to be faced with such obstacles as these. Life is already hard enough; doing or hoping for something just to make it harder would be silly. The point applies to the ethical sphere of life: it is no easy matter to be a good person even for those who take great joy in helping others. Experiencing those pleasures does not help us solve the enormous moral problems facing us. If one experiences no conflict between one's sense of duty and one's inclinations, if one finds that what one has a duty to do is also a great pleasure, there is no reason to wish that one were differently constituted, so as to be more deserving of praise.

We should also acknowledge that at times we would be defective as moral agents, and open to criticism, if we behaved towards others merely out of a sense of duty, and took no pleasure in what we do for them. Suppose someone was extraordinarily kind to me when I was a child, and later in life I am in a position to help him out of a difficult situation. If I reciprocate merely out of the sense that I have a burden to discharge—I owe him—with no feeling of gratitude and no pleasure in helping him in return, there is something missing in my response to his kindness towards me. I do not feel towards him as I should, even if I give him the help he now needs. I might even tell him, as I pay him back, how grateful I am. But if I do not *feel* grateful, and am not happy that I can return his kindness, there is something amiss in how I stand in relation to him. Further, even apart from my relation to him, there is something lacking in me, if I assist him only because I owe that to him, and am not pleased to do so. For my *own* good, I should be getting more pleasure than I do from my ethical response to other people.

This is not to deny that our obligations and duties to others, and our answerability to them if we wrong them, are one aspect of our moral relationships. A sense of indebtedness to others is one component of the experience of a good person. Moral norms can constrain our options and when they do so they are experienced as barriers that frustrate our desires. But that is not the only way in which we experience our moral relations to others, and we would be unfortunate if our interactions with them—with our parents, children, colleagues, and neighbors—had only this burdensomeness, or were the predominant mode of our moral sensibility. To recall a point made earlier in this chapter (section 7): if ethical life were entirely or mostly a matter of burdensome duties and offered no enrichment of our experience, adding nothing to the goodness of being alive, that fact should make us hesitate to bring children into the world. It is the duty of parents to prepare their children for the moral life of adults, and if that cannot reasonably be expected to constitute a great good for them, then the "gift of life" is not much of a gift after all.

9. Do bad people have bad lives?

Here is another way to question the significance of my thesis that being a good person is a great good: for all that I have said, it might be the case that being a bad person is also a great good, perhaps even greater in value than anything a good person can have. After all, suppose someone (A) lacks a conscience, or easily puts it out of mind; (B) cheats, steals, lies (and worse) but escapes detection; (C) and uses these methods to live a life full of aesthetic experiences, gustatory pleasures, intellectual pursuits, romantic escapades, and other non-moral goods. Will that not be a good life? Will it not be better than the lives of morally admirable people who have little of prudential value beyond what accrues to them by their having the experiences that come with being a good person?

Plato tried to show not only that justice in the soul is a great good, but also that the farther one departs from this ideal, the worse off one is. At the other end of the scale, opposite to the fully just individual, is the tyrannical soul, a tormented man who must constantly do battle against himself. He is "maddened by his appetites and passions" (*Republic* 578a), and filled with fear, regret, insatiable desires, and other disorders (579d–580a). Similarly, Aristotle holds that thoroughly bad people "flee from themselves" because "when they are by themselves they remember many disturbing things and foresee others like them" (*NE* IX 4, 1166b14–16). Both philosophers give us portraits of the experiences that they believe accompany extreme moral badness, and the states of mind they depict are the opposite of those we think constitute a good life.

Unfortunately, what they say is unconvincing. Not that they are entirely off the mark. There are many different ways of being a bad person, and one of them consists in being filled with hatred of individual people or whole groups of people merely out of prejudice, or free-floating hostility, or a sense of grievance. Such a person will take pleasure in perceiving the misfortunes of those he hates, but he will also be disturbed by their good fortune. And to the extent that his consciousness is a locus of anger and ill will, it mars his experience of life.

But there are other ways of being a bad person, and many of them do not leave the bad person worse off with respect to the introspectable quality of his life. Think of someone living in a slave society who wrestles, for a time, with doubts about the justice of this institution. Suppose he becomes convinced that slavery is a great evil, but cannot bring himself to free his slaves or to take up the abolitionist cause. He puts the whole issue out of mind and carries on with his life, which is full of the best that life has to offer. He has a grave moral deficiency, but is not the least bit worse off for having it. His complicity with an evil institution need have no bad psychological effects on him. To assume otherwise would be wishful thinking.

It does not follow that I must now retract my claim that it is a great good to have the consciousness of a good person. All the points made in section 7 above remain intact. When one cares about and is interested in other people, and has the variegated conscious life depicted earlier (taking pleasure in the good one sees in others, enjoying being with them and helping them, being patient with them, feeling close to them), that is undeniably a good state of mind to be in. In fact, the slaveholder depicted in the previous paragraph may have this kind of relationship with many others. If he does, he is not completely evil. He is virtuous in some of his relationships (and that is good for him), and the opposite of virtuous in others. (In his relationship with the people who are his slaves, he fails to achieve the good that ethical relationships bring.) That there is grave injustice on the negative side of his moral record does not by itself make him worse off, but it remains true that the positive side makes him better off.

There is a decisive objection to what the slaveholder does: slavery is a horrible violation of a fundamental moral norm. That a slaveholder need not be made worse off by his wrong is one of many counter-examples to the thesis of Plato and Aristotle that injustice harms its perpetrator. To generalize: *any* character defect that harms others might do so without harming oneself. But that provides no basis for taking an investigation into well-being off the agenda of moral philosophy, and no reason to doubt that being good is among its components.

10. Is pleasure always good?

Pleasure is certainly not the only component of well-being. Perhaps there are experiences that partly constitute well-being that have no pleasure in them at all. So, at any rate, I have argued (Chapter 1, section 7). But I have not addressed a further question about pleasure: Does it always have some prudential value? It is a familiar feature of life that pleasant experiences have painful or other unwelcome consequences, and therefore, all things considered, we are better off to avoid them. Even so, those pleasant experiences might be good to some degree. There is nothing preposterous in the thesis that *all* pleasant experiences have at least some small prudential value. But some philosophers claim that although this thesis is not *obviously* false, it is nonetheless false; and to support their denial, they point to morally objectionable pleasures. A torturer, for example, might enjoy witnessing the agonizing pain and humiliation of his victim. If all pleasure has some prudential value, we are forced to admit that sadistic pleasure enhances the well-being of a torturer to some degree. It is understandable that we have some reluctance to grant that claim.[33]

---

[33] Aristotle offers several ways of defending the thesis that pleasure is good even if shameful pleasures are not: (A) One can deny that they really are pleasures. (B) One can hold that pleasure is good, but pleasures achieved in these ways are not. (C) One can point out that only a good person can have the pleasures of a good person. See *NE* X.3 1173b20–31.

The fact that torture pleases someone (the torturer or anyone else) does nothing whatsoever to justify torture. It is not a weak reason in favor of torture, but no reason. But that by itself does not force us to conclude that the pleasure the torturer feels is not at all good for him. For there is another option: we could say that although the torturer gets something good for himself (pleasure), that fact is no reason (not even a weak reason) in favor of his infliction of pain.

It would be misguided to argue: the sadistic torturer's pleasure is morally wrong; therefore, it is not good for him to get pleasure from what he does. It is unfortunately true that people sometimes benefit from the horrible wrong they do.

The best way to approach this issue, I suggest, is to recognize that there are many better pursuits and projects, not only from a moral point of view but also from a prudential point of view, than the infliction of suffering on others for its own sake. The experience of the sadistic torturer—even if it has some small degree of prudential value—is lower in overall quality than many other human experiences. If the pleasure the torturer feels continues to attract him to this activity, then, like many drugs, it is an impediment to his having experiences that are better for him. In that respect, it is not like the wonderful meal that later brings on indigestion. There is something bad for him in what he is doing at the very time of his doing it.

But the fact that there is something bad for him in his activity of torturing is compatible with the possibility that there is also something good for him as well—the pleasurable experience he has. Phenomenologically, that pleasurable experience belongs together with other pleasures, including ones that are morally innocent. Since it resembles them with respect to what they are like from the inside, and since what they (the innocent pleasures) are like from the inside supports the judgment that they have prudential value, the thesis that it (the sadistic pleasure) is bad for someone, whereas the others (the innocent pleasures) are good, is suspect. What underlies this difference in prudential value could only be the difference in their moral status—and that moral difference, we have agreed, does not by itself support the conclusion that the sadistic pleasure is bad for the torturer.

The thesis that all pleasures have some degree of prudential value is therefore not undermined by the example of shameful pleasures. But experientialism is not threatened by this result. It holds that pleasure is not the only component of well-being—far from it. In fact, I have argued that, considered on its own and in isolation from other features of one's experience, pleasure has little prudential value (Chapter 1, section 11). There is no need to go farther by denying that it is one factor that determines the quality of a life, and no reason to single out shameful pleasures as the one kind of pleasure that is devoid of prudential value.

3

Experientialism and the Experience Machine

We turn now to the doctrine I am calling "experientialism" and the challenges it faces. The experience machine will be our first concern. In Part One of this chapter, I will discuss in considerable detail what this thought experiment involves. In Part Two, I argue that it is a thought experiment that counts *in favor of* experientialism—not against it, as often supposed. We will also consider a variation on Nozick's thought experiment proposed by Roger Crisp. Then, in Part Three, I will turn to other objections to experientialism—counter-examples in which one is mocked by friends behind one's back, or in which good things are done for us after we die. I will also return, in Part Three, to some similarities and differences between experientialism and Aristotle's treatment of posthumous and "external" goods.

Part One

1. Strong and weak experientialism

Recall that experientialism makes three claims: (A) well-being is composed of many goods; (B) all of them are experiential; but (C) pleasure is only one element of good experience. Nozick's thought experiment seems to undermine (B). It purports to show that much more matters to the quality of our lives than the quality of its purely experiential aspect. If he is right, the value of machine-induced experiences greatly diminishes, perhaps disappearing altogether. I will argue that it does not diminish at all, but if others insist that experiences inside the machine have less prudential value, but only a bit less, than their phenomenologically identical counterparts outside it, that will be a significant concession.

Not everyone agrees that the experience machine provides us with material that is helpful for philosophical reflection. It may be fun to think about it, but do we need to indulge in this fantasy—might it be inferior as a philosophical tool to more realistic examples? Suppose the people you take to be your friends often snicker about you when you are not present. That fact by itself seems to take something away from you. Would you want that to be your situation, even if you never detect their falsity, and they otherwise give you everything that true friends give?[1] Or consider someone whose long-term projects remain unfinished because of his untimely death. Suppose others bring his work to fruition, and through their efforts he lives on in people's memories because of his accomplishments. Would you not want that to be included in the story of your life, if you were he? These two sorts of examples by themselves seem to undermine (B). They appear to make the experience machine redundant at best.

Furthermore, the experience machine is not a mere set of headphones, of the sort already in use, by which one experiences vivid simulations of the real world—"virtual reality" or "enhanced reality." It is a science fiction fantasy in which the brain is manipulated or stimulated by a human being using laboratory instruments in a way that creates an ongoing alternative reality indistinguishable from the real thing. Will anyone ever be able to do that? Might it be impossible? Could it be that some or many of the experiences we have can only come about through the brain's encounter with distal objects and only when the brain is attached to a body that interacts with the world? Why should we pay attention to a thought experiment whose realizability is in question?[2]

One proper reply to that challenge is that our imagination can construct things whose contemplation teaches us something, even if those things could never exist. We may put together in our minds, for example, the picture of an animal that could never arise in a world governed by evolutionary biological forces; and our emotional reaction to the picture we construct can reveal to us something about our aesthetic sensibility. Similarly, if thinking about the experience machine is a way to raise important questions about the place of experience or the reality behind experience in the right conception of well-being, it will have served its purpose. A second proper reply is that dreams and hallucinations are familiar phenomena. We already have illusory experiences; the experience machine gives us something more vivid and elaborate than anything we have ever known, but that does not show that there is some confusion in the very idea of it.

---

[1] Nozick himself appeals to such examples in *The Examined Life*: "Few of us think that only a person's experiences matter. We would not wish for our children a life of great satisfactions that all depended on deceptions they would never detect: although they take great pride in artistic accomplishments, the critics and their friends too are just pretending to admire their work yet snicker behind their backs; the apparently faithful mate carries on secret love affairs; their apparently loving children really detest them; and so on" (105–6).

[2] Such doubts as these are expressed by Sumner in *Welfare, Happiness, and Ethics*, 94–5. However, his emphasis is different from mine. Noting that one is not allowed to change one's mind about spending the rest of one's life in the machine, he points out: "We immediately begin to imagine the many ways in which things could go horribly wrong.... What if there is a power failure? Suppose the operators of the machine are really sadistic thrill-seekers...?... In real life we cannot eliminate all possible malfunctions and screw-ups. For the thought experiment to yield any results at all, we must therefore imagine ourselves in a world quite alien to our own—and who knows what we would choose in a world like that?" (95). In section 14, we will examine a variation on Nozick's thought experiment that puts the experience machine in a third-person rather than a first-person setting, with the result that these doubts about Nozick's version do not arise.

We will see that that Nozick's thought experiment involves issues of considerable philosophical interest—questions that other sorts of arguments against experientialism do not pose. Even so, we will need to return to false friends and posthumous goods, for they are often regarded as decisive refutations of the thesis that all the components of well-being are experiential. I will argue that their evidential force is open to question (sections 18–21).

Notice an important difference between these examples drawn from everyday life and the science fiction of the experience machine. Those examples seek to undermine (B) by describing components of well-being that are non-experiential. By contrast, Nozick's experience machine is best interpreted to concede, at least for the sake of argument, that although all of the components of well-being are experiential, there is an empirical but non-experiential condition they must satisfy, and if they fail to do so, the prudential value of those experiences diminishes or perhaps even disappears altogether. One might concede, after reflecting on Aristotle's example of the virtuous man who ceases to actualize his virtue and remains asleep for the entire duration of his life, that well-being is composed entirely of *conscious* activities. But that would leave one free to say that these conscious activities must correspond to a reality that lies beyond themselves, and that if they do not, one's well-being declines (even though those experiences are phenomenologically indistinguishable from their more valuable counterparts).

We should therefore complicate the definition of experientialism, and distinguish two forms of this doctrine. The strong form holds that (B1) all components of well-being are experiential, and (B2) if an experience is illusory, that does not in itself diminish its value. The weak form accepts (B1) but drops (B2) and says instead that (B3) non-veridical experiences are lower in value because they are non-veridical; or they have no value at all. The strong form is the one that I am defending. Those who are persuaded by Nozick's thought experiment can adopt weak experientialism or they can reject both of its versions. Those who are persuaded by common sense examples (false friends, posthumous goods) thereby oppose both strong and weak experientialism. Henceforth, when I describe my theory as experientialist, I am referring to the strong form of this doctrine.

What is meant by "in itself" in (B2)? Why is the issue whether the illusory nature of an experience "in itself" diminishes its value? Those words acknowledge that illusory experiences can easily have bad consequences for their subject and often do so. If it looks as though there is a bridge in front of you but this is an illusion, you might fall off a cliff. If you think a stranger who asks for your help is sincere, you may be mugged or worse. What we want to know is whether the experiences produced by the machine have little or no prudential value because of what is inherent to them—because their illusory nature necessarily brings with it an impoverishment of your life, robbing you of great goods.

Even if experientialism is not, strictly speaking, true, it might nonetheless be very close to the truth. (This point, made in Chapter 1, section 6, bears repeating.)

It is possible that although there are non-experiential components of well-being, its experiential components are incommensurably superior to them. Or it is possible that Nozick is right, but non-veridical experiences are only slightly less valuable than veridical experiences. In that case, a very long life spent in the experience machine will contain more prudential value than its far shorter but phenomenologically identical counterpart in the real world. (Here we combine McTaggart's insight about the effect of time on overall well-being with Nozick's thought experiment.)

Notice as well that my efforts to show what is experientially good in being a good person would not be undermined even if we accepted the experience machine as an argument against experientialism. The virtuous individuals whose mental life was portrayed in Chapter 2 were assumed to be participants in relationships with real people—not with the simulacra created in the experience machine. It might be wondered, then, why we need to discuss Nozick's thought experiment at all. The answer is that the question, "What has ethical virtue to do with well-being?" is not the only or even the most basic problem confronting a theory of well-being. We want to have general answers to these questions: What are the components of well-being? Do they differ significantly in value? (If there are posthumous goods, for example, are they less good for being posthumous?) What, if anything, do they have in common, aside from the fact that they constitute well-being? Do they have value only under certain conditions? Or is their value reduced if certain conditions do not obtain? The experience machine requires discussion because it suggests that either something beyond experience—the right kind of contact with reality—is a condition that must be met by any component of well-being, or that its components are vastly reduced in value if they are not produced by reality in the normal way.

In Chapter 1, I suggested that experientialism of some sort seems to be present in Plato and Aristotle. At any rate, that is a plausible interpretation of them if weak experientialism is the doctrine in question. Speaking more generally, it was widely accepted in antiquity that "internal" goods—the ones that reside in the soul, the ones we are conscious of—are the only true goods, or that little else has value. That is the view not only of Plato and Aristotle, but of the Epicureans, the Stoics, and Plotinus. The Epicureans would not satisfy my definition of "experientialism" because they hold that only pleasure is good; and the Stoics would also fail to meet my conditions, because they hold that there is only one component of well-being (virtue). But all of these ancient figures and schools were convinced that "goods" of the body (such as health) and external "goods" (honor) were of little or no value in themselves. Aristotle's thought experiment—the good man asleep for the rest of his life (discussed in Chapter 1, section 2)—is an insight that leads to the thesis shared by weak and strong experientialism: all components of well-being are experiential.

In Plato's *Republic*, the value of justice is said to reside in a felt harmony of the soul, and in the *Symposium*, the ascent of the soul to the form of beauty affords us an intellectual vision, an experience that we would wish to last forever (a passage I will discuss below, section 16). For the Stoics, the one true good—the virtue possessed by a sage—is accompanied by a great sense of tranquility and a joyful affirmation of the universe and one's place in it. For Plotinus, well-being resides entirely in a noetic experience—a sense of unification with the Good—not with "goods" that belong to us as embodied beings.

Yet this is a view that now receives little attention. Why so? Perhaps there is no single explanation, but no doubt Nozick's experience machine is part of the story. It is called the "experience machine"—not the "pleasure machine." It is presented as powerful evidence not only that hedonism is widely off the mark, but also that any theory like hedonism must be equally misguided. The problem with hedonism, it tells us, is that pleasure is just an experience, and experiences have little or no value in themselves, because they can be detached from reality. Contemporary theories of well-being, impressed with the apparent power of this thought experiment, take experientialism to have been refuted along with hedonism; the latter is portrayed as an illustration of the errors of the former.[3]

Experientialism might also seem to lack plausibility because it is mistakenly thought to embrace a questionable form of "subjectivism" about values in general or prudential value in particular. Experiences are of course subjective in the sense that they are psychological phenomena—they are mental states, even if they are also correlated with or identical to states of the brain and the body. But subjectivism *about values* holds that each individual has a kind of sovereignty about the correctness of value judgments—what an individual values is what makes things valuable-for-that-individual. A subjectivist about prudential value would say that an experience is good for someone to have in virtue of his wanting to have it, or his believing that he should have it.[4] But the experientialism about well-being that I will defend does not accept that standard for the goodness of experience. (This point will be developed more fully in section 9 below.)

2. Trade-offs

In his presentation of the experience machine, Nozick acknowledges that his readers will find *something* to like about the prospect of plugging into it. In fact, he goes out of his way to address concerns they might have. His first task is to make the machine sound enticing. You can have any experience you desire. Are you reluctant to be plugged in because on your own you might not invent good experiences to have inside the machine? Not to worry. "Business enterprises have thoroughly researched the

---

[3] The experience machine does not figure in every dismissal of experientialism. For a notable exception, see Shelly Kagan, 'The Limits of Well Being.' One of the conceptions of well-being he discusses is "mental statism," which holds that only mental states (pleasure being one of them, but not the only one) are components of well-being. Kagan argues that a person is more plausibly said to be a body and a mind—not just a mind—and rejects mental state theories for this reason.

[4] Sidgwick might seem to accept such subjectivism when he says that the "judgment of the sentient individual must be taken as final" as regards "how far each element of feeling has the quality of Ultimate Good." See *The Methods of Ethics*, 398. But he can be read to mean that "the sentient individual" is uniquely situated to *assess* how good his feelings are—not that his judgment is what *determines* "the quality of Ultimate Good."

lives of many others" and you can choose among them.[5] Furthermore, you are allowed to return periodically to a fully embodied state and choose once again which experiences you will have after you re-enter the machine. So, you don't have to make a once-and-for-all decision about which experiences to have for the rest of your life. Are you concerned about what will happen to your friends in your absence? They too, Nozick assures his readers, can plug into their machines and have any experiences they want. You could choose "a lifetime of bliss."[6]

Nozick asks, "What else can matter to us, other than how our lives feel from the inside?"[7] He then goes on to answer this question: in fact, there are extremely valuable things, which we already care deeply about, missing from a life spent in the machine. He does not claim that our initial attraction to the machine is *entirely* misguided—that *nothing* of value would be available inside it. That, after all, would be implausible. It is hard to see how the way "our lives feel from the inside" could not matter at all. So, I take Nozick to concede that although we should not spend our lives in an experience machine, *something* can be said in favor of doing so. Something would be gained. But, he insists, much more would be lost.

What would be lost? Nozick replies:

First we want to *do* certain things and not just have the experience of doing them . . . . A second reason for not plugging in is that we want to *be* a certain way, to be a certain sort of person. Someone floating in a tank is an indeterminate blob. There is no answer to the question of what a person is like who has long been in the tank . . . . Thirdly, plugging into an experience machine limits us to a man-made reality, to a world no deeper or more important than that which people can construct. There is no *actual* contact with any deeper reality.[8]

I take Nozick to be pointing out to his readers that they already have excellent reasons to refuse the enticing opportunities offered by the experience machine. They already want to do certain things—to be agents; they already want to be something more than an "indeterminate blob"; they already want "actual contact" with the real world. And they are right to want these things. They *should* not plug in, and he expects them to agree with him about that, because they will acknowledge that they *would* not do so.[9]

Notice that Nozick does not say, in so many words, that inside the machine the *quality of one's life* would decline, or that one would undergo a diminution of *well-being*, or that it would be *bad for* someone to enter the machine, or that one would not *flourish* inside it. Rather, he claims that if we bear in mind what "matters to us," we will not and should not plug ourselves into it. It might be said, then, that although he has definite ideas about how we ought to live our lives, these are not ideas about well-being.

---

[5] *Anarchy, State, and Utopia*, 42.   [6] Ibid., 43.

[7] Ibid., 43. Nozick puts the entire sentence in italics.   [8] Ibid., 42–3, author's emphasis.

[9] It is possible that Nozick tacitly accepts a theory of well-being according to which it consists entirely in the satisfaction of one's preferences. In that case, he holds that it is better for us not to plug in *because* we prefer not to do so. But I think he is more plausibly understood to mean that we should prefer not to plug in because if we did so we would be missing major components of well-being and accepting poor substitutes for them.

Fortunately, we do not have to settle that interpretive question. We are free to appropriate his words for our own purposes. *Our* topic is the quality of life, or well-being, whether or not that is Nozick's, and we can ask whether his thought experiment can teach us something about that topic. Furthermore, we need not confine ourselves to the question whether the reasons Nozick offers for rejecting the machine are good reasons. The more important question, for our purposes, is whether one or more elements of well-being would be affected, either positively or negatively, when someone enters the machine.

When I ask myself what would be missing from the life of someone living in the experience machine, the answers that occur to me are less abstract than the ones Nozick gives. I would not actually be with the people I love, although I might think I am. I would be socially isolated—it would be just me and the technician manipulating my brain.[10] I would be living in an illusory world, not realizing that I am just "a brain in a vat."[11] I would not have a body, and so I could not do any of the things that require embodiment. I could not hug anyone or be hugged, could not play tennis or the piano, eat or drink with my friends, have sex, cook a meal or make things with my hands, and so on. Perhaps, however, these examples are covered by Nozick's statement that "we want to *do* certain things and not just have the experience of doing them." And perhaps my desire not to live in an illusory world is what Nozick is getting at when he speaks of a "deeper reality." Even so, I am doubtful that Nozick makes the best possible case against plugging in. Would I really not be a certain kind of person, but only an "indeterminate blob"? And if someone's world is limited to things that are human constructs, is that really much of a limitation? We will return to these questions.

However, as soon as I rehearse to myself all that would be unavailable to me inside the machine, I remind myself that phenomenologically my experiences would be indistinguishable from those created by my normal encounter with reality. All that is wonderfully rich in real life would be presented to me. I could not hug anyone or be

---

[10] Jonathan Glover writes: "On the experience machine we inhabit a private world, and never again make contact with others.... Our desire is to *have* relationships, not to think we are having them." *What Sort of People Should There Be?*, 95. Glover also asks (ibid., 96–101) a question Nozick ignores: Would the individual inside the machine be the same individual as the one who chose to plug in? I will assume that the experiences of anyone who enters the machine are robustly continuous with those he had outside it, and so, whatever stand one takes about the identity of persons through time, the individual in the machine will unquestionably be the individual who chose to plug in. The only loss of memory the individual will suffer is that of having chosen to enter the machine, and this loss is posited only for those cases in which the experience in the machine would decline significantly in value if one knew that one was inside it.

[11] This is a phrase often used in the philosophical literature about whether and how we have knowledge of a world that exists beyond our mental states. For a widely discussed attempt to prove that we are not brains in a vat, see Hilary Putnam, *Reason, Truth and History*, 1–21. Nozick does not himself speak of an individual who is plugged into the experience machine as a "brain in a vat," and perhaps he assumes on the contrary that such an individual is fully embodied. (I am grateful to Susan Wolf for this point.) But that assumption (if he is making it) plays no role in his discussion; someone in the machine *could* be a brain in a vat, lacking arms, legs, and other parts of the gross anatomy of a human being. I will henceforth assume that he *is* a brain in a vat, for, as we will soon see (section 5), this enhances the thought experiment. See too section 17 regarding the possibility that all the denizens of one's social world are zombies.

hugged; but I would have exactly those experiences. No arms would be pressed against my body, since I would be a brain without a body, but all of the tactile and emotional benefits of being hugged would be mine. Should I care about the actual physical contact that would be missing? My body would not be out there on the tennis court, but somehow or other the experience machine would make it seem as though I were. (I discuss this case more fully below in section 9.) And similarly for the other examples I gave.

Furthermore, there is this to be said in favor of life in the machine: it gives us far more power over our future than we normally have. In the real world, we always face the possibility that the future will bring us more suffering than it would be good for us (or anyone) to experience. Some bad experiences play a useful role in our lives: we learn from them; they provide a contrast with the good in our lives, so that we appreciate the good all the more; they are part of an experience whose joyfulness cannot be separated from its painfulness. Even so, we know that many human lives contain bad experiences that are simply that—they add nothing good to these lives, but only detract from well-being. The experience machine offers us the opportunity to keep our personal suffering within useful limits: the suffering that we, while outside the machine, prescribe for ourselves when we are within it always has a point, and is always limited in intensity and duration. We will encounter some unexpected bumps, even some major challenges and moments of doubt, but we have arranged in advance (when we were outside the machine) that we will come through with flying colors and achieve a deep sense of fulfillment. Similarly, if we prescribe an experience as if of intimate relations with friends and children, we can also insure that we do not feel *them* to be undergoing useless suffering. We can have the illusion, when we are in the machine, that we belong to a wider social world that unfortunately contains misery and tragedy for many *others* on a large scale (the world as we view it from inside our heads)—and although that will sadden us, it will also give us a greater appreciation of how lucky we are to suffer so much less.

When we ask not only whether something is good for us, but whether its value to us is small or large, it is useful also to ask what we would be willing to give up in exchange for it. That feature of Nozick's thought experiment should not be overlooked. He himself does not point out that the experience machine would eliminate all unnecessary and meaningless suffering. So even if he is right that something of value is missing inside the machine (whether that is so is not yet a question we have explored), there is a further question to be asked: would more be gained than lost?

If you remain outside the machine, you are taking an enormous risk. Reality can be very hard on human beings, and there is no way to insure against great suffering. Inside, you can feel uncertain about how life will go—a certain amount of uncertainty is good for you—but you have already guaranteed that the experiential good in your life will greatly outweigh the bad. The bad will be there only to enhance the good (although you will not know that). This is what you trade away when you decide not to enter the machine.

Is it on balance worth it to give up these advantages of life inside the machine? I do not claim that this is an easy question to answer. To address it, we will have to consider more fully and carefully the ways in which the machine would detract from the quality of our lives—or whether it would detract at all. In any case, we can now see that Nozick's thought experiment raises questions different from those posed by false friends and posthumous events. The experience machine provides us with a way of examining the value of embodiment and our power to determine our future lives, and these are issues that do not arise when we ask whether well-being is diminished by the disloyal acts of our friends or the completion of our projects after we die. Those examples seem to cast doubt on the thesis that all components of well-being are experiential, and the experience machine can be used to raise the same issue. But that does not make Nozick's thought experiment worthless. Why should we care about embodiment when we can have all the experience that embodiment normally makes possible, and at the same time have just the right balance of good and bad experience in our lives? Although Nozick can be read to mean that the machine offers us a trade-off, we might decide upon reflection that in fact nothing is traded away—that there is *no* loss of prudential value inside the machine, if one chooses one's experiences wisely.

The value of embodiment is hardly a philosophical issue raised by Nozick for the first time. The Pythagoreans of antiquity regarded the body as a kind of prison, and in several dialogues—*Phaedo* and *Phaedrus*—Plato argues that we must strive to separate ourselves from the sensory world and rise to the level of purely intellectual vision. Thus too Plotinus and Augustine. Descartes argues that we are essentially thinkers, not embodied beings, and that only the most careful reasoning will bring us to the conclusion that we have bodies in contact with other material objects. What if we cannot reason our way to this result—would that show that our mental lives are worthless? Berkeley denies the reality of anything but ideas and the minds that have them. For upholders of the Platonic and the idealist traditions, the loss of the body that Nozick contemplates by way of the experience machine would not be a loss of anything worthwhile. Nor is the philosopher whose ideas are most fully in play here—Aristotle—a huge fan of embodiment. Goods of the body (health, strength, beauty) are not components of *eudaimonia*. The unmoved mover is a soul without a body, and that enables it to achieve for all time the highest possible level of well-being. When he compares the two best lives available to human beings—the philosophical life of contemplation and the political life of ethical engagement—he takes it to be a deficiency of the ethical life that its virtues are expressions of our embodiment (X.8 1178a14–20). Of course, these historical points do not prove that Nozick is wrong. But we should not dismiss without a hearing the great philosophers who hold that we could do just as well (or even better) without the material world.

Perhaps what bothers some people about the experience machine is simply the fact that life inside it is confined to a tiny portion of the world. There you are with the technician who stimulates your brain—you never depart from that small physical space. But does that really matter? Hamlet says: "I could be bounded in a nutshell, and count myself a king of infinite space, were it not that I have bad dreams."[12] His quality of life would be of the highest order ("a king of infinite space") despite his physical confinement ("bounded in a nutshell"). He would be sufficient unto himself, but there is a downside: in the nutshell, he would still be afflicted by bad dreams. Like Hamlet in a nutshell, someone inside the experience machine would be confined to the narrow limits of the technician's laboratory, but his experiential world could be unbounded. He would be better off than Hamlet, because he could tell the technician to give him only the sweetest of dreams.

We should not take Nozick to be saying that no one should ever plug into the machine, whatever his circumstances. That exceptionless thesis is easily refuted when we recall that some miserable people face a future that will almost certainly bring them years and years filled with meaningless suffering and nothing of value. They would be far better off in the machine for the rest of their lives, despite the illusory nature of their experiences. So too would people who are made miserable, for significant portions of their lives, by chronic physical ailments and impediments. Beethoven, for example, could have made very good use of the experience machine: deafness and abdominal distress would be replaced by the rich experience of his own music and a robust sense of physical well-being. (We will discuss musical experiences and artistic creativity inside the experience machine in sections 4 and 14.) But Nozick could easily accept this point. He could say: any life lived inside the machine would be vastly improved if those same experiences connected one with reality in the normal way. True, some unfortunate people would do well to plug into the machine, if they could. But it would be far better for them, Nozick believes, if instead of escaping into the machine they escape to a part of the real world that gave them the experiences they would choose to have in the machine.

The question we must discuss, therefore, is not: should someone plug in? The answer to that question varies according to one's circumstances. We are engaged in this thought experiment because it is thought to show that this component of experientialism is false: if an experience is illusory, that does not in itself diminish its value. (This was proposition B2, in section 1 above.) So, we could take Nozick's general thesis to be, not that one should never plug into the machine, but that if an experience is illusory, that *does* always in itself diminish its value. That, at any rate, is one plausible way to read him, and it is a thesis worth discussing. We will see, however, that it is not the position he takes in a passage less well known than the familiar four paragraphs of *Anarchy, State, and Utopia*.

In this work, Nozick does not hold that veridical experience is ever so slightly better than illusory experience. He claims that one can always do *far* better for oneself outside the machine than inside. Whatever experiences one has in the machine, so much is missing from life inside it that one should, for one's own good, choose to live in the real world, even though one cannot there have the complete control over one's experiences

---

[12] Act II, scene 2, lines 254–6.

that one would have inside the machine. That uncertainty, that risk of excessive suffering, is worth the price, because the inferiority of illusory experience is so great. Much of life's value would be missing inside the machine.

As we have seen, we can combine McTaggart's thought experiment with Nozick's, asking whether a sufficiently long life in the experience machine would have more overall well-being than a far shorter life containing phenomenologically identical but veridical experiences. That is a question that can be raised retrospectively about two lives that have come to an end, one inside the machine, and the other outside it.

So, there are a number of closely related questions here. The one we should concentrate on first is the thesis that any experience produced by the machine is of diminished value, at least to some degree. That same experience, Nozick seems to say, would be better were it not illusory.

3. Moore and the experience machine

We can wonder whether knowledge is better than other cognitive states, or whether contact with reality is better than illusory experience, and we can do so without asking whether life on the experience machine is better or worse than real life. Here is an example from G. E. Moore:

We can imagine the case of a single person, enjoying throughout eternity the contemplation of scenery as beautiful, and intercourse with persons as admirable, as can be imagined, while yet the whole of the objects of his cognition are absolutely unreal. I think we should definitely pronounce the existence of such a universe, which consisted solely of such a person, to be *greatly* inferior in value to one in which the objects, in the existence of which he believes, did really exist just as he believes them to do…[13]

I take Moore to be assuming that the illusory experience of beauty is phenomenologically identical to the experience of scenery in the real world, and so too the "intercourse with persons as admirable, as can be imagined." In this respect, his thought experiment anticipates Nozick's, and it does so without any element of science fiction. But could someone have an imagination as powerful as would be required to replicate our vivid encounter with beauty in the physical world? That is doubtful. Moore's thought experiment has, in this respect, its own drawbacks. The technician in Nozick's example can see to it that we have the same brain activity that is normally caused by the vision of great scenic beauty. There is therefore no reliance on the ability of an individual to produce in his own mind an imaginary scene as vivid and detailed as one that our eyes reveal to us.

There is a further difference between Moore's example and Nozick's. I have assumed that the experience machine is meant to support a point about well-being: for one's

---

[13] *Principia Ethica*, 246, author's emphasis. The passage is compared to Nozick's thought experiment by Hurka, *British Ethical Theorists from Sidgwick to Ewing*, 202. (He cites *Principia Ethica*, 197, but this page reference is an error.)

own good, it is better to experience reality outside the machine than illusion within it. Nozick, as I noted, does not himself use such terms as "well-being" or "the quality of life," but even so, it does not seem contrary to the spirit of his discussion to enlist his thought experiment as a contribution to this topic. By contrast, Moore is asking about whether one kind of universe has more value in it than another. He holds that a world that contains both objects of great beauty and someone enjoying that great beauty contains more value than one that contains only the latter. Similarly he holds that a universe with two admirable individuals engaged in social intercourse has more value than one that contains just one individual who falsely believes he is conversing with an admirable conversational partner. His question is not about what is now called prudential value. It is about impersonal value—what is absolutely good (good, period).[14]

Even so, we could appropriate what he says and apply it to the question we are interested in here. Suppose someone has an experience as of great scenic beauty, but this is an event in his mind that does not correspond to reality. Someone else has that same experience, but in his case the experience is caused by an object of great beauty. If you had to choose which of these two experiences to have, and you made the decision entirely in terms of the quality of your life, would there be a reason to prefer one to the other? (The same question can be asked with respect to social conversation, but this raises complications to be addressed later. I will set it aside for now.) Let's suppose, further, that it would cost you a large sum of money to have an experience of beauty caused by physical objects, and nothing at all to have that very experience caused by the stimulation of your brain. You would have to forego something of significant value, and in exchange the cause of your experience of beauty would be something beautiful that lies behind it, rather than something un-beautiful. It does not seem implausible that you should prefer the simulation. What we should want for ourselves from beauty is the experience of beauty: this is what enhances the quality of our lives. It adds very little to the value of the universe that in my mind there is a picture of great beauty, but what is present in my mind is of enormous value *to me*. That leaves us free to agree with Moore, if we wish to do so, that a universe that contains beauty and the experience of it is a better world than one that contains only the latter.

4. Music in the experience machine

Let us return to Nozick's statement that we would not plug into the experience machine because "we want to *do* certain things and not just have the experience of doing them."[15] I take him to mean that inside the machine we would be entirely passive. We would be receptacles, not agents. Taste sensations, sounds, sights, smells, back rubs—all such things would be delivered to us, as we sit back and enjoy them in bovine bliss. But if this is what he has in mind, he is severely restricting the realm of experience to a narrow

---

[14] See my *Against Absolute Goodness* for a critique of the thesis, which Moore upholds, that goodness (period) is a property that gives us reason to act. Moore thinks it is the only reason. I argue that it is no reason.

[15] *Anarchy, State, and Utopia*, 43, author's emphasis.

portion of what is normally available to us. If the experience machine can provide only a few of the kinds of experience that we value, it poses no threat to experientialism.

When we listen to music, for example, we are both experiencing something and at the same time *doing* something—we are listening. At any rate, the most rewarding musical experiences are the ones that require attention and concentration. They call upon us to reflect on what we are hearing—for example, to recognize the reappearance of the opening motif of a sonata in a new guise, to appreciate surprising changes in tempi and keys, to recognize similarities and differences between one movement and another, and so on. These sophisticated thoughts are as important to the quality of musical experience as the sheer reception of auditory signals. If we plug into the experience machine and are exposed to the music we love outside the machine, but have been rendered no more capable of understanding it than an animal or a baby, then we are simply not having the phenomenologically identical experience there that we normally have. We would be experiencing meaningless sound, a mere buzz in the ears.

We should therefore acknowledge that the experience machine, properly imagined, could give us everything that a trained listener normally experiences when he actively attends to and understands a musical performance. Cognitively and acoustically, his experience inside the machine will be indistinguishable from its counterpart in the real world. Suppose someone chooses to have the experience machine deliver the illusion that he is sitting in a small, acoustically perfect auditorium in which a musician is playing Bach's sonatas for unaccompanied violin. Each note and phrase sounds as though it were traveling through space and produced by a musician and her instrument; each is utterly clear, vivid, expressive, and artful. It seems to be a live performance, with all the excitement created when lovely music is produced second by second as the musician responds to the rapt attention of the audience. In fact, no sounds are traveling across a room—it merely seems that way. Yet, it would be implausible to suppose that the enjoyment of this illusory experience is a less valuable component of well-being than the phenomenally indistinguishable experience that is produced by a violin and a musician. The music lover just described is no worse off because of the error he makes about the source of his musical experience. (The same point applies to illusory experiences, produced in a vat by human manipulation, in which one seems to be seeing beautiful landscapes. Those things that seem to be trees, sky, cloud are just as beautiful as the real thing, and the enjoyment of them is no less a good thing.)

Why would someone use the machine in this way? His musical experience inside it is of the sort he could have outside it, when he listens to music in the normal way. Plugging into the machine in this case seems pointless.

My reply is that it does not matter that this individual does no better inside the machine than outside. Nozick must show that inside the machine the quality of life declines. If we describe an experience in which there is no such decline, we show that he is mistaken, at least in this one sort of case. There is a further reply that can be made as well. Someone might be offered the opportunity to listen to music in the machine free of charge; the phenomenologically identical experience available in the concert hall might be very expensive.

The question why someone would plug into the experience machine requires a fuller answer, and that will be our next topic.

5. Altruistic uses of the experience machine

One impediment to using the experience machine to reflect on the quality of life is that we cannot help thinking that someone who would plug into it would have to be a self-absorbed, irresponsible, heartless, irresolute person. He would abandon his friends and renege on his commitments, just to have a good time. He would either have no projects in the real world to which he felt committed, or he would set them aside just to be amused and soothed. That of course is not our only worry about such a person. He embraces a life full of self-delusion. He is socially isolated. He can do nothing that requires embodiment—climb a mountain, play tennis, build things with his hands, have sex. But let us set aside, for now, those further charges against him. What about the accusation that he would have to be selfish?

As I noted in section 2 above, Nozick briefly addresses this question. He says that you should not worry about other people, when you decide whether to plug in, because they too can choose to plug into their machines. That is hardly an adequate response. You and I were working together on some project that we greatly valued. Should I plug into the machine and walk away from what we had been trying to achieve together? It is not satisfying to be told that you can do the same, if you choose.

At the same time, it also seems that we would be failing to exploit the experience machine for its value as a thought experiment if we dismiss it so quickly and for these reasons. It does seem to pose important philosophical questions about the prudential value of embodiment, as I have said. What is needed, then, is a transformation of Nozick's thought experiment that allows us to focus on those important questions without distracting us with extraneous worries about the selfish motives of anyone who is tempted to plug in. Here is what I suggest, then: Let us suppose that when someone is in the experience machine, the parts of his body that are detached from his brain are put to good use in medical research that eradicates diseases and saves lives. He has volunteered to perform this great service for reasons that are largely if not entirely altruistic. We can then ask whether he would be making a great sacrifice, a small sacrifice, or none at all, when he is plugged in. (He himself presumably has some view about that, but our question is not answered just by finding out what he thinks.)

Nozick's thought experiment has a feature that has not yet been mentioned: someone who decides to plug into the machine chooses the kinds of experiences he will have inside it, but he knows that those sorts of experiences will be produced in him for some limited amount of time, after which he will be unplugged, so that he can make his next choice about what sort of life to have during his next encounter with the machine—and so on. "After two years have passed, you will have ten minutes or ten hours out of the tank, to select the experiences of your *next* two years."[16] The rest of his life will be spent in the machine, except for the brief periods when he is unplugged and chooses what he will experience in the next stage of his life. These aspects of the thought experiment will need some attention, and I will turn to them later (section 8). At this point, I mention them only to fill out my story about how the thought experiment should be altered so that we guard against thinking of someone who plugs in as a very unappealing sort of person. The story should be filled out as follows: someone who enters the machine lets his body be used for the whole time he is inside it, and then he gets his body back for the period of time during which he makes his next decision about what sorts of experiences to have inside the machine.

Here is one further detail that should be added: in the society that has experience machines available to it, the need for a cadre of volunteers who enter the machine is widely recognized and volunteering is regarded as an admirable way of serving others. Young people know of this social need, and if they choose to do so, they can commit themselves to become volunteers several years in advance of plugging in. In this way, they can avoid undertaking projects or making commitments that would have to be abandoned and left incomplete when it is time for them to plug into the machine. If in July someone knows he is going to begin his life in the machine this September, he should not start making plans and preparations for climbing Mt. Everest in a few months. He might instead ask to have a mountain climbing experience on the machine. Outside the machine, he will not set his heart on actually being on top of the mountain when he is inside it. He knows, when outside, that he will be in the technician's laboratory, although he will think he is sitting on top of the world.

6. *The illusion of climbing a mountain*

We can now compare two individuals: Both would like to have the experience of climbing a difficult and dangerous mountain. But the first chooses to have that experience administered to him on the machine, so that his body can be used for the good of others. The second wants his climbing experience to be caused by his body actually moving through space and up to the top of the mountain. Does the second person have a higher quality of life? From the inside, there is no difference. Even so, one has illusory experiences, the other veridical experiences. If Nozick is right, the individual who has volunteered to go through a mountain-climbing experience without actually climbing a mountain has sacrificed his well-being at least to some degree.

Would we counsel people we love not to have the illusory experience but instead to climb the mountain? I certainly would not, for two reasons. First, the actual climb could easily result in death or serious injury, whereas the illusory climb is guaranteed not to do so. Second, actually having one's body move up a mountain can make no difference to one's well-being. The value of climbing a mountain seems *entirely* experiential.

---

[16] Ibid., 42, author's emphasis.

That second point is controversial. It might be said, against it, that actually climbing a mountain requires genuine fortitude, stamina, and courage. Having the illusory experience of climbing a mountain might seem to be "a piece of cake": one just sits back, relaxes, and enjoys images of mountain scenery. Someone who takes this line of thought is conceding that the value of real mountain climbing does not rest on a mere fact about the spatial location of one's body. Rather, its value lies in the great effort that is required to climb a real mountain, and the ability to cope with fear, hunger, cold, pain, and so on.

But to say that is to speak of the experience we have when we climb a mountain. And it is an essential feature of the experience machine, if it is to serve its philosophical purpose, that phenomenologically there is no difference between veridical and non-veridical experiences. So the feeling of effortfulness and the thought that you ought to summon all of your power and energy to overcome your desire for comfort and warmth are available on the experience machine. You have the feeling of your hands and legs pushing against boulders, and you sense their resistance to your efforts. The appearance of snakes or other dangers will produce a feeling of fear, and you will need to keep your attention focused on overcoming such obstacles. You will sometimes have the feeling of slipping, sliding, falling. You will be faced with hard decisions about which path to follow, or whether to turn back, and it will take courage not to let fear, cold, and pain distort one's thinking. Of course, it is also true that you told the technician in the laboratory, before entering the machine, that this story ought to end with success rather than death. But you are not aware of that while you are in the machine. For all you know, you could die if you press ahead, and yet you summon up your willpower and decide to push on. This is no "piece of cake." Whatever might plausibly be called a component of well-being that is offered by climbing a real mountain is also offered on the experience machine. Nozick's complaint that inside the machine one is "an indeterminate blob" must be rejected.

If someone volunteers to have the experience of climbing a mountain and foregoes "the real thing" in order to allow his body to be used by others, is he making a huge sacrifice in his well-being? That strikes me as implausible. In fact, it is hard to see how he is making any sacrifice at all. In volunteering, he sees that everything worthwhile that can be experienced in a real climb will also be experienced in a virtual climb. That is part of his reason for volunteering. He once had the desire to climb—to get his body up there—but upon reflection he sees that a change in physical location is not the point of climbing.

We have seen, then, that two of the alleged deficiencies of the experience machine are not deficiencies at all. We can be active, and we would not be mere blobs. Its third alleged deficiency—the way it "limits us to a man-made reality, to a world no deeper or more important than that which people can construct" will receive our attention later (section 12). But we must not restrict ourselves to Nozick's reasons for believing that life inside the machine is impoverished. As I noted earlier, there seem to me to be better ways than his of expressing discomfort with the idea of living inside the machine.

It is an illusory world, and many activities that human beings treasure inherently make use of the body (playing tennis, playing the piano, swimming, building, cooking, and so on). Would it not be a great loss no longer to be doing such things, however much it seemed one was? I will begin to address these questions in section 9.

7. Self-deception and social illusions

Inside the machine, one has the false belief that one is not inside it but somewhere else, and that one's sensory information is derived in the normal way from contact with a distal reality. Does this by itself diminish or extinguish the prudential value of one's experience?

There is nothing to be said against being deceived by others when one has chosen, for innocent purposes, to participate in deceptive social practices. In certain games we withhold information from each other or deliberately induce false beliefs in the other players. (Bluffing is an essential element of poker.) Does this detract from the value of such experiences? Of course not. Nor is there any moral objection to such deception, because participation is voluntary and some good is achieved (recreational fun). Similarly, if you choose to plug into the experience machine, you are giving the laboratory technician permission to deceive you, and in this sense you are deceiving yourself. We are assuming that you have excellent motives for doing so, and that as a result of your service inside the machine you do the world much good. This is entirely different from cases in which self-deception really is blameworthy. In everyday life, hiding from reality is often a reflection of weakness, cowardice, laziness, or irresponsibility. One ends up harming not only others but oneself. But none of these defects necessarily belong to the character of someone who chooses to enter the experience machine.

On any reasonable conception of well-being, having a false belief does not by itself diminish the quality of life. You may seem to recall from grade school that there are nine planets, but in fact there are eight. Of course, the false beliefs you have inside the experience machine are not like that. You think you are on top of the world, but you are in the technician's basement. But is it valuable to know where one is located in space?[17] Is the quality of your life lower because you think you are in one place but you are in another? A naïve and inexperienced traveler from the Midwest might take the wrong train and think he has arrived in Boston whereas in fact he is in New York. He might nonetheless have a wonderful time there, and think that Boston is a great place for a holiday. The experiences he has there, in restaurants and the theater, are of no less prudential value because he is mistaken about their location.

What about false beliefs about one's social world? We will later consider the so-called friends who snicker about you behind your back, but let us now imagine that you are

---

[17] For an affirmative answer, see Thomas Hurka, *The Best Things in Life*, 70 and 76; and *British Ethical Theorists from Sidgwick to Ewing*, 208. Hurka holds that the experience machine has two further disadvantages: first there are goals (e.g. climbing Mt. Everest) that cannot be achieved in it; second you do not have "real relations with other people" (*The Best Things in Life*, 70). He rejects Nozick's charge that inside the machine one is characterless (ibid., 69).

deceived about a different sort of social situation. You are giving a lecture. It seems to you that the members of your audience are following your ideas with perfect understanding. They seem to be enjoying your lecture, and they often nod in seeming approval. But in fact they are merely being polite. They have wandered into the wrong lecture hall and are making the best of the situation by pretending that they understand you. Because there is no time for questions or any later engagement with your audience, you never discover that you utterly failed to connect with them.

This is of course not something you want to happen to you. When you give a lecture, you are not doing so to hear the sound of your own voice. You are trying to give something to others. (If there is a question period, you hope to learn from it.) But it could have been worse. You might have had a different sort of audience: some of them falling asleep, others showing their annoyance, others looking off into space. That would have given you an inferior experience. But you would have a correct picture of your communicative failure: you would know that your audience is getting nothing of value from you.

Although both are bad scenarios, the first has something in its favor, and the second, I believe, does not. In the first, your experience was phenomenologically indistinguishable from the one you would have undergone, had your audience understood you. Something good goes on inside your head when you are lecturing to an audience that you take to be responsive and sympathetic. You feel at one with others, you feel that you are giving them something worth thinking about, and you are pleased. In the second scenario, one has the opposite feelings.

One lecture is a good experience but illusory. The second is a bad experience but veridical. Which should we prefer? Which has more prudential value? The first, I suggest. If one's audience has no idea what one is talking about, it is better for you to believe that they do than for you to suffer through an hour facing a group of people who exhibit hostility, boredom, annoyance, and incomprehension. The first audience is being kind to you, doing you a favor by pretending that they understand; they are, in other words, giving you something good. The second is mistreating you—they are inflicting a bad experience on you.

It might be said that even so, the best kind of experience for a lecturer to have is one in which he both thinks he is connecting with his audience and is really doing so. According to this view, some diminution of prudential value in the experience of giving a lecture occurs while it is going on, simply in virtue of the fact that the speaker is not understood, and even though he does not recognize that his audience is not following him. But that seems implausible. There are, I suggest, three reasons for a lecturer to want to be understood. First, he hopes that he is giving something of value to others. Second, he hopes that he will learn something from their questions and other reactions. Third, he hopes that the experience of delivering the lecture will be a good one. When a speaker is not understood by his audience, the first two potential benefits are absent. But the experience of delivering the lecture is not affected simply because it does not have the later causal consequences the speaker hopes for. That explains why it is better to give a lecture that gives one the illusion of being understood than to give a lecture in which the hostility or indifference of the audience is manifest. If the illusory nature of the experience could detract from its value, it could also detract so much from it that on balance it would not be better to give the first lecture (a good but deceptive experience) than the second (a bad but veridical experience). We should not make the ad hoc assumption that illusoriness diminishes the value of an experience but only by a bit. For then we would have to say: why only a tiny amount? Why never more than that? It is better to side with common sense and say that if two experiences are phenomenologically indistinguishable, they cannot differ in their intrinsic value to the subject.

8. The rest of one's life

Nozick asks: "Should you plug into this machine for life, preprogramming your life's experiences?"[18] For life? Why should our thought experiment include that stipulation? Why is there no going back on one's decision, after the initial commitment? The point of reflecting on the experience machine is to learn about the value of embodiment, sociability, veridical experience, and our place in a spatially extended universe. It is not obvious why we must stipulate that once you plug in, you must remain plugged in for the rest of your days. What does that aspect of the thought experiment teach us?

Admittedly, Nozick allows one to exit the machine from time to time. These are brief intervals during which one decides which kinds of experiences to have when one is plugged back in. But one does not have the option of remaining outside.

In *The Examined Life*, Nozick admits that there may be good reasons to spend *some* small portion of time inside the machine: "It might teach you things or transform you in a way beneficial for your actual later life. It might also give pleasures that would be quite acceptable in limited doses." But then he adds: "This is all quite different from spending the rest of your life on the machine; the internal contents of *that* life would be unconnected to actuality."[19]

But Nozick is off the mark here. When he stipulates that "the question is not whether to try the machine temporarily, but whether to enter it for the rest of your life,"[20] he is making his thought experiment a less useful tool than it could be. Many of us are reluctant to make decisions that can never be reversed, and reasonably so. We hope to learn from experience, and we realize that we may later regret, for good reason, having made an earlier commitment from which we cannot be released. Of course, there may in some cases be countervailing considerations—reasons to make commitments that cannot later be renounced. But in any case, were we ever given an opportunity to enter the experience machine, we would rightly prefer to do so without forever being committed to remaining inside it for the rest of our lives (with a few brief interruptions). Nothing is gained by renouncing, once and for all, the opportunity to return to everyday

---

[18] *Anarchy, State, and Utopia*, 42.
[19] *The Examined Life*, 108, author's emphasis.   [20] Ibid., 105.

reality and to spend the rest of one's life outside the machine. The smart thing to do would be to enter the machine for a while, and then, after being detached, decide whether to enter it again. If the technician in charge of the machine does not offer us that option, it would be prudent to decline his offer, and look for a different technician who gives us better terms. (We should also recall our stipulation that when one is in the machine, one's body will be put to good use by others. There will be fewer volunteers, and so less good will be done for the community, if a lifetime commitment is demanded.)

Nozick's view is that, for one's own good, one should not re-enter the machine *too often*. Certainly one should not spend the rest of one's life inside it—so he claims—because then, for too much time, one would be severed from the real world. There is, in other words, no loss of prudential value merely because one is inside the machine and disconnected from reality for a time. For moderate stretches, experiences caused by the machine are just as good as phenomenologically identical experiences caused by everyday reality. But when one piles up too many of these sessions inside the machine, something goes wrong, and there is an overall major loss of prudential value. Each session by itself brings no diminution in the quality of life, but when they are taken as a whole, one's life is significantly worse than it would have been had one spent less time inside the machine. What one needs, then, is the right balance between veridical and illusory experience over time.

But why use the machine sparingly? Why not to the hilt? (The more often one returns, the better for others. But now we are asking about the well-being of the individual in the machine.) Why, if no single session lowers the quality of one's life, do a sufficient number of them have that effect? These questions have no obvious answer, and in the absence of an answer, Nozick's stipulation that one must make a lifetime commitment when one first enters the machine seems arbitrary. Nothing of interest in this thought experiment is lost if, against Nozick, we stipulate that one always has the option, after each session, of not returning. That would leave one free to say, at some point, "I've been in the machine often enough. Now I have to start thinking more about my own good." So, the question to be asked is whether that would ever become the right thing to say.

We can easily see the rationale for allowing you to emerge periodically from the machine and decide again not only whether to return to it, but what sorts of experiences to have next, if you do return. It is not too taxing to ask of yourself: Which sorts of experiences should I have next, for a period of rather limited duration? Answering that question would not over-burden your decision-making abilities. You would not have to plan the entire remainder of your life at one go. If the thought experiment did require you to make such a momentous decision, you would be quite tempted to decline the opportunity to enter the machine and instead take your chances with everyday life. But in that case your rejection of the machine would have nothing to do with the place of experiential or non-experiential factors in well-being. It would only reflect the advantages of a piecemeal and short-term approach to your future, as opposed to having the whole of it mapped out all at once in a single decision.

Recall what Nozick says about the intervals during which you are outside the machine: "After two years have passed, you will have ten minutes or ten hours out of the tank, to select the experiences of your *next* two years."[21] But which is it? Ten minutes or ten hours? Nozick does not care, and why should he? We are asking about the advantages and disadvantages of being in the machine. How much time one needs to decide whether to return, and what sorts of experiences to have if one returns, seems not to matter.

But that cannot be right. When one is outside the machine, one has a body, one is reunited with one's friends, one's experiences are brought about in the normal way. A few paragraphs ago, we saw that Nozick recognizes that there may be no loss in prudential value, and even a gain, if we plug into the machine occasionally. We need "the right balance" in our lives between veridical and illusory experience. But now we must ask whether the right balance can be achieved if we stipulate that the periods spent back in the real world are long enough—not ten minutes but several hours or days. Suppose, for example, you commit yourself to spending your weekday mornings and afternoons for the next year inside the machine. Each evening, Monday through Friday you emerge from it and think about what sorts of experiences to request the following weekday. While you are outside the machine, you have dinner with friends, or play tennis, or listen to music, and so on. Going to the technician's laboratory each morning is rather like the everyday experience of going off to your place of work. You spend more of your weekday waking hours there than you do at home. So too in our thought experiment, most days you would spend many more hours inside the machine than outside it. Nozick admits that there is no loss of prudential value when one is not inside the machine for too long. Perhaps then a regime of twelve hours in the machine, four hours of everyday social intercourse back home (where one discusses with friends which machine-induced experiences to have the next day), and eight hours of sleep, is the kind of balance that would be optimal. If one followed this regime for the rest of one's life, it would be a lifetime filled, for the most part, with illusory experience. If something very valuable is missing from one's life when one is inside the machine too often or for too long, then it would presumably be missing in a life with this high ratio between illusory and veridical experience. But in fact, having experiences of one's choosing does not seem a bad way to spend the work week.

We should also explicitly state an assumption that we have been tacitly making for some time: when you are given the opportunity to plug into the machine for the first time, you are a mature adult, not a child or adolescent with too little experience of life to make wise decisions about what sorts of experiences to have inside the machine. (I will return to this point in the next section.) So, even if, after one's initial session, one spends a very high proportion of one's time inside the machine, there was a significant portion of one's life spent *entirely* outside it. When one looks back at one's life as death approaches—let's suppose one is eighty-five—it will be seen as a life with a long early

---

[21] Ibid., 42.

segment spent outside the machine. If there must be a good balance in one's life between real and illusory experiences, perhaps it is achieved by spending all of it outside the machine for a good long time, and then nearly all of it inside the machine for the rest.

What thing of value does embodied experience gives us that disembodied experience does not? Why should we have rather more of the former than the latter? Why not the reverse emphasis, as imagined in the thought experiment just described (with twelve hours in the machine each workday)? It is not apparent that there are good answers to these questions, and so far we have found none. One point in favor of experientialism is that if we accept it, these questions do not arise. But we should continue to explore what life inside the machine could or could not be like, looking for something important missing there.

9. Food, chess, and tennis

Plugged into the machine, one can have any gustatory experience of one's choosing. Do you like chocolate cake and wish you could eat more of it without ill effect? Inside the machine you would have exactly those taste sensations, and many more like them, without gaining weight or feeling sick. Nothing would enter your body, which has been detached from the rest of you and is now being used for medical purposes—thank you very much. One could, if one so chooses, have the illusion that there is a cake sitting in front of one's eyes (beautifully presented). It could seem as though one were eating it—moving one's mouth, breaking up bits of food with one's teeth, swallowing them, digesting them. None of that would happen, but it is hard to find any value in its actually being the case that one's teeth are breaking up pieces of food when one eats. What is desirable, and what we want, in an encounter with real pieces of chocolate cake is just a sensory experience (largely gustatory but partly visual), not a physical action in which we move our mouths and fill our bodies.

There are several lessons to be learned here. First, suppose someone says that inside the machine he wants to have many more taste experiences exactly like the ones he has in his everyday life, and also says (correctly) that his enjoyment of them will be just as great whether he takes himself to be really eating something or not. He does not need the illusion of eating chocolate cake; it would be just as good if he thought to himself, inside the machine, "I am not really eating anything, but these taste sensations are just as wonderful." He would have no false beliefs regarding the source of his experience. What we can now see is that it is not an essential feature of the experience machine that inside it experiences are illusory. Rather, what is essential is that they are not mediated, as they normally are, by one's body and its encounter with other physical substances that impinge on it. A kind of disembodiment (that is, the absence of parts of the body not causally necessary for the production of consciousness), not illusion, is the essential feature.

Why, then, is it widely assumed (by Nozick and others) that in the machine one is living in a world of illusion? The answer is that many of the experiences we would ask to have inside the machine *would* diminish in value, or have none, if we realized, while having them, that they are illusory. Recall our discussion of the illusion that one is climbing a difficult mountain (section 6). That experience would be far less desirable if one knew that the snake one seems to see is just the appearance of a snake; that every fall one seems to be taking is unreal and will not result in unbearable pain or death; that a successful climb and safe return are guaranteed.

I suspect that many of the experiences we would choose to have inside the machine would be enhanced if we mistook them for experiences caused by the external world and its interaction with the body. So I will continue to describe life inside the machine as illusory and the experiences had there as non-veridical. But we should keep in mind that this characterization varies from one case to another, and holds only for the most part.

A second point to notice regarding the experience of eating chocolate cake inside the machine is that sometimes it is actually *better* to have those experiences than their phenomenologically identical real-world counterparts. One would not get sick or gain weight. So, although it may be true that in many instances an experience inside the machine is no worse but also no better than its veridical counterpart, there are exceptions. (If one listens to music while one is in the machine, one is doing no better than one could do outside it.) In this respect, there is a similarity between going into the machine in order to have more chocolate cake sensations and plugging in because one's life is filled or will be filled with meaningless suffering. The chocolate cake lover is escaping from the future suffering he would have, were he to eat that much cake in the real world. But he is not currently suffering because he does not eat as much cake as he would like. Someone who is miserable and faces a bleak future is escaping from misery he now experiences or will experience unless he plugs in.

A third point is that one would be making a very poor use of the experience machine if one used it for only one purpose—to have the sensation of chocolate cake and nothing else. One can imagine a small child making that choice. She might think that this is the best experience she has ever had, and she might be delighted by the prospect of repeating it day after day without interruption, without ever feeling stuffed or ill. Suppose after one year of a life filled with the taste of chocolate cake she is unplugged from the machine and is given the option of returning to it. It would not be far-fetched to suppose that she would choose to do so, and to have those same experiences again. Just as an oyster might get as much faint pleasure from its nourishment each day of its life, so too our little girl might never tire of her experience. She would be getting exactly what she wants, but that would be an impoverished oyster-like existence. Well-being is not constituted simply by the satisfaction of desire (as I noted in Chapter 2, section 1), nor is it the achievement of whichever goals one happens to adopt. An individual can have too small an experience of life or be too thoughtless to realize that the quality of his life is not as high as it could be.

I turn now to a very different sort of experience: that of playing chess. It provides an interesting contrast with gustatory experiences, because not only is it not a sensation, it is essentially an intellectual activity that could in principle be carried out without a chessboard or the movement of pieces through space. Mental chess is still chess, whereas having the sensation of chocolate cake is not eating chocolate cake. Of course, very few people have the intellectual and imaginative skill that would be needed to play chess without using a physical chessboard. If one entered the experience machine and played chess inside it, one would very likely want to have a picture in one's mind of a chessboard, and one would want it to seem as though one is extending one's hand and moving the pieces. This is a case in which one's experience would not decline in quality by knowing that one is inside the machine and that the movement of pieces on a board is illusory. One would regard it as a helpful illusion, and that is what it would be.

I will assume that chess is a valuable experience only if one knows how to play it, and has achieved a certain level of skill. Not a high level—but enough to give one an appreciation of the game and an interest in playing it. Only someone who has at least a minimal level of skill would choose to play chess inside the experience machine. Of course, someone who does not know anything about the game might enter the machine and request the experience of learning how to play. But we will instead assume that it is a skilled player who is plugging into the machine in order to play at his level.

Chess is essentially interactive—there are two players working at cross purposes. If you play this game on the experience machine, against whom are you playing? Let's suppose that it is the technician in the laboratory (although we will see later in this section that this is not the only possibility). Does the technician produce in you an experience in which you do not think about your moves before making them? Of course not—that would not be a phenomenological duplicate of what it is like when one really plays chess. Should we suppose, then, that the technician makes it seem as though you are thinking about your strategy, your tactics, and your next move, but in fact it only seems to you as if you were doing these things? That idea is incoherent. What the technician must do is give you, at every stage of the game, a picture of the board so that the position of the pieces is apparent to you. That visual input is what you will need in the absence of your body. But if the technician made the decisions about where your pieces will move, and you did not, you would not have anything close to the full experience of playing chess. You would just have a picture of pieces being moved. Since you know how to play chess, the technician decides what moves he will make against you, but there would be no point in his also deciding what moves you should make. He lets you do that. Otherwise he would need to play against himself, constantly acting at cross purposes. We should keep in mind a point made earlier (section 4) about the appreciation of music inside the experience machine: it involves active thought and not the mere reception of auditory signals. The attentive listener *decides* what to focus on. Similarly, a chess player inside the machine does something—he thinks about what moves to make. He has a sense of irresolution and tension when he is undecided about what tactics he should use in the next stage of the game, and what his next move should be. He reviews his options and then feels a sense of resolution as he chooses his next move. His moves cohere with each other in his mind as constituting a strategy that expresses the style of attack and defense that has become familiar to him, the same style he has outside the machine. Without this complex phenomenology, there is no inner life of a chess player.

To insure that you have the thoughts that constitute the experience of playing chess, the technician must allow certain events in your brain to cause other events in your brain. You have the thought, "the best move for me now is to advance my bishop." You really do have that thought—it makes no sense to say that you think you have it but you don't. Some event in your brain is the physical manifestation of this thought. Next, your thought about what you ought to do is followed by a conative experience: you will your hand to move your bishop. (That conative experience is what we undergo when we play chess in the normal way, outside the machine. A thought about what one ought to do does not move the pieces—rather, one must will a movement of one's hand.) The technician did not have to intervene in your brain for your thought to cause the exercise of will. He can let some neural events cause others. But at the next stage, the technician does intervene: he gives you the visual impression that your hand is moving the bishop. And you now have the illusion, created by the technician, that pieces in front of your eyes are being moved by your hand. The technician now knows what move you have made in response to his. He thinks through his next move, and then produces in you the image of your opponent's hand moving his piece. And so on.

Chess, as I have said, is essentially an interactive mental game in which the body plays no essential role. But now let us turn to an interactive game that is essentially physical. Tennis is played by embodied human beings holding a racquet and standing on a court with a net. Even so, there is a psychological aspect to the game—overall strategy, observations about how one's opponent is playing, thoughts that precede every stroke about where to hit, feelings of joy and frustration, the sense of physical effort, kinesthetic sensations, the sound of the ball coming off the racquet, fatigue, thirst, pain, and so on. There is such a thing as what it is like, from the inside, to play tennis. All of this would be available on the experience machine. Against whom would you be playing? You can choose as your technician a skilled player who will know how to respond to your shot selection in a way that makes the game challenging but not overwhelmingly difficult for you. Or we can imagine that the technician employs a smart device that receives information about simulated oncoming tennis balls, makes instantaneous shot selections in response to that information, and then transforms those selections into visual information fed to your brain. Inside the machine, you are conscious of the thought that your opponent's backhand is weak today, and that you should take advantage of it. You really do have that thought, and it can lead to the next experiences you have—that of making an effort to move your arms and legs just so. Moment by moment, you are interacting with an opponent, just as you do when you play chess inside the machine. What is missing is that your body is not out there on the court but inside the technician's laboratory. What you have, nonetheless, is every possible mental aspect of the game.

This is what lovers of tennis love—not holding a racquet in their hands, and the movement of the body through physical space, but the mental experience that in our world is available only when one has a healthy body, an opponent, a racquet, balls, and a place to play. A player whose injuries keep him side-lined would be thrilled by the opportunity to plug into a machine that would give him exactly those experiences. He could let others put his body to good use, while he plays mental tennis. Since he would have the very same kinds of experiences and (as we saw in section 8) the fact that experiences are machine-induced does not on its own detract from their value, there would be no decline in the quality of his life.

Would those experiences lose their goodness if they occupied too many of his days? Should he, for his own good, spend only so much time playing mental tennis, in order to have the right balance between it and real tennis? Well, what is the right balance, and how can one tell? And why should this matter, if there is no mental difference between the two experiences?

Gustatory sensations can be just as good even if one knows that they are not produced by real food, but the sense of adventure and danger that accompany climbing a mountain would disappear if one knew oneself to be safe inside a laboratory. What about tennis? It must of course really seem as though the ball is coming at you. It won't be a worthwhile experience unless you throw yourself into it and make every effort to play well and win. If you constantly had it present to your consciousness that this is all an illusion, that would certainly not enhance your experience, and very likely it would weaken your resolve and enjoyment. Nonetheless, if it occurs to you, while you take a break between games, that you are really in the experience machine, that might do no harm, so long as you set that thought aside as you resume play.

It is worth recalling that one of the advantages of life inside the experience machine is that it eliminates needless suffering. Out on the tennis court, injuries are almost inevitable for serious players. Contact sports are far more dangerous. And it is not only athletes who can suffer permanently from their activities. Musicians must sometimes abandon their instruments because of the effects of repetitive motion. The experience machine eliminates all these misfortunes.

I have been assuming that your virtual tennis partner is the technician in charge of your brain, who may or may not use a smart device to play tennis with you. What should be noticed next is that you could also play mental tennis with your normal tennis partner. Here is how: Outside the machine, you chat with a tennis friend about what your next experiences will be. Let us assume that he too has volunteered to spend time in his experience machine, in order to make his body available to others. Collectively, you decide to play tennis *with each other*. How is that possible? You need only have your respective laboratory technicians coordinate their activities. There you will be together in the same room. Information about your "serve" is delivered to your friend's technician, and as a result your friend has an experience as of the ball coming to him just as you have "hit" it. It will seem as though your friend is over there on the other side of the net, trying his best to win the point. Each time one of you "hits" the ball, he will be responding to the thoughts and efforts that the other player actually has. The causal arrow will not be what it usually is; it will go from one player's mental actions to his technician to the other technician to the other player. Your experience is phenomenologically indistinguishable from what it is normally like to play tennis with the other person. Not only that, but in addition you really are interacting with each other. Your body has no effect on what is happening, because it is being used elsewhere, but even so your mental activity must be part of the causal story to be told about why your friend has the experiences he has.

I will consider two more examples. The first involves an architect, someone who wants to design buildings and oversee their construction. If he wants to build a home of his own design with his own hands, he will not opt into the experience machine. But if he wants to design a structure, leaving it to others to build it, the design process can take place entirely in his head. It will seem to him that his hands are working with pencil and paper (or a computer program), just as it seems to a player of mental chess that there is a board in front of him. But these are illusions that facilitate his mental activity. Now, suppose the architect who has no interest in creating a building with his own hands nonetheless wants it to be the case that the building he envisages is actually erected. He wants his mental activity to bear real fruit. He can be assured, before he enters the machine, that this will happen. The laboratory technician will see to it that the building designed in the experience machine by the hands-off architect will be created by others. The causal story about how the building came into existence will include the purely mental activity of the architect. He will create it in a more indirect way than is normally the case, but even so his experiences in the machine have real-world effects.

The second example is rather indelicate. Sex with another person inside the experience machine? Yes, it can be done, along the lines suggested when I discussed the two tennis players. Two individuals can interact even when they are without bodies. It can feel as though they are being hugged and desired. They seem to see each other and to be intertwined. They can feel intense pleasure. Their mental responses to the other person can be coordinated by their two technicians. If one's body is not functioning normally, this would be an improvement over the real world. The simulation of physical contact would give one everything—emotional, cognitive, and sensual—that is desirable in a sexual relationship. As it is, much of human sexuality is in the head. The experience machine builds on the fact that the body merely plays an instrumental role.

As I noted earlier (section 2), when I ask myself why the prospect of plugging into the machine and spending much of one's time inside it initially seems repellent, even if it seems to have attractions as well, I think of the social isolation that I would undergo. True, I could ask to have the illusion that I am surrounded by people, and so I would not feel lonely, but in fact my real situation would be quite different: the only other individual actually in my life would be the technician. But on reflection, we can now see that you could be constantly interacting with the technician. He or she is a real person and you are really there together—perhaps playing chess, perhaps playing tennis, perhaps doing other things. You could have a conversation about any topic of your choosing with the technician. You could become good friends. Or someone who is already your friend could become trained as a technician, and you could have conversations, play tennis and chess with him. In such circumstances as these, you are *never* isolated when you are in the machine, as you sometimes are outside it.

Now that we have seen that experience-by-experience social interaction between you and another person can occur in the machine, we can make one further leap of the imagination, going well beyond Nozick's version of this thought experiment. In principle, the technician need not actually exist; the cause of your brain functioning so as to give you realistic illusions might be an unintelligent and accidental combination of physical forces (wind currents and the like). That would be the production of something meaningful in the way monkeys striking the keys of a typewriter might produce a novel. So, we might suppose that you tell the technician, before you enter the machine, what sorts of experiences you would like; you are then plugged into the machine; the technician dies; but impersonal forces just so happen to cause your brain to undergo the experiences the technician would have given you. Whether your experiences are good ones for you does not depend on whether you are alone in the laboratory or whether instead a technician is there operating the machinery that causes you to have those experiences. In what follows, I will continue to assume that the technician is alive and is the cause of your experiences. But that assumption could be dropped.

Part Two

Now that we have more fully described the ways in which the experience machine must operate, if it is to duplicate the phenomenology of life outside the machine, we are in a better position to consider whether it greatly (or even slightly) detracts from the quality of one's life, as it is often thought to do. We will also examine a variation on Nozick's thought experiment that might seem to be more philosophically significant than his. In this modification, one is asked to assess the quality of lives of two *other* people. (The issue is not whether *you* should plug in.) Their experiences are phenomenologically identical, but one of them lives in the "real world," the other in the illusory world of the machine. Our discussion of objections to experientialism that do not rest on the experience machine, but on familiar features of our everyday world, will be postponed to Part Three of this chapter.

10. Objections to the experience machine

Let us return to Nozick's explanation of why we would and should reject the option of plugging into the experience machine (more than a few times). He says:

First we want to *do* certain things and not just have the experience of doing them.... A second reason for not plugging in is that we want to *be* a certain way, to be a certain sort of person. Someone floating in a tank is an indeterminate blob. There is no answer to the question of what a person is like who has long been in the tank.... Thirdly, plugging into an experience machine limits us to a man-made reality, to a world no deeper or more important than that which people can construct. There is no *actual* contact with any deeper reality.[22]

We have not yet discussed this third alleged defect of life inside the experience machine, but I will soon turn to it (section 12). For now, let us revisit the first two points Nozick makes here—that we do nothing inside the machine, and that we fail to be "a certain sort of person."

We have seen that we can do quite a few things inside the machine: listen to music attentively and understand it; summon forth the courage, strength of will, and tolerance for suffering needed to climb a difficult mountain; play chess; play a mental version of tennis; make love; and design a building. We could go on constructing similar examples, but there would be no point in doing so. Along the way, we have also found a few things one cannot do on the machine: climb Mt. Everest or any other real mountain, play tennis with a real racquet on a real tennis court, build a house with one's own hands. If you put into your description of an action something that makes it essentially an action performed with one's body, then it is true that without a body one cannot engage in it. But that is a tautology, a trivial observation. We should be impressed by the realization that many worthwhile experiences would be available to us even if we had no body. And it would be absurd to suppose that there is little or nothing of prudential value available to people who do not climb a mountain or play tennis. They can find many alternatives that would give them the highest quality of life, and they could do so on the experience machine.

What of the claim that when one is inside the machine there is no answer to the question of what kind of person one is—that one is "an indeterminate blob"? Again, that is not so. Courage is shown when one pushes ahead in the face of imaginary danger. Other examples point in the same direction. There is a courteous way of playing tennis and a mean-spirited way. If one plays mental tennis on the machine, one can display the virtues of civility and good sportsmanship. If one designs a building while on the machine, one can give ethical considerations great weight, searching for the most effective way one's building will serve human needs. We have seen that sexual relations have an analogue on the machine. An ethics of love-making will apply there no less than it does when bodies are actually in physical contact. With sufficient ingenuity, many more such examples can be constructed. We should also keep in mind our assumption that the very act of volunteering to be plugged into the experience machine is an expression of one's concern for the good of others. If we assume that this act of supererogation is not a mere whim but reflects one's good character, then it would be implausible to suppose that one loses one's virtuous disposition when one is inside the machine. At every moment in the machine, you are the sort of person who acted and stands ready to act again for the good of others as well as your own. Of course, someone might plug into the machine and choose experiences in which moral

---

[22] *Anarchy, State, and Utopia*, 42–3, author's emphasis.

character plays only a small role, or none at all—chess, listening to music, and the like. But that does not mean that there is no answer to the question, "What sort of person is he?" He is someone who loves to do these things.

Here is a rather different example that demonstrates that moral character can be put into operation inside the machine. Suppose a woman would like to conceive, nurture, and raise a child, but instead of doing so, she plugs into the machine and has experiences of the same sort she would have were her child real. Her motivation is the same as the one we have been ascribing to all those who choose to plug in: she wants her body to be used for medical research in the public interest. But we can also imagine that she has an additional motive: her part of the world has far too many people, and she wants to cooperate with the government's efforts to limit the size of the population. Furthermore, she may be highly averse to risk: there is much that can go wrong as a child develops, and parents suffer greatly because of the misfortunes of their children. As I noted in section 2, an attractive feature of life in the experience machine is that it allows only as much misfortune as will contribute to one's overall long-term well-being. An illusory relationship with a child inside the machine will have only as much frustration as is needed to make that relationship emotionally rewarding. But the point that should be noticed for present purposes is that someone who has, inside the machine, the experiences that are typical of parental life will have many opportunities for making ethical decisions and feeling ethical emotions. She can have the mental life of a good parent—loving, patient, firm but not rigid, and so on. There is a definite answer to the kind of person she is.

I noted that my initial reaction to the experience machine is not as abstract as Nozick's. What strikes me at first is that I would be socially isolated, living in an illusion, unable to do any of the wonderful things it normally takes a body to do: engage in affectionate physical contact, play tennis or the piano, eat or drink with my friends, have sex, cook a meal or make things with my hands. But we have now seen that social interaction with others is possible without a body. We can play chess with the laboratory technician or a friend. Mental tennis and mental sex are possible. There is no reason to reject illusory experience simply because it is illusory; if it enhances the quality of our lives, its non-veridical character is not a reason to reject it. And it is important to bear in mind that there will be periods of time when we are unplugged from the machine. We could be with others face-to-face and in physical contact for a few hours a day, spending the rest of our time on the machine. If one's time in the machine is spent in solitary activity, that would not detract from its quality.

We have also discovered that Nozick does not deny what experientialism as I have defined it affirms: that if an experience is illusory, that does not by itself diminish its value. In *The Examined Life*, he admits that the machine: "might teach you things or transform you in a way beneficial for your actual later life. It might also give pleasures that would be quite acceptable in limited doses."[23] But he holds that for your own sake

---

[23] *The Examined Life*, 108.

you ought not to spend "the rest of your life" on the machine. What this concedes is that the illusoriness of an experience does not necessarily make it a less good experience. And that is a concession that ought to be made, as we saw by comparing the experience of a speaker who mistakenly believes that his audience understands him with the experience of a second speaker who is made all too aware of the hostility or indifference of his audience (section 7). The uncomprehending listeners do the first speaker a kindness by feigning interest in his thoughts. Other examples point to the same conclusion. Someone who thinks the sounds of a musical instrument are arriving from across the room does not have a worse experience because they are not (section 4). Someone who plays mental chess may mistakenly think that there really is a chessboard in front of him, but that does not make his experience a worse one. Similarly for someone playing mental tennis.

Nozick believes that *great* goods would be missing if one spent the rest of one's life on the experience machine. That is why one should spend little time inside it, even if outside it one cannot guarantee, as one can inside, that one will have just the experiences one hopes for. But so far we have not found *any* sorts of good, great or small, that would be unavailable inside the machine. (*Sorts* of good: you cannot play tennis with a racquet but you can play a sort of tennis.) What we have found instead is that many wonderful components of a good life would remain available inside. There would therefore be no need to extend by vast numbers the length of life inside the machine, à la McTaggart, in order to compensate for its alleged impoverishment. It would not be impoverished at all.

11. *Free choice*

The third reason Nozick offers in *Anarchy, State, and Utopia* for declining an offer to plug into the experience machine (or, as he later says, a reason for not plugging in too often) is that it would limit us to a "man-made reality, to a world no deeper or more important than that which people can construct. There is no *actual* contact with any deeper reality."[24] That issue is still on our agenda, but before we consider it, let us turn next to a different point he makes about what we would lack inside the machine.

In *The Examined Life*, he gives what seems to be a fourth reason: "It seems too that once on the machine a person would not make any choices, and certainly would not choose anything *freely*. One portion of what we want to be actual is our actually (and freely) choosing, not merely the appearance of that."[25] Let's consider this point, and then return to the idea that the experience machine would cut us off from the part of reality that is not a human construction.

I take his thought in *The Examined Life* to be that *outside* the machine we do not merely seem to ourselves to be making free choices—we really are. And we have this freedom despite the fact that the states and processes of the brain play a causal role in

---

[24] *Anarchy, State, and Utopia*, 43, author's emphasis.
[25] *The Examined Life*, 108, author's emphasis.

producing the experiences that we know "from the inside." Why, then, might it be thought that inside the machine we have only the illusion of choosing freely?

I suspect that Nozick is thinking along these lines: Outside the machine, one makes a choice about the kinds of experiences one will have after one plugs into it. One says, for example: "Give me the experiences I would have if I were climbing a mountain." Or: "... if I were playing tennis." Or: "... if I were spending an afternoon looking at art in a museum." Then, one is plugged into the machine, and one makes no further choices for the duration of one's interaction with it. The technician manipulates your brain so that you have certain visual experiences, auditory experiences, and so on. Your reaction to those experiences is also something that the technician decides on— not you. You have merely given him a general command, and he fills in all the details. He may make it seem as though you are choosing how to return the tennis ball to your opponent's side of the court, but it is he who is making that choice. It feels as though your muscles are moving, as though you are extending your arms, as though you are choosing which side of the court to hit to. But you have no muscles or arms, and it is the technician who is deciding where you will seem to be hitting the ball.

If this is what lies behind Nozick's claim that inside the machine there are no free choices, then he would also have to say that when, inside the machine, you seem to be playing chess, you are not really doing so, because the technician is the one who is deciding how you should move. Thoughts go through your mind about what moves to make, leading to the conclusion that you should move your bishop. Nozick would presumably say that these are not your thoughts, because it is the technician who is in control of your brain. They are his thoughts, his decisions about how you should move. I have proposed a rather different description: the technician feeds you all the sensory information that normally comes to your mind by way of the body, and then *you* take that information into account (section 9). You do not cease to be a subject of experience and an agent. If that were not so, your experiential life would be that of someone to whom thoughts occur as though from some unknown external source. Similarly, when you take in sounds and understand them as music, it is your musical training, acquired outside the machine, that is activated. If it were the technician who had musical thoughts and you had none, the machine would not be giving you experiences phenomenologically identical to those you normally have.

Or, to take a different example, inside the machine you may wander through a virtual museum, filled with apparent paintings of this or that genre, historical period, and style; and your preferences for one kind of work or another (encoded in your brain) will be the cause of your spending more time in one wing of the museum than another. You are no more compelled to look at some particular painting than you would be in a real museum; your *taste* in painting (which, we can assume, was developed by you before you plugged into the machine) interacts with the apparent sensory input provided by the technician to produce the experiences you have.

In all such cases, the technician feeds the brain sensory information indistinguishable from what normally arrives from distal objects, and this gives rise to further events in the brain that are the vehicle of thoughts, willings, feelings, images, and other mental events that have a phenomenology. If we are not deprived of free choice outside the machine—if it is not taken from us simply because we are subject to sensory input—then we are not deprived of it when we are inside it either.

Nozick is right that there is a difference between seeming to make a choice and really doing so. We can deceive ourselves here. Suppose that hidden psychological forces within me, rooted in early childhood, are so powerful that I could never reject my father's advice. I may think that I am freely choosing to accept the reasons he gives me because I judge them to be sound. But this is just a story I tell myself; I am not really making a choice, but being compelled by an irresistible need. But this is not what is going on inside the experience machine when I wander through the virtual museum it creates in my mind. I react to the "paintings" that immediately appeal to me and have the thought that I should look at them more carefully. There is no reason to suppose that this is not a free choice—assuming, at any rate, that outside the machine we make free choices about such matters. Although it is not I who makes these images appear before me, my responses to them are my own. When I decide to concentrate more on some than others, that is my decision and reflects my taste. It is freely made, if decisions in everyday reality ever are.

12. Contact with a deeper reality

Now let's consider Nozick's claim that in the experience machine one is limited to a "man-made reality, to a world no deeper or more important than that which people can construct. There is no *actual* contact with any deeper reality."[26] Unfortunately, he does not clarify what he has in mind by "actual contact," or "deeper reality," or what makes it "more important" than what human beings construct. Perhaps his complaint is that the technician is at all times part of the causal story of your mental life. It is he who constructs your inner world. If we take flowers, mountains, stars, and the other wonders of nature to be among the objects Nozick puts into the category of "deeper reality," then his point is that inside the machine you never see such things. You do not have "actual contact" with them through the normal, direct causal link between them and your body. What is presented to you is not a flower out there in the real world, but a mere construction of a human being.

This is a puzzling idea. In the everyday world, you perceive a flower because your eyes are responsive to light, and your brain, reacting to information that comes through the eyes, constructs the conscious experience of the flower. In the experience machine, the technician can look at a flower in his laboratory (or he can move his apparatus outdoors and see flowers there), and make your brain operate in just the way it does when you normally see a flower. It is not clear why the value of your experience would be diminished because the technician is part of the causal story behind your experience. Perhaps Nozick's worry is that you only seem to be seeing a flower, because

---

[26] *Anarchy, State, and Utopia*, 43, author's emphasis.

you have no eyes. In that case, the problem he is raising is simply that your experience is illusory, and we have already seen that illusory experience can be no less valuable for being illusory.

Or perhaps what bothers Nozick, when he makes this third complaint, is that the experience machine limits us by preventing us from *intervening* in the physical world and shaping it to reflect our ideals. The physical world is the deeper reality he has in mind, and the "actual contact" he is thinking of is a more robust engagement with it than we have when we experience the simulacra created by the technician. In the experience machine, you never get outside a world constructed by your wishes, fantasies, and imagination. You are just a contemplator of what you have selected to fill your own mental space. There is more to reality than your inner world, and more to living a full life than merely observing the passing mental scene.

Whether or not this is what he has in mind, it is an objection to life in the machine that is worth exploring. Would it really place a severe limitation on the range of lives that are rich in prudential value, confining us to a rather narrow band of human experience, and restricting the exercise of our causal powers?

One point to notice—even though it may not by itself entirely lay to rest Nozick's complaint—is that inside the experience machine one can learn many of the same truths about the natural universe (that is, parts of physical reality not constructed by human beings) that can be learned outside it. One can do so by reading books— or virtual books. Nozick himself mentions this possibility. To make the experience machine initially appear attractive, he notes that it could "stimulate your brain so that you would think and feel you were writing a great novel, or making a friend, or reading an interesting book."[27] Let's take his last example—reading an interesting book—and ask how we are to understand what it would be to have an illusory experience of this sort.

It might involve nothing more than having images of ourselves, as we sometimes do in dreams, opening a book, turning its pages, thinking to ourselves "how interesting," and telling a friend who approaches us that he would enjoy it too. We would not take into our minds any words in the illusory book; we would just have a picture of ourselves reading it, as an external observer might. But this is not the same experience as the one we have when we really read a book, and it would have no value. We should assume instead that inside the machine we can read with full understanding and that we would have the same emotional and intellectual reactions that readers outside the machine normally have.

There would still be something illusory in our experience. The machine would make it seem as though we were sitting somewhere, perhaps in a comfortable chair, with the light on, holding and reading a book. But all the while we would just be floating in a tank, seeing nothing, and having no book in our hands. We would mistakenly take ourselves to be embodied, in a library or study or café. But we would have only a brain,

[27] *Anarchy, State, and Utopia*, 42.

and be located in some laboratory. Even so, one's experience would replicate the one we have when we really read a book, taking in words on a page (or reading device) as light reflected from them impinges on our eyes. We could ponder what the author is saying, wonder whether we should accept her point of view, be surprised by her unexpected ideas, entertain mental images of characters described, react with displeasure or delight by the way the book is written or organized, and so on.

In this way, one could learn, while inside the machine, all there is to know about physics, chemistry, astronomy, geology, the life sciences, and so on. It is the real world, the world that exists independently of oneself and the technician, that one has full access to—or, at any rate, as much access as normal readers have. Recall what Hamlet says: "I could be bounded in a nutshell, and count myself a king of infinite space.... " He adds: "were it not that I have bad dreams," but even so the image of a "king of infinite space" who has this great authority in spite of his narrow physical confinement is a fitting portrayal of someone who comprehends the universe simply by reading about it. One could occupy this kingly position inside the experience machine. When you read, you are making minimal use of any part of your body beyond your brain; you might as well be detached from it. Admittedly, inside the machine, one would not see or smell an actual flower, since one would have no body. But intellectually one could understand and marvel at the whole physical universe and all its parts.

13. Fictional worlds

Perhaps, however, this does not fully address Nozick's third complaint. When he says that inside the machine "there is no *actual* contact with any deeper reality" (his emphasis) he might mean that there is no *causal* contact. Without a body, you cannot change the world. You cannot build bridges, make musical instruments, or create new drugs in the laboratory. He also complains that one is confined to a "man-made reality, to a world no deeper or more important than that which people can construct." One is limited to a contemplative life inside the machine, enjoying the constructions summoned forth into your experiential world by your wishes and then devised by the technician.

We should keep in mind that we are asking about the *prudential* value of the experience machine—not whether it is good for other people outside the machine. (And we are assuming that one enters the machine partly because doing so benefits others by giving them the use of one's body. Good things come to others because of what one foregoes.) So, even if one cannot make things that are valuable to others when one is inside the machine, that by itself does not show that it is bad *for you* to be there. It should also be recalled that things can be built by others in accordance with the thoughts you have inside the machine. (An architect's designs created inside the machine can be followed by others, as we noted in section 9.)

Inside the machine, one is not a causal agent bringing about good in the world, but Nozick would be ignoring an arena of human existence of enormous interest and value, if he is implying, in his third criticism, that a contemplative existence—a life that does not change the world or seek to do so—is impoverished. That would overlook or degrade the value of aesthetic experience. A life dominated by the love of literature, for example, has many of the same features as a life lived within an experience machine. If Nozick's arguments lead to the conclusion that a life absorbed with fictional characters and stories is to be avoided, there must be something wrong with it.

When you read works of fiction, as opposed to works of science, history, and biography, you become emotionally engaged with and seek to understand characters and situations that are the products of an author's imagination and would not exist were it not for that author's creativity. It might be said that you are in a "man-made reality, . . . a world no deeper or more important than that which people can construct. There is no *actual* contact with any deeper reality." There is nothing you can do to alter an already finished work of fiction—it has an effect on you, but not *vice versa*. While you are engaged with that work, you can be in total isolation. You are in these respects somewhat like Aristotle's unmoved mover, assuming that you have achieved and enjoy a deep understanding of the author's fictional world. Aristotle's god seems to many students of the *Nicomachean Ethics* a strange and repellent figure, socially isolated and inactive. At the same time, we realize that a contemplative, solitary, literary life is rich in experiential value. One of the proper missions of a university is to prepare many students to appreciate literature, and to train some students to make it their life's work.

One could engage with works of literary fiction as fully inside the experience machine as outside it. We can assume that one would not put those experiences to further use outside the machine. One would not enhance one's skill as a moral agent in the real world. And it might be said that in that case the experience of literature loses much or all of its value. Nozick's thought experiment has in this way led us to reflect on the non-instrumental value of an engagement with fictional worlds.

We love stories, even as children, and putting events into a narrative order may be crucial to our ability to navigate our social world. But for this purpose we do not need *fictional* narratives of the sort produced by literary artists. Good biographers and historians also give us the pleasures of a good story well told—and they give us a deep understanding of things that really happened and people who really exist. Why bother, then, with the fantastical creations of writers of fiction? There is a sense in which they do not give us—to use Nozick's phrase—"contact with reality." Even if it could be said, truthfully, that Madame Bovary exists—that is, that the fictional character of this name exists—she is still a fictive entity rather than a "real human being" who exists in space and time. What good does it do to spend one's time thinking about her, when one could be learning about real people—people who exist in space and time?[28]

In reflecting on this question, we must steer clear of the philistinism that Dickens clumsily satirizes in *Hard Times* through his depiction of Thomas Gradgrind, the educator who values nothing but "facts." A conception of well-being that is forced to

---

[28] Whether Madame Bovary exists is a question within the field of metaphysics (not ethics or aesthetics), but I do not believe that if a negative answer is correct that would diminish the value of reading Flaubert's novel. For opposed views on the metaphysical question, see Amie L. Thomasson, *Fiction and Metaphysics* (Madame Bovary exists); and R. M. Sainsbury, *Fiction and Fictionalism* (she does not).

conclude that the arts or playful exercises of a child's imagination have no place, or at best a merely instrumental role, in human life would have no plausibility. Without composers, musicians, novelists, poets, playwrights, and painters, there would be fewer opportunities for us to so enrich our experience that our lives become immeasurably superior to that of McTaggart's oyster.

So, there must be *something* right in the "formalist" approach to aesthetics set forth in the works of Oscar Wilde and other figures of the nineteenth and twentieth century who defended "art for art's sake." What should we learn from this movement? As a first step, we should acknowledge that great beauty and other important aesthetic virtues can be found in what came to be called "absolute music"—music that is not "programmatic," not about anything but its own content.[29] Some of the most treasured compositions of the western canon—Bach's suites for solo instruments, Beethoven's quartets, Shostakovich's preludes and fugues—fall into this category. No truths about our everyday lives can be learned by listening to them, but that does not demote them to an inferior order of art. In saying this, I am rejecting the thesis—prominent in Schopenhauer and dating to the Pythagoreans of antiquity—that music is valuable only because it reflects and reveals the true nature of the world (whether that be futile striving or mathematical proportion). As the experience of music lovers attests, what is valuable in absolute music is already there in the way it sounds to a trained ear—it need not be sought in something non-musical that lies behind it. If you ask what use such music has, you are looking in the wrong place for its value.

We can infer from this a more general conclusion. The insight to be found in the slogan, "art for art's sake," is that what is true of absolute music is applicable to the other "fine arts" as well. Works of fiction, so understood, need not achieve excellence by teaching us general lessons useful for the conduct of our lives in the real world. When they lack didactic value, that does not make them defective as works of art, or unworthy of study because they do not help us find our way among flesh-and-blood human beings.[30]

That does not show that music ought not to be programmatic, or that we should avoid novels that will shape our lives when we are not reading them. If a work of fiction teaches us, for example, what life was like in the trenches of World War I, that is a good reason to read it. We will learn something about the real world, and this is not a motive to be despised. A novel might also be more directly useful, for example by describing

---

[29] See Mark Evan Bonds, *Absolute Music: The History of an Idea*; Peter Kivy, *Music Alone: Philosophical Reflections on the Purely Musical Experience*; Peter Kivy, *Introduction to a Philosophy of Music*; Peter Kivy, *Antithetical Arts: On the Ancient Quarrel Between Literature and Music*.

[30] "All art constantly aspires towards the condition of music." Thus Walter Pater in his essay on the School of Giorgione. See *The Renaissance: Studies in Art and Poetry* (London, Macmillan and Co., 1888), 135–61. The sentence quoted occurs (all of it in italics) on 140. He means that in music alone a perfect unification of form and content is possible, and it thus serves as a model for the other arts. As I read him, he advocates a more radical thesis than the one I endorse in this paragraph: in all art the form (the "mode of handling" its matter) "should become an end in itself," and a work is deficient to the extent that it falls short of this goal. A more accessible edition of Pater's book is available (Mineola, NY: Dover Publications, 2005), a republication of the fourth edition of 1893. In that edition, the sentence cited appears on page 90.

an unfamiliar part of the world that we are about to visit. Authors have no reason to eschew works that offer readers these sorts of insights about reality. Similarly, it does not count against Beethoven's Ninth Symphony that it might inspire listeners to feel a sense of unity with all humankind. If it succeeds, all the greater is its accomplishment.[31]

The conclusion we should draw is that works of art can be valued solely for their internal aesthetic features, or for the further good they do, or for both reasons. Those that, like absolute music, are to be valued simply because of the rich experience we have when we attend to them, can be, on balance, as worthy of our admiration as those that have some further value as guides to reality. That is the kernel of truth in the slogan, "art for art's sake."

With this in mind, we can return to the experience machine. Absolute music can be as fully appreciated inside the machine as outside. Other forms of artistic excellence can be appreciated in the way absolute music is, their value lying entirely in the works themselves and not in what they reveal about a further reality beyond them. Someone inside the machine whose experience is filled with the love of such works as these does not change the world or acquire knowledge of it. But it would be a form of philistinism to hold that the life of such an individual would have little or no prudential value. If Nozick's low assessment of the value of the experience machine entails that we should read only those books or listen only to that music that instructs us, or prepares us to change the world, he is uncomfortably close to Mr. Gradgrind.

14. Crisp's revised version

Nozick says that we (he and his readers) would not plug into the experience machine.[32] He of course also thinks that this is the right choice: we *should* not plug in. Why, then, does he bother talking about what we *would* do? Perhaps he is assuming that if there is a nearly universal rejection of this hypothetical choice, that is good evidence that we would be right to reject the option of plugging in. But the question, "What would you choose for yourself?" is nonetheless a feature of his description of this thought experiment—and that creates a problem. For some people might say "I would not choose to plug in" out of a fear of change, or out of status quo bias, or because they have children to take care of, or because they find it hard to believe that the machine would really give them the experiences they would like to have.[33]

---

[31] Proust writes: "Real life, life at last laid bare and illuminated—the only life in consequence which can be said to be really lived—is literature..." (*Time Regained*, translated by Mayor and Kilmartin, 298). Or: "Real life, life finally uncovered and clarified, the only life in consequence lived to the full, is literature" (*Finding Time Again*, translated by Patterson, 204). Literary works, in other words, give us the opportunity to contemplate and understand human action in a way that is not equally on offer outside the world of fiction. Proust can be taken to mean that if we read literature even partly in order to achieve some non-literary good, our priorities are the reverse of what they should be. That goes too far.

[32] "We learn that something matters to us in addition to experience by imagining an experience machine and then realizing that we would not use it" (*Anarchy, State, and Utopia*, 44).

[33] These distortions are discussed by Jennifer Hawkins, 'The Experience Machine and the Experience Requirement,' in Guy Fletcher (ed.), *The Routledge Handbook of Philosophy of Well-Being*; and Felipe De Brigard, 'If You Like It, Does It Matter If It's Real?'

In order to correct for these limitations in Nozick's description of the thought experiment, Roger Crisp has proposed a new version of it. The key feature of his variation is that you are asked, not whether *you* would plug in, but whether you think there is any difference in the quality of lives of two *other* people: one of them lives his life entirely within the experience machine, and the other has the very same experiences but has them outside the machine, just as we all do. The latter "writes a great novel, is courageous, kind, intelligent, witty, and loving, and makes significant scientific discoveries."[34] The former has the experience of writing a great novel, being courageous, and so on—but this results from the technician's manipulation of the brain, not interactions with the real world. The question to be asked about these two individuals, whose inner lives do not differ, is whether they have the same level of well-being.

That is a better question than the one Nozick asks, Crisp believes, because it is impersonal—not about oneself but about two strangers. One's answer will not be distorted by one's fear of change, or distrust of the technician, or sense of obligation to others. Furthermore, he proposes that when Nozick's thought experiment is modified in this way, it presents a serious challenge to the thesis that he (Crisp) wishes to defend: pleasure is the sole component of well-being. "According to hedonism, [these two individuals] have exactly the same level of well-being. And that is surely a claim from which most of us will recoil."[35] The remainder of Crisp's essay is a response to this challenge. He argues that although our initial reaction to his modification of Nozick's thought experiment poses a problem for hedonism, there are still powerful reasons to regard it as the best conception of well-being, and to distrust our initial reaction.

We should examine Crisp's thought experiment more closely, but before we do so, notice one further difference between it and Nozick's original version—beyond the fact that it calls for a judgment about the lives that have been lived by two other people, rather than a choice between alternative paths that one's own future will take. Nozick's thought experiment asks whether a trade-off would be worth making. There seems, at least initially, to be something quite appealing about plugging into the experience machine: your future will contain the experiences you would like to have as elements of your well-being. But the "down side" is that these will only be experiences—they are not caused by the reality that we normally take to be presented to us through our experiences. If Nozick is right that the negative features of life inside the machine far outweigh the positive ones, that teaches us an important lesson: the immense value of our normal connection to the real world. It *has* to be of great value in order to outweigh the evident and significant value of having the opportunity to shape one's future experiences exactly as one chooses.

By contrast, in Crisp's version, the value of being connected to the real world can be as small as you like: it will still be enough to break the tie between the two experientially identical lives being compared. As a result, his version leaves it open that if just a few of the experiences inside the machine were sufficiently better (as experiences) than

---

[34] Crisp, 'Hedonism Reconsidered,' 635.   [35] Ibid., 636.

those outside it, that would compensate for our not having contact with external reality when we are inside the machine. Not having such contact might in itself be only a bit worse than having it. Crisp's version takes no advantage of the potential boost in well-being that Nozick's version of the experience machine offers. That familiar version allows us to control what happens to us so that the only bad experiences we have are those that are needed to make life better.

Life lived outside the experience machine, on Crisp's version, has everything that life inside it has (all the same experiences)—and more. There is no reason, then, to say that the life of the individual who is confined to the machine is better. Another way to put the point is to express it in terms of philosophical method. We must acknowledge that when we take a stand on philosophical issues, there is a significant possibility that in some cases—perhaps many—we are wrong. The possibility is greater when other philosophers who have studied the matter disagree with us. So, when we need to make practical judgments whose truth or falsity depends on the correctness or incorrectness of the philosophical theories those judgments presuppose, we ought to keep in mind our vulnerability to philosophical error, and opt for a practical conclusion that will not be regrettable, if it turns out that our background theory is wrong. Now, in Crisp's version, the judgment that life outside the machine is better is one that could make no one worse off, were it used as a basis for choosing to live such a life. By contrast, the judgment that life *inside* the machine is better *could* make someone worse off, if it were used to justify putting or keeping someone in the machine. So, even if we think that the only components of well-being are good experiences, we should, out of philosophical humility, recognize that well-being is a difficult topic about which we can be in error—and therefore we should, as a practical matter, take lives that have both good experiences and more to be better than lives that only have those good experiences.

Recall the details of Crisp's thought experiment: one individual "writes a great novel, is courageous, kind, intelligent, witty, and loving, and makes significant scientific discoveries," whereas the second is inside the experience machine and has the same experiences as this first individual. Let's take the first item on this list—writing a great novel—and (for the sake of brevity) leave the others aside. We are to imagine two individuals, each writing a great novel (and, Crisp adds, doing so with equal enjoyment).[36] Since their experiences are identical, the works they are composing are identical—all of the same sentences, and all of the same thought processes that produce those sentences.

It might be asked: how could a brain in a vat write anything—let alone something as long and complex as a novel? The technician will create the illusion that the novelist plugged into the machine is working at a computer screen or with traditional writing materials. That novelist will not have everything he has drafted committed to memory (that is not how novelists work), but will be fitted with a device that brings before his

---

[36] Ibid., 636.

consciousness the experience of re-reading earlier drafts, or notes, and so on. What will the completion of the novel consist in, when it has been composed on the experience machine? It will not take the form of a computer file or a collection of pieces of paper with words on them. It will be constituted by all of the sentences in the mind of the novelist that he has finally chosen to be the sentences of his novel. He does not have all of them in his head at the same time, but he can have the experience, any time he chooses, of "reading them." He will have the illusion that they are there on the screen or in a hard copy—but although that will be an illusion, there really will be such a thing as the novel that he has constructed. It is not something that sits on his desk, available for anyone to read—although it will seem to him that it is.

The question to be asked now is this: when we consider the life of the conventional novelist insofar as it has been devoted to writing that novel, and compare it to the life of the novelist in the machine insofar as it has been devoted to writing that novel, is one of them superior with respect to prudential value? The two novels are identical in literary value, since they are identical in content. Each of them enjoyed the experience of writing his novel in the same way and to the same degree. Each struggled as much or as little as the other with the challenges and frustrations of composition. The difference between them lies not in their experiences (which, by hypothesis, are identical), but in the fact that in one case there was the physical act of writing (at a keyboard or with pen and paper), and a physical product (a computer file or a hard copy), whereas in the other case there were only mental processes and only the mental analogue of a book (the sentences in the mind of the plugged-in novelist). It is implausible to suppose that because of these differences, the novelist outside the machine is better off than the novelist inside the machine.

Perhaps, then, when Crisp says that "most of us will recoil" from the claim that these two novelists have the same level of well-being, he is relying on the tacit assumption that the conventional novelist has not only produced a great novel, but that it is a novel that others can read and appreciate. The novelist in the machine has, as it were, shaped his mind into a novel, but the conventional novelist has brought into the world something that can be shared, understood, and treasured by others. But we should be careful here: the fact that the conventional novelist has produced something that *could* be read by others does not mean that it actually *will* be read by anyone. Suppose it is not. It simply sits there in his computer, or on his desk, and no one ever reads it. In that case, there is no significant difference between the lives of these two individuals, and so they cannot differ in their level of well-being.

Alternatively, we might suppose that the work of the conventional novelist *is* read and appreciated by others. That might be thought to constitute an increase in his level of well-being, in comparison with the level attained by the novelist in the machine. But that would be an illegitimate inference. It is one thing for a novelist's work to be read and appreciated by others, and another for the novelist to realize or believe that his work has reached an appreciative audience. Suppose, then, that although the work of the conventional novelist finds an audience of admirers, he himself has no awareness of this fact. (It could be that he dies before his work is discovered.) In that case, it could plausibly be denied that his level of well-being has increased. (If he is dead, how can he acquire more of what is good for him? If he is alive, how could the bare fact that someone is reading his work do him any good?) On the other hand, if we imagine not only that his novel is admired, but that he recognizes this fact, and basks in the glow of the recognition and fame he has earned, we are no longer in the business of arguing that there are important non-experiential components of well-being.

There is something to be learned from this attempt to work out the details of Crisp's comparison between two lives, one lived inside the machine, the other outside, but identical in experiential quality. It might seem at first that the life that produces publicly accessible goods (novels, feats of courage, witty remarks, scientific discoveries) will be judged by most people to have a higher level of well-being. But at least in the case of two novelists, that judgment cannot be sustained; on careful examination, there is no such difference. My conjecture is that were we to look closely at the other cases Crisp mentions (and more examples along these lines), we would reach the same conclusion. Outside the machine, you obviously can contribute to the lives of others, with your great novels, acts of courage, and scientific discoveries. But do you yourself benefit simply by doing these things outside the machine rather than inside? It is not obvious that you do.

To return to the point I made earlier in this section: the experience machine would certainly enhance certain aspects of our lives, if we made use of its potential to diminish the amount of fruitless suffering we experience. Suppose you are a talented novelist, and are offered the opportunity to plug into the experience machine. Let's further suppose that you know that you have only a few more years to live, and you want to devote them to creating a new work. Your choices are these:

First, you can enter the machine and ask the technician to insure that your novel-writing experience is for the most part good. You will encounter challenges, frustrations, set-backs, but you will also feel exhilarated; you will thoroughly enjoy getting to know the characters you are creating, and in the end you will have a great sense of fulfillment at the completion of your work. (You are the one who is thinking the thoughts that constitute the novel. The technician merely supplies the sensory experiences that you transform, through your creative thinking, into artful prose.) After that, it will seem to you that your work is well received by others: the "reviews" will be excellent, and "sales" will be high.

Second, you can take your chances on writing your novel in the real world. You will work with your hands at a computer, or with pen and ink. You might become so ill that you can no longer write; or you might have writer's block; or you might decide that your writing is so bad that you throw it all in the trash; or you might finish a work that you are satisfied with, but others will ignore or belittle what you produce. Of course, things could go very well for you. It could turn out that you have as good an experience outside the machine as you would have been guaranteed to have inside it. If you are lucky, your work will be read by others; you will be admired and honored.

Is the possibility that your work will be admired by actual people—who might discover your novel only after you die—of such great prudential value that it is worth it, for the sake of your well-being, to risk having a miserable time producing it, and possibly having nothing to show for your efforts? It is doubtful that being admired is even a small component of well-being; and far more doubtful that it is a major component. What cannot be denied is that needless pain, frustration, suffering, and mental anguish in themselves diminish well-being. Nozick's original version of the experience machine allows us to rid our future of these useless evils and so it tacitly admits that a great benefit is in store for us if we enter the machine. That is what makes the thought that we would nonetheless decline to plug in quite powerful. It is not nearly so interesting to learn that when nothing is to be gained by spending one's life in the experience machine rather than in the real world, one is better off to be in a position to reap the advantages of living in the real world (if there happen to be any).

15. Rescued from death

Another way to see the value of life inside the experience machine is to recognize how much better it would be for someone to be within it than to die, or to go on living in a state of minimal awareness. Suppose we come across someone whose body has been severely damaged in a car accident, but whose brain could remain unimpaired—if he is hooked up to a support system and plugged into the experience machine. Suppose further that the experiences he will have, if we rescue him and connect him to the machine, will be continuous with those he had prior to his accident. He is forty years old, and we can expect him to have the same sort of rich experiences on the machine for another forty or fifty years. The financial cost of doing all this, let's suppose, is modest. Should our health care system supply him with an experience machine—will it do him enough good to justify the modest social cost?

Compare this hypothetical case to one in which the alternative to death is an oyster-like existence. Again, we have a forty-year-old man who has been severely injured, but in this case the best we can do for him is to keep him alive and allow him to experience the pleasure of eating a simple kind of food—the same minimal pleasure that McTaggart's oyster might feel. That is the *only* experiential good available to him. In this case, it is far from clear that we should pay even a modest price to keep him alive. Even if we embellish the example, by extending this oyster-like existence for thousands of years, it remains the case that investing in the continuation of such a life is of little value, when compared with the well-being available to human beings (of normal longevity) who live in favorable circumstances.

Compared to an oyster's life, or a human life reduced to that of an oyster, both a life lived on the experience machine and an experientially identical life lived in "the real world" can be vastly superior—and will be, if they include experiences of the right sort, and little in the way of suffering beyond the kind that enhances our lives. An extended period of well-selected experiences on the experience machine is incommensurably superior in prudential value to the life of an oyster (however long the oyster lives); and that point of course remains true when made about a life filled with good experiences caused in the usual way by ordinary reality. So, even if there is more to human well-being than good experiences—a thesis I have challenged—those additional elements are not needed to make our lives vastly (and incommensurably) superior to a life, however long, of ongoing simple pleasures. On a scale of well-being, an oyster's life sits near the bottom, and a life on the experience machine, when those experiences are of the best sort, is at or almost at the top. Whether a human life outside the experience machine is superior to an experientially identical life within it—that is a matter of dispute. But we should not lose the proper perspective on this issue: if there is a difference in well-being here, it is small.

But suppose someone refuses to concede this point. For such a person, it must be terribly important that we are not brains in a vat, for if that is what really lies behind our experiences, then our lives are robbed of much of their prudential value. On the scale that ranges from human life at its best to an oyster's simple existence, life inside the experience machine, according to this picture, must be moved from the top (where I would place it), or nearly the top, to a position far closer to that of an oyster. It might be better than an oyster's life, but if so, not by much. Someone who thinks of life in the experience machine as seriously deficient in prudential value has no basis for resisting the conclusion that if an oyster's life is sufficiently longer than a human life spent on the experience machine, it will be the better of these two lives. According to this view, we cannot judge our lives to be at or near the top of a scale of prudential value simply by attending to the quality and variety of our experiences—the phenomenology that belongs to loving relations, generosity of spirit, intellectual stimulation, music, art, poetry, and sports. If these experiences come to us in the laboratory of a technician, the contribution they make to our well-being is vastly diminished—so say Nozick and those who agree with him.

That position, it seems to me, has no plausibility. As I noted in Chapter 1, section 6, we know certain things by observation, and one of them is that our experiences make our lives far better than they would be if they contained only the kind of pleasure felt by an oyster. That important piece of self-knowledge is available to you and me (who are not living in experience machines) and to someone who *is* living in such a machine. Inside the machine, he might wonder, "Am I only a brain in a vat?" The correct reply is: "yes, but your well-being is not thereby diminished much, if at all." We too wonder (some of us): "Am I only a brain in a vat?" The answer, in this case, is: "no, but our well-being is not thereby increased much, if at all."

16. Intellectual intuition and the ascent to beauty

One type of experience one can have inside the experience machine has been neglected until now, but should be acknowledged: this is what we are aware of when something is presented to the "mind's eye." That phrase alludes to a quasi-perceptual experience—a mental apprehension of a fact in which we "see" that it obtains, or of an object (a concept or idea) that we inspect and assess with respect to its plausibility or truth. Our power to engage in this sort of mental operation is sometimes called our faculty of intuition, and according to the philosophical tradition (beginning with Plato) that sets great store by this faculty, the truths it apprehends have a self-evident status. Those truths are not justified by any inferential path from other, more basic truths; they need no such justification, because they merit our credence in themselves. The epistemology proposed by this rationalistic tradition is of course controversial, but it cannot be rejected out of hand.[37] Let's accept it provisionally; doing so will allow us to see that if there is a faculty of intuition that can apprehend self-evident truths, it can operate within the experience machine, and the richness of life inside the machine could be greatly enhanced by that operation.

The power of one's mind (its store of ideas, its ability to think) is not destroyed by the experience machine. If, before entering the machine, it could behold intellectual objects and truths, and could engage in a priori reasoning, it will not be prevented from doing so when it is inside the machine. Admittedly, there is no reason to enter the experience machine merely in order to avail oneself of these mental powers, for one already has them outside the machine. But, having decided to plug in (partly for altruistic reasons, we have been assuming), one thing one can do inside it is to engage in the kind of philosophical activity posited by the rationalist tradition. If, for example, there is an a priori argument for the existence of God (as the ontological argument is taken to be), one can think the thoughts that contain that argument, and rejoice at the realization that a perfect being exists. One would not be cut off from that all-important part or aspect of reality. And one could enjoy this contemplative and meditative activity without encountering the annoying distractions and interruptions of quotidian life outside the machine.

Recall Nozick's complaint: "plugging into an experience machine limits us to a man-made reality, to a world no deeper or more important than that which people can construct. There is no *actual* contact with any deeper reality."[38] He is assuming here that anyone who chooses to enter the machine would desire to have within it nothing but sensory, perceptual, and emotional experiences, and would renounce all other aspects of mental life. But there is no reason to limit life inside the machine to these simple forms of consciousness.

To make vivid to ourselves the richness that life could have within the experience machine, we can transpose Plato's description, in the *Symposium*, of a lover's encounter with a series of beautiful objects, so that this encounter is an experience enjoyed within the machine. The lover-in-training is first drawn to the beauty of one body; then sees that such beauty is present in many other bodies; then recognizes the greater value of the beauty that is present in souls; then moves on to appreciate the beauty of social norms and spheres of knowledge; and after gazing on this "great sea of beauty" he ultimately arrives at a vision of the most astonishing and fulfilling beauty of all—the very thing (the form of beauty) in virtue of which all else is beautiful (*Symposium* 210a–211b). What the lover undergoes is a gradual enrichment of his experience

---

[37] For a defense, see Elijah Chudnoff, *Intuition*.   [38] *Anarchy, State, and Utopia*, 43.

(guided at each stage by rational thought), until he achieves a profound encounter with an object of the greatest possible beauty, grasped by mental vision.

We can alter Plato's portrait of this transformative experience by supposing that during its initial stages, it is induced by the experience machine. Those beautiful bodies the lover apparently sees are not distal objects, but the result of the technician's manipulation of his brain. Those souls whose beauty he appreciates are likewise fictional characters mistaken for real people. To Plato, that illusory aspect of the lover's ascent would not in the least detract from the value of the whole experience. It would still be beauty that the lover encounters at each stage, and it would still be beauty itself that lies at the culmination of the ascent. The experience of beauty (or series of experiences) one could have inside the machine would be no *more* valuable than the kind of experience Plato is discussing—but it would also be no less so. If someone were physically unable to go out into the world and encounter the beauty of the human body and soul by meeting real people, he could stay at home, plug into the experience machine, and be none the worse than Plato's ideal lover—someone Plato takes to be at the peak of human existence.

With a little imagination, we can also locate in Plato's *Symposium* a counter-ideal that would be impossible to achieve, if one were "bounded in a nutshell" by one's confinement within the experience machine. According to the speech of Aristophanes (189d–193e), what a lover seeks is reunification with a unique part of a whole: the other half of the large, spherical body that each human being once had. If you experience the longing of love, Aristophanes says, that is because there is one individual in the world whose absence is intolerable to you. Your sense of incompleteness and need of your other half will come to an end only if you encounter and become reunited with him or her, by throwing your arms around and embracing that person's body. According to that picture of human well-being, we will always be afflicted with a crushing sense of dissatisfaction—of unfulfilled desire—unless we remain in the real world of human souls with human bodies, find the one who was part of our original self, and physically reunite with him or her. You cannot find that individual and hug him when you are in the experience machine, and so for lovers there would be every reason to remain outside it, and none to enter it.

Aristophanes has an anti-experientialist conception of human well-being: a major component of one's good is *actual* physical reunification with the right individual, not an experience *as if* of such reunification. But this counter-ideal to the one Plato endorses will not survive careful reflection. The physical relationship he posits as the goal of *erôs* is by itself without value. If it is important to well-being, that is only because it produces the kind of conscious experiences one can have when one's body is joined with that of another. What can be wonderful about hugging and being hugged is the intimate sense it conveys of treasuring and being treasured—not the physical fact (whether one is aware of it or not) that one's body bears a certain spatial relationship to another's. If those experiences are available on the experience machine, plugging in would leave one no worse off.

17. Zombies

How do you know that you are not a mere brain in a vat, your sensory input the product of a technician's manipulation? Or, to ask a related question, how do you know that there is more than one conscious being in the world—yourself? The only experiences you are aware of from the inside are your own. Perhaps other people are zombies, mere machines that lack all forms of consciousness but mimic behavior similar to your own.[39]

We have not been concerned here with this epistemological problem, but the questions we have discussed are connected to it. If all other "people" are zombies, is the prudential value of one's own life significantly reduced? It might seem so. After all, you are alone in the world and have always been so. You thought your life was lived among friends and a community of like-minded individuals. All along, it was just you. You thought that your life was going well for you, but it was a fool's paradise.

But why exactly would the quality of one's life be worse if everyone else is a zombie? You have had experiences of a certain sort, and the quality of those experiences is not diminished by facts about other people. How then can the quality of *your* life be diminished if others are not real people but zombies?

Perhaps the assessment of the quality of your life must be revised downwards because the love you have had for others has never been reciprocated. But consider some ordinary cases in which love is felt even when there is no hope of mutuality. Aristotle refers to mothers who give up their children to other families because that is best for their children, and in spite of their wish that they could keep those children for themselves (*NE* VIII.8 1159a28–30). It would be implausible to suppose that these mothers suffer a loss of well-being, not because there are experiences of intimacy that they will never have, but simply because "X loves Y but Y does not love X" holds true of them in relation to their children. The point applies more generally. We can and do admire people (many of them no longer living: great composers, philosophers, public benefactors of the past) even when we know that they do not admire us, and our attitudes towards them can be fully justified by their wonderful qualities. Such unreciprocated admiration does not constitute a diminution of well-being. There is no reason to suppose otherwise regarding unreciprocated love. So, if we shrink in horror at the thought that we might be brains in a vat, or that our social world is populated by zombies, we should not try to justify this reaction by saying that in these scenarios our love and admiration for others is not reciprocated.

---

[39] Our perceptual experiences are, I believe, correctly assumed to derive from our encounter with distal objects. The common assumption that we are living in an "external" world is not only correct but has sufficient warrant; also warranted is our belief that we know this. That is because the contrary hypothesis— that there actually are experience machines, that we have been placed inside one of them for reasons unknown, and cannot recollect having been so treated—is one that there is no reason to accept. Here I follow John Skorupski, *The Domain of Reasons*, 494–9. For fuller treatments, see Duncan Pritchard, *Epistemic Angst*; and Penelope Maddy, *What Do Philosophers Do? Skepticism and the Practice of Philosophy*.

What we ought to say instead is that if we became solipsists, abandoned our conception of ourselves as one mind among many, and interacted with others in the full awareness of their having no inner life, our lives would be turned upside down, and what we normally value in our social existence would be unavailable. Take the simplest sort of case: on the assumption that other people feel pain or are suffering, we normally look for ways to alleviate their bad experiences. If in fact they feel nothing, but are merely acting in ways that typically express pain and suffering, then nothing good is accomplished by our efforts. Nothing bad is happening to someone simply because he emits the sound "ouch" but expresses nothing, feels nothing, has no sense of aversion, does not dislike anything. Even if his body moves away from the knife that caused him to emit this sound, that is no reason to come to his aid, because there is nothing bad about one body moving away from another. Similarly, if you have been trying to make people feel happy, but became convinced that they are totally without affect or feeling, and their smiles and body language express nothing within them, then your efforts did not achieve the good you were hoping for.

Furthermore, if you are convinced that the others around you are zombies, and they therefore have no idea what it is like for you to be you, you can no longer have the rich experiences of feeling comforted by them, or receiving their understanding and sympathetic support. You can take no joy in the presence of a kindred spirit, because there aren't any. You could no more feel loved by others whom you take to have no inner life than you can feel loved by machines. And although you can love your children even if you expect no love in return, that love is an expression of the hope that they will have rich, flourishing lives. We could love a zombie only in the way in which we love a car—something we replace when it no longer meets our needs.

If one becomes convinced that one is alone in the world, or if one feels serious doubts, whenever one deals with others, about the existence of their inner lives, the quality of one's life will certainly suffer. But if you are, without realizing it, the only person in the world, that by itself does not make your life worse, because it does not by itself affect the quality of your experience. What these points imply is that there is a good practical reason not to become worried about the truth of solipsism. A serious everyday concern about whether one is all alone would detract from one's well-being. One should be intrigued and fascinated by the "problem of other minds," but not fearful and distressed that there might not be any.

If there is just one person in the world, there is less well-being in it than we normally suppose. That would be a great shame. But if the world contains many people, all of them either a brain in a vat or a technician in a laboratory, there is no less well-being in the world.

Part Three

We completed, in Part Two, our long examination of Nozick's thought experiment. His claim that one can always do *far* better for oneself outside the machine than inside must be rejected—in fact, there is no reason to think that one can always do *somewhat* better. Illusory experiences are not lower in value simply because they are illusory.

But our results were not entirely negative. We have come to recognize something of considerable philosophical interest by means of this thought experiment. Having become mature adults, if we are able to carry on with the rest of our lives without the help of the body, we would suffer no loss of well-being. We would need only the brain and neural system—whatever is the minimal physical basis for our experiential life. Our everyday social and physical world contributes to our well-being, to the extent that it does, by giving us the experiences that constitute the quality of our lives. The Platonic idea that our good resides in the soul rather than the body—an idea with which Aristotle entirely agrees—is not far from the truth, and has been largely vindicated. (Not entirely: we do need the brain.) It remains true, of course, that we care deeply about what is external to our experience. We *should* care, because more should matter to us than our own well-being.

In the remainder of this chapter, I turn to further objections to experientialism, and to doctrines of Aristotle that differ only slightly from the conception of well-being I am defending.

18. *Well-being and the satisfaction of desire*

Several sorts of arguments have appeared in the philosophical literature purporting to show that some of the components of well-being lie outside the awareness of the individual whose well-being is in question. Like Nozick's, these arguments take the form of counter-examples. One sort asks us to reflect on cases in which an individual is the subject of invidious thoughts or utterances, of which he is and remains unaware. A second sort asks us to imagine ways in which posthumous events seem to add to or detract from the total amount of good that accrues to someone. These thought experiments, unlike Nozick's, do not conjure up a fictional world. It is a familiar fact that someone can be the unwitting victim of hostile attitudes, both while he is alive and after he dies. Isn't it better not to be the object of those attitudes? Another sort of example is the posthumous completion of someone's long-term project: the deceased cannot take satisfaction in that accomplishment, but it might nonetheless be thought better for him that his labors come to fruition.

These sorts of arguments differ from Nozick's in a further respect (beyond the fact that they are not pieces of science fiction). His thought experiment does not challenge the thesis that all components of well-being are experiential. Rather, it purports to show that the prudential value of an experience is diminished (and not just marginally) if it is produced by a technician who is manipulating one's brain. If two experiences, one produced inside the machine and the other outside, are qualitatively indistinguishable, the machine-induced experience is alleged to be far inferior in value to the one that connects one to the real world in the usual way. Even if that were so, the thesis that all the components of well-being are experiential would remain standing. By contrast, the familiar sorts of cases we are about to examine are thought by some philosophers to show that there are elements of a person's well-being and ill-being that lie outside that individual's conscious life.

Our discussion of the experience machine has some bearing on one sort of alleged counter-example to experientialism—the sort in which someone's well-being is said to diminish because he is unwittingly the object of scorn, disrespect, or other unfavorable attitudes. It might be thought that it is bad to be the unsuspecting target of these attitudes at least partly because in such cases there is a bit of social reality pertaining to oneself that one is ignorant of. When you have false beliefs about what the people in your social world think of you, that fact, it might be said, by itself detracts from your well-being. According to this line of thought, social illusions are in themselves of negative value. That is a position that I have rejected, but the experience machine was not the only thought experiment that figured in my argument. Recall our discussion of the lecturer whose audience politely feigns understanding and approval, but has no idea what he is talking about (section 7). That speaker has false beliefs about his audience's reactions to him, but that does not by itself make his experience less good for him. So, if there is (as some believe) some diminution in one's well-being when one is the unwitting object of invidious attitudes, what is amiss is not simply the fact that one has a false belief about how one is regarded by others. The invidiousness of their attitudes must play an important role in the explanation of why one is supposedly made worse off.

In what follows, I will not take it for granted that experientialism is true—that all components of well-being are experiential. To do so would beg the question. But I will be assuming that a certain conception of well-being ought to be rejected, namely the thesis that it consists, wholly or partly, in the satisfaction of one's desires. By "the satisfaction of a desire," I mean a state of affairs in which (A) one wants it to be the case that X, and (B) it is the case that X. It often happens that we get a feeling or sense of satisfaction when we are conscious of the fact that something we have wanted has now been achieved. But that is not the sense of "satisfaction" that is relevant here.

Let us examine the thesis that well-being consists *entirely* in the satisfaction of one's desires (in the sense of "satisfaction" just specified). Once we see why this is a highly implausible conception of well-being, we will be in a position to examine the weaker thesis that *one* element of well-being is the satisfaction of desire.[40]

According to this theory, whatever is good for us is made good by the fact that we desire it, and whatever is bad for us is made bad by the fact that we want it not to be the case. It would fit with this conception of well-being to say, in addition, that one thing is made better for us than another if we prefer it, or want it more strongly than we want the other. (Needless to say, the theory in question does not hold that well-being consists in the satisfaction of desires for merely instrumental goods. Rather, it claims that well-being consists in the satisfaction of what we desire partly or entirely for itself, not as a mere means.)

[40] For a presentation of the theory that is sympathetic to it, see Chris Heathwood, 'Desire-Fulfillment Theory,' in Guy Fletcher (ed.), *The Routledge Handbook of Philosophy of Well-Being*, 136–47.

Ill-being, I have been assuming, is constituted by a large variety of bad experiences. Here is the partial list I mentioned earlier (Chapter 1, section 8): pain, nausea, dizziness, itchiness, soreness, discomfort, disgust, boredom, anxiety, stress, worry, loneliness, frustration, alienation, anguish, sorrow, despair, irritation, annoyance, anger, hatred, fear, shame, guilt, embarrassment, humiliation, depression, weariness, disorientation.

According to the desire-satisfaction conception of well-being, however, there are only two kinds of things that are bad for us, and neither appears on the above list. One is the state of affairs in which (A) we desire that X not be the case, and (B) X is the case. The other is the state of affairs in which (C) we desire that X be the case, and (D) X is not the case. These are what is *basically* bad. The other items mentioned above might also be bad—but when they are such, they are *derivatively* so, and are made such by our wanting not to experience them.

That conception of well-being and ill-being is deeply at odds with common sense. The ordinary view is that some introspectable quality of the negative experiences mentioned above grounds our normal aversion to them. We of course want to avoid experiencing such inner states as anguish and depression, but these are not whims or fancies directed at objects that in themselves are neutral in value; rather, they are grounded in the way these states are experienced. The desire-satisfaction theory, however, says that there is nothing bad about the way they feel. Prior to our wanting to avoid them, they are not bad to experience; they take on negative value only as a result of their happening to us while we baselessly want them not to happen. The implausibility of this view is immediately apparent.[41]

If I were to hate someone, I would wish him to be afflicted with all of the experiences mentioned above on my list of the components of ill-being. Similarly, if someone were to hate *himself*, he would wish upon himself all of those negative experiences. They would not become good for him by virtue of his wanting to suffer through them.

Something's being desired is not the same thing as its being desirable. That it is desired is compatible with its being something that ought not to be desired, just as what is believed may be a proposition that ought not be believed, and a person who is admired may be someone who does not merit admiration. So, it is not surprising that well-being and ill-being are not constituted by the satisfaction or dissatisfaction of desire. Well-being is not merely something desired—it is desirable. It is natural to assume, then, that its components must pass a more demanding test than that of being the object of the desires of the individual whose well-being is in question. (It might be true that if you want to do something on a mere whim, and there is nothing to be said against your doing so, you should do it simply because you want to. What you do may not be desirable, but your desire could make it true that you ought to perform that action. It does not follow that the quality of your life is improved by the satisfaction of

---

[41] This objection is acknowledged by Heathwood, ibid., p. 145. "When we are thinking just about ourselves and our interests, don't we want the things we want because they are good for us? But the desire theory suggests the opposite, that these things are good for us because we want them." He does not propose a solution to or dissolution of the problem.

your desire. If, however, you get some pleasure from satisfying your whim, that *does* enhance the quality of your life.)

These reflections show that ill-being does not consist *entirely* in the failure of desires to be satisfied (and well-being in their satisfaction). But they also undermine the weaker thesis that one component of well-being and ill-being is the satisfaction of desire and the failure of desires to be satisfied. For our discussion of the stronger thesis has rested on the premise that when the satisfaction of a desire has a bearing on our well-being, that is because there is something about what is desired that promotes or constitutes our well-being. *Each* component of well-being ought to be desired because it has a nature in virtue of which it is such a component.

The desire-satisfaction theory of well-being might have some superficial appeal if we mistakenly assume that whenever a desire is satisfied (in the relevant sense), that brings with it a *sense* of satisfaction as well. That is often the case, but there are many exceptions. We can be disappointed when we get what we want; we thought it would please us but it leaves us cold. Or, to take another sort of example, we may wish events in a remote part of the world to go a certain way, but remain forever unaware of the fact that our wish has been fulfilled.

The point is made vivid by Parfit's example of an individual whose life is dominated by his chronic addiction to a drug in plentiful supply. He always has a burning desire for the next fix, but when he takes the drug, this brings no felt satisfaction but only a desire for yet another dose. Day after day, throughout his life, he gets what he fervently desires, and he knows that this is so, but this brings him no pleasure or any other good experiences. If getting what one wants is even one of the basic components of human well-being, we must say that such a life is of very high quality (and especially so if it is a long life). But it is a paradigm of an empty life. There is nothing good about taking a drug one wants to take if the experience it produces is not itself a good one to have.[42]

Some philosophers hold that well-being consists not necessarily in the satisfaction of actual desires but rather the desires it would be best for someone to have—his ideal desires, or the desires of the prudentially ideal transformation of his present self.[43]

[42] See *Reasons and Persons*, 497. Parfit says that a desire-satisfaction theory that is confined to what he calls "global" desires can avoid this difficulty, but that restriction also yields implausible results, as Katarzyna de Lazari-Radek and Peter Singer point out in *The Point of View of the Universe*, 221–2. Chapters 8 and 9 of the latter work argue that hedonism is a better theory of well-being than any version of what they call a "desire-based" theory. For their discussion of the experience machine, see 254–61.

[43] A theory of value (not just prudential value) of this sort can be found in Richard Brandt, *A Theory of the Right and the Good*, 1–162. In *The Methods of Ethics*, Sidgwick defines well-being in terms of the satisfaction of ideal desires (111–12), but does not embrace an "ideal desire satisfaction theory" of the sort I have described. Rather, in Book III, chapter 14 he argues that pleasure is the good: this is what desire should ultimately aim at because it is best. (He defines pleasure as a feeling apprehended as desirable; for my discussion, see Chapter 1, section 8.) For him, the desires one would ideally have, from the point of view of one's own well-being, are the ones that maximize states of mind one regards as to be desired. Another "idealized desire" account of well-being is offered by Peter Railton, who writes: "an individual's good consists in what he would want himself to want, or to pursue, were he to contemplate his present situation from a standpoint fully and vividly informed about himself and his circumstances, and entirely free of cognitive error or lapses of instrumental reality." See 'Facts and Values,' in *Facts, Values, and Norms*, 54.

These might include some of his present desires—but only if they would remain his were he to undergo this transformation. We should not accept this conception of well-being, because it retains the problematic feature of the actual-desire-satisfaction conception of well-being we have been discussing. Both the actual-desire and the ideal-desire theory implausibly claim that prior to something's being wanted by someone (whether actually or ideally), it has no features that make it something that he should want to have or want not to have; they claim that it is made good or bad for him only in virtue of being desired (by the actual or ideal self). But, to repeat, such experiences as anguish, boredom, frustration, nausea, and the like are already bad for someone as experiences, apart from one's motivation to avoid them. The ideal self will not want them because experiencing them makes life worse for that individual. One might want to feel them out of self-hatred, but in that case one would not be an ideal self; one's desires would be for the elements of ill-being.

If some readers nonetheless cling to the thesis that well-being consists in the satisfaction of the desires of one's ideal self, they nevertheless will agree with a premise that I will exploit in my discussion of the arguments against experientialism: what is desired for its own sake (and not as a mere means) may be undesirable—it may have no prudential value. These readers recognize that actual desires have objects that might be neutral or negative in value—that is why they hold that it is the satisfaction of the desires of one's ideal self rather than one's current self that constitutes well-being. That common ground is what matters in the arguments to come.

One further point should be acknowledged before we examine the sorts of examples that allegedly make trouble for experientialism. When we ask ourselves what the components of well-being are, certain states of mind that have an introspectable quality strike us immediately as plausible candidates. Consider, for example, the idea that pleasure is one basic element of well-being. It would be odd for someone to resist this idea on the grounds that pleasure is something that we experience. How could something's being part of our inner lives be a reason for *doubting* (rather than affirming) that it partly constitutes the quality of our lives? By contrast, there is nothing odd about wondering whether a non-experiential feature of our lives can qualify as a component of well-being. "That is something he will never be aware of, so how can its occurrence by itself detract from the quality of his life?" is very different from "That is something he is aware of, so how can it enhance or detract from the quality of his life?" The first question immediately seems reasonable, the second unreasonable. The credibility of a proposal that something is a component of well-being is supported by its experiential nature; what we will never mentally encounter lacks that

---

Unlike Sidgwick, Railton offers no general theory about what in fact each individual would ideally want himself to want. Presumably that is because he assumes that this will vary from individual to individual, and cannot be specified in a philosophical essay. So understood, Railton holds that nothing is such that one ought to want it because of its prudential value. Rather, what has prudential value is made such because under certain conditions one would want it. Rawls's conception of well-being in *A Theory of Justice* has, I believe, this same character. See 408–9.

introspective backing, and so its eligibility as an ingredient in a good life is more vulnerable to challenge.

That these non-experiential states are on the surface weaker candidates does not show that they should be rejected without a hearing. What we must do, then, is ask whether there is a strong enough reason to count these candidates as genuine components of well-being, in spite of the fact they are non-experiential. We will see that they fail this test.

19. Nagel on the betrayal of friends

According to Thomas Nagel, "the common remark that what you don't know can't hurt you" ought to be rejected, because:

> . . . it means that even if a man is betrayed by his friends, ridiculed behind his back, and despised by people who treat him politely to his face, none of it can be counted as a misfortune for him so long as he does not suffer as a result. It means that a man is not injured if his wishes are ignored by the executor of his will, or if, after his death, the belief becomes current that all the literary works on which his fame rests were really written by his brother, who died in Mexico at the age of 28.[44]

These, Nagel adds, are "drastic restrictions" on what counts as a misfortune or injury.[45] With a bit of reflection, we can see what you don't know (and will never know) *can* hurt you.

I agree with him that we should reject this adage. Suppose someone I take to be my friend belittles me in a letter he sends to my employer, and as a result I am never promoted to a position that would have enhanced the quality of my life. My well-being is not diminished as a result of this betrayal, but it would have increased had it not been for that letter. In that sense, I have been harmed by what my "friend" has done, even though I have no awareness of what he did or the fact that he deprived me of a good. This sort of example presents no threat to an experiential conception of well-being. Experientialism can say that one is harmed whenever others deprive one of the better experiences one would have had, but for their interference.

Nagel may have something different in mind, however. He might say that I have already been made worse off even before I lose my promotion, in virtue of the very fact that my "friend" wrote and sent that letter. This was an act of betrayal or disloyalty; and that by itself, it might be said, is a mistreatment of me and a misfortune for me. Suppose he wrote and sent that letter to my employer, but it was lost in the mail. A day after writing it, he realizes that the surge of hostility he felt towards me was completely unjustified. Even so, I was betrayed. Nothing bad for me results from that hostile act,

[44] 'Death,' in *Mortal Questions*, 4. Nozick gives similar examples in *The Examined Life*. See Part One of this chapter, note 1. I give an example of the same sort in 'Two Conceptions of Happiness.' There I argue that Aristotle and contemporary subjectivists about well-being disagree about what happiness is—Aristotle, I say, has an "objective" conception. My views about how to bring his theory of well-being into a dialogue with other conceptions have changed over the years.

[45] 'Death,' 4.

but Nagel's idea seems to be that acts of betrayal are misfortunes for those betrayed apart from any ill consequences. It might be said that for a period of time I lost a friend and as a result one component of my well-being (his friendship) was lost to me, without my realizing it.[46] If so, experientialism is false.

Nagel writes: "the natural view is that the discovery of betrayal makes us unhappy because it is bad to be betrayed—not that betrayal is bad because its discovery makes us unhappy."[47] But how should we interpret the statement that "it is bad to be betrayed"? Someone who says this might merely mean that an act's being an act of betrayal is a strike against it. Betrayal, in other words, is a wrong-making feature of an action. Experientialism is not threatened by that way of understanding the badness of betrayal. But it is undermined if the badness of betrayal is taken to mean that the very act of betraying someone counts as a diminution of that individual's level of well-being. Perhaps this is what Nagel has in mind when he says that "it is bad to be betrayed."

If we asked people to consider the possibility that their friends might betray them behind their backs without detection and with no ill consequences (as in the example above—the letter is lost in the mail), most would say that this is something they do not want to happen. From this, we might infer that most people have a standing desire not to be betrayed—even when a betrayal is undetected and inconsequential. So, should such a betrayal occur, a desire they have fails to be satisfied. But if the argument of the preceding section was correct, this does not show that their well-being would be diminished by a friend's betrayal. Ill-being does not consist in the failure of desires to be satisfied.

It is essential, at this point, to recognize that although the effects of being mistreated often diminish the well-being of the person mistreated, that is not always the case. Here are several examples that show that this general rule has exceptions.

You have been nominated for a literary prize, and your work deserves the highest honor. But a member of the awards committee dislikes you and sees to it that the award is given to an inferior writer. You have been treated unfairly. But had you been granted the award, you would have incurred many unpleasant obligations—to attend the award ceremony, to serve on literary committees, to appear on talk shows. No benefits would come to you as a result of receiving the award. You are no worse off for not receiving it—in fact, you are better off.

A company that manufactures dangerous chemicals fails to do all that it is morally and legally obliged to do to protect residents of the neighborhood in which it has its plants. Fortunately, no accidents happen, and no one is harmed. The company wrongs those residents by putting them at risk, but their well-being is not diminished.

Someone breaks into your bank account, appropriates some of your savings, quickly makes a fortune, and then returns what he stole from you. All of this escapes your

---

[46] See Philip Pettit on what he calls the "robust demands of attachment" in *The Robust Demands of the Good*, 11–42. To use his terms, I do not receive "the benefit" of love when a friend does not respond to my situation as a friend ought, or would not respond appropriately in counterfactual situations.

[47] 'Death,' 5.

notice. Your property rights have been violated and so you have been wronged. But you do not lose a penny, and suffer no anxiety. Your well-being is undiminished.

Some forms of mistreatment make their victims worse off and others do not. But if we are not careful, we can fall into a trap that blocks our recognition of this fact. We can easily move from an obvious truth to a false conclusion by a series of small steps, as follows:

A. They ought not to have done that to you.
B. What they did to you ought not to have happened to you.
C. What ought not to happen to you counts as a misfortune for you.
D. A misfortune for you diminishes your well-being.

The "logic" seems impeccable, but if we apply it to any of our examples, we must reach the opposite conclusion from the ones those examples at first seemed to support. The chemical company—to return to our second example—ought to have installed equipment to protect your safety. They put you at risk without your knowledge or consent, and this ought not to have been imposed on you. When what ought not to happen to you does happen, that is your misfortune. And when you suffer a misfortune, that is a reduction in your well-being. So, we must apparently reverse our initial reaction to this example. Even though you suffered no physical injury at the hands of the chemical company, and even though it did not cause you any loss of sleep or worry you in any way, it robbed you, to some degree, of a portion of your well-being. You were living a worse life than you realized.

The better course, I suggest, is to stick to our initial reaction to this example and the others. We can do so by finding something illicit in the movement from one step of the above argument to another. One option is to say that (C) is not entailed by (B). The awards committee ought to have given you the highest honor, but it was no misfortune that it did not. The chemical company ought to have installed equipment to insure your safety, but you suffered no misfortune as a result. The thief ought not to have appropriated your bank account, but caused you no misfortune. Alternatively, we could make a distinction between different types of misfortune. One type occurs whenever what happens to someone ought not to have happened. A second type occurs when someone's well-being is diminished. If we make this distinction, we can say that there is an equivocation in the transition from (C) to (D). It is not important that we decide which of these two options should be chosen. The important point is that both are superior to the view that whenever someone is mistreated, the very fact of mistreatment detracts from the quality of his life, even if there are no ill consequences.

Nagel's view seems at first to have some plausibility because no one wants to be betrayed by his friends, or slighted by an awards committee, or put at risk by a chemical company, or the victim of theft. We don't want these things to be done to us even if being mistreated in these ways does not lead to some harm. When such things happen to us, we can correctly say that "bad things" are being done to us. As a result, we can easily be led by these and similar examples to reject an experientialist conception of well-being. To avoid making that mistake, we must be brought to recognize the implausibility of a desire-satisfaction conception of well-being, and we must realize that when betrayal and other wrongful acts are called "bad," that might merely mean that they are wrongful and ought not to be done. We want our friends not to betray us even when their doing so escapes our detection and has no ill consequences because we do not want to be wronged by them, and we do not want to be wronged by them simply because we ought not to be wronged by them (or anyone else). Even when the betrayal of a friend is no loss of well-being for us, we correctly believe that we ought not to be treated this way, and wish for that reason not to be so treated. Nagel is mistaken, if he holds that every betrayal of a friend or every wrongful act is bad for us in that it is a diminution of our well-being.[48]

I have focused on only one of the examples Nagel uses. He also speaks of someone who is "ridiculed behind his back, despised by people who treat him politely to his face"; someone whose "wishes are ignored by the executor of his will"; and someone whose fame diminishes after his death because it is widely believed that his books were written by his brother "who died in Mexico at the age of 28." These further examples need not be construed as cases of betrayal (except for the executor who ignores the will of the deceased). I take Nagel to be proposing that it is a misfortune to be ridiculed by *anyone*, or despised by *anyone*, even if one is unaware of being the object of these acts and attitudes, and even if they have no ill effects on one's life.

All of these cases—including the posthumous "harms"—can be handled in the same way as that of the betrayal of a friend. All of us believe that we do not deserve to be ridiculed and despised. We also believe that the executor of a will has an obligation to adhere to its terms, and that literary fame properly belongs only to those who have merited it because of their hard work and talent. Since in each case there is a violation of a valid social norm, having to do with desert, obligation, or merit, we can agree that all of them are "bad things," and we can even agree that when these norms are violated that is a "misfortune" for the victim. But we can then add that bad things and misfortunes are not all of the same sort. Some (but not all) bad things and misfortunes are bad and unfortunate simply because they ought not to happen. Other bad things and

---

[48] The posthumous disesteem of friends can be blameless and dreaded nonetheless. Dickens's *Great Expectations* contains a marvelous example. When Pip fears that he is about to be killed by Orlick, he reflects: "Estella's father would believe I had deserted him, would be taken [i.e. apprehended by the police], would die accusing me; even Herbert would doubt me, when he compared the letter I had left for him with the fact that I had called at Miss Havisham's gate for only a moment; Joe and Biddy would never know how sorry I had been that night, none would ever know what I had suffered, how true I had meant to be, what an agony I had passed through. The death close before me was terrible, but far more terrible than death was the dread of being misremembered after death. And so quick were my thoughts, that I saw myself despised by unborn generations,—Estella's children..." (chapter 53). What Pip fears most is the prospect that those he loves will think far worse of him than he deserves. Their estimation of his character would be revised downward, never to rise again; that would be a grave injustice, however faultless. We could take Pip to be assuming that he will be harmed posthumously by these attitudes, but his dread of being disesteemed can also be explained (as I would prefer) as the expression of a deep desire to be loved and admired by these people for its own sake, apart from any difference that makes to his well-being.

misfortunes ought not to happen, but in addition they take something away from the well-being of their victims.[49]

An anti-experientialist might hold that it is not only *undeserved* ridicule and hatred that are prudentially bad and detract from someone's well-being even when that person is unaware of them—*any* ridicule and hatred, it might be thought, are components of ill-being. Of course, ridicule and hatred might be directed at someone not only when he is alive (and thus "behind his back") but after he has died. If these are elements of ill-being, they can continue to accumulate posthumously, and a person's overall ill-being can steadily sink lower and lower through decades and centuries. Correspondingly, well-being can continue to accrue to admired literary or political figures through the ages, as more people in each generation sing their praises or silently register their approval as they read their works or biographies of them. The well-being of Sophocles keeps growing and growing, according to this theory. Similarly, when we rehearse in our minds the villainous deeds of people like Hitler, and heap scorn on them, they sink to ever lower levels of ill-being. If he ought to be punished for his horrible crimes, we all ought to do our part to punish him, by frequently bringing our scorn for him to the center of our attention. These are of course absurd conclusions. But we are inevitably led to them if non-experienced goods and evils are no less prudentially good or evil than their experienced counterparts.

An anti-experientialist can avoid these absurdities by invoking the concept of incommensurable superiority in value—the notion that we discussed in Chapter 1 in connection with McTaggart's oyster (section 6). That version of anti-experientialism would say of posthumous goods and harms, or of non-experiential goods and harms in general, that the experiential sphere of life is incommensurably more important than its non-experiential sphere. That would allow us to say that when others have feelings of hostility to you or are filled with admiration for you, whether you are aware of those attitudes or not, and whether you are alive or not, a certain amount of good or

---

[49] I can now explain my objection to Darwall's definition of well-being (see Chapter 1, note 31). He says: "what it is for something to be good for someone *just is* for it to be something one should desire for him for his sake, that is, insofar as one cares for him" (*Welfare and Rational Care*, 8, his emphasis). Should I desire that my revered teacher be unfairly maligned after he dies? Of course not; I genuinely care for him. That is why I do not want this to happen to him—not for my sake, or anyone else's—but for his sake. Darwall's definition therefore yields the conclusion that if my teacher's reputation is damaged after he dies, that is bad for him—it is a diminution in his welfare or well-being. Whether one should accept his definition therefore depends on whether there are posthumous goods and harms—an issue that needs to be considered on its merits. It would be misguided to reason in the reverse direction, starting with his definition and then, on that basis, inferring that there are posthumous goods and harms. Part of the problem with his definition is that the phrase, "for someone's sake," has a broader use than "for someone's well-being." If you ask me to do a favor for your son, I might do so for your sake—that is, out of a sense of indebtedness, respect, or friendship for you (not in order to increase your well-being). Similarly, I do not want my teacher to be maligned posthumously—not for my sake, but for his; that is, out of respect for and gratitude to him. I should want this not to happen to him for his sake, insofar as I care for him. But if this does befall him, and I am right that there are no posthumous goods and harms, that is not a diminution in his well-being.

bad accrues to you; but that experienced goods are incommensurably better than those of which we are unaware, and experienced ills incommensurably worse.

That would concede that whether something enters, or is prevented from entering, one's conscious life makes an enormous difference to one's well-being. The gap between experientialism and this sort of anti-experientialism would be small. So small, in fact, that trying to resolve the conflict between the two theories would be an idle exercise.

20. *Feeling loved and being loved*

"My truly having close and authentic personal relations is not the kind of thing that can enter my experience." Thus James Griffin.[50] I take him to mean that one has a "close and authentic personal relation" only if one truly loves another and is truly loved in return. Although feeling loved can of course "enter my experience," really being loved cannot. I can have very good reason to believe that another person loves me, but that is because I infer from that person's actions and words that what she is expressing is love. Just as it does not enter the experience of a mathematician or logician that her train of reasoning constitutes a proof—however much she thinks it is a proof—so the love of another person for me (unlike the feeling of being loved) is not something I can detect by introspection. Griffin is presumably also assuming that really being loved is a component of well-being, but that merely feeling loved is either not a component or is far inferior in value. If feeling loved had just as much prudential value as being loved, or nearly as much, it would hardly matter that "having close and authentic personal relations is not the kind of thing that can enter my experience."

We can test this idea by imagining a mother who is afflicted with the kind of emotional coldness that Kant refers to (Chapter 2, section 8). Her misfortunes have robbed her of her capacity to have warm feelings towards others, even towards her own young son. But suppose that, although she feels no love for her child, she is an excellent actress, and she behaves towards him in exactly the manner that a truly loving mother would. Her son feels loved as fully as any child can. That is of course instrumentally valuable for him—assuming, as seems reasonable, that when children feel loved they acquire many psychological assets (self-esteem, confidence, and so on) that they will need as adults. But—and here I depart from Griffin, as I understand him—it also seems plausible to suppose that when a child feels loved, this feeling is a component of his well-being at that time of life. In fact, it is wonderful to feel loved at *any* point in one's life, just as it is wonderful to feel admired or respected. These are among the experiences that enrich human life and lift it immeasurably above the impoverished psychological life of an oyster. If another person loves you but makes you feel unloved, or admires you but makes you feel worthless, you suffer a great misfortune.

An anti-experientialist might nonetheless protest that feeling loved is a genuine prudential good, but only if it results from real love. Or that feeling loved is only a small prudential good if it is not the expression of the real thing. But the previous paragraph's

[50] *Well-Being*, 19.

example of the unloving mother counts against those anti-experientialist claims. This woman has managed to make the inner life of her child everything that it would be had she felt real love for him. It is implausible to suppose that *he* has an impoverished childhood simply because of a deficit in *her* mental life. Matters would be quite different, of course, if our discussion of the experience machine had arrived at the conclusion that life inside the machine is inferior to life outside it. But this was not our conclusion. We should also recall the example of the lecturer whose audience has no idea what he is talking about, but, out of kindness, makes him feel understood. He at least has a good experience, and is better off than a lecturer who has to suffer through the blank or hostile gazes of an uncomprehending audience (section 7).

The anti-experientialist must say that the son of the unloving mother in our example receives less good from her than truly loved children receive from their parents because that son's feeling of being loved has the wrong sort of cause. The cause is not real love but a sense of duty and an ability to create an experience indistinguishable from love. But what it is like for the son to feel loved is not affected by facts about what causes him to feel that way. How good an experience is for us, not as a means to something further, but in itself, is not diminished because it has a non-standard causal history. Its prudential value as an experience lies entirely in the phenomenology of the experience. That is what we should learn from Nozick's thought experiment.

We can embroider the example of the unloving mother by supposing, further, that there are times when she has strongly negative feelings towards her son. (He is such a burden; caring for him prevents her from pursuing her other interests, and so on.) But when she is in his presence, she is always able to put these feelings of hostility aside, and her sense of duty prevails, so that there is no diminution in his sense that he is loved. It would be implausible to suppose that the very existence of those negative feelings by itself constitutes a diminution of his well-being. His psychological development is not impeded by her occasional feelings of resentment, and his experience of childhood as it is lived is not affected.

The mother in this example is less than an ideal mother, but we do not blame her because her lapses from the ideal are (by hypothesis) excusable. By contrast, in the sorts of examples used by Nagel and others (your friends are snickering about you behind your back), we tacitly assume that the hostile and hidden feelings in question are culpable. Your friends should not snicker at you behind your back, and you would not wish them to do so. But there is no reason to suppose that, because the mother in our example is not to be blamed, whereas the snickering friends *are* to be blamed, the two sorts of case should be treated differently when we ask whether someone's well-being is affected by the hidden attitudes of others.

Philosophers who believe that it is in itself bad for you to be the object of the hostile feelings of friends, family, and lovers may have this picture in mind: How intimate members of your circle treat you and feel about you is part of "the story of your life." That narrative includes your social milieu, not just your thoughts and actions in isolation from others. Your life story, or this portion of it, is not going as well as you suppose, if within your intimate social circle you are the object of hostile attitudes, even though you are unaware of them and they have no ill effects on you. Since your life is not going as well for you as you think it is, *you* are not faring as well as you suppose. Alternatively, it might be said that although *you* are faring as well as you suppose, *the story of your life* is not as good as you think it is.[51]

What we should say instead is that some parts of the story of a life are a record of that individual's well-being and other parts are not. Returning to the unloved son of the dutiful mother: it is part of the story of his life that his mother did not love him but only acted as though she did. No full narrative about his childhood could omit that fact. But, as we have seen, his well-being was not affected by her hidden feelings. A life story can have a regrettable element without the individual whose story it is suffering a loss of well-being. There is no real paradox here. If the son discovers, after his mother dies, that she did not love him, but made him feel loved, he will wish that a different story of his life had been true. He will do so for his mother's sake—she was the one who suffered, not he. We want our life stories to go a certain way partly for our own good, but only partly. We do not want to be wronged even when that does us no harm. And we want others not to be forced, from a sense of duty, to put on a show of love when that is not what they feel.

21. Opus posthumous

Simon Keller proposes the following example as evidence that good can befall someone after he dies:

Imagine someone who spends his life trying to get a book published. He works hard at writing the book and marketing it to publishers, and if you ask him what he wants in life, he says that more than anything he wants to be a published author. His goal is self-directed; he wants to publish the book because he wants his life to include the writing of a published book. His goal does not change over time; even when his death is imminent, he works as hard as ever to get the book published, undeterred by his knowledge that the book will not appear during his lifetime. And his book, imagine, is published after his death, in just the way he wants.[52]

---

[51] Shelly Kagan argues that prudential value is two things: how *you* are faring (what he calls your "well-being") and how *your life* is going (what he calls the "quality of your life"); furthermore, he holds that these may come apart. See 'Me and My Life.' If the conception of well-being I defend here is correct, there is no reason to bifurcate prudential value in this way.

[52] 'Posthumous Harm,' in Steven Luper (ed.), *The Cambridge Companion to Life and Death*, 181–97. The passage cited is on page 190. See too John Broome, *Weighing Lives*: "…Perhaps it adds to the goodness of a person's life if she completes a book she is working on, rather than leaving it uncompleted at her death…. There is backwards causation of wellbeing" (46). For a contrary view, see Ben Bradley, *Well-Being and Death*. He writes: "If you are planning to write a great novel just so you can defeat death, you will be doing it for a bad reason…. Some people would say that just completing the novel is intrinsically good for you. Those people are wrong" (180). Bradley's book rejects the possibility of posthumous harm. "It is impossible to harm someone after she has died" (177–8)—and, he might have added, impossible to benefit her.

Keller adds: "by virtue of the posthumous event, the story of the man's life becomes a story of fruitful effort, of achievement, of work that pays off."[53] He is certainly right that when the author's book is published, the project to which he devoted his life has succeeded. But Keller is trying to arrive at a stronger conclusion than that. He believes that it is good for the author he describes in this passage that his work is published after he dies. His life has gone better for him because of what has been done after his death. If we are keeping track of the total amount of prudential value that accrues to him over time, we ought to add to the good that he had while he was alive the further good he had after his death.

Keller takes it for granted that "the story of the man's life" has as one of its components the completion of his project after his death. This is a contentious use of the phrase "the story of someone's life." It might be said that the story of our lives includes only events that occur while we are alive. It is a fact about Sophocles' plays that they are still read and performed, but it is not a fact that forms part of his biography, which tells a story that comes to a close at his death, when his *bios* is over. There is of course a story to be told about the posthumous *reception* of Sophocles' plays, and similarly there is a story to be told about what becomes of the manuscript left behind by Keller's imagined author. But is that a part of "the story of the man's life"? I believe it is not. But I will set this verbal question aside. The truth or falsity of experientialism should not rest on it.

Keller says nothing about whether the book in question is a *good* book, or whether anyone will read it, or think well of it. He is right to omit these details, because if he had done so, that would have altered the issue before us. If the book in question is a good book, it is worthwhile for other people to read it. But we want to know what the publication of the book has to do with the *author's* well-being, not its effect on the lives of others. So let's assume that it is mere publication that this particular author has made his lifelong goal—a goal that is achieved even if the book is a bad one, or even if no one reads it, or even if all copies of it are destroyed before anyone has a chance to read it. (We will consider the posthumous publication of a book that does then find an audience, after we have discussed the present case, in which there is publication but no readership.)

We can achieve greater clarity about the force of Keller's example if we ask whether we would invest our resources in the completion of the author's project after he dies. Suppose you have a large sum of money at your disposal, but you are permitted to use it in only one of two ways. First, you can have the author's manuscript published, knowing that no one will ever read it. Second, you can pay for an operation that will cure someone's disease, thus insuring that the suffering he feels will permanently disappear. Both the author and the individual who needs an operation are complete strangers to you. It is obvious that you should choose the second of these options.

Now suppose that your options are somewhat different. Again, you can use the money at your disposal to cure a disease and thereby relieve someone of suffering. Alternatively, you can publish the books of one hundred authors each of whom is in the same situation

---

[53] 'Posthumous Harm,' 191.

as the man in Keller's example. Even if publishing one of their books does only a little good for the author, publishing all of them will do one hundred times as much; and we can make this number as high as we like. Even so, it remains the case that you ought to use your money to help alleviate suffering. No one will read any of the one hundred books that will be published. If you choose that option, you will have done no good.

Recall Keller's statement that "by virtue of the posthumous event, the story of the man's life becomes a story of fruitful effort, of achievement, of work that pays off." All of these phrases are open to question. Was it a fruitful effort, or an achievement, or work that pays off, if no one reads the book?

Evidently the force of Keller's example is diminished by the assumption that no one reads the author's publication. So, let's now consider a case in which an author has devoted his life not merely to the completion and publication of a manuscript, but to the further goal of reaching a wide audience of readers. He completes his work before he dies, but he has made no arrangements for its publication. If you then see to it that his work is published, and it does find a readership, then the phrases Keller uses will be apt: "by virtue of the posthumous event, the story of the man's life becomes a story of fruitful effort, of achievement, of work that pays off." We can now say that by arranging for the publication of his book, you have made it the case that the author made good use of his life. His life has gone well, by virtue of something that has occurred after he dies.

But this version of Keller's example should not convince us that there are posthumous prudential goods. We can agree that when the book in question falls into the hands of others who benefit from it, then it becomes the case that the author "made good use of his life." But that is because he used it to benefit others. It does not follow that *he* benefits as well as his audience, when they read his work. We can also agree that "his life has gone well"—because he devoted it to the service of others, and they really did benefit as a result of his efforts. One way for someone's life to go well is for it to go in such a way that it produces good things for others. It then goes well for them. Another way for a life to go well is for some of the components of well-being to accrue to the individual whose life it is. It then goes well for him. One should want one's life to go well in both ways. But if it goes well in the first way, that is not by itself a reason to suppose that it also goes well in the second.

Suppose writing this manuscript was an entirely hellish experience for our author. If it is published after his death, and becomes a work of great value to others, he did not suffer in vain. His labors did after all pay off—for others, not for him. However, if his work is published but finds no audience, its appearance in book form does not redeem his suffering or make it the case that on balance his literary efforts outweighed the badness of his misery. Even if what he fervently desired was mere publication (not a readership) and he devoted himself to this goal, its achievement does him no good, for, as we have seen (section 18), the realization of someone's desires, goals, or aspirations is not what well-being consists in, partly or wholly.

Finally, let us consider one further variation on the theme of the posthumous career of a literary work and its bearing on the well-being of its author. If a book brings an author great fame and admiration after she dies, is that posthumous success something that should figure positively in our assessment of her overall well-being over time? Conversely, if a book is widely read but is an object of scorn and condemnation (think of Hitler's *Mein Kampf*, for example), should that figure negatively? The good or bad posthumous reputation of a work and its author can continue for centuries, and so, if they figure in the overall assessment of well-being over time, they will, over the course of centuries, become the most important component of that assessment. How much prudential value accrues to an author over time will depend largely not on her experience of life when she was alive, but on her posthumous reputation, because her experiential life is short in comparison with the duration of her fame. It would be worth it, from the point of view of one's own well-being, to endure depression and other forms of mental anguish, if one will be posthumously praised and admired for centuries. Imagine a father who brings up his daughter with that kind of career in mind. He knows how greatly she will suffer, but she clearly has great talent, and posthumous admiration is a likely prospect. Is he acting as he should to promote her well-being, when this is the kind of life he arranges for her? Clearly he is not. He is sacrificing her on the altar of literary achievement and fame.

If there are posthumous goods and evils, their potential longevity must enter the plans we make for our lives and the lives of those we care for. The experiential components of well-being last only so long, and those that are non-experiential have no such limitation. That conception of well-being would require us to attend not only to our brief future as it is lived but also to the prospect that we might become the objects of other people's thoughts long after we die. Our perspective would be analogous, in this respect, to that of a religious believer who takes our embodied existence to be a brief episode in the eternal career of the soul. But traditional religious believers are experientialists; they hope we will have the greatest experience of all after we die, when we will be eternally unified with the divine source of our being. By contrast, the literary artist who foregoes the riches of ordinary human experience in the pursuit of the posthumous literary fame that comes with aesthetic excellence might bring great joy to others, if her art is appreciated, but, unless I am mistaken, nothing is added to her well-being after her death. Belief in posthumous well-being can do great damage, if there is no such thing.

22. Aristotle on posthumous benefits and harms

In saying that after one dies, no further benefits or harms accrue to one, I bring myself into disagreement with Aristotle, but I am glad to say that our differences are very slight. He says:

If anything good or bad does actually affect them, it will be pretty unimportant and insignificant, either in itself or in relation to them; or if not it must at least be of such an extent and kind as not to make happy those who are not happy already nor to deprive those who are happy of their being blessed. So when friends do well, and likewise when they do badly, it does seem to have some effect on the dead. But it is of such a nature and degree as neither to make not happy those who are happy, nor anything like that.   (*NE* I.11 1101b1–9)

With these words, Aristotle clings to an observation he made in the preceding chapter: "Both good and evil are thought to happen to a dead person, since they can happen to a person who is alive but is not aware of them. Take, for example, honours and dishonours, and the good and bad fortunes of his children and of his descendants generally" (I.10 1100a18–21). He adds that to deny this "seems excessively heartless and contrary to what people think" (I.11 1101a22–4). This commits him to saying that if your children fare well *when you are alive*, that counts as a small good for you as well (whether you ever learn of this or not). So, his idea is not that benefits accrue to us posthumously in virtue of the completion of projects we left unfinished while alive. It is rather a doctrine of *vicarious* benefits and harms. Some small proportion of the good or harm that accrues to one's children accrues to oneself as well, just because they are one's children.

Aristotle does not offer a persuasive defense of this doctrine. His argument above is that (A) it would be "excessively heartless" to deny this, and (B) this is "what people think." These points count for little or nothing, individually and jointly. Furthermore, notice this difficulty for his thesis that good accrues to us when we are dead in virtue of the good that accrues to our children: When someone is dead, we can make true statements about what he once desired, but any attribution of a desire to someone who has died is false. The dead once wanted things, but they no longer do so. So, after you die, the good fortune of your children satisfies a desire you used to have, but no longer have. There is no plausibility in the idea that if what you once desired to be the case really is the case, that is good for you. Aristotle is presumably not relying on that idea, but is instead assuming that some portion of one's well-being is constituted by the well-being of one's children, regardless of one's desires.

The more important point, however, is that the disagreement between Aristotle and me regarding posthumous goods is small. For he is at pains to keep his acceptance of posthumous good and harm within limits: even if good and harm can befall us after we die, their degree of goodness and badness is such that the overall quality of the lives we have lived cannot be transformed from good to bad or bad to good. If the goods we possess make it the case that we have been *eudaimon* up to the point of death—if we have lived well throughout our lives—then any harms that accrue to our children after death, however large, cannot make it the case that we were not *eudaimon* after all. And that, Aristotle says, is because of the comparative smallness of the harms that can occur to us after we have died.

Here we have something very similar to the point I made about the relative importance of experiential and non-experiential goods (section 19). I believe that the goods that constitute a good life for a human being are all experiential, but if someone demurs, we have only a minor difference of opinion, so long as it is accepted that non-experiential goods are in some way second-rate. They might be second-rate in this way: if the experiential goods and harms in your life are such that it is on balance a good life (well worth living), then whatever non-experiential harms accrue to you, however large and however long they last, it will remain the case that your life is on balance a good life. The experiential sphere of life, in other words, is incommensurably more important than its non-experiential aspects.

23. Aristotle on honor

Just as Aristotle comes close to the truth about posthumous goods, but needs correction, so too with respect to honor (*timê*). This good, as he conceives it, is a public bestowal of recognition, and often takes a political form. If one is chosen by one's city, for example, to serve as a general in the army, then one is the recipient of a great honor. To be honored is to receive the gift of high public repute. It is, in this respect, rather different from the private phenomena that contemporary authors typically discuss when they put experientialism about well-being to the test by considering private acts of disrespect, contempt, or betrayal—acts performed by colleagues, friends, and lovers that express hostility or violate norms governing human relationships. The question these authors raise, as we have seen, is whether these hostile acts in themselves constitute a harm—a diminishment, to some degree, in the level of well-being of those who are the object of their disrespect, contempt, or disloyalty. Even if the individuals at the receiving end of these attitudes never detect them, and even if those attitudes have no further consequences, does the very existence of those attitudes by itself constitute a diminution in their level of well-being?

But in spite of the differences between honor as Aristotle conceives it and the private disrespect that typically figures in examples used by recent authors, it is not far-fetched to find a connection between them. In both cases, the question is whether a phenomenon that is in an important respect external to an individual can on its own increase or decrease that individual's level of well-being. Aristotle wants to show that honor, which he counts as an external good, is in some way a lower-order value, and therefore not as important as many wealthy and elite citizens (attracted to the political life) assume.

Honor, he says, "seems too shallow to be an object of our inquiry, since honour seems to depend more on those who honour than on the person honoured, whereas we surmise the good to be something of one's own that cannot easily be taken away" (*NE* I.5 1095b23–6). Later he adds that goods of the soul (not external goods like honor, or goods of the body like health) "are the ones we call most strictly and especially good" (I.8 1098b14–15). Although he does not explicitly say that one can be the recipient of an honor without ever realizing it, surely a public memorial to a great figure of the distant past and no longer alive would count as an honor. So, there is a common element in his treatment of this external good and my discussion of contempt and disloyalty when they never reach the consciousness and have no effect on the mistreated individual. I would say, following him, that these attitudes of others are "too shallow to be an object of our inquiry" (too shallow to be components of well-being), because they are external to the consciousness of the dishonored individual.

I believe that these parallels to Aristotle's dishonor (our disrespect, contempt, disloyalty) are not in themselves bad things—not harms, not bad for the individual at their receiving end, not diminutions of his well-being. By contrast, Aristotle never denies and seems to feel no temptation to deny that honor is in itself a good thing (for the honored individual), and therefore that dishonor is in itself bad (for the dishonored individual). He calls it shallow and denies that it is good "most strictly" or "especially." That creates a difficulty that he does not address. Suppose someone receives honor from many people and for a very long period of time. Since the quantity of honor he receives is great, it matters little that honor is not the greatest prudential good, and not itself the ultimate end of human life. A sufficiently large quantity of honor should compensate for its failure to be the most valuable prudential good. Aristotle could solve the problem by emphasizing his claim that it is not good "most strictly"—meaning, by this, that strictly speaking it is not in itself a prudential good. (It would then be trivially true that it is not "especially" good.) Were he to do so, his position would the same as the one I have defended: our standing in the eyes of others is not by itself something that makes us better or worse off.

There is another way in which Aristotle could solve the problem I have raised for him, and it parallels the solution I offered him in my discussion in the previous section, of posthumous goods and harms. He wants to say that good and harm can befall us after we die, but he also needs to keep their degree of goodness and badness within limits. Similarly, he counts honor and dishonor as in themselves prudentially good and bad, but he needs to limit their value and disvalue. He could do so by employing the concept of incommensurable superiority. Honor, Aristotle can say, is good, but because it is not a good of the soul, its prudential value is immeasurably inferior to the value of the ones that constitute our inner lives.

24. Aristotle's god and the sense of control

One further feature of Aristotle's ethics has some bearing on the issues we have been discussing. I referred to it above when I noted that he takes the best life in the universe to be not that of a human being but that of the unmoved mover, who engages in no social interaction, is incorporeal, and is not an efficient causal agent (sections 2 and 13). This supreme being endlessly and uninterruptedly lives a rich life of the mind, filled with the joys of scientific understanding. There are cognitive, hedonic, and aesthetic dimensions to its experience, as it immensely enjoys contemplating the remarkable order of the universe. Aristotle's god has no ethical virtues, no friends, and no body, but it has no need of these goods and does not suffer from their absence. These are, for Aristotle, important features of human life because of our sociability and embodiment, but we humans do not have the best possible mental powers or the best possible internal life.[54]

Aristotle may be right that human life even in the most favorable circumstances is not the best kind of life there is or can be. Perhaps elsewhere in the universe there are forms of existence richer in prudential value than our own. But it is not easy to agree with him that god's life, as he conceives it, is better than even the best life available to human beings. We can set aside one advantage he believes the unmoved mover has over us: the good it has is possessed eternally, whereas our well-being comes to an end when we die (with the slight exception of posthumous goods). *That* difference is not the only one that leads Aristotle to his conclusion that divine life is better than human life. Rather, he takes divine life to be superior simply because it contains nothing but the best good (contemplation), and we have less of that good because we do not have it at every moment of our existence. We may reasonably doubt that contemplation is in fact the best good. Even if it is best, the absence of all other goods from god's life might make it a worse life than ours, all things considered. We can contemplate and do many other wonderful things, whereas god can only contemplate; its one greater asset (conceding, for the sake of argument, that it is greater) might not be so much better than ours that it outweighs the absence of the many wonderful goods we have but it lacks.

Even if we reject this part of Aristotle's theory of well-being, we should acknowledge that there is something to be said in favor of one of his arguments. This is his claim that if one life is more self-sufficient than another, that is a point in its favor. One can contemplate, he points out, even when one is by oneself. By contrast, one cannot perform the acts typical of a good person on one's own—one needs others, either as collaborators or beneficiaries (*NE* X.7 1177a30–1177b1, X.8 1178a28–33). There is a good point to be made here: if two prospective ways of life differ in that one is less likely to be sustainable over time, because it is more dependent on factors beyond one's control, that is a point in favor of the more self-sufficient way of life. If they are equal in value, one should choose the one that is more self-sufficient. If one is superior in value, its greater self-sufficiency is a further point in its favor.

There is a related point that could be made here, although it goes beyond what Aristotle says in his discussion of the contemplative life. One way to experience one's life is to have a high degree of confidence that one's well-being is a matter that is in one's hands—both because of what it consists in and because of the instruments it needs. If the things we take to be good are experienced as fragile, fleeting, easily taken from us, our inner lives are burdened with a sense of unease. If, on the other hand, we can assure ourselves not only that we are living well, but that little or nothing outside ourselves can ever undermine or detract from our good, our experience of life is all the better. Of course, it is better to have *justified* confidence that our well-being will continue than

---

[54] See *NE* X.7–8 for a series of arguments for the superiority of the philosophical-contemplative life to the ethical-political life. For Aristotle's conception of the unmoved mover, see *Metaphysics* XII.6–10.

to have a false sense of confidence; for there is great *instrumental* value in having a realistic view about what the future is likely to bring, and about the steps one must take to make the future more secure.

Suppose someone does not realize that the means he needs to live well could easily be taken from him, but, in fact, he is lucky, and those means remain available throughout his life. He has a firm sense of control, but is not really in control. Is his life less good for him because of this? Not at all. He is lucky that he continues to have a good life, but his life is no less good simply because he is more vulnerable than he realizes. By contrast, consider someone who is filled with anxiety about what he takes to be the fragility of the goods he enjoys, but whose anxiety is ill founded and imprudent, because in fact no one and nothing can take those goods from him, and there is no reason for him to think otherwise. That individual's life certainly *is* made less good than it otherwise would be, because his experience of it is marred by his sense of uncertainty.

There is a difficulty here for the anti-experientialist who says that if you believe that someone admires you, but he does not, the quality of your life *is* diminished, in spite of your feeling admired. We want it to be the case that the prudential goods we have are under our control—it is not merely the feeling of control that we want. Similarly, we want to be admired, and not merely to feel admired. The anti-experientialist claims that well-being is diminished if we merely feel but in fact are not admired. But, the well-being of someone who has a sense of control that is not backed by reality is not diminished by that error. Why should there be this difference between the two cases?

Thus far, experientialism has, I think, responded successfully to the challenges it faces. But there is another sort of argument that can be given against it: it is thought by some that the upward or downward direction of well-being over the course of a life partly adds to or detracts from it, even apart from its effect on one's experience. If that is correct, then even if all the constituent parts of well-being are experiential, their arrangement (and not just our experience of their arrangement) is a feature of a life that must be included in any assessment of its overall lifetime quality. That will not be our main concern in the next chapter—our principal task will be to find the best response to McTaggart's thesis. We will see, however, that the relation between well-being and time is many problems, not just one. Whether pattern (an upwards or downwards trend) *by itself* matters—and as a result we should not simply add together the good times and subtract the bad—is one of them (Chapter 4, sections 5, 8, and 10–12). Having addressed that issue, our discussion of experientialism will be complete.

4

Well-Being and Time

We turn now to the way in which well-being is affected by time. Plato and Aristotle connect these themes. For Plato, *eternal* possession of the good is best. For Aristotle, *eudaimonia* consists in rational activity over the course of a "compete life." Plato's thesis can be challenged—as we will see, the Stoics and Plotinus do not accept it—and Aristotle's notion of a life's completeness is obscure. Their ideas will therefore need our attention. But for the most part this chapter will be devoted to McTaggart's thesis and my favored alternative to it. We will need to consider whether goods diminish in value over time, whether all times of a life have equal importance, and whether the temporal shape of a life (its narrative arc) should enter into our assessment of its quality. My treatment of these issues has profited enormously from the work of Pierre Hadot, Tom Hurka, Dennis McKerlie, Jeff McMahan, Thomas Nagel, Derek Parfit, Michael Slote, Larry Temkin, and David Velleman. All of them will figure in the discussion to come.

In Part One of this chapter, I return to McTaggart's thesis and several ways of resisting it. Part Two begins with a question posed by Velleman: "Is a good life just a string of good years?" My discussion of this and related questions will bring us back to a final consideration of McTaggart's oyster. We will then turn to Aristotle's claim that *eudaimonia* requires a "complete life." That might be thought incompatible with a thesis I defend: that a good life overall is an aggregate of the quality of life over briefer periods. But we will see how little distance there is between Aristotle and me on this issue.

Part One

1. Do goods lose their goodness over time?

Let us turn back to McTaggart's thesis that an oyster's life of simple pleasure, if long enough, is superior to the best possible human life of normal duration. If we are to reject it, we ought not to say merely that we disagree. We should also offer some diagnosis of his mistake—citing some error of omission or commission that he makes, and that we avoid when we deny his thesis. Our task is to take apart his reasoning and identify the deficiency in the oyster that cannot be overcome by its longevity.

Four possible strategies will be examined. (I list them here in an order different from that of Chapter 1, section 5.) First, perhaps at a certain point in time the oyster's pleasures lose all value; it continues to feel pleasure beyond that time, but pleasure is no longer good for it. The second possibility is a variation on the first: the oyster's pleasures have diminishing value over time, never sinking to zero, but ever approaching a limit, never reaching or exceeding it. Third, perhaps the oyster's well-being does not extend beyond the present moment because it has no conception of time and cannot want future pleasure. Fourth, the pleasures available to the oyster belong to a lower order of value; human goods are incommensurably superior. We will consider the first two alternatives immediately. Discussion of the third will be postponed to section 14. The fourth is the one I favor. I will elaborate on it and defend it as we proceed. Once we understand it better, it will appear inherently plausible, far more so than its competitors. If we hold firm in our confidence that McTaggart's thesis must be wrong, then recognizing the implausibility of the first three strategies will not serve a merely negative purpose. It will be one part of the argument in favor of the fourth approach that it provides a more satisfactory diagnosis of where McTaggart's error lies.

The first strategy is not one that anyone has ever adopted, so far as I know. Perhaps, then, it is the least promising alternative. But we should not dismiss it without a hearing. It is, after all, very similar to the second alternative, and so it is worth asking which is better and why. The idea is that once you (or any other creature) have had a good—*any* good—for a certain period of time, having it for an additional period of time is less good, and at some point no good at all. So, the oyster's pleasure is good for it for a few hours or days, but beyond that it ceases to be good (even though the pleasure itself, by hypothesis, endures). It is not as though the oyster gets bored, and the food it once enjoyed is no longer appealing. Rather, this is a thesis of a priori axiology: each good comes, as it were, with a shelf life, beyond which its goodness diminishes, and eventually reaches zero.

It is certainly true that certain human activities or products decline in quality because they do not end when they should. A novel may have characters and situations that require two hundred pages for their artful development and elaboration, but the author's decision to devote four hundred pages to them may undermine the success of his work. Similarly, a pleasant meal with friends would be ruined if it continued for too many hours. Some philosophers think that human life is like this: it too needs a narrative structure in order to be well-lived, and so it is better, on balance, that we die than that we live forever. Accepting these examples would naturally lead to the idea that an oyster's pleasures, being always the same, are good for just a few minutes or hours. (Narrative structure will be discussed in sections 11–13.)

But we would be moving too fast if we extrapolated from the easy cases (about good novels and good dinners) to the more difficult ones (about death and pleasure). A good novel is a work of significant length and narrative heft (longer and more complex than a novella); it has a beginning, middle, and (if the author has completed it) an end. How these cohere counts towards its artistic success. That is why an author can be faulted for not knowing when or how his work should end. But we would beg the question if we simply assumed that a good life must have not only a beginning but also a middle that leads at some point to a final stage. The most successful novels have a satisfying end, but it doesn't follow that our lives would be worse were they everlasting.

On what grounds could it be argued that it is best for each of us, all things considered, that we die at some point in the future? Let's assume that we could remain in good mental and physical health forever; the aging process would cease and there would be no loss of vigor or competence. (The world would have in it plenty of resources to provide for our children, and their children, and so on.) Would we eventually become bored with life? So some say.[1] Another possible drawback is that without any limits on the time available to us, making choices between different ways of life would become arbitrary. We could have them all, in the fullness of time, and so we would lose the feeling of urgency that now accompanies such decisions. It would not matter to us what we do, because it is guaranteed that the opportunities we give up now will be available later.[2]

But suppose, *per impossibile*, that neither of these alleged psychological consequences of infinite life would in fact occur. Nothing in our experience of life would go sour over time. In that case, there is no doubt that we would be much better off living forever rather than for a limited period of time. (I return to this point in section 21.) When we worry that in living forever we would at some point no longer have a good thing, our worries presuppose that it is the experiential component of existence that matters for well-being—this is what we fear would deteriorate in quality. That shows how natural and plausible it is to assume that well-being is constituted by the quality of one's conscious existence.

One difficulty with the idea that the goodness of the same kind of pleasure diminishes over time is that it is inherently arbitrary to say when that diminution occurs. Several paragraphs ago, I considered the possibility that an oyster's pleasures, being always the same, are good for just a few hours or days. But which is it: a few hours or a few days? Or why not say that an oyster's life loses all value in just a few minutes? (Would it be ten minutes? Twenty?) The problem is not that there is a small gray area, as there is whenever a concept lacks precise boundaries; rather, in this case, the gray area is almost entirely all-encompassing. If we think that a pleasure loses its value simply because it goes on being pleasant for too long, we will be unable to find any basis for saying, of any pleasure beyond the shortest possible, that it remains good or loses the goodness it once had.

There is a further, related difficulty for the idea that the goodness of having the same kind of pleasure diminishes over time: when applied to particular cases, it gives the wrong advice. Suppose I must choose between enjoying a half-hour back rub seven days a week and enjoying a half-hour back rub one day a week. Assume as well that the price of the two alternatives is the same, and that if I choose the one-day-a-week

---

[1] So Bernard Williams argued in 'The Makropulos Case: Reflections on the Tedium of Immortality,' in *Problems of the Self*; see too Shelly Kagan, *Death*, 234–46.

[2] Samuel Scheffler, *Death and the Afterlife*, 98–9.

option, that does not give me additional time to pursue any other activity. It seems obvious that, in these circumstances, I have a good reason to prefer the seven-day-a-week option to the one-day-a-week option, and no reason to prefer the opposite ordering. Keep in mind that by hypothesis I will enjoy the back rub as much each subsequent day as I did on the first. It would be irrational to choose the less frequent over the more frequent pleasure. But someone who thinks that the value of a pleasure diminishes when one keeps having the same kind of pleasure is not entitled to any confidence that this is so. Such a person has no basis for rejecting the hypothesis that the pleasure of a back rub is good for only half an hour a week.

Since this strikes me as obvious, I must agree with McTaggart that the longer an oyster enjoys a pleasant form of consciousness, the better its life is. It is his claim that a long enough oyster life would be better than a well-lived human life of normal length that I reject.

2. Does well-being have a diminishing marginal value?

Suppose we make a slight modification in the proposal that over time what is good for us is less and less good, eventually losing its goodness *entirely*. According to this modified proposal, what has prudential value at one time has less the next time, and so on indefinitely. (We can set aside for now the question how long these units of time are.) Once this process of diminution begins, then at each later time there is less value, but it never gives out—it is always some fraction of an earlier value. This is the application of a familiar arithmetical point: the aggregation of an infinite series approaches but never reaches a limit if each additional element is sufficiently smaller than the last. When the first member of a series is one, the second one half, the third one half of that, and so on, no matter how long the series is continued, some smaller amount is always available to be added, and the sum approaches two as a limit. When we apply this idea to the question of how good a life an oyster can have, if it is sufficiently long-lived, we obtain the result that there can be a low limit to the quality of its life, however long it lives. It keeps getting better, but by less and less.[3] If that is the correct way to look at things, there is no need to accept the thesis that some kinds of goods are incommensurably superior to others.

Before we examine this proposal, we should make sure that there is no misunderstanding of the idea that a longer period of well-being is better than a shorter period. A loose way of expressing that idea would be to say that well-being grows or increases over time. But if we want to speak of well-being in this way, we had better make sure that we are not misunderstood. Well-being does not grow or increase in time in the same way that the size of a bank account increases over time, as money continues to be added to it. If you have $1,000 in your account, and add $100 each day, then with each

---

[3] Temkin says: "We don't believe there would be a *significant* difference between the goodness of an oyster-like life that lasted 100 years, or 1,000 years, or 10,000 years…" *Rethinking the Good*, 121, author's emphasis. On the next page, he indicates that this judgment rejects "additive aggregation." The oyster's life at some point gets better by less and less.

new deposit, you retain everything you had before, and you add something else to it, yielding a greater sum. It would be absurd to suppose that when someone retains the components of well-being over time, his well-being inevitably increases, just as a bank account increases with each new deposit.[4] If well-being consists in X and Y, and someone retains both X and Y, at the same level, over time, then at each later time his well-being is no greater than it was at earlier times. If we want to say that his well-being increases over time, that must be taken simply as a way of expressing the idea that the amount of time in which he possesses the elements of well-being continues to increase, and that it is better for well-being to last a longer than a shorter time.

We can now turn to the suggestion that the elements of well-being—some or all of them—progressively lose their prudential value over time, although that value never sinks to zero. The thesis in question is not that we know a priori that the components of well-being, whatever they happen to be, are (some or all of them) available to us in smaller and smaller amounts. For example, it does not claim that every kind of pleasure (assuming, for the sake of illustration, that it is a part of well-being) is felt to a smaller and smaller degree, as time passes. Rather, to stick with this example, it holds that even if a pleasure continues to be felt to the same degree, it becomes less and less good for an individual to feel it (without ever becoming no good at all). That is purportedly why McTaggart's oyster has very little well-being over the course of its incredibly long life.

Suppose we interpret this thesis in the following way: it is not a claim about this or that component of well-being, but a more abstract claim that holds that *whatever* well-being consists in, it is less and less good for an individual to go on living; and, to be more precise, the goodness of a life for an individual keeps diminishing by halves. You've been faring well already—and since you've "been there, done that," it is not nearly so good for you to go on faring well. So construed, the thesis in question is too implausible to be taken seriously.

That, I believe, is an important point to bear in mind. It is not the case that prudential value *must* diminish over time. The fact that the valuable thing you now have in your life (namely, well-being) is something you've had before is no reason, in itself, to conclude that it will be less valuable for you to continue to have it. The point applies to any component of well-being: it could be something that will be just as good to have in the future.

The idea that *some* things have "diminishing marginal value" is of course widely accepted, and for good reason. Money is a good example: if someone has only one thousand dollars to his name, adding ten thousand dollars to his bank account gives him the opportunity to greatly increase his well-being; but if ten thousand dollars is added to the account of a billionaire, it has almost no value for him. How much a fixed

---

[4] Plotinus makes this point in *Ennead* I.5, which bears the title, 'On Whether Happiness Increases with Time.' The contrast between the accumulation of money in a bank account and an increase in well-being over time is made by Eyjólfur K. Emilsson, 'On the Length of a Good Life,' 128, in Steven Luper (ed.), *The Cambridge Companion to Life and Death.*

sum of money can enhance someone's life depends on how much is already possessed by the individual who receives it.[5] The important question, for our purposes, is whether the same point applies not only to instrumental means but also to the components of well-being as one continues to possess them over time.

Some philosophers say that the same point *might* apply. Here is what Gustaf Arrhenius and Wlodek Rabinowicz write: "the marginal contributive value of adding one unit of pleasure to a whole consisting of five units of pleasure doesn't have to be the same as the marginal value of adding one unit to a whole consisting of ten units of pleasure."[6] They do not claim that the marginal value *is* less—only that it *could be*. But I want to ask: what grounds could there be for thinking that it *is* less? After all, we have seen the implausibility of the idea that well-being itself becomes less good for you in the future simply because you've had it in the past. It would, in other words, be wrong to say of well-being what Arrhenius and Rabinowicz say of pleasure—wrong to say, "the marginal contributive value of adding one more year of well-being to a life that has been going well for five years doesn't have to be the same as the marginal value of adding one year to a life that has been going well for ten years." It is not the case that with each year or day of our lives, we have a less weighty reason to add another year or day of well-being. The value of another day or year of well-being does not vary according to how much of it someone has already had. Why should pleasure (assuming, for current purposes, that it is an element of well-being) behave any differently? How *could* it behave differently, given the assumption that it is an element of well-being?

We know how to continue this diminishing series of numbers: 1, 1/2, 1/4, 1/8, ... But we would be at a loss to specify the rate at which the marginal value of well-being diminishes. If someone persists in thinking that well-being or one of its components is of less marginal value with each successive unit of time, we must ask: "By how much does it diminish? Does it diminish each minute, or each day, or each month? On what basis do you answer these questions?" Any answer will be arbitrary. We should conclude that this way of providing an alternative to McTaggart's thesis fails. If the long life of his oyster is far worse than human life at its best, that is not because the marginal value of each day of its life progressively diminishes.

Consider again the statement made by Arrhenius and Rabinowicz: "the marginal contributive value of adding one unit of pleasure to a whole consisting of five units of pleasure doesn't have to be the same as the marginal value of adding one unit to a whole consisting of ten units of pleasure." Surely there is *something* to what they are saying. Suppose you have been enjoying a lovely summer day. For three hours, the sunlight has felt good on your skin, the breezes have been soothing, the air has been shimmering with light. It is likely that the next (fourth) hour of this good weather is going to be of less value to you than was an hour earlier in the day. That is because later in the day

---

[5] Although it is generally true that the value of money diminishes at the margin, it is not invariably so. For exceptional cases, see Harry G. Frankfurt, *On Inequality*, 16–34.

[6] 'Value Superiority,' in Iwao Hirose and Jonas Olson (eds.), *The Oxford Handbook of Value Theory*, 230.

you are not rejoicing in the beauty of the day as much as you had done earlier. The pleasure you've been feeling has begun to wear off; the fourth hour is still an hour of pleasure, but because there has been no change in the weather, your attention is not being drawn to it.

What this familiar sort of example shows is that adding one further temporal unit (one hour, for example) of a *source* of pleasure can bring less additional value (pleasure), when what it is added to is larger (three hours), because that additional unit contains a less pleasurable experience than earlier ones had done. In the fourth hour, the sun (let's suppose) is shining just as brightly as before, the breezes have not changed, and the air is no less clear. The causes and duration of pleasure are the same at the end of the morning as they were at the beginning, but the pleasure itself has diminished, and that is why less good comes your way in the fourth hour.

But Arrhenius and Rabinowicz seem to be suggesting that even if you rejoiced in the fourth hour just as much as you had done earlier, nonetheless that fourth hour of pleasure *might* have less "marginal contributive value" for you than the third, which in turn had less "marginal contributive value" than the second. It is of course a truth of arithmetic that when three of something is increased by one, the percentage by which the group increases (33 percent) is smaller than the percentage by which a group is increased when it expands from two to three (50 percent). Their thought is not this trivial, mathematical point—rather it is the substantive axiological idea that there *could* be less and less reason to welcome pleasure as a day goes on because each additional hour of pleasure, though fully as pleasant as the preceding one, has less value than its predecessors. (Recall their words: "it doesn't have to be the same.") Yes, that *might* be true—but only in the sense that there is nothing incoherent in the thought itself. There is no reason to suppose that it is a true thought. It will *not* be true unless there is some detectable change in the quality of the later experiences of the day—a diminution in the pleasures one feels, or a change in the attitude one has towards those pleasures, or some other subjective alteration that explains the decline in the value of one's state of mind. Just as well-being itself does not become less good over time simply because later periods of well-being are added to an increasingly larger whole, so too pleasure—which I take to be one of its components.

Consider another illustration of the familiar point that certain activities pay diminishing rewards as they are repeated. If you have read *Pride and Prejudice* twice within the past year, you will find a third reading less rewarding, and a fourth still less so, and so on. Perhaps there is no point at which you will have exhausted the riches of this novel, but even so the value of each additional reading over the course of a year will diminish. This is no evidence that even when what is good remains unchanged its degree of goodness diminishes over time. What is good, in this example, is a moral and aesthetic experience, but it does not remain the phenomenologically identical experience when the novel is read again and again within a year. Of course the value of re-reading it declines—that is because later readings are spoiled by a sense of repetition and a loss of interest.

Suppose then we alter the example. We are now to imagine that a second and third reading of the novel gives one just as much pleasure and insight as the first. To keep the example close to common experience, we can imagine that one first reads the novel in one's twenties, and again a decade later, and so on. With each new reading, let us suppose, one recalls nothing from one's previous encounter. That is why one enjoys it and learns from it just as much as one did in one's first reading. There would in this case be no diminution in the value of reading it again. It would not be a good reason against re-reading it a decade later that one had already read it several times before. If one had to choose between reading it again and a worse book one had not read before, it would be a mistake to avoid *Pride and Prejudice* merely because one had read it before. What difference should that make to you, if a further reading would be exactly as thrilling and eye-opening as one's first encounter, and the other novel is aesthetically inferior?

Of course, if you spend a year studying Spinoza's *Ethics* for the first time in your life, others will have more reason to admire you than they would if instead you had spent that year re-reading *Pride and Prejudice* for the fifth time in five decades. You will have exercised philosophical skills over the course of your life, and not only literary skills; that is a greater achievement. But our topic is well-being, the quality of someone's life. What is admirable has a place in our discussion only to the extent that doing what is admirable is not only admirable but also good for you. Accordingly, if you would greatly enjoy Austen but would only suffer through Spinoza because his doctrines and method of argument would repel you, it is the former reading experience that would be the greater constitutive element of your well-being. Here is a case in which the greater amount of pleasure that an experience affords is appropriately included in our judgment about which of two alternatives is better for you. You might decide to devote the year to the more admirable activity, if that is what reading Spinoza is. But you would have not chosen the alternative that gives you the best quality of life.

We might ask why you should do what is admirable, if no one will in fact admire you for doing it. You should of course do what is morally right even if doing so will earn no one's admiration. But why read a book because it is admirable to do so? If the answer is that you would then have a powerful *sense* of accomplishment and would feel the *glow* of your own admiration, that would concede that phenomenological considerations are providing the standard for making this judgment. The idea would be that one should struggle through the rebarbative book because of the psychological dividends it will later pay. That reason for reading Spinoza (rather than Austen) would be grounded in an experiential conception of well-being.

A different sort of issue is whether increases in the intensity of a pleasure are proportionately greater in value. G. E. Moore holds that they are not. Thomas Hurka reports that according to Moore, "the value of a fixed increase in a pleasure's intensity gets smaller the more intense the pleasure is."[7] Suppose pleasures vary in intensity from 1 to 10.

---

[7] *British Ethical Theorists from Sidgwick to Ewing*, 198. He cites G. E. Moore, 'Mr. McTaggart's Ethics,' 358.

Someone in control of the pleasure center of your brain begins by giving you the feeling of scratching an itch, and you accurately report that its intensity is at level 4. He increases the intensity for the next minute and you report that it is now at level 6. In the next minute your pleasure center is manipulated once again, and you report that the intensity of the pleasure you feel is now at level 8. This is a "fixed increase in pleasure's intensity": it rises by 2 and again by 2. Moore says that the second of these two increases brings you less good than the first increase. But why should we agree? Is this an a priori claim that has nothing to do with your subjective reaction to increases in the intensity of pleasure? In that case we have no reason to accept it.

It is more likely that Moore has something else in mind. We can suppose that the technician in control of your pleasure center is turning the dial on the apparatus he is using from 4 to 6 and 6 to 8. The neural activity in your pleasure center then rises from 4 to 6, and then 6 to 8. Correspondingly, you judge that the intensity of the pleasure has increased from 4 to 6 and then from 6 to 8. But you also find by careful introspection that the second increase, though to your liking, is not as much to your liking as was the first. There are two mental phenomena here, both of them properly called pleasure. One is the pleasurable sensation of having an itch relieved; this is what increases in intensity by two units each time. The other is not a sensation but the feeling of pleasure *that* one has that sensation.[8] (We can have many different attitudes to pleasant sensations as we experience them. We can feel shame, surprise, pride, and so on.) The first kind of pleasure (the sensation) has undergone a fixed increase in intensity, but the second (the liking for the sensation) has not increased proportionately. That is the empirical phenomenon that underlies the judgment that the value of the second increase is smaller than the value of the first increase. For if you had liked the second increase as much as the first, Moore's statement would be a baseless a priori assertion. His claim is plausible only if the second increase in the total amount of pleasure— which combines the intensity of the sensation with the degree to which it is liked—is smaller than the first increase. Little wonder, then, that the value of the second increase is smaller—it brings one less total pleasure.

I said earlier (section 1) that the first strategy for rejecting McTaggart's thesis, which holds that goods eventually lose all their value, might seem the least plausible of the four. But now that we have examined both the first approach and the second, can we find any reason to suppose that one of them is closer to the truth than the other? The first says that goods diminish in marginal value over time and eventually stop adding to one's lifetime well-being. The second instead claims that goods diminish in marginal value but never stop increasing the total amount of good in one's life, at least to some small degree. Why suppose that the second of these options has more to recommend it than the first?

---

[8] The distinction between the attitude and the sensation is important to the defense of hedonism presented by Fred Feldman, *Pleasure and the Good Life*, 55–6.

It might be replied that something in our experience points towards the second strategy and away from the first. Introspection—so the argument goes—tells us that the pleasure we take in the same things over time diminishes but never gives out entirely. One continues to like the massage one is getting less and less, but one does still go on enjoying it to some small degree. Therefore it will continue to be good to some degree. But if that is the basis for choosing the second strategy over the first, its advantage is illusory. A massage that goes on and on might continue to give someone a pleasant sensation, but having grown tired of it, he might no longer be at all pleased by it. He will then want it to stop. At that point, the claim that the whole of this experience remains good but is a smaller good is not more plausible than the claim that it ceases to be good. In any case, both strategies should be rejected, and for the same reason. Good experiences that remain phenomenologically unaltered over time neither lose all value nor diminish in value just because they continue through time. Their goodness is grounded entirely in what they are like, and if that remains unaltered, so too does their degree of value.[9]

The components of well-being, we should conclude, do not have diminishing marginal value over time. But we should be careful not to infer that in the decisions we make about what we owe others, we should disregard the number of years of good life they have already had. Suppose I can save only one of two strangers who are in danger of losing their lives. One of them has already had eighty years of good life; the other has had twenty. Suppose, further, that in both cases only one more year of good life will be added, if I intervene. The fact that one of them has already had eighty good years, and the other only twenty, surely ought to have some bearing on my decision. I would do as much good for the eighty-year-old as I would do for the twenty-year-old, but how much good we do for others is not the only factor to be considered—there are also questions about how the good we do for others should be distributed. That is a familiar point. To take a common example: if I can rescue only one of two individuals who are in danger of drowning, one of them my son and the other a stranger, I should save my son, because he has a stronger claim to my assistance. Similarly, in certain situations we ought to give a year of good life to someone who has had less of it than someone who has had more. When I save my son, that is not because I am doing more good for someone than I would be doing by saving the stranger. And similarly, if we give another year of good life to a twenty-year-old in preference to offering the same benefit to an eighty-year-old, that is not because life necessarily becomes less good with each passing year, even when the quality of one's experiences remains unchanged.

[9] A corollary of the thesis that the components of well-being do not diminish in value over time is that the components of *ill*-being do not diminish in *dis*value either. Reflection confirms that this is so. Consider torture, for example—an experience that involves not just physical pain but anguish, humiliation, fear, and the like. No one could believe that after a few seconds or minutes or an hour, this horrible experience begins to be less bad for the victim—even when the pain, anguish, humiliation, and fear remain at the same level. It would be arbitrary to pick some temporal period—for example, ten minutes—and stipulate that torture that lasts longer than that is less bad.

3. Hurka on the well-rounded life

"Goods matter more the less of them you have."[10] Thus Thomas Hurka. They come in four basic categories, according to his theory: pleasure, knowledge, achievement, and virtue.[11] Since, as he says, they "matter more the less of them you have," he infers that we ought not devote ourselves to just one kind, but should instead seek a "balanced variety of them all."[12] He acknowledges that "aiming for balance will be counterproductive if it reduces the amount of each you achieve."[13] What we need, then, is a mixed strategy, one that goes between the extremes of concentrating single-mindedly on just one type of good, and giving equal attention to them all. "You should be neither a pure specialist nor a pure all-rounder, but should give a moderate preponderance to one good over the other."[14]

Let's test this idea by imagining someone who has devoted much of his life to making the world a better place. He is a model of virtue, and not only that, his efforts have been successful and personally rewarding, full of marvelous interactions with like-minded colleagues and allies. So he has an abundance of three of the four goods on Hurka's list: pleasure, achievement, and virtue. But there are many branches of knowledge (Hurka's fourth good) that he has almost entirely neglected. His way of life has left no time for intellectual pursuits, and his knowledge of mathematics, science, philosophy, history, and so on, is rudimentary. Suppose, further, that having reached the age of fifty, he is unexpectedly given an opportunity to make a great change in his life. He can withdraw from public service (honorably, in a way that violates no moral obligations) and devote himself fully to the pursuit of knowledge for its own sake. (A wealthy relative is willing to support him, if he makes this change.) He is going to make this decision entirely on the basis of what is best for him.

Hurka's claim that "goods matter more the less of them you have" certainly has a bearing on the question that confronts him. He has little knowledge—and so the acquisition of knowledge will be of great value to him. A corollary of Hurka's statement also applies: goods matter less the more of them you have. Therefore a life of ongoing virtue, pleasure, and achievement will be of little value to him. As their value approaches zero, the choice this man ought to make, for his own good, is to abandon his current way of life and devote himself to a life of study.

We may suppose, further, that when he is faced with this choice, he has no interest in the pursuit of knowledge. He does not experience his lack of intellectual education as a gap in his life; it is not a deficiency that upsets him. And he foresees that although he would make excellent progress in his study of this or that intellectual discipline, the experiential quality of his life would not improve—on the contrary, it would decline.

---

[10] *The Best Things in Life*, 169. The ideal of a proper balance is more fully presented in 'The Well-Rounded Life,' in *Drawing Morals*, 37–54.

[11] These goods are discussed in *The Best Things in Life* and more fully in *Perfectionism*, chapters 8–10; and throughout *Virtue, Vice, and Value*.

[12] *The Best Things in Life*, 167.   [13] Ibid., 169.   [14] Ibid., 173.

For him, intellectual work is a grind. Even so, Hurka's theory advises him to give up his career, for his own good, and devote himself to the life of the mind.

This is a highly implausible consequence. The advice he would receive from common sense would tell him: if continued devotion to the common good would give you as much joy as ever, if you would be just as virtuous, if you would achieve as much as you have done thus far, and if you would get little enjoyment from your engagement with intellectual pursuits, then you should make no such change in your life.

We should reject the parts of Hurka's theory that get him into trouble. One of them is his claim that "goods matter more the less of them you have" and its corollary, that goods matter less the more of them you have. That underestimates the prudential value of the felt quality of our lives. It holds that only one aspect of our inner lives is a component of our good—pleasure—and it calls on us to pursue goods that we lack, or have little of, regardless of the effects this will have on our inner selves. It requires us to seek novelty just for its own sake—regardless of its effect on the quality of experience.

Hurka does not present his theory as a departure from common sense. He says, for example: "If you've already studied World War I for eight hours today, how much will you gain from an extra hour? Wouldn't you do better to switch to a different activity?"[15] What he implicitly suggests by asking this question is plausible enough: probably you would learn less in that extra hour because you would experience fatigue and your attention would flag. If those psychological claims are correct, then less knowledge will be gained in that extra hour. But this is not an illustration of the thesis that goods matter less the more of them you have. You will acquire less knowledge in that extra hour—but what needs to be shown is that even if you acquired the same amount of knowledge, doing so would be less valuable, because as you acquire more knowledge, the value to you of that increment diminishes.

To return to a point made in the previous section: if it were true that all goods (including the components of well-being) matter less the more of them you have, then an individual's *well-being* matters less as each day goes by. (After all, well-being is a good.) But surely *this* good does not behave in this way; someone who has achieved a certain level of well-being for N months does not have less reason, with each passing month, to care about his future. Admittedly, there might be *some* reason to care less, as time goes by, about one's future well-being. Perhaps as we move through life, we ought to become increasingly devoted to the good of others—and in some cases that might require caring less about one's own good. But that is an entirely different idea from the one we are discussing. It lends no support to the thesis that each successive period in which our lives go well for us is less good for us than the previous one.

There is nonetheless something to what Hurka says: someone who excels in many different areas of life is more deserving of admiration than another person who excels in only one such area. He uses such examples as these: "Leonardo da Vinci, with his varied accomplishments in painting, science, and engineering...Benjamin Disraeli

---

[15] Ibid., 170.

(novelist and prime minister)... Bill Bradley (basketball star and senator)."[16] It is a tautology that if someone excels in many different fields, his life has more excellence than it would have had, had he excelled in fewer of those fields. To return to the example used earlier: if a political activist, having excelled in this area, changes his life and takes up various intellectual pursuits, excelling in them all, then he has more excellence in his life as a result. He excelled in one area during one stage of his life, and if he continues his career as a political activist, he will not increase his level of excellence (or so we have supposed). But if he gives this activity up, and studies various branches of learning, he may become excellent in those new areas of life as well. He will be more like Leonardo, Disraeli, and Bill Bradley—more admirable for his multiple skills and talents.

It might be suggested, at this point, that Hurka's theory and the one I have been defending do not come into conflict because they are not talking about the same thing. He is defending a thesis about what is excellent and admirable; I am defending a thesis about the quality of life. Both topics might be spoken of as "a good life" or "a life that is good for the one who is living it." But, it might be said, we should not be misled by this superficial verbal point of contact. Those are names for two very different things.

That suggestion should be rejected, for two reasons. First, although it might reasonably be said that Hurka's theory is *primarily* about human excellence—being good at something—it does include pleasure in its conception of a good life; it is one of the four goods, along with virtue, knowledge, and achievement. The felt quality of one's life has some prudential significance for Hurka—but less significance than it does according to my theory. So that is one issue about which we disagree. The second point of difference is related to this: we give conflicting advice about how one should live one's life, when this is a question not about one's moral obligations or duties to others, but about what one should do with respect to oneself. The example I used earlier, of someone devoted to public service but deficient in knowledge, brings out this difference between us.

It is a merit of Hurka's theory that it attempts to answer a question that arises for any pluralistic account of prudential value. If a theory holds that the components of well-being are several in number, it should not leave us in the dark about their relative value. It should not evade such questions as these: Are the elements of well-being equal in value—at least roughly, if not exactly? Or are some significantly better than others? Can we say, for example, that one of them should always be preferred to the others? Or that one is twice as good as another?

Hurka tacitly gives a negative answer to these questions, but he does have something to say about how we should balance one good against another. He does this by positing that "goods matter more the less of them you have" (and matter less the more of them you have). That is how he arrives at his prescription: "You should be neither a pure specialist nor a pure all-rounder, but should give a moderate preponderance to one good over the other." It is an admirable feature of his conception of a good life that it

---

[16] Ibid., 167.

addresses questions about degrees of goodness, and does not merely offer a list of goods. Unfortunately, the answer it gives to these questions is unacceptable.

Hurka's conception of a good life—set forth in four basic goods—fails to learn from Aristotle a lesson that has been guiding me throughout this study: well-being cannot consist in a state of mind that one can be in even as one sleeps. Sleep can be long-lasting—it could endure the rest of one's life. Should it do so, one would no longer be living a good human life, a life rich in prudential value. (I assume here that this long-lasting sleep would be dreamless or contain only brief moments of dreaming.) Yet one could continue to have three of the four items on Hurka's list: virtue, knowledge, and achievement. (One would have little of the fourth good, pleasure.) An honest person does not stop being honest when he sleeps—what stops is the activation of his honest disposition. Someone who has acquired a body of knowledge remains a knower while he sleeps. A high achiever (suppose he has won the Nobel Peace Prize) still has those achievements to his credit while he sleeps. These points must lead Hurka's theory to the conclusion that someone who falls into a permanent state of sleep retains much that is good—he is very far from having a life devoid of value. In that case, a disease that induces a permanent state of sleep would not be one that we urgently need to combat. This theory underestimates the harmfulness of such a disease.

It does acknowledge the existence of one reason for fighting this disease: it would deprive us of the one remaining good on his list—pleasure. But here Hurka's theory has the same deficiency that hedonism has: the only basis on which it values conscious life is the pleasure it affords. Other aspects of our rich and variegated consciousness are deemed to be without a value of their own. In any experience worth having for itself, pleasure is the only feature that explains why it is worth having.

Hurka's theory does have this arrow in its quiver: it can draw upon the idea of diminishing marginal value to reach the conclusion that at *some* time or other there will be a strong case for waking up a sleeper. Goods, we are told, matter less the more of them we have. So, as our long-term sleeper sleeps, eventually the goods he has (virtue, knowledge, accomplishment) are less good, since he has had them for such a long time. But what is the rate at which their value diminishes? Is there no significant decline in their value for a month? a year? a decade? Any answer proposed would be an arbitrary stipulation, because we have nothing in our experience of life to guide us.

There is an obvious way to improve this theory: it should become an experientialist conception of well-being. It would be better to say that the basic goods are pleasure and the kinds of consciousness available to those who are virtuous, knowledgeable, and accomplished. That is not my theory (I do not propose a complete list of goods), but it would bring our theories closer together.

4. McTaggart, love, and Parfit's "Century of Ecstasy"

My use of McTaggart has drawn on only a minuscule portion of *The Nature of Existence*—the two pages in which he speaks of an enormously long "oyster-like life."

To many readers unfamiliar with this massive treatise, it may be of some interest to learn how that example serves his general ethical purposes. It may also come as a surprise that McTaggart formulated and embraced the thesis that when goods (certain goods, that is), increase in quantity their value does not increase proportionately. His adherence to this doctrine creates a puzzle: why does he not arrive at the conclusion that a million-year oyster-like existence has little lifetime well-being, because, as time passes, the value of its pleasures diminishes, never reaching and therefore never surpassing a rather low limit? My discussion of this question is much indebted to an essay by Dennis McKerlie.[17]

McTaggart holds that there is a shortlist of "qualities which are good or evil—that is, which give a good or evil value to the selves, or parts of selves, which possess them." The good qualities are knowledge, virtue, "the possession of certain emotions," pleasure, and "amount and intensity of consciousness, which we may call 'fullness of life'."[18] But they are not on a par. Some twenty pages later, he adds: "those thinkers are right who attribute a unique and supreme goodness to love." He then asks an excellent question: "In what way can love be supremely and uniquely good?"[19] Several possibilities are rejected in short order. (A) It is not the only good. (B) The other goods are not all dependent on it. (C) It is not unique by being "really eternal, for everything is really eternal."[20]

His next suggestion, he says, comes closer to the truth. He asks: "Can we say that love is incommensurably better than any other good?" And replies: "That seems attractive, but I cannot think it correct. If it were so, it would follow that, starting from any standpoint—my own at present, for example—the smallest conceivable increase in love would be better than the greatest possible increase in knowledge, virtue, pleasure, or fullness of life. And it does not seem to me that this is true." But a modification of this proposal, he believes, does capture what is supremely and uniquely valuable about love: if there is *enough* love in a person's life, that is better than the possession of all the other goods combined, however large their quantity. This, he notes, is what "many people, mystics and non-mystics" have held. "It seems to me that when love reached or passed a certain point, it would be more good than any possible amount of knowledge, virtue, pleasure, or fullness of life could be."[21]

What does McTaggart have in mind here, when he speaks of an "increase" in such goods as knowledge, virtue, and pleasure? What is it for love to have "reached or passed a certain point"? Following McKerlie, I assume that McTaggart is tacitly assuming that *one* way a good can increase, or pass "a certain point," is by enduring.[22] So interpreted, he takes the supremacy and uniqueness of love to consist in the fact that when it

---

[17] 'McTaggart on Love,' in Thomas Hurka (ed.), *Underivative Duty: British Moral Philosophers from Sidgwick to Ewing*, 66–86.
[18] The two passages cited are from *The Nature of Existence*, vol. 2, 412.
[19] Both statements are at ibid., 436.   [20] Ibid., 437.
[21] All statements cited in this paragraph are at ibid., 437.   [22] See 'McTaggart on Love,' 84.

reaches a "certain point" of intensity or duration (or both), it is better than "the greatest possible increase" in the other goods.

Having arrived at this conception of what makes love special, he next asks whether it is consistent with a thesis he had defended earlier: every good can keep increasing indefinitely in its degree of goodness.[23] Knowledge, virtue, certain emotions, pleasure, and fullness of life have no intrinsic limit: no matter what their quantity is, one can always have more of each of them, and it is better to do so. It might seem, then, that "whatever the good belonging to an amount of love, there would be some amount of each of the other qualities which would be better."[24] But, McTaggart replies, that is not so. Love alone is limitless in value, whereas all the other goods, as they increase, approach a limit in their value, but never reach it. "If, in the case of the other qualities [knowledge, virtue, pleasure ...] the good, after a certain point, should only increase asymptotically—each successive increment of the quality yielding a smaller increment of good—then, in the case of those other qualities, there would be a limit to the good it yielded."[25] All goods other than love, in other words, have diminishing marginal value. One's lifetime well-being increases as one continues to have them, but by less and less.

As McKerlie notes, this creates a puzzle: Why does McTaggart insist that a sufficiently long oyster-like life, one that is devoid of love, is better than a shorter human life that contains love and the other goods? McTaggart has the resources he needs to reject his thesis that the oyster-like existence is better. Why does he not use them? McKerlie proposes that the best explanation is this: McTaggart believes that only in the final stage of the universe—the stage when the universe's great potential for value is fully realized—will the supremacy of love take hold.[26] All goods other than love are subject to the law of diminishing marginal value, but that law, as McTaggart formulates it, says only that "*after a certain point*, all goods other than love" increase in value only asymptotically. We should therefore take him to be assuming that the oyster's life has not yet reached this point. Its lifetime well-being increases just as much with each passing day of pleasurable nourishment, because the final stage of the universe—the stage at which only love's increasing value is proportionate to its increasing quantity—is not the stage it has reached.

Notice that McTaggart proposes two different theses: one of them identifies the respect in which love is better than other goods; the other affirms that this conception of love's supremacy is consistent with his claim that every good increases in value at least somewhat without limit, as its quantity increases. The first says nothing about diminishing marginal value—only the second does. The first is about a relation, the relation of superiority that love bears to all other goods; the second makes no comparisons between goods, but says of each good other than love that its quantity is never at a maximum, and that the value of having it is never at a maximum, but ever approaches a limit.

---

[23] For his defense, see *The Nature of Existence*, vol. 2, 413–15.   [24] Ibid., 438.   [25] Ibid., 438.
[26] McKerlie points out the difficulty in 'McTaggart on Love,' 77. He then examines and rejects several possible solutions before arriving at his own solution on page 85.

What bearing do these two propositions have on one another? McTaggart replies that the only reason to accept the diminishing value of goods other than love is to uphold love's supremacy.[27] He thinks he must say that if love is supreme in the way he supposes, then although the other goods increase somewhat in value as they increase in quantity, they can never attain or exceed a maximum value. I believe he is wrong to assume that the kind of unsurpassable value love has requires the diminishing value of all else, but before we turn to that issue, we should recognize that for McTaggart the supremacy of love—its superiority (once it reaches a certain level) to all other goods combined—stands on its own as a plausible insight into value. It is not inferred from the thesis that the goods other than love at some point diminish in value as they increase in quantity.

Recall his statement: "It seems to me that when love reached or passed a certain point, it would be more good than any possible amount of knowledge, virtue, pleasure, or fullness of life could be." He immediately adds: "This does not, so far as I am concerned, spring from any belief that I have reached such a point. It is a conclusion which seems to me to follow from contemplating the nature of love, on the one hand, and of the other quantities on the other hand."[28]

McTaggart then starts a new paragraph with a new section number: "But is not this inconsistent with the results we reached in the last chapter?" To which he replies: there is no inconsistency.[29] He had earlier claimed that any good, no matter how abundant, can increase in goodness as it becomes more abundant. He continues to affirm that thesis. And he points out that the doctrine that a good can always increase in goodness by becoming more abundant is compatible with holding that its value increases less and less, approaching but never reaching a limit. The points he makes in this paragraph need not be taken to mean that, in his opinion, diminishing marginal value is the *grounds* on which the special supremacy of love rests. Recall that when he explains his grounds, he says: "It is a conclusion which seems to me to follow from contemplating the nature of love, on the one hand, and of the other quantities on the other hand." That suggests that for McTaggart the supremacy of love is self-evident: if, upon careful reflection, we fully understand the five things that are good, we will recognize that they do not have equal value, because love has a certain kind of supremacy. He does not argue that love has this primacy by applying the law of diminishing value to all but love. Readers are meant to accept the supremacy of love because of the intrinsic plausibility of that thesis.

We can now turn back to McTaggart's assumption that we ought to accept the doctrine of diminishing marginal value of all goods other than love because otherwise love would not have the great superiority we perceive it to have. This, I believe, is a mistake. In affirming the doctrine of diminishing marginal value, he assumes, without warrant, that there must be some single exchange rate among all goods in virtue of which their overall comparative value is determined entirely by the greater quantity of

---

[27] *The Nature of Existence*, vol. 2, 438.   [28] Ibid., 437.   [29] Ibid., 437–8.

good. Accordingly, although he thinks that a certain quantity of love is better than any quantity, however great, of other goods—and that this is self-evidently so—he also thinks (mistakenly) that this would not be the case unless those other goods suffer, but love does not, from some handicap that eventually limits their ability to compete with love in the exchange of one good for another. They must at some point in time grow less in goodness, whereas love does not. He fails to avail himself of the idea that if a good belongs to a lower order of value, then however much it continues to accumulate over time, never bringing less of that lower value than it had done before, its lower quality will continue to make it rank below a good that belongs to a higher order, if there is a sufficient quantity of the latter.

This is the very mistake McTaggart makes when he says that the pleasures of a sufficiently long-lived oyster have greater value than the combined lifetime good that accrues to a much shorter but well-lived human life. His assumption, when he proposes this example, is that the value of the oyster's pleasures has not yet begun to diminish over time. Each day brings just as much as the previous day to the lifetime well-being of the oyster. These amounts are not to be discounted, and so when they are aggregated, their total must at some point exceed the total good achieved in a much shorter life. He assumes here that when the value of a good is not discounted over time, nothing can stop it from eventually ranking above better but shorter-lived goods.

McTaggart, as we have seen, does not argue that love has the kind of supremacy he attributes to it. He thinks that if we contemplate the nature of love and the nature of the other goods, and come to understand them adequately, its supremacy should become evident to us. Presumably he would agree that to understand these different goods requires a good deal of experience of them all. Someone who has come to know what it is like to love another person is in a far better position to assess its prudential value—and similarly for the other goods that have an experiential nature. (On my view, all goods have such a nature—though McTaggart does not agree. Knowledge is on his list of goods, but it is not an experience.) According to this way of thinking about our knowledge of value, we do not need an explanation of why some good has the kind of supremacy over other goods that McTaggart assigns to love. Explanations cannot be expected of everything; some propositions merit acceptance on the strength of their own plausibility.

The phrase "higher order of value" is used by W. D. Ross to express the relationship between virtue and pleasure. He finds it likely that "*no* amount of pleasure is equal to any amount of virtue, that in fact virtue belongs to a higher order of value, beginning at a point on the scale of value higher than that which pleasure ever reaches."[30] Citing this statement, McKerlie writes:

McTaggart would find Ross's view implausible because it makes virtue incommensurably better than pleasure. Also, Ross's comments about positions on the scale of value do not really explain

---

[30] *The Right and the Good*, 150, author's emphasis.

why aggregating the value of pleasures would not eventually lead to a total amount of value that was equal to the value of a given amount of virtue. McTaggart has an explanation of a sort—if the value of increases in pleasure diminishes in the way he supposes, the total amount of value that can result from aggregation will be constrained by a limit.[31]

Suppose Ross had said about virtue what McTaggart says about love: when it is present in someone to a *sufficient* degree, it "belongs to a higher order of value." That would address the first problem McKerlie raises. (When McKerlie complains that Ross makes virtue "incommensurably better" than virtue, he is using "incommensurable" as McTaggart does—to mean that even the smallest possible amount of the higher order good is superior to the greatest amount of the lower order good.)

What of McKerlie's second objection—that Ross does not explain why aggregated pleasures cannot eventually surpass virtue in value? Here McKerlie assumes that if there are higher and lower orders of value, as Ross maintains, there must be a reason why that is so. But as we have seen, McTaggart's theory also contains a thesis for which no grounds are offered: it is the thesis that love is the supreme value in that a sufficient amount of it is superior to any quantity, however large, of other goods or combination of goods. We are expected to recognize the truth of that proposition simply by contemplating the nature of love and the other goods. If that epistemological position has merit, Ross can avail himself of it, just as McTaggart does, and say, in reply to McKerlie's objection: if we have an adequate understanding of virtue and pleasure, we can see that a sufficient amount of the first is better than any amount of the second.

McTaggart does not offer any explanation for why the four goods inferior to love (knowledge, virtue, pleasure, and "fullness of life") at some point begin to diminish in value. That does not mean that he has no reason for believing that they do. He says: "the only reason for believing this theory to be true is that it seems the only possible way of reconciling two conclusions"[32]—namely (A) each of these goods can continue to increase without limit, and as each does so its value also increases at least somewhat; and (B) love is supreme in that a certain amount of it is better than any amount of another good or combination of goods. So, although he does not say that his selectively applied law of diminishing value is inherently *implausible*, he claims for it no inherent plausibility (as he does for the thesis that love is the supreme good).

Here he overlooks the legitimate doubts that can be raised about the thesis of diminishing marginal value. These have been rehearsed in sections 1 and 2 of this chapter. Chief among them is the point that well-being cannot plausibly be thought to diminish in value as time passes. Of course, someone who has lived well for forty years might start to live less well in his fifties. But if the goods in which well-being consists are as abundant in his fifties as they were in his forties, he cannot be worse off in this later decade. Anyone who thinks otherwise will need non-arbitrary answers to these questions: *When* does a good begin to decrease in value? *Why* does it diminish in value? *Why* does it diminish *just then*? *How much* did it diminish? McTaggart does not

---

[31] 'McTaggart on Love,' 76.   [32] *The Nature of Existence*, vol. 2, 438.

struggle with these questions—and for good reason. There is nothing to think through, because any answer would be arbitrary.

McTaggart's theory of diminishing marginal value provides a nice illustration of that doctrine's inherent implausibility. He holds that at some point the value of pleasure begins to decline, as does the value of every good but love. When does it decline? He arbitrarily assumes that it takes at least a million years. His long-lived oyster is better off than any human being because the pleasures it enjoys are to be aggregated at an undiscounted rate—the diminishing value of pleasure has not yet taken hold even after a million years. This is an absurd view, but there is bound to be something odd in any theory that proposes that at some point (why then?) a component of well-being becomes less good (how much less?) for someone than it used to be, simply because he has already had it for a certain length of time. The fact that someone has had a good does not explain why it is less good for him to continue to have it.

It is tempting to suppose that McTaggart's denial of the reality of time plays a role in explaining why he believes in the superiority of a sufficiently long-lived oyster-like existence. He is perhaps assuming that if time were real, one would never reach the point at which the pleasures of an oyster-like life would begin to diminish in value. He would in that case agree that it is absurd to suppose that this deterioration in value begins to occur after a few million years, or any other period of time. So read, his idea is that the length of time one possesses a good makes no difference to one's well-being, because the temporal markers of present, past, and future have no basis in reality. For him, the true way to assess the comparative value of the life of a human being and that of an oyster is to dismiss the duration of their lives entirely, since that has no basis in reality, and to make a timeless comparison instead. In that case, our lives, when filled with love, can be recognized as superior. For however intense a pleasure an oyster might have, the value of that pleasure is not greater in proportion to its intensity; for any degree of intensity, it could be greater, but its value only approaches and never reaches a fixed limit. This allows a certain intensity of love, which is not subject to diminishing marginal value, to be superior to any amount of pleasure. (The idea that time is illusory, and that we must live our lives with a view to eternity or a timeless present, is a central theme of Neo-Platonism. We will return to it in section 15.)

Returning now to Ross's thesis that there is a "higher order of value," we should note that it is endorsed by Derek Parfit when he speaks of different "scales" of prudential value.[33] He asks us to compare two possible future lives: "I could live for another 100 years, all of an extremely high quality. Call this *the Century of Ecstasy*. I could instead live forever, with a life that would always be barely worth living. Though there would be nothing bad in this life, the only good things would be muzak and potatoes. Call this *the Drab Eternity*."[34] He adds that there would be "no limit to the total value" that

---

[33] 'Overpopulation and the Quality of Life,' in Peter Singer (ed.), *Applied Ethics*, 145–64. For his rejection of a single "scale" of value, see page 161.

[34] Ibid., p. 160, author's emphasis.

accumulates in the Drab Eternity—no diminution in marginal value, no asymptotic approach to a fixed quantity of good.[35] Even so, he says: "The Century of Ecstasy would be better for me in an essentially qualitative way."[36] That, he points out, departs from Sidgwick's view that "all *qualitative* comparison of pleasures must really resolve itself into quantitative [comparison]."[37] Parfit notes: "This would be so if the value of all pleasures lay on the same scale."[38]

In effect, Parfit rejects the merely quantitative approach to value that Sidgwick (a hedonist) and McTaggart (not a hedonist) share. There is, as he puts it, a "qualitative way" in which some goods, in a sufficient amount, are better than a greater quantity of other goods. That, as Parfit notes, is similar to Mill's point, in *Utilitarianism*, that there is a difference in quality between human and porcine pleasure.[39] Parfit's opposition to an entirely quantitative approach to the comparison of values is a rejection of McTaggart's belief that to uphold the superiority of one kind of good (love) to any quantity of all others, he must posit a quantitative limit to the value of the others.

McKerlie sides with McTaggart rather than Parfit. He says: "if the drab life were eternal it would contain an unlimited or infinite amount of value, and this makes it harder to explain why it is worse than the other life."[40] Of course, there is no time at which the drab life has accumulated an "infinite amount of value." Rather, its lifetime well-being continues to increase with each passing day, without end or limit. McKerlie wants to know: if the drab life is worse, as Parfit holds, why is it worse? If we respond by saying: "because its goods are qualitatively inferior" or "its goods belong to a lower order of value," he could legitimately question the explanatory value of such phrases. But Parfit's thesis does not diminish in plausibility even if there is no explanation of why the Century of Ecstasy is better than the Drab Eternity.

To repeat: some propositions recommend themselves to us because of their inherent plausibility; when they do so, we may, upon careful reflection, accept them even if we cannot defend them by inferring them from other propositions. This, as we have seen, is the basis on which McTaggart accepts the supremacy of love (its being better, when there is enough of it, to any quantity of other goods). There is no reason why it has that supremacy in value—it simply has it. He believes (mistakenly) that for it to

---

[35] Ibid., 161. In another essay, Parfit discusses a thesis of diminishing marginal value that he finds credible, but it is not *prudential* value that is said to diminish. He uses the term, "diminishing marginal moral importance," to describe one view about how well-being is best distributed across populations. According to that theory, which he calls "the telic version of the priority view," "if benefits go to those who are better off, those benefits matter less. Just as *resources* have diminishing marginal *utility*, so *utility* has diminishing marginal *moral importance*" (author's emphasis). See 'Equality or Priority?' in Matthew Clayton and Andrew Williams (eds.), *The Idea of Equality*, 81–125. The statement cited is on page 105. I take him to mean that, according to this theory, there is, from an impartial (moral) point of view, less reason to want a benefit to go to a better off individual, the more benefits that individual already has. This is not the view that a component of well-being diminishes in value as it increases in duration.

[36] 'Overpopulation and the Quality of Life,' 161.

[37] See *The Methods of Ethics*, 94 (Sidgwick's emphasis).

[38] 'Overpopulation and the Quality of Life,' 161.

[39] Ibid., 161. Mill's comparison is made in *Utilitarianism*, chapter 2.

[40] 'McTaggart on Love,' 78.

have this supremacy in value, the quantity of its goodness must also be supreme, and so he stipulates that the value of other goods cannot surpass (or reach) a limit as they increase in intensity or endure over time. But he does not treat love's unique exemption from the law of diminishing value as the reason why it is supreme in value. In siding with McTaggart and against Parfit, McKerlie assumes, without argument, that (in Sidgwick's words) qualitative comparisons "resolve into" quantitative comparisons.

We can elaborate on Parfit's thought experiment by imagining a music lover who is offered two alternative futures. The first will contain one hundred years of the kind of music he loves most: the works of Monteverdi, Purcell, Handel, Bach, Haydn, Mozart, Beethoven, Schubert, Verdi, Wagner, Mahler, Debussy, Ravel, Bartok, Shostakovich, and all the other composers who have a place in the history of this kind of music-making. The second will contain unending years of the mildly pleasant music that might be heard on an "easy listening" radio station. (It will remain no less pleasant as time passes.) He has good reason to choose the first future over the second: he has experienced both kinds of music, and he judges that one hundred years listening to the better music is time better spent than any number of centuries spent with the worse music. He need not provide an explanation of why the first alternative is better than the second (and perhaps there can be none). Even so, he is making the right choice, and his experience of music warrants his judgment. The quality of experience in the first life will be of a higher order, although the quantity of one kind of good experience (pleasure) in the second life will, because of its far longer temporal span, be greater.

When a choice must be made between different kinds of music, what they sound like matters—not just their duration. Sound can be so high in quality that a sufficient amount of it is more desirable than any amount of lower quality sound. (A sufficient amount: not just a bagatelle. I will say more in section 17 below.) Here we can see how dubious is Sidgwick's "resolution" of qualitative into quantitative comparisons. There is more music, all of it pleasant, in Parfit's Drab Eternity. But there is music of far higher quality in his "Century of Ecstasy." Even with an iron-clad guarantee that one will never become tired of the easy listening available in a Drab Eternity (comparable to the stipulation that each day in the life of McTaggart's oyster brings it as much pleasure as any other day, over the thousands of years of its life), one ought not forego the far superior musical experiences on offer for a hundred years. Those experiences provide a smaller quantity of pleasure over the course of one hundred years than is available in the Drab Eternity, but pleasure is only a part (and often not a large part), of what makes our experiences good for us to have. There is something about what it is like to listen to the great music of the great composers that grounds a music lover's refusal to give it up in exchange for limitless auditory enjoyment that has nothing to offer the ear or the mind besides bland pleasure. One could not be said to love, understand, or properly appreciate this music if one thought otherwise.

Can we say that although there is, in the fullness of time, more musical *pleasure* in the Drab Eternity, there is a greater quantity of some *other* good thing in the century of great music? Of course: it contains more profound and inspiring music (because there is none of that in the Drab Eternity). It might next be asked: since pleasure is one of the goods, why is it not the case that a sufficiently large temporal dose of that good is more choiceworthy than a far shorter period of great music? To this question, there is no reply—and none is needed. It is simply the case that a certain quantity of one type of good constitutes a better life than any quantity of the other, as our experience assures us. (This is what entitles us to call the first kind a "higher order" good and the second a "lower order" good.) It would be absurd to look for some third type of value—the genus to which great music and pleasant listening belong as species—and to assume that only by having a greater quantity of that generic good can great music be more choiceworthy than bland acoustical pleasure. Mill's appeal to the quality of pleasures as a second factor that deserves weight, in addition to quantity, is therefore a move in the right direction, if we sever it from his hedonism. A higher order good is not made higher by having a greater quantity of some third thing than a lower order good.

There is something that McTaggart, Ross, and Parfit agree about—and I am glad to join them. McTaggart's doctrine of love's superiority, Ross's thesis that virtue is better than any amount of pleasure, and Parfit's preference for the Century of Ecstasy have this in common: some amount (a sufficient amount) of one kind of good is preferable to any amount of other goods. With Parfit, and against McTaggart, I believe that this does not require that some goods diminish in prudential value as they increase quantitatively by virtue of their being possessed for longer periods of time. We may call certain goods higher in *quality* when, being abundant enough, they are superior to any quantity of other goods. We may also say that they belong to a higher *order*. What stands behind these assertions is simply a judgment, based on our experience, of what is or is not worth giving up in exchange for something else.

5. Life's ups and downs

A life can go well for a period of time and then decline. Or it can improve; a miserable childhood or adolescence does not doom one to unmitigated suffering as an adult. Further, we seem to be able to add together, retrospectively, the different levels of well-being achieved in this and that portion of someone's life, and arrive at a rough overall assessment of how good a life that individual has been having, or once had. We can, for example, say that Mr. X, now deceased, had a good life up until his last six months; if it was a long life, filled at every stage with much good and little bad, except during its last six months, we would judge that overall he had a good life.

It is tempting to suppose that the prudential value of a whole length of life is nothing more nor less than the sum of the prudential value of its temporal parts, just as the length of a line that stretches from A to Z cannot be anything other than the sum of whatever smaller segments we conceptually divide it into. That idea is open to question, as we will soon see, but let us provisionally accept it.[41]

---

[41] How to calculate total lifetime well-being is an especially important matter in political philosophy, if one holds that human beings ought to have an equal amount of well-being over the course of their lives, but

Is the best lifetime—the lifetime that is best with respect to well-being—simply a quantitative matter? Is it, in other words, the life that has the greatest quantity of prudential value over time? It might be thought that this is self-evident, but there is an alternative way of thinking that deserves consideration. According to that alternative, a desirable prudential feature of a whole length of life is to have no significant temporal portion that is far worse than the others; the various stages of life (childhood, adolescence, and so on) should instead contain roughly equal amounts of well-being.[42] Certainly it would be a great burden to endure a whole decade of pain and suffering, and we might think it better to make some sacrifices in total well-being to avoid living through lengthy bad periods.

Suppose we frame the issue this way: A pregnant woman learns that the child she is bearing will have one of two kinds of life, depending on which medical procedure she elects before she comes to term. If her child has life A, he will go through a decade of severe mental illness filled with misery and little joy, but before and after that decade his prospects for a life of physical and psychological health are excellent. If he has life B, he will be free of that severe mental illness; there will in this case be no terrible decade, but from beginning to end he will have chronic conditions that detract from the quality of his life. Let's assume that the best guess she can make is that her son's overall lifetime well-being will be slightly greater if he has life A (the one with a very bad decade).

The right choice, I believe, is the procedure that gives her son life B. She has a parental duty to protect him from serious harm. If she chooses the procedure that leads to an entire decade of suffering for her son, it would be misleading to say that she allows such harm to occur to him; rather, she is the cause of his misery—she inflicts it. It would be an inadequate justification for her doing so to note that as a result of her choice his life eventually attains a greater balance of good over bad. As her son suffers through his bad decade, he could rightly blame her for his misery.

But the point made in the previous paragraph does not answer the question I have raised. To repeat: "Is the best lifetime with respect to well-being the one that has the greatest quantity of prudential value over time?" The previous paragraph is about how one individual ought to treat another, when doing so would result in different levels of well-being. My question, however, is not about interpersonal relations; it is about what counts as the best life. So imagine that you are trying to form a retrospective judgment about someone's life, which is now over. (It is therefore someone else's life, not yours.) It turned out one way, but could have gone another. More specifically, it had one very bad decade, and you ask yourself: would it have been better, all things considered, for that

need not have an equal amount at each temporal segment. For discussion, see Iwao Hirose, *Egalitarianism*, 136–51; and Kasper Lippert-Rasmussen, *Luck Egalitarianism*, 152–6.

[42] This idea is presented by Michael Slote as follows: "In the determination of…the goodness of lives… the roughly equal intertemporal distribution of goods carries weight quite independently of good-maximizing considerations." See *Goods and Virtues*, 11. Slote offers this as a reading of points made by Amartya Sen in 'Utilitarianism and Welfarism,' 470–1. Sen suggests that there was a maldistribution in the life of King Lear (so much suffering at one time!), and points out that among economists an individual's poverty typically "is not weighed up or down in terms of the deal he has got in the past or is expected to get in the future" (471).

individual not to have had so much misery within that period of time, if the price to be paid for that improvement would have been less well-being overall?

I suggest that the quantity of well-being over time is the single criterion to be used here. The best life with respect to prudential value, in other words, is the one that has more prudential value than any other.[43] That, at any rate, is the right criterion to use, if we are assuming that the individual in question is to be counted as one person enduring over time, rather than a series of two or more persons. For once we make that assumption, it is implausible to suppose that the various decades of a person's life (or other temporal divisions—infancy, childhood, adolescence, and so on) have a claim to roughly equal shares of well-being. Separate individuals who are fellow citizens ought to have equal opportunities and equal rights, but the periods of a single individual's life are not fellow citizens. You do not mistreat yourself if you accept a certain diminution in well-being, for a time, in order to have, on balance, more well-being over time. Similarly, although citizens might plausibly be said to have a duty to insure that their fellow citizens have sufficient resources for well-being—guaranteeing them some floor below which they cannot sink—there is no similar intrapersonal requirement. We do not owe it to ourselves to guarantee that no period of our lives is only so bad and no worse. So there is no reason to object to the policy of using quantity of well-being as the sole factor that determines which sort of life is prudentially best.

That point applies, in a way, not only to retrospective but also to prospective judgments. If I could know *with utter certainty* that my options, going forward, are to have life A or life B (as above), I should choose A—the one that has more overall well-being, in spite of the fact that it also contains a very bad decade. But that does not entail that one should make decisions about one's future in this way, for the utter certainty (or anything close to it) that it presupposes is impossible in such matters. How can I give the proper weight to the future misery I will endure for a decade, if I choose life A? Like most people, I am likely to discount it unjustifiably simply because it is far in the future. Even if I can accurately assess how bad it will be, I might find myself experiencing regret about my earlier decision, when I find myself living through that painful decade. On each day of my ten decades of misery, I might add to my sufferings by berating myself for having brought them on myself; and that additional suffering is something I might have ignored when I made my decision. For several reasons, then, it is a bad strategy for living one's life to take upon oneself long periods of suffering in the

[43] James Griffin writes: "We can never reach final assessment of ways of life by totting up lots of small, short-term utilities.... Our final, authoritative calculation of utility...has to take a global form: this way of living, all in all, is better than that." See *Well-Being*, 34–5. A footnote to this passage adds: "we cannot focus on experiences" (324 n. 31). That suggests that Griffin rejects the overall assessment of lifetime well-being by breaking it down into shorter segments of life, and that he does so because he takes that method of reckoning to presuppose what he calls "the Experience Requirement," which he also rejects (chapter 2, n. 20). But perhaps Griffin's opposition to "totting up" is compatible with my thesis about the composition of well-being over a lifetime. He later adds: "One does not aggregate...by totting up many small values from various quarters of one's life; instead, one's important global desires already incorporate the major magnitudes that determine one's choice" (144–5). This passage suggests no opposition to "totting up" how one has fared during different periods of one's life to arrive at an overall conclusion about the whole duration of that life.

hope that on balance they will pay off by producing the most prudential good over the long run. We do better to act *as though* in the distant future we will not be the same person we are now (similar in many respects, but not the same) and protect that future person's well-being in a way similar to the way we protect other people.[44]

6. Nagel's brain-damaged man

A tacit assumption I have been making should be brought into the open before we move on: I find it natural to suppose that when we assess someone's level of well-being during some portion of his life, we are to consider only the quality of his inner life during that interval, and not also his mental state at some earlier time. But obvious as it sounds, that might be questioned. One way to challenge it is to reflect on an apparent paradox that Thomas Nagel brings to our attention. He points out that although we would pity "an intelligent person [who] receives a brain injury that reduces him to the mental condition of a contented infant," a child in that same condition is not unfortunate and is not to be pitied.[45] How can that be? They have (we are to assume) the same inner life, and exercise the same cognitive and emotional capacities. Nagel also points out that the man whose mind has degenerated "is in the same condition he was in at the age of three months, except that he is bigger. If we did not pity him then, why pity him now...?"[46]

He suggests a solution: "most good and ill fortune has as its subject a person who is identified by his history and his possibilities, rather than merely by his categorical state of the moment...."[47] These words can be read as an expression of ideas with which no one would disagree. Obviously, the injured adult is worse off than he used to be, whereas the infant is on an upward trajectory. We can say, in addition, that the adult is faring poorly *for an adult*; whereas the baby is faring well *for a baby*. But I want to consider a different idea that might be read into Nagel's words. We might say that after the adult has been injured, he henceforth has a lower level of well-being than does the infant. He is contented, as is the infant, but now there is an evil in his life that detracts from its current prudential value: he is now someone who was once much better off. We look not just to his mental condition now, to assess the quality of his present life, but we also compare it to his earlier state and judge his present state to contain a great disadvantage that must figure in our assessment of it. It is bad for him now that he used to be so much better off. That would explain why we pity the adult and not the child.

The injured adult and the child experience the world in the same way. If we accept an experientialist conception of well-being, we will say that during a certain period of

---

[44] Here I am close to what Griffin says: "Distribution can matter in prudence as well as in morality. I might prefer a life with a lower sum [of prudential value] to one in which the bad periods got very bad— the sort of 'minimum acceptable level' requirement often imposed between lives now applied inside a life." See *Well-Being*, 35. But unlike him, I hold that as prudent planners of our long-term future, we *ought* to guard against long periods of suffering (not merely that we *might* have this preference). Also unlike him, I claim that our retrospective assessment of lifetime well-being must be arrived at by considering the value of each of a life's temporal segments. (He does not deny this, but neither does he affirm it.)

[45] 'Death,' in *Mortal Questions*, 5.   [46] Ibid., 6.   [47] Ibid., 5.

time (the time after the adult's injury and before the child outstrips him in cognitive functioning) they have the same quality of life. Nagel can be understood, however, to be using this example as an argument against experientialism. So read, he is claiming that there is a non-experiential aspect to the injured adult's life, post-injury: it detracts from his well-being now that he once was better off.

It would be a mistake to argue: "The adult's present condition is worse than his earlier condition. The three-month-old child's present condition is better than his earlier condition. Therefore, the child is now better off than the adult." Since this cannot be what lies behind Nagel's example, where does its evidential force lie?

What requires explanation is that we pity the adult but not the child. One possible explanation is that the injured adult has a lower level of well-being than does the child, because our assessment of the adult's present condition must be sensitive to a relational fact: he is in a far worse state than he once was. That is not an introspectable feature of his mental life (he is unaware of the reduction in his cognitive functioning), but, it might be said: so much the worse for experientialism.

But there is a far more plausible way to explain why we pity the adult but not the child. Our emotions are sensitive to changes in people's circumstances, our own and those of others. An adult whose recent injuries have left him with the life of a contented child, not just momentarily but for the remainder of his days, evokes our sympathy or pity because that is a radical break from the recent past, and the future has nothing better in store. The narrative arc of a life story is what engages us emotionally, not the degree to which someone is, for a period of time, above the zero point between well-being and ill-being. The injured adult is above that point, just as the infant is. If we ask ourselves which condition we would choose to be in for a day (or some other brief period in which there is little change in mental life), and we consider only the level of well-being we would attain during that period, there would be no basis for choice. But that is no reason to react with the same emotions to an infant who is developing normally and an adult who has fallen from a very high to a very low level of well-being.

The alternatives between which we must choose are these: (A) The well-being of the injured adult and the normal child are not comparable. It is not the case that one is better off than the other, or worse off; or that they are equally well off. (B) They are at the same level of well-being. (C) The adult is better off than the child. (D) The child is better off than the adult. Positions (A) and (C) have little or no plausibility. So, we must choose between (B) and (D). And once we become clear about the question we are asking, it should be apparent that (B) is the superior answer: the adult and the child are at the same level of well-being. For our question is about how these two individuals are faring now, during this segment of their lives. It is not a question about their whole lives or about how their current stage of life compares with their earlier or future stages. We should not let the fact that the adult has suffered a great misfortune and evokes our sympathy mislead us into thinking that during this interval of time, when the adult's mental life is the same as that of the child, the child has a higher level of well-being.

A further point is that pity, the emotion that Nagel assumes to be appropriately felt for a man "reduce[d] to the mental condition of a contented infant," can distort and damage our personal relations. A wife who seeks to give loving care to a husband who has suffered this misfortune should not rehearse to herself thoughts about how pitiable his decline has been; she would do far better to bear in mind that the mental state he has returned to (that of the infant he once was) is filled with the cognitive, sensory, and social delights that are typically experienced at that stage. Nagel writes: "The intelligent adult has disappeared, and for a creature like the one before us, happiness consists in a full stomach and a dry diaper."[48] But of course there is more to the mental life of an infant than that, much of it marvelous. It would be well for a loving caregiver to reflect on the fact that the quality of life of a brain-injured adult who is in the same mental condition as his earlier infant self is just as good as it once used to be.

7. Temkin on exceptionally bad years

My approach to the assessment of overall lifetime well-being might be thought vulnerable to an objection drawn from an argument of Larry Temkin. He writes: "Suppose one is faced with a choice of living one of two lives. In the first, one will get to live at the exceptionally high level of 91 for 100 years, in the second one will get to live at the slightly higher exceptionally high level of 93 for 99 years, where the cost of doing so is a year of *exceptionally* bad pain and suffering…at a level of –90."[49] There is a total of 9,100 units of good in the first life and a balance of 9,117 in the second. The additive approach I have proposed holds that the second life is better, but Temkin says this is "deeply implausible, and I believe that most people would strongly agree with me."[50]

Temkin frames his example prospectively, so there is something we can agree about. As I have said, when we make choices about our long-term future, we should not condemn ourselves to long periods of severe suffering in the expectation that this sacrifice will bring us just a small increase in total well-being. But Temkin's example, although expressed in prospective terms, might be thought no less applicable to retrospective assessments of lifetime well-being. Suppose we alter his words so that the issue is this: which of two individuals, both deceased, was better off: one who was at the level of 91 for 100 years, or the one who was at 93 for 99 years, but –90 for one year? The purely additive-subtractive approach makes the second life better, despite its horrible year. Would Temkin be right to say that this is deeply implausible?

The general principle at work in this example is that when a continuous portion of a life contains much bad and little or no good, and that period of time is of significant length, then our overall assessment of the quality of the whole life should take that into account. In the second life, there is a year in which (let us assume) each day and week is overwhelmingly bad; the misfortunes keep coming without relief for the whole of that lengthy period. Does that individual suffer all the more because of that? If the example is meant to be realistic, the answer should be yes. As his year of relentless suffering

---

[48] Ibid., p. 6.   [49] *Rethinking the Good*, 113, author's emphasis.   [50] Ibid., 114.

unfolds, he looks back to recent days, weeks, and months, and finds nothing to sustain him—only bad memories. Looking forward, he might not know when, if ever, the bad days will end. Furthermore, the almost complete absence of relief from suffering is bound to degrade the psychological resources of anyone in this situation. Each new day of pain will be harder to bear than the previous one, just as a heavy weight becomes more difficult to lift again and again, as one's arms weaken through repeated exertion. The additional suffering felt because of the concentration of bad in this extended period of time must be included in any assessment of how bad that year was for him. Recall that Temkin represents the burdensomeness of that bad year as –90. If, when we combine its badness with the goodness of other years, that negative figure represents everything we need to know about that year—if it takes into account the compounded suffering that one experiences when it is long-lasting and unrelieved—then Temkin would be wrong to judge the first life better. There would be nothing else to do but compare the total amount of good in each of the two lives.

There is, however, a different way to think about Temkin's objection. Just as some people hold that it is *in itself* unjust and therefore morally objectionable for the world to contain people whose level of well-being is unequal through no fault of their own (whether or not they are aware of it), so, it might be said, it is a bad feature of a life that the suffering in it is distributed unequally over its various temporal portions.[51] In a life that has 93 exceptionally good years, each represented by the number 91, and one horrible year, represented by –90, there is a stark inequality between one year and the rest. That, it might be said, counts as a bad feature of such a life, and it is bad enough to make this life worse on balance than the first life Temkin describes, even though the second life would be judged better were we merely to add and subtract units of goodness and badness.

That idea, however, has nothing to recommend it, as I noted in the previous section. Years of a life do not have a claim to equal treatment. Nothing is amiss if someone decides to live through some bad times in order to have a better life on balance, thus creating an inequality of goodness between one year and the rest. Doing so would certainly not be unjust. Nor would it be imprudent.

There is one further feature of Temkin's argument that must now be considered. He says: "…it is better to live a life *all* of which is at an exceptionally high level than to live a life that is slightly better most of the time but includes a full year of terrible pain and suffering, during which one's life in not worth living."[52] Here he makes explicit what he takes to be a salient similarity and a salient (but small) difference between the two lives: (A) The salient similarity: they are alike in having many *exceptionally* good years. (B) The salient but small difference: although in one life those years are consistently better than the years in the other life, they are only *slightly* better. (Recall that one is at level 93 for 99 years, whereas the first is at level 91 for 100 years.) For nearly every year,

---

[51] Temkin explores the meaning of this egalitarian ideal in his earlier work, *Inequality*.
[52] *Rethinking the Good*, 115, author's emphasis.

the two lives are a mere two units out of 93 apart—hardly any difference at all. (Of course, there is also this all-important difference: the second life has one terrible year, while the first has none—a huge disparity in well-being for that one year.)

We might ask: so what? Although both lives are exceptionally good, one is somewhat better not just once or twice, but repeatedly. Should we lose sight of that repeated difference? Further, although one life has a terrible period and the other does not, that difference lasts for only one year. Should we lose sight of there being only one such year? Temkin's point that both lives are at "an exceptionally high level" (except for one terrible year) suggests that, to his mind, when a sufficiently high threshold of well-being is achieved over a sizable stretch of time, marginal increases in well-being above that threshold matter less and less. The superiority of the second life to the first by two units for each of many years ought to be discounted, one might suppose, because there is already so much well-being in each year. By contrast, if a continuous segment of someone's life is bad (in negative territory) and remains bad as that segment continues, each additional burdensome day should receive at least the same negative weight as the preceding one, when we assess the overall quality of the life. A single bad year therefore counts for a great deal, whereas it matters little whether an already good year could have been made better. That is why a life whose total score (when we merely add and subtract, and prior to discounting) is only somewhat higher than the total score of a different life might nonetheless be worse on balance. That total score would fail to represent the fact that making an already very good year somewhat better hardly matters.

But there is an obvious problem with this way of thinking: the temporal unit selected—one year—is completely arbitrary. It would be absurd to live one's life by dividing it into years, seeing to it that each year had just enough good to bring it up to a certain threshold of goodness, and caring little for how much good accrues the remainder of the year. (Why is the relevant unit a year? Why set the threshold at one level of well-being rather than another?) We look to the whole of our lives, as far as we can foresee the future, and seek as good a future as we can achieve, sometimes accepting some bad stretches (months, years) if they are very likely to bring a sufficient reward in the long run. Similarly, when we look back on someone else's life after his death, and assess its overall quality, we do not divide it into one-year portions (or any others) and treat the good bits that exceed a threshold within that period as lower in prudential value than the other good bits that fall within that stretch of time.

Our discussion has perhaps been excessively abstract, so let us make it more concrete with an example. Suppose a year of suffering is brought about in the following way: A sixty-year-old man spends one week of each year visiting old friends in a distant part of the world. Each week is filled with good discussion, good food, long walks, and so on. When he is eighty, he becomes terribly ill; unbeknownst to him, there is something in the atmosphere of that distant part of the world that gradually accumulates in his body and causes him to suffer for nineteen weeks. He recovers completely from this illness, and lives several more years. Knowing this about him, we look back, after his death, and ask: was he on balance better off or worse off for his having visited his friends? On the one hand, each visit was short—just a week. There were twenty separate visits, but it seems reasonable to add these together and say that he had twenty good weeks as a result of his travels. On the other hand, he suffered quite a bit because of those journeys—for nineteen weeks. Those nineteen weeks were not spread out over a period of nineteen years—they were nineteen weeks in a row. Does the fact that these nineteen weeks were continuous with each other matter, when we make this comparison? Only if that continuity had psychological consequences that made those weeks contain more on the bad side of the ledger than the good that accrued to him over the course of twenty weeks each belonging to a different year.

A retrospective review of the quality of his life must ask: What good did he derive from his visits? Was his friendship as good for him as a friendship can be, or was it a rather superficial relationship? Did each new visit bring as enjoyable and rich an experience as the last? Turning then to his illness, we must ask how much pain he suffered, and whether his pain kept him from having anything good in his life for that period of time. What was the psychological toll of the pain? Depending on how we answer these questions, we might be able to say that on balance it was definitely good for him to have made these visits, or that it was definitely bad, or that no clear conclusion can be drawn. We will add together the good, and subtract the bad. That is all there is to do.

As an afterthought, we might represent our conclusion numerically. If, for example, we are confident that those visits enhanced his life on balance, we might say: each week of his visit brought him 10 units of good for each of 20 weeks, whereas each week of his illness brought him 5 units of bad for 19 weeks. But these numbers would only be another way of conveying what we had already concluded.

We can embellish this story by imagining that the man in question learns, some time after his painful illness, that it was caused by his twenty annual visits. It would then be natural for him to look back and ask himself: "Would it have been better for me not to have taken those one-week vacations, in view of the later suffering they caused?" To answer that question, he must undertake the same sort of review that an external observer of his life might carry out—although, if he is good at recollecting what those visits were like, and what he went through during his illness, he is in a better position to make this assessment. But, like any external observer, he will assume that to answer his question he ought to add together the goodness of each of the twenty good weeks, and then subtract the badness of the later nineteen painful weeks. Suppose he undertakes this review and quickly concludes that he has no regrets about those annual visits to his friends, even though his miserable disease was the price he had to pay. It would be odd to accuse him of having made a mistake because he simply added together the value of each of the separate twenty good weeks and then subtracted the burdensomeness of his nineteen continuous weeks of illness. It would be strange to protest: "But each year in which you made a visit was a very good year! There was therefore little value in each of those twenty visits. You have failed to mark them down. You should have stayed home." To this he would rightly reply: "But the experiences I had during each of those one-week visits were no less wonderful because of how good the rest of each of those years was for me." We would be wrong to tell him that the quality of his experiences—what it was like for him to be with his friends—is a misleading indication of the value of his time spent with them.

Temkin calls the principle of aggregation that he applies to an individual's well-being over time the "Disperse Additional Burdens View." He introduces it as an inter-personal counsel that might be given a longer and more cumbersome name: "Disperse Additional Benefits So as to Prevent Any Individual from Having to Bear a Substantial Additional Burden."[53] But it retains its shorter name when he later applies that approach to the intrapersonal aggregation of good and bad over time. Notice that it is framed as an imperative: what we are counseled to do is "disperse additional burdens." As an imperative or counsel, it is prospective rather than retrospective. This is how we should arrange our lives as we look forward: rather than allow burdens to cluster and densely populate a single period of time, we ought to disperse them widely over many different periods.

What we have found, however, is that interpersonal and intrapersonal questions about the aggregation of well-being must be examined and treated separately. One reason why this is so is that individual well-being over time can be regarded both prospectively and retrospectively. These two perspectives cannot yield different results; it cannot be the case that someone's well-being over time is one thing when assessed in one temporal direction and another when assessed in the reverse direction. The slogan, "Disperse Additional Benefits," tacitly presupposes that we will not go astray if we approach the aggregation of well-being over time from a prospective point of view. But as it happens, it is the retrospective perspective that gives us the proper point of view from which to assess the overall well-being of a single life. When we are looking back on a life, we are not dispersing benefits and burdens—nothing we do affects the quality of that life. We are contemplating its ups and downs, asking how to combine them into a single overall evaluation. That might strike us as a pointless or silly exercise. Why bother?—that life is over, and it is not our own. The prospective problem of aggregation is the one whose significance is easily recognized. But we can now see that although the future-oriented question of aggregation has greater urgency, its backward-looking analogue has much to be said for it. It is the perspective from which we can truly assess the overall well-being of a life.

The retrospective assessment of lifetime well-being is a question that faces Aristotle, because what is salient to him is Solon's dictum, reported in Herodotus, that it is only after a life is over that we can know whether it was *eudaimon*.[54] In the *Nicomachean Ethics*, he shows how his conception of *eudaimonia* can solve a puzzle that might be raised about Solon's view: surely it cannot be the case that one is living well only when

---

[53] Ibid., 67.
[54] Herodotus, *History*, I.30–3. In the *Eudemian Ethics* (II.1 1219b6), Aristotle accepts Solon's dictum, but does not discuss it, as he does in the *Nicomachean Ethics*. We will return to Solon and Aristotle's treatment of this issue in sections 12 and 20.

one's life is over—so what can Solon have meant (I.10 1100a13–17)? The obvious answer is that only after a life is over can we know that it contains no tragedies of the sort that afflicted Priam. The retrospective view of a life is the one that Aristotle must take to achieve his purposes. He never addresses the prospective problem that we take to be of greater practical importance: what should we do when we have reason to expect that by undergoing great hardships for a limited period, we could have more lifetime well-being? That is a gap in his thinking, but we now see how salutary his retrospective perspective is.

8. Equal temporal weight

Do all the temporal parts of a lifetime have equal weight, or are some more important than others? That question can be interpreted in many different ways. Some philosophers say that the present is the only time of life that should matter to us. There is a kernel of truth in this, and later I will try to show what it is (section 16). But in this section, I will explain and defend the thesis that—to formulate it roughly—all times have equal value.[55]

A more precise formulation can be arrived at by taking a retrospective perspective on a life that has come to an end. We ask ourselves: "On balance, looking at the whole of his life, how well or badly did it go for him?" The thesis of equal value holds that, when we make this overall assessment, no temporal portion of a life is to receive more weight, simply in virtue of its temporal location, than any other. Some periods of life are early—very close to the beginning of an individual's existence. When we work out an overall assessment of total lifetime well-being, the well-being of that individual at that early point is not to be given greater or lesser weight than others simply because it occurs at such an early point. Similarly for late periods—the ones close to that individual's demise. And similarly, the fact that one time of life is earlier than another or later than another has no bearing on our overall assessment.

This thesis of equal weight is entirely compatible with the obvious point that during certain periods of our lives there are things that we do or that happen to us that have far more significant causal consequences than others. If a child is sexually abused, that can seriously damage him for the rest of his life. As a general rule, the early periods of our lives are far more important than the ones closest to the end, because they affect our future well-being for many more years. But the thesis of equal weight does not conflict with this familiar truth, because it claims only that an early period of life is not of greater or smaller value than others simply in virtue of its *temporal* relation to the others. When we are young, what we do and what happens to us often has serious *causal* consequences for our future. Their causal influence on later life is what makes

---

[55] This is the view of Henry Sidgwick, *The Methods of Ethics*, 381ff.; John Rawls, *A Theory of Justice*, sections 45 and 64; and Thomas Nagel, *The Possibility of Altruism*, chapter 8. For criticism, see Michael Slote, *Goods and Virtues*, 9–37. Slote's view will be considered in section 9 below.

them contribute so much to our overall well-being—not the mere fact that they occurred at an early point.

We can think of the temporal expanse of a lifetime as a container into which the things that happen to us and the actions we undertake are placed, as time moves on. Looking to the future, we ask ourselves: how do I want my life to go, when I am old? Here we are asking: What do we hope will be inside the container at that time? The thesis that all temporal portions of a life are equal in weight is a thesis about the container, not about what is inside it. Some portions of our lives contain much good, others much bad. But their temporal position within the container does not in itself matter; what does matter is the intrinsic prudential value of what goes into the container, as well as its causal effect on what comes later.

This entails that when we retrospectively assess the overall well-being of a life that has come to an end, we should not overlook the quality of life that individual had when he was a child, nor should we discount it merely because it was early. Because this portion of his life occurred long ago—long before the time when we are making our retrospective assessment—we might give it less than the equal weight it ought to receive. That would be the same sort of illegitimate temporal bias we exhibit when, in making plans for the future, we give less weight to the distant future simply because it is so far in the future. We should remind ourselves that childhood can be a wonderful period of life, and we should give full weight to it when we make our retrospective assessment. A lucky child grows up feeling the love of his parents and grandparents. He is delighted by fantasy but is also curious about the natural world. He enjoys games and sports. He is absorbed by books and adventures. If someone has been blessed with a childhood idyll, those years of joy must figure fully in an overall assessment of his lifetime well-being. They are not to be discounted simply because they occurred during the earliest period of his life.

Aristotle, it might be recalled (see Chapter 1, section 10), says that we should be glad when childhood is over. We should be pleased that we have moved on to the next stage of life, because if all goes well, our lives will be better. "…No one would choose to live the whole of his life with the mind of a child, even if he were to take the utmost pleasure in what pleases children" (X.3 1174a1–3). I suspect that there are aspects of childhood (fantasy, games, feeling loved) that he does not appreciate sufficiently, but even if he does underestimate its potential value, that does not undermine his more important claim that the periods of life that follow childhood are potentially better because of what they will contain. As I noted in that earlier section, a child's social, emotional, and cognitive immaturity places a limit on his well-being during that period of life, and these limitations are gradually surpassed as he matures and the full richness of adult life becomes available to him. In any case, it would not be fair to accuse Aristotle of downgrading childhood simply because of its temporal position. It is what goes into that period of life—not its earliness per se—that makes him regard it as our least rewarding time, with respect to its potential prudential value. He is right about that. Adulthood brings with it richer possibilities, although they may not be realized.

9. Slote on discounting

Michael Slote notes that when we consider "how fortunate someone has been in life" we have "a definite tendency to discount youthful misfortune or success...."[56] That may be true—but is this tendency justified? Slote claims that it is, and his defense of that claim depends in part on assumptions he makes about the kinds of goods children typically value. They care about such things as being captain of the team, receiving prizes, and the like. These, he admits, are good in a way—they are what he calls "period-relative goods,"[57] giving children "childhood-reasons for action."[58] But they are not to be counted as significant goods when we consider someone's life "from the large perspective of life as a whole."[59] That is one reason why he thinks our "tendency to discount youthful misfortune or success..." is justified.

But childhood, as I noted in the previous section, can be a wonderful time. If a child warms to the love of his family, is filled with curiosity about the world, loves sports, delights in reading, he has goods far more valuable than the school prizes or popularity contests Slote refers to. Such goods as a child's sense of wonder and adventure are not to be dismissed or assigned negligible value in an overall reckoning of how well his life has gone, when it is retrospectively assessed. Similarly, the awfulness of an awful childhood ought to figure in full measure in any assessment of overall lifetime well-being. But what especially interests me in Slote's ideas about this matter is a further reason he gives for ignoring how the early period of life goes: it ought not to be taken seriously in our overall assessment of someone's well-being, he claims, precisely because it is early. It is, in other words, not only what is typically put into the temporal container that makes childhood have little or no prudential value in itself, it is also childhood's early position within the container.

Slote also speaks of "the greater importance attributed to later periods,"[60] suggesting, with this phrase, that just as childhood is and ought to discounted, in an overall assessment of lifetime well-being, so the last stage of life deserves to be given additional weight precisely because it comes last. "What happens late in life is naturally and automatically invested with greater significance and weight in determining the goodness of lives...."[61] He also speaks of "the badness or tragic quality of King Lear's life";[62] note that it is his *life* that is called tragic, not just its final stage. That implies that in an overall reckoning of Lear's lifetime well-being, its terrible ending overshadows and perhaps even undoes whatever good came to him earlier.

Not only are the good and bad elements of the earliest stage of life to be discounted and those of its last stage magnified; in addition, he thinks, a third temporal feature of our lives must figure in our reckoning of its overall well-being: it is better for us if there is an upward slope in well-being than a downward slope. Slote illustrates this

---

[56] *Goods and Virtues*, 14. For criticism, see Lazari-Radek and Singer, *The Point of View of the Universe*, 129–33.
[57] *Goods and Virtues*, 21.   [58] Ibid., 30.   [59] Ibid., 30.   [60] Ibid., 34.
[61] Ibid., 23.   [62] Ibid., 25.

third factor by contrasting two political careers: in the first, a man spends the early part of his adult life in the "political wilderness," but then, later in life, he achieves the power he has long sought, and does great things with it. A second man achieves "meteoric success" in his younger years, attaining the same office as the first man and achieving as much good, but then loses power, never to regain it.[63] I take Slote's point to be that the value of a whole life includes not only the combined value of its temporal segments, but something further: the direction of change over the course of the life.[64]

I disagree with all three of these proposals: that the earliness of our younger years diminishes their intrinsic prudential importance; that the lateness of our later years magnifies their contribution to overall well-being; and that an upward or downward slope in well-being by itself enhances or diminishes it.

Several hypothetical cases illustrate the implausibility of these views. First, imagine that our lives had the opposite developmental direction from the one with which we are familiar. In this alternative world, human beings would come into existence at the height of their cognitive, emotional, and social powers; and then, as life continues, they would become increasingly like children. The earliness of our early years would not make their contribution to lifetime well-being negligible.

A second hypothetical case casts doubt on Slote's thesis regarding the upward or downward slope of our fortunes and misfortunes. Return to McTaggart's oyster, but for current purposes, think of *two* of them, one of them experiencing more pleasure with each passing day, the other less. The point of considering these oysters is not, as before, to compare the value of their lives with ours, but to compare each to the other. (It is no longer relevant, then, that they live very long lives.) The first oyster has less pleasure each day, but it has no awareness that this is so. On its first day of life it has a full unit of pleasure; on the second day one half of that; on the third, one half again; until, on the day of its death, it experiences the barest noticeable amount of pleasure. Its total well-being has approached two units of pleasure. The second oyster receives, on its first day of life, the same tiny fraction of one unit of pleasure that the first oyster felt on its last; then, on each subsequent day it is given more, until it dies. Assume that the second oyster's schedule of pleasures eventually produces a total lifetime score of nearly two units of pleasure. There is, then, the same quantity of pleasure and therefore the same amount of good in each oyster's life—if what we consider is only the temporal parts of their lives, and ignore the direction in which their lives improved or declined.

Our two oysters have the same overall quality of life; the difference in the slopes, one upward and the other downward, of the amount of pleasure they felt does not affect our overall assessment of how good each life was. For neither was aware from one day to the next how its level of pleasure compared with what it had been aware of in preceding

[63] Ibid., 23.

[64] See too Temkin, *Rethinking the Good*, 111–12: the "shape" of a life matters as well as its total goodness or badness. In a footnote, he suggests that Aristotle would agree, since he "attaches special importance to how our lives conclude" (111, n. 24). I return to the significance of a life's "shape" in sections 11–13, and to Aristotle in sections 12 and 20.

days. We, as outside observers, note that difference, but it does not affect our judgment of the quality of their lives, because it did not figure in their consciousness.

Does anything follow from this about human well-being? The natural extension of the conclusion we have reached about our two oysters is that the direction of change in well-being of a life—the life of *any* conscious creature—makes no contribution to its overall lifetime well-being, if that creature is unaware of the change. Accordingly, when we *are* aware of the direction of change, that affects the quality of our lives by altering the quality of our experience of life. In addition to feeling good or bad about the events in our lives that are occurring now, we are aware, at the same time, of how they compare with what we know of our earlier days, and so either disappointment or a sense of amelioration, or a complex combination of both, mingles with our experience of the present.

If you visit a beautiful landscape each day to enjoy its beauty, you will not be indifferent to any deterioration it exhibits from one time to another. If it becomes noticeably less attractive, the delight you take in it will be diminished because you will compare it to what it was like the day before. The reverse phenomenon will produce increasing delight. You cannot isolate your current experience and react to it as though it were your first; it is heightened or diminished by your expectations and your recognition of what you could be experiencing now (because you experienced it before), but are not. Conversely, if you think that your life is getting worse with each passing year, the emotional quality of your life will be tinged with disappointment; a sense that things are steadily getting better will have the opposite emotional effect.

If one is acutely aware that one's death is approaching—just a few more years, or months, or days—that may alter the way one experiences one's good or ill fortune during that final period. Time will seem more precious, and how it is filled will matter more than it had before. Perhaps the horrors that Lear lived through were all the worse for his knowing that this was the last stage of his life. But if we imagine that, before he made his disastrous mistake of ceding power to his most professedly loving daughter, his life was filled with wonderful things and had little in the way of suffering, we will say that only the last stage of his life was tragic—not the whole of it. True, Shakespeare's *play* counts as a tragedy, and it is the *whole* play that is so classified, not just its last lines or last act. But that does not entail that our overall assessment of the lifetime well-being of a real person whose final days are like Lear's must count it a bad life. The prudential value of the earlier parts of such a life (the ones that preceded its tragic ending) is not undercut or even diminished by what happens in the end. That the tragic portion of such a life is also its final portion does not by itself magnify the role that period should play in an assessment of its total well-being.

Slote acknowledges that his readers may appeal to the different ways in which we experience upward and downward changes in our circumstances, and in this way question his thesis that when good things enter our lives later rather than earlier, that temporal fact by itself makes our lives better. Such readers may be tempted to think: it is better for good things to come later because we take pleasure in anticipating them, and these pleasures are greater than those we feel when we remember the good things of the past. To address this concern, he returns to his example of contrasting slopes: one man starts out in a "political wilderness" but achieves power and success later in life; to a second man these goods come early in life, but he is then forced out of politics. He now adds: assume that the first man has no hopes or expectations, during his earlier years, of later political success; and assume that the second man, having been forced out of politics, hopes and expects to return to it. Even so, Slote claims, we have a "greater estimation of the former's career."[65] That, he says, shows that we have a "sheer preference for goods that come later."[66]

It is unfortunate that Slote speaks here of what we "esteem" or should esteem in an individual's "career," for the question under discussion is the quality of a *life*, not esteem for a career. We want to know whether the direction of change in someone's well-being (whether it moves upwards or downwards) is an ingredient of his overall well-being, apart from any effect it has on his experience. Returning to Slote's two politicians, as he describes them in the preceding paragraph, we should ask: which has more well-being over the course of his life? The first man has no hope or expectation of political success during the first part of his adult life, but then attains the power he has long sought. The second man achieves political success during the first part of his life, loses it, but is ever hopeful, when he is out of power, that he will succeed again. It is reasonable, then, to assume that the first goes through a long period of frustration before he eventually succeeds, whereas the second is full of hope and optimism when he is out of power. We are assuming that they exercise power for the same number of years, and that the experiential quality of those years is equally high for both. I do not see why we should esteem the *career* of the first man more highly than the second, but what is more important for our purposes is that the second man surely has the better *life*—filled as it is with hope and optimism, rather than frustration and pessimism. I conclude that Slote has not offered a convincing reason for his thesis that it is better for us when goods enter our lives later rather than earlier precisely because they are later, and apart from any effect that temporal difference has on our experience of life.

Slote may nonetheless be right about certain kinds of career: they are more estimable when there is steady improvement, as an individual moves from moderate accomplishments to achievements that are increasingly impressive. Novelist A produces a brilliant work in her twenties, and with each decade publishes a new novel, each less excellent than its predecessor. Novelist B is prolific in the same way (one book each decade) but her accomplishment grows steadily. Which is the more admirable record? Assume that the overall quality of a lifetime of work is the same in each case—B's best and last work is a match for A's best and earliest, and so on. Even so, there is more to esteem in B's ascending career than A's record of decline. B learned from her earlier efforts and became a master of the art of the novel, whereas A luckily hit the mark at first but then failed to learn from her earlier efforts—she in fact became worse at her craft.

---

[65] *Goods and Virtues*, 24.   [66] Ibid., 25.

Perhaps this is what Slote has in mind when he uses his two politicians to support the thesis that it is better for goods to be later than earlier. But we should recall, once again, that our topic is prudential value, not, in the first instance, excellence at some task (although being good at something may in some cases be one ingredient of well-being). Novelist B has a more admirable career trajectory than A, but it does not follow that her level of well-being moves higher with each passing decade, or that she has more lifetime well-being than A. Although the quality of her novels may steadily improve, she may believe the opposite of them; many of her critics may fail to recognize the increasing excellence of her work; and the labor required by each new novel may take a terrible toll on her psychological and physical health. A, on the other hand, might move to a higher level of well-being with each passing decade, because she cares little about the trajectory of her career and has many non-literary activities, each more wonderful than artistic success, in her life.

We must be careful, when we reason from hypothetical examples to conclusions about how well-being *over* time is related to well-being *at* a time, that the lives we construct for purposes of illustration really are clear cases of faring well or poorly. This is a defect in Slote's argument, for it is not obvious that possessing political power is a basic component of well-being. By contrast, it does seem uncontroversial that the quality of someone's experience is at least one (and a very important) element of well-being. Discussions of this topic—well-being over time—will therefore be soundest when the examples they appeal to as evidence are of individuals whose *experience of life* varies from one period of life to another.

10. Steady decline and an oyster-like existence

I noted in the previous section that our experience of our present circumstances is affected by memories and expectations. The quality of our experience—how good or bad it is for us to be in our present conscious state—depends to some extent on whether we react to the present as a period of improvement or decline. A further point should now be recognized: even if one senses that the quality of one's life is not as good as it once was, and even if one expects that it will continue to decline steadily, one may also judge—and judge accurately—that one's overall lifetime well-being will be greater if one carries on with one's life. One should not wish for death simply on the grounds that life will never be as good, going forward, as it is now—and that it will become increasingly less good. At any rate, that one should continue to live one's life, even if its quality will steadily decline, is a conclusion one arrives at if one assumes, as I have been doing, that—as I said in section 5—"the best lifetime with respect to well-being [is] the one that has the greatest quantity of prudential value over time." Even when future periods bring less and less well-being than past periods have brought, they still add to the overall prudential value of one's lifetime.

Suppose, for example, that in one's twenties one loves to play tennis and excels as an amateur. It is, let's assume, one of the experiences that makes one's life a good one.

One might foresee, however, that one's athletic abilities will gradually decline over the course of one's life, and that as a result, it will never be quite as satisfying as it is now to participate in this sport. Someone who killed himself for this reason would be making a terrible mistake. It would also be a mistake to stop playing tennis for this reason. One should simply accept that this part of one's life will not have the same prudential value that it has now, and that it will continue to make a smaller contribution as time passes. Playing tennis, though enjoyable, will be a mixed experience, assuming that one can never stop comparing one's present pleasure with what one felt before. But mixed experiences can on balance be good experiences. If one can keep one's disappointment from dominating one's attention, there remains a good reason not to give up the sport. (There will of course be competing reasons for turning instead to some other sport or some other type of activity, if doing so would increase the overall quality of one's life.)

When, however, the quality of someone's experiences are such that they are no better than those that could be felt by an oyster, and there can be no future improvement in that individual's condition, then what is distinctively good in *human* life is no longer available. There are two competing ways to describe this situation—but for my purposes here, there is, fortunately, no need to decide between them. According to the more radical alternative, the individual in question (suppose he was called Jones before he declined) has ceased to exist, because the mental life sustained by the physical organs that once belonged to Jones is too unlike the mental life they now sustain. If that is the correct diagnosis of what has happened to him, then of course we must conclude that the oyster-like pleasures that are now felt by Jones's successor are not to be added to Jones's overall lifetime well-being. After all, what we want to know is how Jones's life went—not the combined total of Jones's well-being and that of some other individual.[67]

By contrast, according to the second alternative, Jones still exists—he simply has become unable to possess any sort of good other than the kind available to an oyster. In this case, the overall lifetime well-being of Jones continues to increase. Even so, it would make good sense to refuse to mingle together into a single sum the well-being that accrued to Jones before his experiences became oyster-like and the quality of life he has after he enters his oyster-like phase. He himself may not care to extend his oyster-like pleasures for as far into the future as possible; what matters to him instead may be his distinctively human well-being, and that will have ceased to increase. We too may think it best, as he does, not to mingle together these two "scores"—the amount of well-being that accrues to him before he becomes oyster-like, and the amount that comes afterwards. It would be implausible to suppose that keeping these two assessments apart from each other is arbitrary, as though it were akin to keeping

---

[67] There is a large recent literature that seeks a general answer—one applicable to all of us—to the question, "When did I come into existence, and when will I cease to exist?" (Often the question takes this form: "What is it for a person to continue through time?" But there is an important difference between these formulations. The first leaves it open that one might not always have been or remain a person.) Part III of Derek Parfit, *Reasons and Persons*, has played a central role in the debate. I have also learned much from Jeff McMahan, *The Ethics of Killing*; and Marya Schechtman, *Staying Alive*.

track of someone's well-being on the Tuesdays of his life and on his Fridays. If McTaggart's thesis is rejected, oyster-like pleasures are immeasurably lower in value than the goods that constitute a good life for a human being. Jones can reasonably suppose that at the time when the only goods that will be available to him are of the lower order of value attained by an oyster, his well-being no longer has a claim to his attention or anyone else's.

Part Two

We are (roughly) at a midpoint in our discussion of the relationship between well-being and time. I have been defending, and will continue to defend, the thesis that the total well-being of a whole life is an aggregate: we assess the overall quality of someone's life by adding and subtracting—adding up the duration of his good experiences and subtracting the duration of his bad experiences. (Of course, it also matters *how* good or bad these experiences are—not just their duration.) The point applies no less to non-human lives—to McTaggart's long-lived oyster, for example. He is right to assume that the longer an oyster feels pleasure, the better a life it has overall. But I have not yet completed my defense of this claim; our discussion of this issue will continue almost to the end of this chapter.

A statement made in Chapter 1, section 6 still requires explanation and defense: "the quality of human consciousness," I said, can be "so good (provided that it endures over a sufficient period of time) that no amount of simple oyster pleasure, however long-lasting, will give it a better life." What is a sufficient period of time?

And we still have on our agenda Plato's thesis that eternal possession of the good would be best (and so death is an evil); Aristotle's claim that *eudaimonia* needs a "complete life"; and the doctrine, endorsed by the Stoics and Plotinus, that once the proper goal of life has been reached, it does not matter how long or briefly one remains in that state. We will find some truth in the ancient idea that Goethe endorses when he has Faust and Helen jointly affirm that "only the present is our happiness."

11. Velleman on narrative significance

David Velleman argues for a conception of lifetime well-being radically at odds with the one I have been presenting. The question he raises is exactly the one I have addressed here. As he puts it: "What is the relation between the value ["welfare value," as he sometimes calls it] of a period and the shorter periods it comprises? Is a good day a day during which one is frequently well off? Is a good week just a week in which the good days outweigh the bad? Is a good life just a string of good years?"[68]

He also speaks of "momentary welfare" throughout his essay—the welfare of an individual *at* a time, rather than "over an extended period."[69] That phrase, "momentary welfare," might be used to refer to someone's well-being at a durationless point in time.

---

[68] 'Well-Being and Time,' in *The Possibility of Practical Reflection*, 56–7.   [69] Ibid., 56.

Suppose someone was feeling pleased at noon last Friday. His experience must have had *some* duration, however brief, but even so, it would be correct to say that *at* noon (that durationless point) his experience was a good one. Durationless instants of time, of course, cannot be added together to form something that does have duration. Moments of welfare, in this sense, cannot be strung together to constitute longer-term welfare.[70] I will assume, then, that Velleman's use of "momentary welfare" refers to the *shorter* periods in which we can say that things were going well or badly for someone. These vary in duration, depending on what one is experiencing. Someone might tell a joke, for example, that is fifteen seconds in the telling. That can count as a good experience, but it is experienced as a cohesive unit rather than as an accumulation of staccato seconds or micro-seconds. Velleman's question, then, is about how long-term well-being—and, most important of all, lifetime well-being—is related to the shorter periods within it. Do we just add together the value of shorter periods? No, he replies; something more complex is involved.

"The value of an extended period," he writes, "depends on the overall order or structure of events—on what might be called their dramatic or narrative relations."[71] To illustrate, he, like Slote, asks us to imagine two lives, one with an upward trend (beginning with a horrible childhood but ending in "peaceful retirement"), the other with the reverse trajectory (ending with "misery in old age").[72] The sum of momentary well-being, he asks us to assume, is equal; but, according to Velleman, the life that improves is plausibly thought to be superior because of the narrative relation among its earlier and later parts. At any rate, he notes, this possibility cannot be ruled out a priori.[73] It is at least *possible* that a life is made better because its parts have a certain structure; there *could* be something other than the aggregated value of the temporal parts that enhances or degrades the quality of the whole, just as a novel whose beginning, middle, and end fit together as an integrated artistic whole has more to offer than the combined quality of each sentence or chapter.

If Velleman's argument consisted solely of this example, its force would be open to question. As I noted (section 5), when the quality of our lives steadily improves, our awareness that this is the direction in which we are moving changes the way we experience each period that is present to us. He therefore asks us to assume that when we add together the short-term well-being of the improving life, the overall sum is the same as the combined short-term well-being of the declining life. For that to be the case, the segments of the improving life need some features that would make them significantly worse than the segments of the declining life—were it not for the effects of comparing them with what preceded them. And in that case the total well-being of the two lives

---

[70] Durationless instants of time are sometimes called the "mathematical" or "strict" present, as distinguished from the phenomenal present, which has duration. Psychological studies of our experience of time often use William James's term, "the specious present," to designate the brief but temporally extended unit in which time is experienced. See for example Barry Dainton, 'Time Passage and Immediate Experience,' in Craig Callender (ed.), *The Oxford Handbook of Philosophy of Time*, 392–3; and Jenann Ismael, 'Temporal Experience,' ibid., 461–7.

[71] Velleman, 'Well-Being and Time,' 58.   [72] Ibid., 58.   [73] Ibid., 59.

would be equal simply because the improving life was enhanced by its repeatedly containing the joys that come with rising good fortune, whereas the declining life was degraded by the ongoing sense of deterioration that accompanies the experiences of which it is composed. The "overall order or structure of events" or "their dramatic or narrative relations" would not make a *further* contribution to the assessment of their relative lifetime well-being. Their upward or downward direction will have made a difference because of the different ways in which they enhance or detract from each short-term period of life. The prudential value of the whole life would simply be the sum of the value of its parts.

Here is an analogy: Mr. A studies two paintings, one in the morning, the other in the afternoon. The second painting is artistically superior, but before it is presented to him, his memory of the first is wiped clean. Somewhat artificially, let's say that he receives two units of pleasure in the morning and three in the afternoon. The next day, these two paintings are shown in the reverse sequence to Mr. B (whose memory is also wiped clean midday). He receives three units of pleasure in the morning and two in the afternoon.

Was A's day better, even though he experienced no more pleasure than B, because his contemplation of the better of the two paintings came after his contemplation of the worse? By hypothesis neither compared his afternoon experience to his morning experience. So the difference in the shape of their days should make no difference to them. Neither would be rational to pay a certain amount of money to have his day go from the worse painting to the better. However, if we want to change the example, eliminating the hypothesis that their memories are wiped clean, then the order in which they view the paintings will make a significant difference to them. Each would then have a reason to pay to see the better painting in the afternoon: for then he can fully enjoy what the inferior painting has to offer, without any sense of its inferiority; and his appreciation of the second painting will be enhanced because he cannot help but compare it to the first.

If we want to retain the assumption that the total pleasure each receives over the course of the day is the same, that will require us to make some further assumption as well: there will have to be something negative about A's experience that explains why on balance he did not have a more pleasant day than B, in spite of the fact that he was not aware of the first painting's inferiority when he viewed it in the morning, and was delighted by the superiority of the painting he viewed in the afternoon. However we choose to explain this, it would be wrong to look for the explanation in the fact that the better of the two paintings entered his life later in the day. It would be absurd to suppose that it is better for someone to look at the worse of two paintings first simply because the artistic merit of what we view should have an upward direction, regardless of how this affects our way of experiencing them. How good a day A and B have is a mere sum of the quality of their mornings plus the quality of their afternoons, and the opposite order of what they encounter over the course of the day makes a difference to their total well-being only insofar as it affects the value of these temporal segments.

There is no reason to suppose that some other approach applies to larger temporal segments of a life than mornings and afternoons. What we have said about adding the quality of a morning to the quality of an afternoon, to arrive at an overall evaluation of how the day went, should apply to weeks, months, seasons, years, life stages, and so on. At any rate, we have found no reason, as yet, to suppose that some other approach is appropriate for larger units. (What would those units be? Selecting temporal expanses shorter than a whole life would be arbitrary.) I am not proposing that it is self-evident and in no need of argument that overall lifetime well-being is to be assessed simply by adding together the prudential value that accrues, stage by stage, over the course of a life. Rather, I find this thesis plausible because it applies to one's longest temporal period of all—one's entire lifetime—the method of aggregation we use to answer such smaller-scale questions as, "How did his day go?," "How good a year was it for him?," and the like. Perhaps we do need a different method for answering the question, "How good was his life?," but if so, we should expect some explanation for that shift.

We must turn, then, to additional material in Velleman's essay, if we are to be convinced that total lifetime well-being is not simply the combined value of its shorter parts. To support his position, he offers several examples in which "the narrative relation" between earlier and later events is such that the significance of an earlier event is altered by what follows it.[74] In one sort of case, he calls our attention to the value of learning from one's misfortunes. "If a life's value were a sum of momentary well-being, learning from a misfortune would be no more important than learning from other sources.... On being invited to learn from a personal tragedy, one would therefore be entitled to reply, 'No, I think I'll read a book instead.' "[75]

There are times, however, when this reply would be justified. Suppose a doctor, knowing that she has just one more year to live, ends her medical career by performing a complicated and novel operation on a patient. The operation goes badly and the patient dies. Obviously, she should be deeply troubled by her failure. But Velleman is imagining a narrative in which one learns from a tragedy—drawing a lesson from it—not one in which grief is the only response. What lesson, then, should this doctor learn? "Now I know never to do that kind of operation again" would be a silly and frivolous response. She knew in advance that this would be her last operation. "I am going to spend the year acquiring the skills that will keep me from making the same mistake again" would also be a poor reaction—that would be a wasted year. But if, in addition to feeling great remorse, she resists whatever urge she feels to improve her medical skills, and devotes herself instead to the study of a great work of literature, that would not be a terrible use of her time. She would be adding to her overall lifetime well-being. Whether it is in one's interest to devote time to learning from one's mistakes is a matter to be decided by looking to the *future* benefits of doing so.

A second example: "In one life your first ten years of marriage are troubled and end in divorce, but you immediately remarry happily; in another life the troubled years of

---

[74] Ibid., 63.   [75] Ibid., 64.

your first marriage lead to eventual happiness as the relationship matures. Both lives contain ten years of marital strife followed by contentment; but let us suppose that in the former you regard your first ten years of marriage as a dead loss, whereas in the latter you regard them as the foundation of your happiness."[76] Two lengthy periods of life, each having in equal measure an unhappy and then a happy portion; but in the first, Velleman says, "the bad times ... are cast off, and in the other they are redeemed."[77]

I take him to be assuming that when a husband and wife remain with the same partner despite their troubled marriage, and their relationship improves, that is because each partner has admirably learned how to alter his or her behavior and attitudes for the better. The second couple—the one that stays the course and eventually achieves marital contentment—draws upon such moral qualities as loyalty, courage, compassion, and a willingness to compromise; by contrast, the first couple might have ended their relationship because they lacked these admirable traits. But the conclusion Velleman wants to draw is not that one couple is morally superior to the other. It is that when the story of a life is that of the second marriage, it is the story of a better life for each partner. They achieve a higher degree of well-being than does the first couple, even though, by hypothesis, there is just as little happiness during the first ten years of marriage, and just as much after that. Happiness, Velleman assumes, is a component of well-being, and its opposite has negative valence, but the second couple "redeems" the bad years, whereas the bad years of the first couple are simply "cast off." The second couple, looking back at their first ten years, has a new perspective on it, and treats it as an integral component of an organic unit, a dramatic element of a narrative structure. When they were living through those first ten years, they were bad years, but when those same years are taken as part of the larger whole to which the happiness of the later years also belongs, that earlier period of time was time well used, because they learned from their mistakes.

It might sound as though Velleman is committed to a contradiction: the first part of the marriage was both bad for the couple and not bad for it. But he believes he can solve that potential problem by insisting that "well-being" is the name of two different conditions: momentary well-being and holistic or lifetime well-being. "Self-interest is not a unitary dimension of value."[78] They had little momentary well-being during the first part of the marriage; these were mainly bad years as they experienced each day, moment by moment. That of course was bad for them. But those same ten years then become components of a new stretch of time—the continuing marriage viewed as a whole—and from that longer perspective, they do not diminish the value of that whole but contribute to it, because they learned from them. By contrast, the first couple has ten bad years that never become components of a longer narrative unit. They were bad years to live through moment by moment, and even though they then move on to new

---

    [76] Ibid., 65.   [77] Ibid., 65–6.
    [78] He continues: "a person has two distinct sets of interests, lying along two dimensions—his synchronic interests, in being well off at particular moments, and his diachronic interests, in having good periods of time and, in particular, a good life" (ibid., 71).

partners and have as many new good years as does the second couple, those earlier bad years forever remain a bad part of their lives.

It is difficult to assess the force of this thought experiment because there are goods that are available to couples who have stood by each other through good times and bad, and who as a result develop stronger emotional bonds and a richer store of memories. They draw on some of their fond memories (even if there are few of them) and their awareness that their partner has been loyal through all these years. That is what the second couple can achieve if they remain together after their first ten rocky years, and that is what the first couple cannot have, after they "jump ship" and start new relationships. These differences must be ignored—if we can—when we assess the force of Velleman's argument. After all, these second-decade emotional experiences of the second couple add to their overall well-being simply by enhancing the quality of their lives after they have found a better basis for their marriage. They do not also enhance the quality of life they experienced during their troubled years, or somehow redeem their badness by incorporating them into a larger organic temporal whole. There is no need to say, as Velleman does, that "self-interest is not a unitary dimension of value," to explain why there are goods available to couples who stick together.

Think of all the unnecessary suffering that occurs when couples become enemies as well as lovers—the rage, the horrible things they say and do, the feelings of hating and being hated. If a couple survives this nightmare and eventually transforms their marriage into a happy relationship, and they think back to their bad times, they must feel anguish at the needless suffering that they inflicted and endured. They have learned *something* from all that suffering, and have put it to good use, with the result that now their relationship is a good one. But if our thought experiment is to be realistic, it must be one in which much of that early suffering was a dead loss. Those periods of suffering do not become a component of a further "dimension of value" in which they no longer detract from but enhance the quality of their lives. And to the extent that the bitter times did have some instrumental value—because they learned a lesson from them—it is *only* instrumental value that they have. They are not components of well-being.

It might help to reflect on an example that has a structure similar to the one we have been discussing. You stand in a queue all day because you want to get a ticket to tonight's performance of one of your favorite singers. There you are, spending ten hours on your feet in the cold and rain. Our story now branches into two alternative denouements. First: you succeed in getting a ticket, and you enjoy a wonderful performance. Second: at the end of the tenth hour in the queue, you are told that no more tickets are available, but just then a friend phones you and offers you a ticket to a concert being given that night by another of your favorite singers. In the first scenario, the time you spent on the queue has not been wasted; you put it to good use. In the second scenario, it has been wasted. Had you spent the day curled up in bed with a good novel, you would have done better. Even so, in both cases there is a miserable morning and afternoon followed by a wonderful evening. They differ in that in one case the wonderful evening results from what you did, and in the second case it does not. Should we say, then, that in one scenario you have a better day?

If Velleman's way of thinking is correct, you have a better day by attending the concert you hoped to hear all through the day. For in that scenario, the suffering you endured was redeemed, whereas it was a dead loss in the other scenario. You earned a ticket in one case, but not in the other; and it is better for you, he thinks, to have a good by earning it than by good luck. But it is more plausible, I suggest, to say that there is no such difference. Of course, if your enjoyment of a concert is diluted because, as you listen, you keep thinking about how you wasted your morning and afternoon standing in the cold and rain, then your evening would have been better for you had your efforts been successful. But that is because the quality of your experience over the course of the evening would be lower. Similarly, if your enjoyment of a concert is enhanced because you are aware, as it proceeds, that what you are now hearing is the result of your painful efforts, then you are better off attending that concert than the other. But again, in this case, what makes you better off is not the very fact that your suffering produced results, but your *awareness* of that fact all through the performance. What gives you a better day is simply the better quality of your experience in the evening.

This example and Velleman's exhibit the same structure: a bad period followed by a good one; but in one case during the good period one builds on what one did in the bad one, whereas in the other case one does not. It seems obvious from the example of queuing for a performance that early suffering does not lose its badness because of what results from it. Velleman's example has the potential to mislead us because we so easily bring to it assumptions that should not be allowed to affect our thinking. These are the assumptions I mentioned earlier: our admiration for loyalty, courage, perseverance; and the deeper bonds that may grow as a relationship endures. The example of queuing for a concert reminds us that suffering that leads to a good result is not redeemed simply by having that outcome.

That point can be strengthened by changing the example slightly: you have been queuing in miserable weather, you are about to receive a ticket, but just at that moment a friend offers you a ticket to a performance that evening that you know you would enjoy much more. Should you nonetheless stick to your original plan because you have suffered through so much of the day? That would give you an evening that you earned through hard work—but by hypothesis that is not going to affect the way you experience the concert. If you really will have a better evening at the other concert, that is the one you should attend. It would be a mistake to stick to your plan simply because you have sunk so much time and effort into it, and suffered so much.

The structurally similar question about staying with a marriage partner is filled with complexities that my example of queuing for a ticket lacks, for reasons we have already noticed. Whether to sustain or abandon a long-term relationship is a moral and not merely a prudential question; which of two concerts to attend is not. If one stays in a relationship, the quality of one's life will be affected by one's past experience of it in a way that has no parallel in the case of hearing a performance after having spent the day waiting in a queue. Nonetheless, if we stipulate that by ending one relationship and entering another, the quality of your experience will be better for you, and the only question is how best to serve your own good as you move forward, then that is what you ought to do.

12. Velleman and Solon

Let us turn now to Velleman's thesis that the full span of a human life is something that either goes badly or well as an integrated whole, and is not merely a string of good or bad years. In this respect it is like a story; it has a narrative structure, and is made good or bad not by the accumulation of separate events, but by the proper relations among its seasons and stages. So, if someone has had a happy childhood—let's say that it is a period of fifteen years—it is not as though he has fifteen years of *unitary* lifetime well-being "in the bank." Those are fifteen accumulated years of *momentary* well-being, but in a final reckoning of the holistic goodness of that individual's life, their contribution may be positive or negative, depending on the way they are structurally related to what comes later. The same point applies to later stages of life. (Recall Velleman's statement that "self-interest is not a unitary dimension of value." For him, there are two kinds of well-being, not one.)

It follows that it is only at the end of a life that one can make a completely secure judgment of its lifetime holistic well-being. If things go very well in the final period, that could cancel all the bad that had come earlier; similarly, misfortunes that shortly precede death can cancel all previous good. Velleman therefore remarks, "...we are inclined to perceive some wisdom in Solon's refusal to declare Croesus happy without knowing how his life would ultimately turn out."[79] It is only some wisdom, not the whole story of well-being, for momentary well-being remains unchanged with the passage of time; the bad days you had as a child remain bad days. But when life is assessed along another dimension of well-being, those early bad days can be an enhancement of well-being, just as good days might make no contribution to (perhaps even detract from) the quality of the whole. There is just a single "score," be it high or low, that can be assigned to unitary lifetime well-being, because it is only in virtue of the whole story of a completed life that its level of holistic well-being is achieved and fixed.

How plausible is this way of assessing the well-being of a whole life? Consider the life of Priam, king of Troy—the example Aristotle uses when he discusses Solon's dictum that no life should be deemed *eudaimon* until it is over and can be seen as a whole (*NE* I.9 1100a5–9, I.10 1101a6–8). His son, Hektor, had been killed in battle. His city, Ilium, had been destroyed, its army decimated, its women and children held captive as slaves. As Velleman notes, when Aristotle reflects on the tragedy that befell Priam, he (Aristotle) sees some merit in Solon's dictum. It seems that something like Velleman's holistic approach to well-being—his thesis that there is a kind of lifetime

---

[79] Ibid., 73.

well-being that is not a mere accumulation of the good and bad in shorter periods—has been around for a long time, and Aristotle sees some plausibility in it. (*Seems*—but only seems, for reasons I am about to give.)

When I reflect on the life of Priam, I find nothing to support the idea that all of the good that has occurred in a life can be cancelled simply in virtue of the fact that it ends badly. Let's suppose that Priam had the happiest of childhoods; make the same assumption about his adolescence (assuming, anachronistically, that there was such a thing in antiquity), early manhood, middle age, and any other stages of life that come to mind. Then there is a reversal of fortune in the last years of his life, and he came to a tragic end, filled with lamentation and grief. I can find no reason to say, as Velleman would, that although Priam had much momentary well-being all through his life, there is a second kind of well-being (unitary, holistic lifetime well-being), and Priam's life sinks to the bottom when it is assessed in that way, despite the fact that for nearly the entirety of his life it went well.

It makes more sense to say that what Priam failed to achieve, despite all the good years he had, was well-being *throughout* his life. For Aristotle, whether or not someone is *eudaimon* is a question that must be answered by seeing how he is faring over a considerable period of time—a point we will come back to (section 20). That is why he thinks there is something to Solon's dictum. He feels some pressure, in fact, to make the period of time in which *eudaimonia* can be achieved the full span of a life.

For our current purposes in this section, the question is not how to interpret Aristotle but whether the life of our partially imaginary Priam—who had a wonderful existence (we suppose) up to its final stage, but then a tragic ending—should be regarded in the way Velleman proposes. Did he have much of one kind of well-being (an accumulation of many good days and just a few bad ones) but no well-being of another kind (because his tragic end made his earlier years prudentially worthless)? I see no reason to describe the good and bad in his life in this bifurcated way. We can accurately and thoroughly assess the prudential value of his life by saying that it was very high for many years and then became quite low at the end. He did not fare well (was not *eudaimon*) *throughout* his adult life—but that is simply because what it takes to fare well (be *eudaimon*) throughout one's adult life is to do well during every stage up to and including its final days. That is what "throughout" means here. But is there some structural, dramatic, narrative feature of Priam's life, taken as a whole, such that when we take that into account, we must say that his early and middle years make no positive contribution to his lifetime well-being, because what would otherwise be positive in them has been cancelled by what came later? No. There is only the plain fact that although he fared very well for a long time, he did not fare well throughout the whole of his life.

Velleman's conception of holistic lifetime well-being has implications, as he recognizes, for the question: When is the right time to die? That decision, he says, "is rather like deciding how and when to end a story." It is not "a decision to be based on the incremental gains and losses that one stands to accumulate by staying in the game.... Hence a person may rationally be willing to die even though he can look forward to a few more weeks or months...."[80] Does he mean by this that you should hope or choose to die when a story teller, relating the tale of your life, would make the best story by having you die just then? No. He notes near the beginning of his essay that his talk of a "better life story" should not be understood in the sense of "a better story in the telling or hearing, but rather in the sense that it is the story of a better life."[81] The idea then, is that the right time to die is when your life is better for ending *then* rather than at some other time. Whether it is the right time is to be decided by looking back in time, not forwards. It is the time that would give one's life the best narrative structure, taking it as a whole—not the time when the sum of future gains and losses falls below a threshold of acceptability. One should look to "the overall order or structure of events...what might be called their dramatic or narrative relations."[82]

Recall that for Velleman, it is better for the trend of well-being to slope upwards rather than downwards, even if the overall quantity of good and bad is the same in both directions. That is the better order of events. That commits him to saying that one should die when one is at the top: if you foresee that life is never going to be as good for you as it is at this moment, you should choose or hope to die—even if there would be decades of good and nothing bad for you in your future. If you are thirty years old, and you see that your thirties will not be quite so good as your twenties, and that there will be another slight dip in the next decade, and the next, and so on, you are at the moment when it would be best for you to die. So, when he says that it could be better to die even if you "can look forward to a few more weeks or months," he has no way to keep this from going further: not just "a few more weeks or months" but also a few more years or decades. After all, a good lifetime, he holds, is not an accumulation of good years. One would do best to die at the moment when life will only get worse, because the important thing is to avoid a downward trend, not having more good years.

There is, nonetheless, this much that Velleman and I can agree upon: I too believe that there can be a time in the life of a human being when there is good reason no longer to add additional days, months, or years to it—even if that additional stretch of time, however long, would bring pleasure and no pain. As I said in section 10, it is not arbitrary to place the oyster-like pleasures that a human being can feel in a separate category from the distinctively human goods that make our lives immeasurably superior to that of an oyster. When all that would be left in a life are those inferior goods, that remainder does not constitute the sort of life a human being should have. There is good reason to hope to die rather than become that simple organism.

I will soon return to Velleman's essay. We next consider a further argument purporting to show that narrative structure is an important aspect of the quality of a life.

13. McMahan on narrative unity and death

According to Jeff McMahan, one "dimension of well-being" is the narrative unity of a life. This sort of unity exists, he says, when "the elements in a life fit together to form a

---

[80] Ibid., 74.   [81] Ibid., 59.   [82] Ibid., 58.

meaningful whole, a series of events that have an intelligible purpose, direction, and overall structure—specifically, as Aristotle demanded of dramatic art, a beginning, middle, and end. When a life has narrative unity, the meaning or significance of each segment is derived in part from its relations both to what has gone before and to what comes after." When its final stage is "jarring, inappropriate, or inharmonious," it is made, to some extent, a worse life.[83]

He illustrates by imagining two people who suffer a stroke:

> Each can be expected to live for about another year in a state of bovine contentment.... Suppose that one of the two people had devoted his earlier life to the experience of passive pleasures. For this person, the additional year of contented dementia seems in harmony with the values that informed his previous life, and thus may be an acceptable, though sadly diminished, extension of that life. Suppose that the other person, by contrast, has previously led a life of the mind, devoted to intellectual and spiritual concerns. Set in the context of this person's previous life, the additional year may seem a travesty of life that is worth living. For this person, the additional year may be a dreadful misfortune.... Within *this* life, the additional year has negative value. It is bad for the person while he lives through it and diminishes the value of his life as a whole.[84]

These examples seem convincing at first, but we should examine them carefully. Many, I suspect, would agree that it would have been better for the second individual to die one year earlier, avoiding a stroke and the dementia that results, because the last year of his life, spent in "bovine contentment," is not what he wanted, or would have wanted, for himself. By contrast, the first individual *would* prefer a year of contented dementia to death, and so in his case, an extra year of life after the stroke extends his total lifetime well-being.

However, if that is what lies behind the initial plausibility of these examples, they fail to serve the purpose for which they are intended, which is to support the general thesis that one component of well-being is the narrative unity of a life. McMahan is not proposing, in the passage cited, that there is prudential value in the achievement of one's goals or the satisfaction of one's desires. He speaks instead of narrative unity, how the parts of a life "fit together to form a meaningful whole" by virtue of its "overall structure," just as the parts of a good play form a unified whole, ending in a way that befits what came before. A play that has precisely the ending its author chooses is one thing; one whose end fits well with the rest is another. If the play has unity, that is because of features there in the play—not in the author's desires. Conversely, if a play has exactly the ending that the author meant it to have, it might nonetheless be completely disunified. McMahan's thesis, then, is that it would be bad for the life of an intellectually active person to end with a year of "bovine contentment" because there is no unified whole formed by these two temporal segments—on the contrary, they are "jarring, inappropriate, or inharmonious." It might be true that the intellectual would

---

[83] *The Ethics of Killing*, 175.   [84] Ibid., 175, author's emphasis.

not want his life to end in this manner, but if so, that is because that ending has a feature that grounds his desire to avoid it.

To evaluate the force of McMahan's proposal, then, we must ask whether lives always lose some prudential value by having less narrative unity, and always gain some by having more. On reflection, it should be clear that they do not. Suppose someone lives, in his twenties, "a life of the mind, devoted to intellectual and spiritual concerns"; then devotes himself, in his thirties, to "the experience of passive pleasures" at entertainment venues; then throws himself, in his forties, into political activism and public service; then becomes, in his fifties, a jazz musician; and so on. There is no unity here. If one were to write a play about such a life, devoting one act to each decade, it would be a series of playlets, not a unified whole. And yet it is not a life whose overall well-being is diminished by its fragmentation into a sequence of heterogeneous interests and pursuits. If there is prudential disvalue in such a life, the explanation for that would be the intrinsic inferiority of what this or that decade contains—not the failure of the decades to cohere into a unity.

Let us return to McMahan's statement that when an intellectually inclined person, having suffered a stroke, lives one final year in passive contentment, that "additional year may seem a travesty of life that is worth living. For this person, the additional year may be a dreadful misfortune.... Within *this* life, the additional year has negative value. It is bad for the person while he lives through it and diminishes the value of his life as a whole." Here he is claiming that the last year of this individual's life is on balance bad for him in spite of the pleasure he feels; and further that the badness of that year reaches back and detracts to some extent from the prudential value of the long preceding segment of that individual's life. A final act that is totally out of joint with what preceded it will affect our overall evaluation of the artistic quality of the play. Analogously, he claims, that extra year of life not only has negative prudential value in itself, but also alters the past, making the overall quality of what preceded it worse than it would have been had he died before the stroke.

McMahan does not claim that there is nothing of prudential value in the final year of the intellectual who has suffered a stroke. He is contented with the passing show, and McMahan can allow that as a result that final year has some goodness in it. His thesis is that, even so, that final year could have *overall* negative value, because it jars so badly with that individual's earlier life. Narrative unity, for him, is one dimension of well-being, not the only one. He can say that pleasure is a further component, and therefore, if the pleasure of that final year is great enough, it could on balance be a good year. On the other hand, the reverse might also be true, if the pleasure is small enough. "...The badness of the year in this respect [its narrative disunity] may outweigh the fact that it is subjectively experienced as good."[85]

How great or small a good is narrative unity? Is the clash between the character of life during that last year and that of earlier years only a small deficiency or a large one?

---

[85] Ibid., 175.

How much pleasure would it take to overcome it? If we could administer to this poor intellectual enough chemically induced thrills, that would at some point outweigh the fact that his final year jars with his earlier life. Should we invest time and resources to developing this medical intervention? There seems to be no way to answer these questions.

A more important point is that McMahan's theory misidentifies what is amiss in the final year of the stroke victim. For him, it is that it is out of synch with his earlier life. The other individual in his example—the one who lived a life of passive pleasures—has a good final year (though not as good as his earlier years), because it is quite in harmony with them. By contrast, according to the conception of well-being that I have been defending, the point to be made about both stroke victims is that their subjective experience is oyster-like and therefore belongs to a lower order of value. As I said in section 10, someone who is reflecting on the prospect that he might suffer a stroke that leaves him in a demented state "can reasonably suppose that at the time when the only goods that will be available to him are of the lower order of value attained by an oyster, his well-being no longer has a claim to his attention or anyone else's." On this account, it would not matter much if the passive and mindless pleasures of the two stroke victims were intense. Both lives would still fall below a significant threshold of value.

A further difference between McMahan's account and mine concerns the quality of the pre-stroke life of the intellectual in his example. The final year of his life is not only "bad for the person while he lives through it"—it also "diminishes the value of his life as a whole." It might have seemed to him and to us, as we carried out, prior to his stroke, an assessment of the quality of his life thus far, that his years were all good ones. But if McMahan is right, we must revise that assessment, for the bad post-stroke year "may seem a travesty of life that is worth living." That bad last year casts its shadow backwards over the whole life and makes it less good. How much less good? The word "travesty" suggests that his stroke and final demented year robbed him of nearly all of his lifetime well-being.

We might be tempted to agree with McMahan because we fear that our memories of loved ones who have suffered from dementia before dying will mainly be of our fraught interactions with them in that final stage of their lives. When we think back on their lives, we might take little pleasure in recollecting their pre-stroke years, because those thoughts are mixed with more recent memories of the time when their lives had so much less value. *They* may wish for death prior to a stroke because they do not want to be remembered in that way.

But that valid observation should not lead us to the conclusion that their pre-stroke years are made worse because of their later dementia. Here the analogy McMahan relies on between the narrative structure needed by a play and the integration he thinks a good life ought to have tells against him. A play can be brilliant for four acts and then fall apart in the fifth and final act. We can justifiably re-read it and return to see it on the stage many times, enjoying its many merits, in spite of being let down as we read or sit through its final component. If a bad final act does not make the first four acts worse, why suppose that a bad final year makes all earlier years worse?

McMahan says, speaking of a life that has narrative unity: "the significance of each segment is derived in part from its relations both to what has gone before and to what comes after." These words do characterize many successful artistic works, and should be kept in mind by audiences as they experience the way plays, novels, and musical compositions unfold. What a line in a play means may not come across with full significance until the play's denouement. The same applies to music and the other art forms that unfold in time. That is the sort of claim McMahan makes about the narrative aspect of lifetime well-being. However, although we should accept his aesthetic point, we should reject its application to prudential value.

Here is why. If a play or a piece of music ends badly, it does not follow that the *quality* of everything that went before is diminished. *Meaning* might be altered by what comes later—but not *quality*. We thought at first that a line in a play meant one thing, but as we later discover, it meant something else, or something more. It is quite another matter, however, to revise our judgments about artistic quality, so that although we thought Acts One through Four were excellent, we discover in Act Five that they were not. That kind of revision does not occur and is not called for. So, if we want to look to the arts as a model of how to evaluate lives, we should not agree with McMahan that a bad last year can devalue all that preceded it.

It might be replied that McMahan's thesis that well-being has a narrative component stands on its own—is plausible even if our judgments about the quality of works of art lack this backward-looking dimension. According to this suggestion, if we reflect on examples like the intellectual who suffers a stroke and enjoys mild contentment for a year, we see, without drawing an analogy with the arts, that these events do cast a shadow on the whole of that individual's earlier life. I believe the reverse is the case. When I ask, "Did he have a wonderful life until his stroke?" I have no trouble imagining that he did, and no hesitation in affirming that his stroke did not make that long part of his life any less wonderful. He did not have a good life *all the way through* (including his last year), but that is no reason to say that *the entire span* of his life, with its many different parts, was not as good as it seemed at the time.

14. Can death harm a cow?

There is one further component of Velleman's essay that now requires discussion, for he rejects a thesis that I have adopted in my reflections on McTaggart's oyster. I believe that the oyster's life gets better with each passing day. Velleman, however, using a cow rather than an oyster as his example of a creature whose psychological capacities are extremely limited, argues that the life of such an animal can be made no better by its continuing to exist, no matter how long and how many benefits continue to accrue to it.[86]

---

[86] For critical discussion of Velleman's argument, see Ben Bradley, *Well-Being and Death*, 147–54.

His discussion of this issue is governed by the following general claim: "Because well-being is a relational value, it is constituted, in part, by a point of view—namely, the point of view inhabited by the creature whose well-being is in question."[87] A cow's "point of view" is highly limited: it "is unable to conceive of itself as persisting through a sequence of benefits."[88] (Let's assume that its good is pleasure and the absence of pain.) It cannot want to enjoy pleasure tomorrow because it has no sense of itself as persisting from today to tomorrow. Therefore, it is not better for its present pleasure to recur again tomorrow rather than not. If it survives from today until tomorrow and enjoys pleasure once again, that is no better for it than its dying before tomorrow begins. For nothing "can be good for a subject if he is constitutionally incapable of caring about it."[89] McTaggart goes wrong, then, because an oyster, like a cow, is not an enduring self—a being that has a conception of itself as moving through time.

This does not commit Velleman to saying that it does not matter if you torture a cow tomorrow. When tomorrow comes, and the cow is still alive, it will be faring poorly if it feels pain, and well if it feels pleasure. But it is not the case that it will be better for the cow to survive until tomorrow.

The argument seems to have a serious weakness. Suppose I tell you that someone (a human being) doesn't care about X. You should not infer that X is not a component of his well-being. After all, it might be good for him and a deficiency of his that he doesn't care about it. Now let's change the example slightly: suppose I tell you that someone (a human being) is *incapable* of caring about X. Again, you should not infer that X is not a component of his well-being. For, again, it might be a deficiency in him that he has this incapacity. If it is impossible for him to remedy this defect and acquire this capacity, that is too bad for him. His permanent incapacity keeps him from ever seeking one of the components of his well-being.

Oysters and cows are permanently unable to think ahead to the future and to form desires to have tomorrow what they lack today. But for reasons we have just seen, it does not follow that dying at the end of the day is no loss for them—that they would be no better off were they to live again tomorrow and enjoy another day of pleasure. Their intellectual limitations should not make us hesitate to say what seems evident: it *would* be good for them to be alive tomorrow and to feel pleasure again, just as it is good for them to feel pleasure today. Additional days of pleasure bring them more pleasure over the course of a life—and since pleasure is their good, a longer life brings more good. We might therefore say: too bad for them that they have conceptual limitations that prevent them from making long-term plans.

But that last statement—"too bad for them . . ."—is too hasty. Creatures can have many other kinds of resources for promoting their well-being besides sophisticated concepts. Suppose oyster A has a good "memory"—not in the sense that it performs intellectual feats of recall, but in the sense that its sensitivity to what it finds in its environment is

---

[87] 'Well-Being and Time,' 79.   [88] Ibid., 81.   [89] Ibid., 81.

stored in its brain and guides it in the future. With this sort of memory, oyster A returns to parts of the environment where it has found food for at least two days of the last three, and does not return to less resource-rich and pleasure-giving locales. It is better off because of its memory than oyster B, which strikes out in this direction or that in search of food, with no memory to guide it. The memory of oyster A does the same job for it as would be done by its wanting a present pleasure to continue tomorrow. It brings it more pleasure and food over time than accrues to oyster B over time. Unless oyster B has been very lucky in its hit-or-miss searches for food, oyster A will have had a better past than oyster B, because A's memory has enabled it to go without food on fewer days, and felt pleasure on more days.

In saying that it has had a better past, we aggregate: we put together what it experienced one day with what it experienced on a different day, and arrive at a retrospective overall judgment of its total well-being to date. We understand how it behaves by seeing its memory as something that serves its long-term good. In the same way, we also make prospective judgments about it: it is likely to be better off in the future than oyster B, because it is likely to have more days of food and pleasure.

Even if oysters do not have the ability I am hypothetically ascribing to some of them, we can nonetheless say: it would be good for them if they did. We think the best life for an oyster would be a very long one—to be McTaggart's oyster. (I posited no long-term memory for oyster B, but to compare it with A we must aggregate in both cases.)

Velleman's statement that "nothing can be good for a subject if he is constitutionally incapable of caring about it" must therefore be rejected. Our initial suspicion that this is mistaken has proven to be correct. We should also reject his claim that "because well-being is a relational value, it is constituted, in part, by a point of view—namely the point of view inhabited by the creature whose well-being is in question." There is of course a sense in which well-being is a "relational value." The components of well-being are non-instrumental benefits—they are beneficial *to* or *for* someone. But well-being is not a "relational value" in the further sense that if a creature does not have a point of view regarding X—if it lacks the concepts needed for having that or any other point of view—then X cannot be part of its well-being.

It might be said, against the thesis I have been defending here, that creatures like oysters and cows that lack a conception of themselves as perduring selves—organisms whose consciousness is confined to their present experience—do not in fact persist. They are creatures of the moment. They have *bodies* that persist through time, but within those bodies there is no ongoing self. And since there is no ongoing self inhabiting those bodies, there is no subject to whom more good accrues as time goes by.

But this is not our normal conception of what it is for oysters and cows to exist through time. According to our common sense metaphysics, they are functionally integrated living organisms, and as long as they maintain their bodily integrity and function as single units, they persist through time. Some of them manage to find food (and the agreeable consciousness that presumably accompanies their intake of food) on more occasions than others. Those are the ones that are better off. And going forward, they will continue to be better off if they are more often successful in their search for food. McTaggart's oyster will have a better life, the longer it lives.

15. Goethe and antiquity: "Only the present is our happiness"

I turn now to an idea that might at first seem ludicrous, but which has struck some first-rate minds as the deepest insight we can attain about well-being and time. It is that once the highest good of human life is attained, it does not matter whether it lasts a short time or a long time, or indeed whether it endures at all. Having reached that peak, you are at the summit of human well-being, and you cannot add to the well-being achieved in your life by remaining in that state for a longer time. This thesis can be found in Plotinus, *Ennead* I.5—the title of which reads: "On Whether Well-Being [*eudaimonia*] Increases With Time." His answer is that it does not. That thesis is endorsed by Stoics as well. In Cicero's *De Finibus* (*On Moral Ends*), Cato, the spokes-man for Stoicism, says: "a happy life (*beata vita*) is no more desirable or worth seeking if long than if short."[90] The same idea might lie behind a dictum of Epicurus: "Unlimited time and limited time contain equal [amounts of] pleasure."[91] Jumping ahead to modern authors, we find the idea reaffirmed by Goethe: "...the spirit looks neither ahead nor behind. Only the present is our happiness."[92] That, according to Pierre Hadot, is Goethe's endorsement of the thesis found in the Stoics and Plotinus.[93]

It is a thesis that has some bearing on the questions we have been discussing. I have argued that the life of McTaggart's oyster keeps getting better as it continues to feel its small pleasures. To make a more general point: it strikes me as obvious that well-being is that sort of good; that is, if the well-being of X continues through time, that is better for X than its not continuing. The longer it continues, the better. But, as I have just noted, that assumption is not accepted by all philosophers, and so we must give a hearing to their point of view.

To begin with some smaller points:

There are some goods that cannot be extended in time beyond a certain limit. For example, when someone completes at midnight the final stage of the book he has been writing, that is good for him (assume that it is a necessary step he takes to achieve some element of well-being), but he cannot continue working on it after midnight. Were he to do so, it would not have been true that he had completed his project at that precise moment. Further, there are some goods that we ought not try to extend in time as long as we possibly can. If you are planning a musical program, it will not be good for your

---

[90]   Book III, chapter 46, translated by Raphael Woolf.

[91]   *The Principal Doctrines*, 19, translated by Brad Inwood and L. P. Gerson, *The Epicurus Reader*, 33.

[92]   *Faust*, Part II, 9381–3. The translation is that of Pierre Hadot. See note 93; and Chapter 1, note 16, for the German text.

[93]   "'Only the Present is Our Happiness'": The Value of the Present Instant in Goethe and in Ancient Philosophy," in Hadot, *Philosophy as a Way of Life*.

audience if you keep adding to its duration, with more and more songs—as many as possible. That would just ruin your program.[94]

But with well-being, I suggest, it is different. There is certainly no conceptual contradiction in imagining someone's well-being continuing without end. And, if I am right, this is one good that (unlike some others) it is better to have for a longer period than a shorter period. There is no cut-off period such that, beyond that, it is no longer good for someone to continue to have it. As I noted earlier (Chapter 1 section 1), this is the view that Plato implicitly endorses in the *Symposium*: he says that we want to have the good *forever*, taking it for granted that we *should* have this desire. It would be irrational to want it for only a thousand years, or a million years. Why would we want there to be a future time when we will not have it?

When Epicurus says, "Unlimited time and limited time contain equal [amounts of] pleasure," he faces an obvious objection. Suppose A experiences pleasure for eighty years and then dies. B experiences pleasure (assume they are the same kind as A's pleasures) for those same eighty years, and then his pleasures go on, never stopping. Is it not the case that B has more pleasure? And if pleasure is the good, does he not have more good? Perhaps Epicurus would respond to this challenge by saying: A is not conscious of missing anything, once he is dead. So, it is no defect in his life that it is of finite duration.

If Epicurus is right about that, this line of thinking leads to the conclusion that no matter how short a life is, it is no less good than a longer one. Someone who lived only a day or a minute or second would be no worse off for the brevity of his existence. But there is a fatal flaw in this argument: it's not true that what happens to you unawares cannot harm you. Someone who arranges behind your back to diminish the pleasure that would otherwise have come your way is making you worse off than you would have been. You are unaware of the fact that he has harmed you, but he has. Similarly, after we die, we do not dwell on the fact that we would have had more pleasure, and a better life, had we remained alive.

Plotinus does not make any simple error of this sort, when he argues that well-being does not increase with time. His defense of this thesis presupposes a metaphysics according to which each of us has a real self that lives the life of a timeless intellect. The goal of life is to be in touch with this noetic self and to dwell so far as possible in the intelligible world, a world where temporal markers (before, now, after) are inapplicable. When that happens, nothing in the temporal world can diminish the joy and value of one's consciousness, and the duration of one's body and the lower parts of the soul is a matter of indifference. "It must not be counted by time but by eternity; and this is neither more nor less nor of any extension, but is a 'this here,' unextended and timeless.... One must take it all as a whole ... not made up of many times, but it is all together ...."[95]

---

[94] I borrow these examples from Krister Bykvist, 'Value and Time,' in Iwao Hirose and Jonas Olson (eds.), *The Oxford Handbook of Value Theory*, 125.

[95] *Enneads* I.5.7, 23–30, translated by A. H. Armstrong.

This is not the place to assess the cogency of Plotinus's metaphysics. If his conception of reality is correct, then it may indeed follow that well-being does not increase with time. What can be said here is that he must pay a high price to reach this conclusion: he must reject as worthless almost all that is of apparent value in human experience. The delicious flavors of food and drink, the sound world of music, the visual splendor of nature and pictorial art, the pleasures of friendship and moral life, the feats of great athletes—all of these take place in time and are grounded in the physical and social nature of human beings. But these experiences are of no value to the noetic self. For Plotinus, it does not matter whether they endure for a long or a short time, because they are only apparently good. This is so deep a departure from our conception of value that we must regard any metaphysics that leads to this conclusion as one to be resisted.

Let us turn to the Stoics: What reasons do they give for holding that a long good life (*beata vita*) is no more desirable than a short good life? In part, what leads them to this view is shared with Plotinus: they think that much that ordinary human beings seek is only apparently good. Only one type of thing is truly valuable: not pleasure, as the Epicureans suppose, but the virtuous condition of the soul, the condition attained only by the sage. Furthermore, when one reaches that stage, one can, within a single brief moment, arrive at the ultimate goal of human existence. One then has an all-encompassing vision of the connectedness of everything in the universe. Thus Marcus Aurelius writes: "he who has seen the present has seen everything, all that from eternity has come to pass, and all that will come to be in infinite time. For everything is akin and the same."[96] Hadot elaborates on this idea: "At each instant we must...resituate ourselves within the perspective of universal reason so that, at each instant, our consciousness may become a cosmic consciousness. Thus, if one lives in accordance with universal reason, at each instant his consciousness expands into the infinity of the cosmos, and the entire universe is present to him."[97]

Would it not be better if one's synoptic encounter with the universe remained present to one's consciousness for a long period of time? The Stoics must reply negatively, but what reason can they offer for doing so? Perhaps their answer is that once your narrow consciousness has "become a cosmic consciousness," it no longer matters how long you, considered as a separate and small part of the universe, endure—or whether you endure at all. What matters instead is the life of this "cosmic consciousness," and this will of course continue to exist far into the future.

This response is in effect a dismissal of the whole project of understanding *prudential* value. Our question, from the start, has been: What is it for an individual's life to go well—to go well *for* that individual? It is not: What is the best state for the universe to be in? Admittedly, someone who hears our question about the good of a single and separate individual, and understands it properly, might react to it dismissively,

---

saying: "I don't care about myself or about any other single human being or any other single animal or organism. We are mere fragments. I want an answer to a different question: what state should the universe be in for *its* sake?" Similarly, if the Stoics hold that we should not care whether we have a good and long-lasting life or a good but brief life, because what we should care about instead is the state of the cosmos, which will continue to exist for a long time after one's body perishes, they have set aside the project of constructing a theory of individual well-being.

But perhaps a different interpretation will salvage the Stoic view. We might take them to believe that the ongoing good state of the universe is good not just for it, but also for you, even after you have died. In that case, they must be counted among those philosophers (discussed in Chapter 3, sections 19 and 21) who hold that prudential good and ill accrue to us posthumously. Aristotle himself accepts this idea, as we have seen (Chapter 3, section 22) although he severely limits its significance. Were the Stoics to take on board the existence of posthumous goods, they could say that you need not care about the length of your life, because after you die, the universe will still be in good condition, and that is a good that accrues not only to it, but to you as well, even though you are dead.

But *why* should we believe that it is also good for you? When you are dead, you have no awareness of the good state of the universe and cannot feel a sense of identification with it. There is a further difficulty for this interpretation: it is rather distant from what Marcus Aurelius says. Recall his words: "He who has seen the present has seen everything, all that from eternity has come to pass, and all that will come to be in infinite time. For everything is akin and the same." What he alludes to here is a certain kind of *experience*: a synoptic vision of the contents of space, time past, and time future. You will not have that experience once you are dead. So, our question remains: Would it not be better for you to have that experience for as long as possible?

16. *The art of valuing the present*

Although we have found no reason to accept the Stoic thesis that a brief valuable life is just as good as a long one, there is an important truth that lies in the neighborhood of Goethe's thought, warmly endorsed by Hadot, that "only the present is our happiness." Here is how Hadot expands on what Goethe means to convey in those brief words of Faust and Helen of Troy:

The characteristic feature of ancient life and art [was] to know how to live in the present, and to know what he [Goethe] called "the healthiness of the moment." In antiquity, says Goethe, the instant was "pregnant"; in other words, filled with meaning, but it was also lived in all its reality and the fullness of its richness, sufficient unto itself. We no longer know how to live in the present, continues Goethe. For us, the ideal is in the future … while the present is considered trivial and banal. We no longer know how to profit from the present … [98]

[98] Ibid., 220.

That one should live in the present is a recurring theme in Marcus Aurelius's *Meditations*. "Practice to live only the present which you are now living, and you will be able to live through to the time of your death in imperturbability and kindliness, and at peace with the divinity which is in you" (12.3). To acquire the art of living in the present, he recommends this exercise: "It is possible to depart from life at this moment. Have this thought in mind whenever you act, speak, or think" (2.11). We will live more fully—have a greater emotional investment in our experience and a greater appreciation of its value—if we think of the present moment as our last opportunity to get what we can from life. By supposing that we have little time left, we will treasure it all the more. Further, when more comes our way—when it turns out that we have not died—we will more fully welcome our next experiences, because they come as a surprise, and are not dulled by habit or expectation. If we can treat each moment as it comes our way with this heightened sensibility, the whole expanse of our lived experience will be more intense and precious. We will see the world anew as a fresh creation. And there are further benefits: We protect ourselves from the dangers of procrastination. We do not allow concern about the future to cast a pall on the present. We do not allow the present to be spoiled by ruminations on what has gone ill for us in the past.

Whatever we make of this way of approaching present experience, it must be recognized that even if we agree with Marcus Aurelius, Goethe, and Hadot that it is the best way to achieve our good, we can still reject the Stoic thesis that a longer period of well-being is no better than a shorter period. Guided by the idea that "only the present is our happiness," and taking this to mean that time brings no increase in well-being, we might achieve more good for ourselves than would otherwise be possible. But our success would only demonstrate the *instrumental* advantages of living with this thought; it would not show that it is a true thought. If, in a moment of philosophical reflection, we temporarily step back from this strategy of heightening our receptivity to present experience, and ask ourselves, "should I hope to live with this heightened sense of the value of my existence for a long time, or does it really not matter?" the answer ought to be: may this continue rather than cease.

Further, this approach to the present has drawbacks as well as benefits. Focusing entirely on the present—if it means never looking back to earlier times—would cut us off from all that we rightly want to treasure from our past experience. One of the best reasons for seeking certain kinds of experience is that they will always be available to us for recall. Similarly, directing our attention forward to the good things we expect the future to hold in store can magnify their value: we reap benefits from them even before they happen. Admittedly, Marcus might reply that this misunderstands his intent. Perhaps he would say: "When you fondly recall the past, or feel excited about the future, you are creating good present experiences. So the dictum that you should live only in the present does not counsel you never to think about your past or future." But if this is how he wishes to be interpreted, he must retract the other statement cited earlier: "It is possible to depart from life at this moment. Have this thought in mind whenever you act, speak, or think." If I remind myself that what I am doing now might be the last action I ever undertake, I cannot at the same time take pleasure in looking forward to future good.

There is yet another problem for Marcus: living only in the present would prevent you from using present time to make plans for the future. When you set yourself the task of planning, you treat present experience as a mere means to an end that will at best pay rewards at some later time. Planning is always a sacrifice of one thing for another; if you had done something else rather than spend your time planning, you would have found a more rewarding experience. Of course, if you have become convinced that a short period of well-being is just as good as a long period, you have already robbed planning of its point. But since we have found no reason to agree that well-being in a moment is as good as well-being that endures, we ought to devote some time, at least now and then, to making plans. Present time devoted to insuring a good future can be time well spent.

Thus far, we have found nothing that can be salvaged from Goethe's thought, "only the present is our happiness," when that is taken to mean that we should forget the past, act as though there is no future, and treat momentary well-being as equal in value to long-lasting well-being. But by setting aside all of the bad advice that might be read into that dictum, we are now in a position to recognize what it gets right. Marcus Aurelius, Goethe, and Hadot have something important and true to teach us: there is such a thing as knowing how to make the most of the present moment, and this is an art or habit well worth acquiring.

What I mean by "making the most of the present moment" is best explained by simple examples in which one fails to do so. You get through your meals preoccupied with the problems that you must address later that day, and fail to savor what you are tasting. You look at a painting in a museum but not with full concentration; your thoughts wander to other subjects. You walk through a lovely park, but instead of responding to its charm and beauty, you think only of the insulting remark someone made about you last night. You grow so accustomed to your friends and colleagues that you never bring their good qualities to the center of your attention and recognize how admirable and unusual they are. You look at your child's drawings and dismiss them as trivialities, instead of delighting in the play of his imagination and his increased control of his hand movements. In each such case, there is something missing from your experience that might have been added, increasing its value to you without diminishing the overall long-term quality of your life. You fail to make the most of your present experience because you lack the outlook, sensibility, or habits that would have enabled you to do so. The potential value in what your present circumstances offer is not realized. You fail to make the most of the present moment.

This, I suggest, is part of what Goethe saw in ancient life and art; and it is part of what Hadot has in mind in his essay, 'Only the Present is Our Happiness.' We don't have a single word for this art of making the most of the present, and perhaps that contributes to its neglect. Perhaps we also neglect it because "knowing how to live in the present" sounds similar to ideas that are in fact significantly different from it, and which must be rejected: that only present circumstances should enter our awareness, that we must live as though we might die tomorrow, that it is not more in our interest to have more well-being over time than less. We should not let the falsity of these ideas prevent us from developing the art of seizing the passing moment and finding in it all that it has to offer.

One more champion of the value of present experience deserves our attention, both because of the grand style in which he expresses this thought, and for the way in which he misunderstands it. What I have in mind is the well-known concluding chapter of Walter Pater's work, *The Renaissance: Studies in Art and Poetry*. He writes:

> Not the fruit of experience, but experience itself is the end. A counted number of pulses only is given to us of a variegated, dramatic life. How may we see in them all that is to be seen in them by the finest senses? How shall we pass most swiftly from point to point, and be present always at the focus where the greatest number of vital forces unite in their purest energy? To burn always with this hard, gemlike flame, to maintain this ecstasy, is success in life.[99]

Pater, in the unpoetic vocabulary I have been using, is an experientialist. If by the "fruit of experience" he is referring to something not present to consciousness, a feature of life one is unaware of, he is saying that by itself it has no prudential value. So far, so good.

It is also clear that he is a devotee of what I have called "the art of seizing the passing moment." But his statement reveals how easily one can slide from that good idea to a different and bad idea. This further thesis is that one's emotional life should remain for as long as possible in a state of great excitation. There is something to be maximized, Pater thinks: passion, drama, energy, vitality. Ecstasy is not to be regarded as one of many feelings, to be sought from time to time, and taking its proper place (when appropriate) among a wide range of many other calmer feelings. No, "to burn always with this hard, gemlike flame, to maintain this ecstasy, is success in life."

I do not mean to suggest that Pater arrived at the thesis that this is how one should live by making a faulty inference from the truth of experientialism to the conclusion that the more ecstasy one experiences the better. It is more likely that he took it to be self-evident, as Bentham did, that the intensity of a pleasure and its duration are the only two dimensions along which the value of an experience can vary. That is a mistake, as reflection on McTaggart's oyster reveals: even if its intake of food were accompanied by intense pleasure, "burn[ing] always with this hard, gemlike flame," its long life would be inferior to human life at its best.

17. "A sufficient period of time"

I said earlier (Chapter 1, section 6): "the quality of human consciousness" can be "so good (provided that it endures over a sufficient period of time) that no amount of

---

[99] London: Macmillan and Co., 1888, 249–50. In the edition of Dover Publications, Pater's statement is on p. 154. The sentence that begins "To burn always..." is the first of a new paragraph, but I reproduce it here without a paragraph break.

simple oyster pleasure, however long-lasting, will give it a better life." But what is a sufficient period of time? At what point in the life of a human being does it become immeasurably better than that of an oyster? On the very first day? When a child is five? Only in adulthood? On what basis can we give even a rough answer to such questions? Of course, we could play it safe, and simply say that a *long* human life—one that endures for ninety years or something close enough to that—has the requisite length. If we are not willing to say even that, we will in effect have abandoned the thesis that human life belongs to a different (and higher) order of value than does that of an oyster. But is it only a ninety-year-old life that has this kind of superiority—not the life of a fifty-year-old, or a twenty-year-old, or a ten-year-old?

My reply is that a transformation takes place somewhere along the path of human development, and it occurs far closer to the beginning of life than to the end. When a child is only a few days old, McTaggart's long-lived oyster has accumulated more prudential good than has yet accrued to the child. However, as that child acquires a richer array of experiences—a matter of months, perhaps—it will take a far greater increase in the length of that oyster's life (years, not just months) for it to surpass that child with respect to prudential value. Eventually, at a certain stage, not much beyond the child's first year, his life will have become immeasurably better than that of any oyster, however long-lived. There is no one moment at which this occurs, no single transformative event that marks this change, as there is when water becomes ice. Rather, with enough mental growth, the life of a child gradually changes, as a higher order of prudential value increasingly becomes available to it.

That is a rough answer to *one* question that arises about a "sufficient" amount of time. There is this further question as well: Once a human being has arrived at that time of life when a higher order of value becomes available, is *every* temporal segment of her life, however brief, one in which immeasurably more good can accrue to her than accrues to the oyster however long it lives? Is every *minute* in the life of a human being of a sufficient age incommensurably greater in value (if it is a good minute) than any length of an oyster's life? Every second? Every nano-second?

The most important point to bear in mind, when we consider these questions, is that duration itself is not what matters. Rather, it is the quality of experience. To illustrate: suppose a musically educated listener attends a performance of Beethoven's Ninth Symphony and fully responds to its emotional depth and intellectual significance. (That listener might be very young—a child prodigy.) In virtue of that single hour of rich consciousness, that person's life has more prudential value than accrues to McTaggart's oyster. Can we go further, and say that our listener had achieved that level of well-being in fifty-five minutes? Forty-five minutes? The sensible way to respond to these questions is to say that the first second does not provide enough time for there to be a profound response to the music, but the listener's experience immeasurably surpasses an oyster's even before the musical work reaches its final moment. Why is one second not long enough but fifty-nine minutes is? Not because there is something about fifty-nine minutes of consciousness that gives any experience of that length, when it occurs in a human being, immeasurable value. It is because it takes far more than one second, but less than an hour, for a musical experience to have its full emotional and cognitive impact.

To give one more example: One does not have to see all four operas that comprise Wagner's *Ring* cycle for it to be the case that experiencing this massive work (with appreciation and understanding) belongs to a higher order of value than can be attained by McTaggart's oyster. *Das Rheingold* is by itself enough. And if one sees all but the last minute of *Das Rheingold*, that is still enough. But hearing just the opening measures and no more is not sufficient. Where exactly does the cut-off point occur, then? There is no precise moment. But by a certain point, one can be confident, through introspection, that the powerful emotional, visual, auditory, and cognitive experience one is having brings with it more prudential value than is available to any oyster, however long it lives.[100]

To guard against misunderstanding: I do not claim that it is *only* intense experience, of the sort that music sometimes affords, that is capable of making the difference between the prudential value of human existence and that of an oyster's life. Pater's ideal of burning always with ecstasy was rejected in the preceding section. Rather, the point is that the period of time that it takes for an experience to have a higher order of value is sometimes a matter of an hour or less, as is made clear by certain encounters with works of profound artistry. Many other kinds of experience, calm rather than intense, can also make our lives superior to that of McTaggart's oyster. How long do these calmer experiences have to last before they have that elevating effect? What I have been pointing out is that there is no answer to that question, and no need to answer it. Increases in the duration of human consciousness have no value in themselves; rather, they should be long enough to make what is felt a valuable experience. How long that is varies depending on what sort of experience it is.

Notice that I have now reached a point of agreement between my account of the effect of time on well-being and a thesis upheld by Epicurus, the Stoics, and Plotinus (discussed above in section 15). They too think that something of great value in human life can take place in a brief period of time. The mental preparation needed to have that immensely valuable experience may be long in coming, but once the groundwork has been laid, it might occupy only an hour or two. I do not reject that

---

[100] What if one has already listened to 20,000 hours of Beethoven over the course of one's life, and one is then offered the choice of either one more minute or an oyster's simple pleasure for millions of years? (I am grateful to Roger Crisp for this question.) In response: Some musical works have such great emotional depth that each new encounter with them is no less a valuable experience than those that preceded it—provided that enough time has elapsed between them (otherwise one's responses are dulled). But these profound works need more than a minute to accumulate their profundity. So, one should choose the oyster's life, if the only alternative is to hear just one more minute of Beethoven and die, especially if one is too familiar with that musical passage through repeated listening. But no matter how many times one has thrilled to one of his great sonatas, if one could be thrilled all over again by listening to a complete performance, that experience should be chosen over the endless pleasures of an oyster.

part of their view—only their further claim that it can do no good for life to continue beyond that brief moment.

There is a further point of difference between my view and that of the Stoics and Plotinus. For them, ordinary human experience has little of value to offer. (Plato's *Phaedo* is an early expression of this outlook.) Life is worth living only if we turn our backs on nearly everything that seems good; we need instead to study the cosmos, or the noetic world. By contrast, according to the view I am presenting, ordinary human lives can be filled with experiences of the sort needed to elevate those lives to a higher order of prudential value. The human capacity to live that better kind of life is rooted in many aspects of our mentality, but one of the most significant is our sophisticated sense of time. Even brief periods of human life can contain experiences that are of considerable prudential value to us because our consciousness during those periods is a mixture of what the world is now presenting to us and memories, expectations, and hopes. Present experience has the felt character not of something arrested or punctuated, but of a continuous, smooth flowing of the past into the future. We conceive of the present extended moment as a portion of a larger whole, and we value it as it happens because we experience it against the background of a sense of our lives as larger than the present moment. The first few moments in which we open a new book can be filled with excitement because we see it as our first step towards the acquisition of a new language and the appreciation of a new author. If we acquire the art of appreciating what the present moment has to offer, part of what we learn is how to attend to the present in a way that brings it together with our memories and hopes. Of course, not every momentary pleasure of a human being has this valuable character—far from it. And *some* temporal segments (a nano-second, for example) are simply too short to be the vehicles of such rich experiences.

The thesis I have been defending (to repeat) is that how well a life goes for someone (its accumulated prudential value) is nothing other than the sum of how well it goes during its temporal segments. What is the length of those segments? Is the proper way to arrive at a conclusion about the total well-being of a life to divide it into so many decades and then add? Or rather so many years (days, seconds)? The answer is that one size does not fit all. The appropriate duration to use in assessing the contribution made by an experience to someone's well-being varies according to the type of experience in question. The value to us of reading a sonnet is not the sum of reading each word one by one, or each line in isolation from the rest. Reading a story is typically a longer experience, and reading a novel longer still. Our consciousness links what we are doing or feeling now to certain portions, but not all portions, of our recollected past and our expected future. What is experienced can be momentary, hour-long, or day-long. But when we are asked, "How did your week (month, year) go for you?," we typically and reasonably respond by dividing that conventionally designated unit of time into smaller components. We say that the week started well, but then went badly; or that every day was wonderful; or that the week had its ups and downs. Similarly, someone's level of well-being over a *lifetime* is the sum of smaller units.

18. McTaggart's thesis defended

I would now like to consider what might seem to be a forceful objection to the position I have taken regarding McTaggart's oyster. It takes the form of an example. Imagine a ninety-year-old man whose life has thus far gone very well, and whose mental powers have declined but little. He has just embarked on a new project: to learn Russian and then to read the major works of Tolstoy. He does not know it, but he has a heart condition that will suddenly and unexpectedly kill him one year from the first day of this undertaking.

Will he have more well-being over that period of time than accrues to an oyster? Let's change that question to one about many oysters—an immense number, each experiencing a simple and faint pleasure as it takes in nourishment. Each has a lifespan as long as you like. It might be thought that when the number of collective oyster years becomes large enough, their combined overall well-being must at some point exceed that of our ninety-year-old admirer of Tolstoy during his final year.

Several features of this example should be noted. First, there are so many of them, and only one of him. Second, he has already had a long life, so one more year will not add significantly more. Third, his long-term project will not even be close to completion by the end of his one remaining year of life. Perhaps none of these features is by itself decisive, but it might be thought that their collective force is sufficient to sustain the conclusion that the aggregation of the oysters' pleasures will exceed whatever well-being will accrue to him. If so, a sweeping general conclusion seems to follow: there is no "higher order" of value available to human beings—no component of human well-being that makes our lives immeasurably greater in prudential value than that of an oyster or any number of oysters.

It is important to see that this objection has no force, because it misunderstands McTaggart's thesis. He asks us to imagine the best possible life that a human being can have. We are allowed to put into it everything we take to be good for a human being (assuming that they are all compatible with each other). He adds: imagine that all these goods endure for a finite period of time, be it as long as you like. Even so, he proposes, the oyster must have a better life, provided that its duration exceeds that of this blessed human being by enough.

In light of this, it should be clear why the objection under consideration fails. For suppose it is conceded (provisionally) that the well-being that accrues to our ninety-year-old devotee of Tolstoy in one year will be less than the aggregated well-being of all the oysters. What that would show is merely that *this* particular year of someone's life does not provide an example of a period of human existence that is immeasurably better than that of McTaggart's oyster. But McTaggart does not claim that *some* human life or other is inferior to that of a long-lived oyster. That would be of no interest. Rather, his thesis is that *any* human life, *however good and however long it is*, is inferior to the much longer life of an oyster.

If we reject McTaggart's thesis, as I think we should, our justification for doing so must appeal to examples of human lives, or temporal portions of them, that have one or more immeasurably valuable goods. Such temporal portions must have sufficient duration, if they are to have evidentiary force—a nano-second will not be enough. As we have seen, some philosophers (the Stoics, Plotinus) hold that it takes only a brief time (greater than a nano-second but shorter than a day) for a *certain* kind of conscious state to give human life immeasurable superiority to that of an oyster. If there are such brief periods of human existence (the example I offered was a fully responsive hearing of Beethoven's Ninth Symphony), that would not entail that *every* human endeavor will in a brief time (an hour, a day, a year) make the person who undertakes it immeasurably better off than a long-lived oyster, or a massive number of them. How much time it takes for a temporal part of a human life to achieve that higher level of goodness depends on which goods that human being is seeking. Perhaps it will take our ninety-year-old devotee of Tolstoy many more years than one before his project allows him, in these late years, to attain that higher level prudential value. Perhaps he will need to have read one or more of Tolstoy's works. In that case, since he will die before he is able to do that, he would not provide a convincing counter-example to McTaggart's thesis. Other counter-examples will have to do that job. But surely there are many such: we need only imagine human lives that stretch from a happy childhood to an adulthood filled with the best that human life has to offer.

What the failure of this counter-example reveals is that we must not let the difficulty of answering the question "How much time is sufficient?" lend any credibility to McTaggart's thesis. That question is one that is legitimately posed about my thesis that "the quality of human consciousness" can be "so good (provided that it endures over a sufficient period of time) that no amount of simple oyster pleasure, however long-lasting, will give it a better life." Marcus Aurelius answers that question by pointing to the time it takes to have a synoptic vision of the cosmos. Plotinus answers it by pointing to the time it takes for the real self to enter the noetic realm. I have proposed instead an encounter with a great work of art. How convincing are any of these replies? That is a matter about which there might be reasonable disagreement. But that should not mislead us. It is far less dubious (not dubious at all, I submit) that if a human life of some eighty years or more, has, at each of its stages, all the richness of experience that a human being can attain, that is a level of well-being that no oyster or aggregate of oysters can achieve, however long their lives, no matter how many of them there are.

I granted several paragraphs ago, for the sake of argument, that a ninety-year-old man embarked on a study of Russian might not, during that final year of his life, have a higher level of well-being than the combined well-being of many oysters. My provisional acceptance of that claim should now be revisited. More detail is needed before we can decide how plausible a claim that is. Is learning a new language a thoroughly unpleasant, boring, and burdensome task for this man? If so, those additional features of the example decisively show that the oysters have more good in their lives than he. However, if we assume that, like many linguistically talented people, he finds it a great joy to learn a new language, then it would not be implausible to say that he does have more good in his life during that remaining year than do the oysters. Every day brings a new and rich array of challenges and delights: a new system of sounds, a new way of looking at the world, new expressive powers.

We should not be misled by a further feature of the example: he is learning Russian in order to read Tolstoy in the original, and had he known that he would never reach that goal, he might have chosen to spend his time differently. That fact does not detract at all from the quality of his experience of Russian. Obviously, reading Tolstoy in Russian would have been even better, but the only comparison relevant for our purposes is that between his encounter with the Russian language over a period of a year and the mild pleasures felt by the oysters.

What about the fact that there are *many* oysters (millions of them, if you like) and only one of him? I chose to compare his well-being to that of a great multitude of oysters because some readers might find the purported counter-example far more forceful that way. These readers might think that the life of McTaggart's single oyster does not become much better as time goes by, because the pleasure it feels each day is phenomenologically no different from any of its earlier pleasures. Perhaps they think that the oyster's life is boring. It would bore *us*, and even though the oyster does not *feel* bored, *we* know that its life is (objectively speaking) boring. For readers who think along these lines, the purported counter-example has far more force against me because it substitutes many oysters for McTaggart's single oyster. The pleasure of each of the many oysters, small as it is, is not to be discounted when we add all of them together, whereas there is some temptation to discount the later pleasures of a single oyster because it has already had that pleasure so many times.

But these readers would be mistaken. Admittedly, were *we* to feel the same simple gustatory pleasure every day, recalling that it is just what we have felt as far back as we can remember, and having no experiences other than these, we would feel utterly bored. But McTaggart's oyster is incapable of boredom. It does not have any recollection of the pleasure it felt yesterday or the day before, and so on. So each day's pleasure is experienced as if it were new. There is no difference in total value, then, between the well-being aggregated over the life of a single oyster that lives a million years and the collective well-being of a million oysters each of which lives for a year. I constructed the purported counter-example of this section, comparing the aggregate good of a multitude of short-lived oysters with a single year of language-learning undertaken by a 90-year-old devotee of Tolstoy, in order to address readers who might think otherwise and to point out what their mistake is.

There is more to be said to these readers: my discussion of Velleman's cow in section 14 is pertinent here. The central point, it should be recalled, is that a creature's receptivity to its environment may include an aggregative mechanism—something that enables it to return to environments in which it has more frequently encountered favorable conditions. If it can remember that it received pleasure more days in a row in one location than another, it will return to the more pleasing environment. Something in this creature adds together pleasures felt at different times, and favors more of them to less. It is good for a creature to have this ability to remember and to aggregate. Once that point is recognized, it cannot be denied that the overall lifetime well-being of McTaggart's oyster increases each day.

One remaining feature of this section's purported counter-example remains: the 90-year-old man who embarks on a study of Russian has already had a long life, and so it might be thought that one more year will not add significantly to his well-being. This feature, like the others we have been discussing, provides an opportunity to warn against making a faulty inference. When one adds one year to a life that already has had ninety, the percentage by which that individual's longevity increases is small, in comparison to the percentage by which one year adds to the longevity of a twenty-year-old. It does not follow that there is less good in the older person's year. Suppose that this twenty-year-old is about to embark on a study of Russian, with the eventual goal of reading Tolstoy in the original. He too has only one more year to live, though he does not realize it. If these two (the young man and the old man) have the same love of language, it will be a very good year—and an *equally* good year—for both of them. It will be no better a year for the young man simply because he has twenty years of existence behind him rather than ninety.

19. *The reality of human suffering*

Overall lifetime well-being is the sum of the well-being of its temporal parts, or so I have been arguing. It is important to keep in mind that this assessment involves not only addition but subtraction. The good times are to be added, the bad ones subtracted.

I stipulated that McTaggart's oyster feels no pain. There is nothing in its experience over the course of its long life that detracts from the quality of its existence. That feature of its life must figure in any comparison we make between its well-being and human well-being. The quality of the life of a human being is an aggregate of positive and negative experiences, and so even if someone has many good years, there may be many more bad ones, with the result that, on balance, he has little in the way of overall lifetime well-being. In that case, McTaggart's oyster will eventually have had a far better life.

Consider a human being who has good times and bad. In the good periods, let's suppose all goes exceedingly well: no suffering, no bad experiences of any sort, and many wonderful goods that are immeasurably better than anything available to an oyster. From this description, we might be tempted to infer that no matter what this individual encounters during the bad times, his overall lifetime well-being must be greater than that of McTaggart's oyster. For we have just said that those wonderful goods, which he experienced for a portion of his life, have made him, during the good years, better off than the oyster can be, no matter how long the oyster lives.

This is an inference we are not entitled to make. We have to be careful when we state the thesis that we place in opposition to McTaggart's. It is this: when someone, over a sufficient certain period of time, (A) has goods that are better for him than any length of an oyster's life could bring to it; and (B) little or nothing is very bad for him during that period; then (C) that settles the matter in his favor: his well-being for that period is greater than the oyster's, no matter how long the oyster lives, and even though there is nothing bad in its life. Of course, if the period of time in question is the whole extent of someone's long life, and conditions (A) and (B) apply to it, then again (C) follows. Admittedly, over the course of a long human life, condition (B) may not obtain. Even so, there have been many human beings whose suffering over the course of their lives has not been so great as to put in doubt the immeasurable superiority of those lives to that of McTaggart's oyster.

It might seem puzzling that a human good that is immeasurably more valuable than an oyster's pleasures (no matter how long-lasting) might nonetheless be too small in value to make the whole length of that person's life better overall than the oyster's. But we need only think in more concrete terms to realize that there is no mystery to be explained here. Suppose someone has had a marvelous period of five years in his early twenties. Put into those five years everything that you think makes life good for someone of that age. Now imagine two scenarios: in the first, he dies after those five wonderful years; in the second, his life takes a terrible turn, and he endures fifty years of little but suffering and hardship. If we reject McTaggart's thesis, we can say that in the first scenario this man had a life better than that of any long-lived oyster, but that does not commit us to saying that the same is true in the second scenario. If he lives that second life, the bad in it, in a reckoning of his lifetime well-being, overwhelms the good he possessed in his twenties, because the bad is so long-lasting. For a period of five years, that early segment of his life is better than that of McTaggart's oyster. But the bad years are worse for him than the good years are good, because there are so many more of them.

We would be in trouble if we thought of the goods that fill his five good years as *infinitely* good.[101] If you erase a certain segment of an infinitely long line, that does not diminish it; similarly what is finitely bad for someone could not lower his overall level of well-being, if his life contains something infinitely good. But we need not posit infinitely valuable goods to dissent from McTaggart's thesis. What we posit instead are two orders of goodness, one of which, in a sufficient amount, is always better than any amount of the other. What belongs to the higher order of goodness need not be infinitely good. For its value to be finite means that it might be outweighed, in an overall assessment of an entire existence, by bad things that are bad enough and endure for much longer periods of time.

To see the point more vividly, you might imagine yourself in a race with McTaggart's oyster. You're well ahead of it so far, but that does not mean that it cannot catch up to you and surpass you, if you both keep going. If you exit the race now, by dying, you are the winner, no matter how much farther the oyster keeps going. You win because there can be no future suffering that detracts from the overall quality of your life. That, however, does not mean that it would be best for you to quit while you are ahead. If your

---

[101] Hadot writes: "Because the sage lives within his consciousness of the world, the world is constantly present to him.... The present moment takes on an infinite value: it contains within it the entire cosmos, and all the value and wealth of being." See "'Only the Present is Our Happiness': The Value of the Present Instant in Goethe and in Ancient Philosophy," 230.

future will continue to be good, it is in your interest to carry on. If the goal of human existence were to have more well-being than McTaggart's oyster, you should long for death as soon as you are ahead of it. What this image of a race shows is that having a better life than an oyster is not our proper goal. We should aim instead at having a good future.

I have assumed, in these remarks, that nothing in life is so good that it immunizes us from harm. That has long been a contested matter. Socrates, as described by Plato in the *Apology*, has no fear of death or any other purported evil, because he takes himself to be a good man, and he believes that no harm can befall those who are virtuous (30c–d, 41c–d). He stands at the beginning of one important strand of Greek and Roman moral philosophy. The Stoics follow his lead when they insist that virtue alone is good, vice alone bad; it follows that if you are virtuous, nothing can detract from your well-being. For Plotinus, no evil befalls the soul that dwells in the noumenal world.[102] Aristotle is closer to common sense in his claim that should great misfortunes (like those of Priam) befall a virtuous man, he cannot be congratulated for living well—he is not *eudaimon* (*NE* I.5 1095b31–1096a2).

I side with Aristotle. In my view, when suffering of some form is not an indispensable and good-making part of a good experience (like the adverse conditions that confront someone making a difficult ascent up a mountain), it detracts from the quality of life. Being a good person or having a vision of the highest good does not make one invulnerable to misfortune—including deep and long-lasting suffering. At any rate, accepting the thesis that some goods are immeasurably good in relation to certain others does not entail that nothing is bad for those who possess or have at some time possessed those goods.

It is not a naïvely rosy view of the human situation to conjecture that many human beings, during certain portions of their lives, have experiences that make their lives, at those times, immeasurably better than that of McTaggart's oyster. To reach that higher level, one does not have to be an exceptionally virtuous person, or a master of the art of finding great value in the passing moment, or a devotee of the arts, or the master of some field of intellectual expertise. The fortunate child who feels loved, delights in fantasy, is filled with curiosity—and is not burdened by illness, exploitation, or neglect—has a childhood incomparably superior to the entire life of McTaggart's oyster. This rosy picture represents only one temporal part of human life. It says only that for most people there are some good times, and while they last, that portion of life is raised to a level immeasurably better than what is available to an oyster. But the bad times may occupy a larger portion of many lives than the good times, and they can be far worse than the good times are good. When that happens, the long, painless, unburdened life of an oyster will have more overall lifetime well-being. For human beings who suffer so much, it would be far better to plug into the experience machine.

---

[102] *Ennead* I.4.6.

20. Aristotle on a complete life

After his reflections on the human *ergon* (function, task) lead him to the conclusion that the human good is activity of the soul in accordance with virtue or excellence, Aristotle adds, in one of the few poetic images of his treatise, that this "must be over a complete life. For one swallow does not make a summer, nor one day. Neither does one day or a short time make someone blessed and happy" (I.7 1098a18–20).[103] But what is it for a life to be complete (*teleion*)? Aristotle explains that word in temporal terms. For virtuous activity to constitute the human good, it must be virtuous activity that endures over a substantial period. How much time is that? And why is the human good (*eudaimonia*, happiness) not achievable in less time?[104]

I proposed (in section 17) that in a human life rather short periods of time are sufficiently long to contain goods that belong to a higher order of value. My example was the profound experience of listening to a great musical composition. It might be thought that in saying this I am contradicting what Aristotle claims when he says that *eudaimonia* must be in a complete life. In fact, there is no such conflict. We must recall another statement he makes later in the *Nicomachean Ethics*, when he argues that a virtuous person willingly accepts certain sacrifices, because though he loses something, he gains more. "He would prefer a short period of intense pleasure to a long period of mild pleasure, a year of living nobly to many indifferent years, and a single noble and great action to many trivial ones" (IX.8 1169a22–5). Needless to say, he is not here making a comparison between the experience of a virtuous person and the pleasures of an oyster. But he is comparing two experiential states, one of them brief, the other long. He does not say of the long experience: make it as long as you like, and it will still not contain more good than the short experience. But (as I claimed in Chapter 1, section 6) we can plausibly take that to be his tacit assumption. So read, he rejects McTaggart's thesis. Furthermore, as the statement just cited shows, he believes, as I do, that a brief experience is not prevented by its brevity from belonging to a higher order of value. We must therefore look for a way of understanding his remark that "one swallow does not make a summer" that makes it consistent with his recognition that brief experiences can have an immeasurable superiority to longer ones.

I suggest that when Aristotle says that *eudaimonia* requires a "complete" period of time, he is guided by the assumption that any life that we call *eudaimon* ought to be ideal or not too far from ideal. There can be degrees of *eudaimonia*—Aristotle needs that idea, because he holds that although the life of philosophical contemplation is best, there is a second-best life (devoted to politics) that is also *eudaimon*. But if a life

---

[103] Aristotle occasionally uses *makarios* (as he does here) in addition to or instead of *eudaimon*. (The conventional translation of *makarios* is "blessed.") How these differ—and whether they differ significantly—is a question I set aside. Often he seems to use them interchangeably (as at I.10 1101a5–9), and that is how I read his statement about a single day or short time.

[104] Although I depart from her in some ways, I have benefited from reading Gabriel Richardson Lear, 'Aristotle on Happiness and Long Life,' in Øyvind Rabbås, Eyjólfur K. Emilsson, Hallvard Fossheim, and Miira Tuominen (eds.), *The Quest for the Good Life*.

has a serious and long-lasting deficiency, then it is vastly inferior to the best, and it is a conceptual truth that it does not qualify as *eudaimon*. Further, one way for a human life to be seriously deficient, and therefore fall short of *eudaimonia*, is for it to be cut short in youth or shortly after the onset of adulthood, well before its natural point of termination. There is a normal span of human life, in other words, and a life that is far briefer than that (only twenty years, for example) is one that could have been much better, had it been longer. It would be an abuse of language to call such a life *eudaimon*. In saying this, Aristotle adopts a position that will later be denied by the Stoics and Plotinus. He agrees with them that a brief experience can, despite its brevity, belong to a higher order of value. But, against them, he holds that it would be far better for us to possess what is good not just for a moment but for the whole course of a lifetime.

Does Aristotle believe that for a life to be *eudaimon*, there must be, over the long course of adulthood, no period during which the activity that constitutes *eudaimonia* is seriously disrupted? Evidently not. Speaking of a virtuous person to whom misfortunes have occurred, he says: "he will not be shifted easily from happiness, and not by ordinary misfortunes, but by many grave ones. He would not recover from these to become happy again in a short space of time. If he does recover, it will be after a long and complete period of great and noble accomplishments" (I.10 1101a9–13). Here he is imagining a virtuous person who has been exercising his excellent qualities for a certain period of time, goes through a difficult period in which his virtuous activities are curtailed by misfortune, and then enters a period of life of considerable length in which he does "great and noble" things. Obviously, this is not ideal, but I take Aristotle to be saying that it is not so distant from the ideal that, looking at the life as a whole, it cannot be called *eudaimon*. I also take him to be assuming that the lowest period of such a life is not one of great duration, in comparison with the rest. If it were very long, and the better periods of life short, how could that life, considered as a single stretch of time, qualify as good?

His picture, then, is this: there can be an initial good period of adult life, followed by a short period of misfortune, and then a third period, of considerable length, in which there is a steady recovery from misfortune and eventual great success ("great and noble things"). Looking at the whole adulthood of someone living such a life, we see that it is marred by a brief period in which virtuous activity is disrupted, but that is only a brief period, and it is followed by many years that culminate in activities of exceptional value. Since a *eudaimon* life need not have the greatest of goods (the political life is one that has no time for philosophical contemplation), it is not out of keeping for Aristotle also to hold that when someone's virtuous activity is impeded for a few years because of misfortunes, that individual can still be counted, at the end of a sufficiently long and (for the most part) very good life, as having been *eudaimon*. He says that a short time does not make one *eudaimon*; he could have added: and neither does it make it impossible to be *eudaimon*.

Aristotle, we have now seen, does not oppose the thesis I have been defending: certain brief human experiences have an immeasurable superiority to the longer experiences of McTaggart's oyster. A single swallow does not make a summer, but some brief moments of human life bring goods of a higher order.

There remains this question: why does he not consider the possibility that *eudaimonia* is a great good (in fact, the greatest) built up out of many little ones? For us, it seems obvious that for a decade or year or month to go well for someone is a matter of smaller temporal segments going well. The very image he uses—a single swallow does not make a summer—could be taken to mean not the point he uses it to make but its opposite. Summertime is an accumulation of many days that bring us lush flowers and languid afternoons. That could be taken to suggest that a life is made *eudaimon* when its days, or a great many of them, contain the good, whatever it is, in which *eudaimonia* consists. That great good, in other words, is made great by having *so many* goods of short duration, just as a long distance is made of many short ones.

One response to that challenge is this: although a decade of well-being is an aggregate of smaller periods that go well, Aristotle is not talking about well-being, but *eudaimonia*, which is a different concept. For him—so this proposal goes—the very idea of *eudaimonia* is the idea of something that occupies the whole length of a life, or the whole length of an adult life, or at any rate a period of time very close to this length. We might make this comparison: a season is not composed of smaller units each of which is itself a season, and a career is not composed of small bits of time each of which is a career. By definition, these are temporal periods of considerable duration. In the same way, it might be said, the concept of *eudaimonia* is the concept of a good possessed for a long period of time.

The objection to this way of understanding Aristotle is that it leaves no room for a satisfying answer to the question, "What is his reason for saying that *eudaimonia* needs a complete life—that is, a long period of time?" We might say: his reason is that this is the way that word is used. But that would make his claim trivial. Instead of giving us a deep insight about how we should live our lives, he would just be telling us how to use a word correctly.

Here is a different kind of response to the question we are asking: when Aristotle says that *eudaimonia* requires a complete period of time, he is making an inference, one that moves from a fact about virtuous activity to a conclusion about *eudaimonia* itself. A virtue, according to Aristotle's theory of character, is a state that is by its nature a long-term condition. When someone acts in a way that expresses a good character, he is bringing forth something from within that is enduring and unshakable (*NE* II.4 1105a33). It will stand the test of time, or has done so already. It follows (according to this way of reading him), that *eudaimonia* also has this long-term feature. It requires a complete life because what it consists in endures over a lifetime.

This interpretation is better than the one just rejected, because it takes him to be making a substantive point and to be defending that point. But it has a serious defect: when he says that *eudaimonia* needs a complete life, he does not support that claim by appealing to the long-term nature of ethical virtue. He has not yet begun to tell his audience what a virtue is. Rather, he simply appeals to the idea that one cannot be *eudaimon* for only a day. "A single day or a short time [do not] make a man blessed and happy." It is a substantive point, and we are expected to accept it right away, because there is something about *eudaimonia* itself that makes it a condition of great duration.

I conjecture that Aristotle takes *eudaimonia* to have this temporal feature because he thinks of it as what we appropriately give an enduring and guiding place in all our practical thinking. That something ought to play this ongoing role is a point he makes at a very early stage in his discussion. The opening chapter of the *Nicomachean Ethics* introduces us to the notion of a hierarchy of goods, and in the next chapter we arrive at the conclusion that there should be an ultimate goal for all that we do, and in reference to which we make all our decisions. He then says (I.4 1095a17–18) that we have a word for this goal—it is *eudaimonia*—and the question we need to answer is what it consists in. So, even before he arrives at the conclusion that it consists in virtuous activity, he has assembled the materials by which he arrives at the conclusion that *eudaimonia* guides us through the whole span of our adult lives. We do not and ought not set before ourselves a different goal each day, or each month, or year. The better way to live our lives is to have a single aim throughout, and to make plans for shorter periods by referring to that unitary lifelong goal.

That, I submit, is the most plausible way to understand the reasoning behind his claim that we achieve *eudaimonia* in a complete life. Having settled that matter of interpretation, we can now ask: Should we agree with him? Should we, in other words, reject the thesis I have been defending, according to which lifetime well-being is an aggregate of the good and bad that accrue to us over shorter periods? We should not. We can wholeheartedly embrace Aristotle's plausible idea about the need to make long-term plans, but to do so we need not say, as he does, that well-being is possessed only over a long period of time, in the way that a career stretches over a long period of one's life and is not a matter of a single day.

When someone is carrying out a long-term plan—one that will take two years to achieve, for example—it can be asked, on any given day, week, or month of his execution of it: During this period, how well did he do, and how did things go for him, with respect to that plan? Did he advance it? Did anything unforeseen or unforeseeable happen to him on that day, week, or month that advanced him or set him back? The fact that he is not just taking each day as it comes, but is embarked on a long-term project does not prevent us from asking how this day or that went for him—with respect to the execution of his long-term project. The same point applies to the assessment of someone's overall lifetime well-being. To have a good life, it is best to make some long-term plans, and not live entirely moment by moment. One need not have a detailed blueprint of the entirety of one's future; one ought to leave room for revisions; and one should not refuse to welcome unforeseen things simply because they were unforeseen.[105] Nothing stops us from accepting these familiar verities and adding: for a whole life to go well is for it to have many temporal parts that go well and few that go badly.

---

[105] See Charles Larmore, *The Practices of the Self*, 177–83, a section entitled 'The Importance of Unexpected Goods.'

That way of explaining the great value of lifelong well-being—reducing it to the sum of temporally smaller values—strikes me as plausible, even though it brings me into conflict with Aristotle. This is neither a merely verbal difference nor a matter of great substance; there are several more significant points about well-being and time that we both accept. Before I say what they are, I will state more fully what I take his theory to be. I imagine him elaborating as follows on points he makes with his usual brevity:

"The human good consist in virtuous activity of the soul—and, I must add, in a complete life. When I say that, I do not mean that there is some precise and lengthy period of time (fifty years, seventy years, or some other number) for which a life must endure in order for it to qualify as *eudaimon*. Any such figure would obviously be arbitrary. I mean rather that the best one can seek and attain is to have the good (virtuous activity) for many, many years; the closer that comes to the complete normal lifespan of a human being, the better.

"I should add that a good length of time is also needed in order to *acquire* the states of the soul that count as virtues; you must have much experience of life and develop good habits of emotional and intellectual response to your circumstances. Then, once you have finally acquired the virtues, you must set long-terms goals, as you seek the good of the political community, your friends, and family. Little that a good person seeks is accomplished in a day. Complete *eudaimonia* will be attained if you live such a life for many years without encountering major misfortunes.

"At any point along the way, the question can be asked: is this life *eudaimon*? We can answer provisionally in the affirmative, if it has thus far been a life filled with virtuous activity and few evils. But for all we know, there could be much suffering in the future, and if a portion of life will be seriously blighted, one cannot call it—that is, the *whole* of it—*eudaimon*. ("What is to prevent us, then, from concluding that the happy person is the one who, adequately furnished with external goods, engages in activities in accordance with virtue, not just for any period of time, but over a complete life? Or should we add that he will live like this and die accordingly?", I.10 1101a14–17).

"Can we retrospectively say, at the end of someone's life, that a large portion of such a life was *eudaimon*—the lengthy part that came before its unfortunate final component? Yes, but that is not a point about how to live, but about the use of a word. We should not make the word *eudaimon* useless by applying it only to a life that is no less than perfect. A second-best life should qualify, and so should a long life that has had only a small number of bad years.

"Regarding the long-term goals you undertake because you are a virtuous person, it must be recognized that your aim is not merely to move them forward, but to bring them to completion. Suppose, for example, that you are overseeing the establishment of a theater or a gymnasium in your city, and your project encounters unforeseeable obstacles and must be abandoned. You cannot feel the pleasure that normally accompanies (and ought to accompany) virtuous activity. Your goal was to benefit your city, and this you failed to do. A life that contained only or mainly such failures would not be a *eudaimon* life. It would be too deficient in one of the great pleasures of virtuous activity—the pleasure of benefiting others. Regular or frequent failure at the tasks of a good person is incompatible with *being* a good person, for there is no virtue in the absence of the practical effectiveness known as cleverness (VI.12 1144a23–8). But it does not follow that whenever a long-term plan fails to reach its goal, there is *nothing* good in the activity devoted to it. Day by day, a good person has thoughts and feelings that are just what they should be, given the circumstances he encounters. If his efforts in service of the common good are going well thus far, he will be well pleased. The later failure of a project does not undo the good that came to the virtuous person along the way. There was less good for the agent than there should have been (and none for those he aimed to serve), but there was still some good."

In view of this last aspect of Aristotle's theory—his acceptance of the thesis that the benefits of being a virtuous person accrue day by day, and are not cancelled by later misfortunes—it would not be a significant alteration if he reduced the great value of lifelong well-being to the sum of temporally smaller values.

He says, "one swallow does not make a summer, nor one day." Another analogy would also suit his purposes: a single successful night of theater does not make a successful theatrical season. The very notion of a season carries with it a stretch of time far longer than the duration of a single day. But we could say that a good season of theater simply is a long succession of excellent performances over the course of the many days of a season. That analogy does not fully serve Aristotle's purpose, because typically the performance of a play takes an afternoon or evening and then it is over, to be succeeded by yet more performances on other days. The activities of a well-lived life do not all of them come in such uniform temporal packages. Some of them take less than an hour, others occupy us for years. Even so, these long-term undertakings can receive interim reports regarding their success to date.

His theory, we can now recognize, has much in common with my own. Most significantly, he would reject, as I do, the thesis of Epicurus, the Stoics, and Plotinus, that if one has the good in which well-being consists, it does not matter whether one has it for the briefest of moments or for a long period of time. Like Aristotle, I hold that the best human lives are the ones that have the components of well-being for a long time. Like him, I believe that we can, at any point in someone's life, look at it retrospectively and assess how well or ill it has gone thus far. Like him, I think that we can judge that a certain portion of a life went badly, but that thereafter it went well (or vice versa).

Our most serious disagreement has to do with childhood: when he looks retrospectively at a life to assess its *eudaimonia*, he does not count anything that happens during that early portion of life as *by itself* a factor to be weighed in an overall reckoning of lifetime well-being. "And for this same reason [because he is not virtuous], a child is not happy either, since his age makes him incapable of doing such actions. If he is called blessed, he is being described as such on account of the potential he has" (I.9 1100a1–4). Childhood is important in his theory, but only because of the effect early education or the lack of it has on later life. On this point, I am certain that he is mistaken. (See sections 8 and 9 above.) It is an error he falls into because he has too narrow a conception of the goods that comprise well-being. He is right that ethical virtue (the inner life of a good person) is a major component of a good life. A child is not yet a fully mature ethical agent, as Aristotle recognizes; that is a good that is not yet available to him. He is also right to hold that adulthood brings with it the potential for greater goods than those a child can have (Chapter 1, section 10). But he goes wrong when he holds that because childhood is not a period of life in which full virtue is possible, *nothing* that a child does and nothing that befalls a child by itself counts positively or negatively in an overall assessment of that individual's lifetime well-being. He does not see how wonderful many of the experiences of childhood are.

21. Death revisited

The lifetime well-being of McTaggart's oyster increases with each passing day, and continues without interruption. There is no good it gains by dying at some point or other. With human beings, must it be different? Do we need to die to gain something of prudential value—something good enough to compensate for the loss incurred by having no further well-being? Plato holds that we want to have the good *forever* (Chapter 1, section 1), and that seems plausible. We have seen that well-being itself does not have diminishing marginal value, nor do its components (section 2 above). So long as there is no decline in the quality of life, more life is better than less. It would therefore be better for me to continue living a good life forever than for my good life to end. That is compatible with the idea that if the quality of experience falls below a certain threshold (making life oyster-like), I have too little reason to want to continue to live (section 10 above). Alternatively, I may already have gone out of existence—that oyster-like creature would not be me.

I find it easy to imagine an unending human life filled with prudential goods. My thought experiment does not envisage a world in which all human beings know that they are invulnerable to death or any sort of deterioration, psychological or physical. (Invulnerability to death, but vulnerability to crippling disease would not be an attractive package.) That transformation in the circumstances of human life would be radical indeed, making it hazardous to arrive at a confident assessment of what the quality of life would be. In a world that has no possible harms, why strive for good? Would goods simply come to us without our needing to make any effort? How good could any such good be?

What I imagine instead is a world in which just you and a small group of your loved ones and friends happen to be so lucky that you all continue to exist without undergoing any physical or psychological deterioration. The quality of your lives never declines, and there is no end to your days. All others, however, are subject to the ravishes of time and die from the usual causes.

To add concrete detail to this picture, imagine that you and your circle of friends and family are artists, writers, dancers, and musicians. You read the best of the latest novels, listen to the leading contemporary musicians, and view the most recent outstanding work at the galleries. (You do not have time for everything, so you must be selective.)

You meet frequently with your friends to discuss what you are writing, reading, listening to, viewing. The aesthetic world never stops changing, and your interest in it remains strong. Since you do not decline physically or psychologically, you assume that you will experience what the next decade will bring—and then, after that decade, you look forward to the next one, and so on. Turning back to earlier centuries, you see how much your experience has been enriched by what writers, musicians, and artists of those times still have to offer. The same increasing enrichment is what you expect from the future. You will be the beneficiary of both the creative geniuses that flourished in the past and the ones that will arise in the future. There will be new Beethovens, new Tolstoys, new Rembrandts (not the same kind of work, but no less worthy of attention), and you are eager to observe the shape that work will take. You also realize that new genres and new forms of artistic expression arise from time to time, and do so in ways that no one could have predicted. That too is likely to be the case in the future. Some of the sources of excitement in being alive are beyond your current imagination or anyone else's. When it occurs to you that you might die and miss out on all that is to come, you fervently hope that your good fortune continues.

If we react to this picture by saying that we must never set our hopes on living in such a world, because that is too good a world to bring to mind, we have conceded the point at issue: the best span for a human life is one that never ends. We might instead react by saying that there is a concealed impossibility in this scenario. But what is it? Is it impossible for the arts to continue to move in new and wonderful directions? Impossible for the body or mind to withstand the forces of deterioration? It would be dogmatic to insist upon these points, but even if the picture painted were impossible, would it lose any of its attraction?

To resist the conclusion that the best human life would be one that goes on forever, we would need to describe the great good that such a life would lack. It would have to be a good so great that we should give up the ones described in this scenario in order to have it. I myself know of no such good.

22. *Long-term plans and the persistence of individuals*

As noted earlier (Chapter 1, section 1), I have modified McTaggart's comparison between the best of human lives and the far longer life of an oyster. I have stayed closer to what we are familiar with, by taking the human life in question to extend over about eighty-five or ninety years—not a million years, as he does. He has a reason for using such large numbers (a human life of a million years and an oyster's life far longer than that). Doing so allows him to make use of a familiar point about our vulnerability to a flawed way of thinking about the distant future. As he says, "we are generally affected more than is reasonable by the present or the near future in comparison with the far future."[106] He then adds: "And a change which will only happen after the end of a million years is in a very far future."

---

[106] *The Nature of Existence*, volume 2, 453. The remaining statements of McTaggart cited in this section can be found on that same page.

Many people, he adds, will mistakenly opt for a million years of wonderful human existence rather than far more years of an oyster's simple life because "men's choice in such cases is very much affected by their imagination." And "it is much easier to imagine the difference between the two sorts of life which we have considered, than it is to imagine the difference between an enormously long time and another time which is enormously longer." That failure of imagination together with our insouciance regarding the far future explains why we are likely to reach the wrong conclusion, pre-ferring a million years of the best that human life offers to many, many more millions of years of the oyster's existence.

When McTaggart says, "we are generally affected more than is reasonable by the present or the near future in comparison with the far future," he is reflecting on defects in our normal practices of planning, and projecting them far beyond that. I take him to mean that if we *know* (by stipulation) that our future will extend for a million or many millions of years, we should not discount even that incredibly remote future, and should therefore choose the life of an oyster. We should no more discount the value of lives one million years from now than we should discount what tomorrow or next year will bring.

The defect in this aspect of McTaggart's thought experiment is obvious: human life and human nature being what they are, it would be impossible for us to make plans that guide us through a period of a million years. At any rate, if our lives continued to have the complexity and richness that makes them (at their best) so worthwhile, many aspects of the distant future would be unforeseeable. Prudence would therefore require us to wait and see how circumstances change before we made irrevocable decisions about allocating present resources. By contrast, we are familiar with how human lives change (sometimes gradually, sometimes abruptly) when they extend over a mere eighty-five or ninety years. Making some sacrifices in our well-being now or in the near future for the sake of a far better middle age or old age makes good sense, because we have sufficient evidence to make justified predictions about what our gains will be.

It does not follow that it could not be better for a human being to live for a million years than ninety (or any other period shorter than a million years). If the argument of the preceding section is correct, we can coherently describe a group of people who are lucky enough to have lives that continue year after year without any diminution in well-being. They make short-term and long-term plans as we all do, looking ahead ten, twenty, thirty years; and their near-term sacrifices reap greater rewards later. These people are better off (have greater lifetime well-being) than those who have a much shorter life of equal quality. There is nothing wrong, then, with McTaggart's idea of a human life that lasts a million years and is filled at every stage with great prudential goods.

His error in using an unrealistically large number lies only in what he implies (with-out actually saying): that we would be at fault, *as decision-makers*, if, looking ahead and planning our distant future, we failed to give a month one million years from now as much weight as one month next year; and that our common vulnerability, in our present circumstances (having lives of some eighty or ninety years), to discounting the distant future underlies our temptation to suppose that his oyster has a worse life. He forgets that we are in a much better epistemic situation as planners of ninety-year lives than we would be as planners of one-million-year lives. As things now stand, we should know better than to ignore what our lives will be like when we are old, and fail to plan ahead. Some sacrifice of near-term well-being is prudent because we can be reasonably confident that it will pay greater rewards later. By contrast, we have no way of knowing what our world or lives might be like one million years from now, if we were to endure that long. We could legitimately decline to make current sacrifices for a future so distant.

I have been assuming that in normal circumstances each human being is a single individual persisting through time: one and the same individual for the whole of a lifetime (which, at best, will be some eighty-five or ninety years). That leaves room for exceptional cases. On some conceptions of personal identity over time, certain psychological changes are so radical that we must speak of the earlier individual as no longer existing and of a new individual arising. Some would say, for example, that if a normal human life is transformed so that the body of that individual enters a persistent vegetative state, that life has ended and a second individual has replaced the first. But everyone agrees that other changes that befall us, significant as they are, are changes that occur to a single continuing individual human being. A one-year-old child and a ninety-year-old man can be the earlier and later temporal segments of a single human being, in spite of the immense psychological and physical differences between them. We do sometimes speak loosely or figuratively of someone becoming "a different person," meaning only that the later person has taken on a rather different personality or character traits—has, for example, become self-confident and outgoing, whereas earlier he was insecure and introverted. In such cases, there is no death of one individual and no birth of a new one. Rather, a single individual changes greatly, remaining that same individual throughout.[107]

Since each of us has a conception of himself as a single individual persisting through time, with a potential longevity of some eighty or ninety years, we can each make long-term plans that involve near-term sacrifices of well-being for the sake of an increase in overall lifetime well-being. It would be an error to do otherwise—to think that only one's present well-being ought to receive one's attention, or that only this month matters, or only one's youthful years, and as a result to allow the rest of one's life to be filled with misery. The period of well-being that we ought to look to, when we make decisions about our future, is overall *lifetime* well-being—where a lifetime is something like eighty or ninety years, not a million.[108]

---

[107] Parfit cites passages in Proust and Solzhenitsyn in which characters speak of their past selves as separate persons who have died, or their future selves as new persons. See *Reasons and Persons*, 305. As he notes, "talk about successive selves can easily be misunderstood, or taken too literally" (305–6).

[108] There is no conflict between this thesis and any of the claims made by Parfit in *Reasons and Persons*. One of the major aims of that work is to refute what he calls "the Self-interest Theory," according to which "for each person there is one supremely rational ultimate aim, that his life go, for him, as well as possible" (4). (That is not a view I endorse here.) To this end, he argues that the psychological connections between earlier and later selves distant in time are often weak; and, partly for this reason, there is no reason to care

But suppose one has reason to expect that many years from now one will be a "different person" (speaking loosely)—would that be a sufficient reason to abandon the normal policy of looking to lifetime well-being? Suppose you are in your thirties and foresee that in your seventies and eighties your interests, tastes, and even your personality will be different. You have seen this happen to your father and his brothers and sisters—you might think, then, that there is some genetic basis for your expectation. Furthermore, you foresee that in later life you will need to move to a new part of the world, where people generally have interests rather different from the ones you have now. Your new social milieu, you believe, will change you—you will become more like the members of that new community. Currently you love parties, card games, basketball, jazz, mathematics. Later in life, you expect that you will instead love solitude, poetry, rowing, classical music, novels. You don't believe that your current interests and personality are objectively superior to the ones that you expect to have later; they are different, but no better or worse. You don't believe that there will be no prudential value, or less, in the life of the "new person" you expect to become in your later days.[109]

In such a case, it remains true that one should look to one's overall lifetime well-being, just as one does when one expects there to be few or no major changes in the kind of person one will be in one's later years. One would be making a mistake not to sacrifice small near-term goods for the sake of securing greater rewards that come late in life. One might, for example, discover in middle age that one has a medical condition that can be treated in one of two ways: An operation can be scheduled for the near future, in which case there will be a painful recovery period that lasts a week. The alternative is to let the condition remain dormant until old age, but in that case the painful recovery period would last a year. Your health is otherwise excellent, so you can reasonably expect to live into your eighties or nineties. So, your choices are to inflict a small period of pain on the person that you are now, or much more pain on the "new you" of your later life. There is only one correct decision: to have the operation sooner rather than later, for the sake of your overall lifetime well-being. The fact that you will be "a different person" later does not give you a reason to do otherwise. In the sense that matters in these cases, you will be the same person.

Each of us is a being extended in time—a lifetime. What we should therefore look to is not just well-being at a time—the present time, or the near future—but also well-

---

supremely about this future self, with no direct concern about the well-being of others. He does not claim that one can have *no* reason to care about a future self that might be called, speaking figuratively, a new self. Rather, he poses a *comparative* challenge to the Self-interest Theory: Why should one care so much *more* about one's future self, who is so different from one's present self, than about those who are literally other people? The success of this challenge would not pose a problem for my statement that "the period of well-being that we ought to look to, when we make decisions about our future, is overall *lifetime* well-being."

[109] In that respect this scenario differs from the example used by Parfit of a young nineteenth-century Russian nobleman who is concerned that his socialist ideals will fade later in life and therefore takes steps to undermine the goals of his later self. See *Reasons and Persons*, 327. I have benefited from reading David O. Brink, 'Prospects for Temporal Neutrality', in Craig Callender (ed.), *The Oxford Handbook of the Philosophy of Time*.

being "in a complete life," as Aristotle says. But although I have arrived at the same conclusion, my reasons differ from his. He believes that as soon as one becomes a mature decision-maker, one should set for oneself a single ultimate goal that remains an unchanging guide for the present and all later times. If one did change it, that (he assumes) would show that one had been mistaken to set it in the first place—or that one is wrong to change it now. And, being a long-term goal, it cannot be achieved in a day or any short period. By contrast, the argument I have used allows for the possibility that a prudent person might have different goals at different times of his life. It rests on the assumptions that planning for the future is often a worthwhile investment of time, and that there is no reason to discount the future. This point is well illustrated by examples in which a short-term loss is compensated by a greater gain that comes later. Aristotle never mentions such cases. Perhaps he failed to recognize them.

23. McMahan on an infant's death

Jeff McMahan asks us to "consider the life of a human being who dies shortly after birth. This brief life contained very little good at all. Yet it does not seem to have been a tragic life; nor does the infant seem to have been a deeply unfortunate individual. Why not?"[110]

This is an excellent question. Here is how he begins his reply:

…a newborn infant, like an animal, is simply not a substantial enough individual psychologically to be susceptible to injustice or tragedy. While the infant's objective loss is great, the infant itself is too shallow a vessel to contain that loss.… It is not terribly bad for the infant to have had that life.[111]

…Most forms of great misfortune—for example, blighted hopes, failed efforts at significant achievement, the loss of something that one cares deeply about—presuppose a psychologically substantial subject.[112]

McMahan is right. When we think of the clearest examples of tragic lives, we imagine individuals who have experienced deep suffering, anguish, misery. Had King Lear died peacefully immediately after dividing his kingdom between his two undeserving daughters, he would not have been a tragic figure. An infant cannot experience the powerful emotions that are the stuff of tragedy. The greatest misfortunes of human life are the ones that are deeply felt, and an infant is psychologically too shallow to have emotions of this sort. The brief life of an infant who dies, having suffered no great physical pain or psychological distress, contains nothing that is very bad for it.

Suppose an infant would have had a wonderful childhood and adulthood, had it lived. McMahan says: "the infant's objective loss is great." He does not claim that it does not matter whether the infant lives or dies, or that there is no reason to lift a finger to save it. Because the objective loss is great, there is a stronger reason to hope that it survives than there would be if, were it to survive, its life would be barely or not at all worth living.

---

[110] *The Ethics of Killing*, 162.   [111] Ibid., 163.   [112] Ibid., 164.

Let's imagine that the infant has been abandoned by her parents and is asleep in the forest. A fire caused by lightning is about to consume her. But a wolf comes across her, drags her to safety, and she is found by a peasant couple who have always wanted a child. She goes on to have a long and wonderful life. Compare this with a second story: this time it is a fifteen-year-old girl asleep in the forest, abandoned by her parents. She too is saved by a wolf, is brought up by a new family, and has an equally long and wonderful life. It would have been no tragedy had the first child died. But had the fifteen-year-old died, that, we could say with some plausibility, would have been a tragedy, even if she was asleep and felt no fear. For in this case, to use McMahan's words, she loses something she "cares deeply about." A fifteen-year-old has an outlook on life, expectations, ambitions, yearnings and plans. Even if she suffers no anguish about her loss of life, we might say that it is a tragedy that her hopes and ambitions came to nothing. Our hearts go out to her because we envisage concretely what she was on her way to becoming. An infant, however, has no hopes and ambitions to be dashed. An infant's death is often heartbreaking for her parents, but it is experienced by them in a different way from the death of an older child.[113]

If a wolf saves the first child (the infant), it brings about more lifetime well-being than it would by saving the second. (We are assuming that these two children live the same number of years. The infant is saved at a point in her life fifteen years earlier than the other, and so receives more benefit from the wolf.) But if the wolf saves the first child, and the second dies, there is more tragedy in the world. Which act produces more prudential value? There is a better outcome for the infant than for the older child if the infant is saved. To make this more evident, we can alter the example slightly by assuming that the first child has *much* more well-being than the second, by living longer and having many more years of good life. In that case, it is all the more evident that if the infant is saved rather than the fifteen-year-old, that is the better outcome.

What does McMahan's theory say about this comparison? He more fully develops his account by emphasizing the infant's immature sense of time:

An infant is unaware of itself, unaware that it has a future; it therefore has no future-directed mental states: no desires or intentions for its future. Because its mental life is so limited, there would be very few continuities of character or belief between itself now and itself as a person. And if it had lived to become a person, it would then remember nothing of its life as an infant. It is, in short, almost completely severed psychologically from itself as it would have been in the future. This is the principal reason why its time-relative interest in continuing to live is so weak. It is almost as if the future it loses might just as well have belonged to someone else.[114]

---

[113] Here is how Darya Alexandrovna feels about it: "Once again there arose in her imagination the cruel memory that weighed eternally on her maternal heart of the death of her last infant, who had died of croup, the funeral, the universal indifference before this tiny pink coffin and her lonely, heartrending pain before the pale little brow with the little curls and before the open and surprised little mouth that could be seen from the coffin at the very moment when they were closing the lid with the lace cross." Leo Tolstoy, *Anna Karenina*, Part VI, chapter 16, translated by Marian Schwartz.

[114] *The Ethics of Killing*, 170. McMahan later discusses an apparent paradox for this account (which he calls a "Time-Relative Interest Account"). "A day-old infant will die unless the doctor saves him. Although

None of this is true of the fifteen-year-old.

Recall his statement that "the infant's objective loss is great." That is because she is robbed of a long and well-lived life. But since she does not care about her future, and would not remember her infancy, there is little lost in the way of "time-relative interest." When he speaks of her great "objective loss," this does not refer to a great loss of prudential value *at the time of death*. He might say that it is very bad *that* the infant dies (for had she lived a long and wonderful life, that would have been good for her), but he holds that her death is not very bad *for* her *at the time of death*, because at that time she has so shallow a future-oriented mental life.

We might ask: if both children are about to die in the fire, and the wolf is poised between them, able to save only one, is it better that it save the infant or the fifteen-year-old? Imagining ourselves as impartial observers of the scene (strangers to both children, and unable to intervene), should we hope for the alternative in which more well-being is eventually produced (the preservation of the infant), or the alternative that is less tragic (the preservation of the fifteen-year-old)? For the moment, we assume that no other moral factors are to be considered, beyond the ones already mentioned. I will soon return to that assumption.

For McMahan, it is important that when the wolf acts, the "time-relative interest" of the infant is meager. At that time, death does less harm to the infant than to the older girl. If one hopes for the less bad death, one hopes that the wolf will save the fifteen-year-old. If, however, one envisages the two alternatives by looking far into the future, and retrospectively considers what the wolf did many years ago, there will be more reason to be glad that it saved the infant (if that is what it did) than reason to be glad that it saved the older child (if that is what it did), for that is the alternative that led to more well-being.

My discussion of McTaggart's oyster and Velleman's cow (section 14) is relevant here. McMahan is unfortunately forced to say that the oyster is no better off living a thousand years than a day, and that an ordinary oyster is no better off for having a good "memory" that allows it to return day after day to favorable locations. For an oyster, like a human infant, has no awareness that it has a future or past, no forward-looking desires, no intentions or plans, no memory of earlier days. Psychologically, it too is a "shallow vessel"—probably more so than the infant. But, unlike the infant who is rescued from the fire, it continues to have a thin psychology for all the days of its life.

the infant can be saved, the condition that threatens his life cannot be cured and will certainly cause his death later around the age of thirty-five" (ibid., 185). The Time-Relative Interest Account cannot explain why the doctor should save the infant, for it holds that he would lose almost nothing by dying in infancy, whereas if he lives to thirty-five his death robs him of a great deal beyond the age of thirty-five. He argues that the paradox is only apparent, because we should use a "Life Comparative Account" of the badness of death as well as the "Time-Relative Interest Account." The Life Comparative Account makes the badness of death "proportional to the difference between the total value the life as a whole would have if the death were to occur and the total value the life would have if the death were not to occur" (ibid., 105). The two accounts are not in conflict, he says, because they "are concerned with different dimensions of the badness of death" (ibid., 186). On this view, the infant's death is only slightly bad in one dimension and very bad in another.

So, the prudential value that accrues to it on one day is, on his theory, not to be added to the prudential value that comes its way the next. He need not deny that it remains the same organism over the entirety of its thousand years. But what he says about an infant applies here as well: "It is almost as if [its] future . . . belonged to someone else." It is one oyster over time, but that matters little to him, for it is "almost as if" it were a new oyster each day. What he thinks matters is that it does not have more well-being by living longer. The infant *would* have more well-being if it lives longer, but that is not something it can care about now.

This, as I argued earlier, is a mistaken view about oysters (or cows). It rests on the assumption that the psychological perspective of an individual (whether an infant, an oyster, or a cow) determines what its well-being is, and whether prudential value accrues to it over time. But an infant need not care about her future for it to be the case that if a nearby wolf might easily have saved her from death but does not do so, the wolf's rescue of the older child instead of her must be counted as a great loss for her. Her death was very bad for her, even though we do not respond to it as a tragedy, and even though she does not care about having a long future.

The example I have relied on has a peculiar feature: it is a wolf, not a human being, whose intervention saves a life. I do not claim that if a human being comes across an infant and a fifteen-year-old, each asleep in a forest, and can rescue only one of them from a fire, he ought to rescue the infant. If that human being is the father of one of these children but not the other, he owes it to his child to rescue her. Other social bonds that have been established between the rescuer and one of the children may similarly play an important role. But what if the human being who comes across the endangered children is a total stranger to both? He sees that one is an infant, the other a teenager. He has no reason to think that the quality of their lives will differ or that one will die at an earlier age than the other. So it can easily occur to him that he will bring about more well-being if he saves the infant. Is that therefore what he ought to do?

It is only one consideration among many that by saving the infant rather than the fifteen-year-old he brings about more prudential value among these two individuals over time. There are other human beings to be considered, and other factors besides the total amount of prudential value. The infant is not yet a morally responsible member of a wide social world tied together by bonds of reciprocity and commitment. But the fifteen-year-old can be assumed to be treasured by her friends and her larger social community. Her parents and teachers have been devoting themselves for many years to bringing her into adulthood. She has incurred obligations to them as they have to her. If these considerations occur to the rescuer, they might outweigh the fact that rescuing the infant would produce more good for her than rescuing the fifteen-year-old would produce for her.[115]

---

[115] For further discussion of McMahan's Time-Relative Interest Account, see Ben Bradley, *Well-Being and Death*, 113–46, and John Broome, *Weighing Lives*, 249–51.

5

Variations on Aristotelian Themes

My agreements and disagreements with Aristotle have been scattered across the preceding chapters of this work, so I will bring matters to a close by assembling many of them and, in some cases, elaborating on and supplementing them.

Aristotle is close to experientialism, but he is not an experientialist. One way in which he departs from this conception of well-being is by accepting the existence of posthumous goods and harms. But at the same time his treatment of this issue also reveals a strong affinity to experientialism. He believes that what happens after one's death can do one some good or harm—but very little. The importance of what I have been calling the "inner quality" of our lives is, for him, enormous. He is certain that if someone is experiencing agonizing pain, his life at that time is not going well for him. His methodology calls upon the arguments employed by an ethical theory to be tested against what he calls the "facts (*erga*) of our life." He holds that well-being does not reside in external goods (such as honor) or goods of the body (such as health). These passages suggest that for him the quality of one's experience—what one is aware of from the inside—has a great bearing on the quality of one's life.

There is a further feature of Aristotle's practical philosophy, not mentioned so far, that sets him farther apart from experientialism. He holds that human well-being consists partly in exercising the ethical virtues and furthermore that one has those human excellences only if one also possesses and exercises the intellectual virtue that he calls "practical wisdom" (*phronêsis*). Someone who is wise in this way has thought carefully about the proper ends of human life, and lives ethically because he understands why it is best for him to do so. This feature of mental life—philosophical reflection on ultimate ends—is good for one only if it yields real wisdom. One's thoughts about how to live must be true, and one must have correctly reasoned one's way to the recognition of those truths. In this respect, having practical wisdom is like having a proof in mathematics or logic: however strong one's impression is that one has demonstrated a theorem, one's efforts are a failure, if they do not conform to an external standard of correctness. For Aristotle, even if someone acts and feels just as a virtuous person would, and even if he enjoys such activity, he does not actually have a genuine virtue, and so does not live well, if that activity does not arise from a reasoned and true conception of well-being.

He is of course right to this extent: part of what makes an act ethically virtuous is its conformity to the correct standard of virtue. Just acts, for example, must distribute goods correctly—it is hardly enough that one has a certain feeling or thought when one tries to do the just thing. But he goes farther, because he adds that these sorts of actions do not count as good for the agent unless he has correctly reasoned his way to an understanding of why he should act justly. However similar his behavior, feelings, and thoughts are to those of a virtuous person, he will merely be acting as a virtuous person acts, but will not be expressing a genuine virtue, unless what ultimately motivates him is a well-reasoned understanding of the proper ends of human life And so the experiences he has as he acts virtuously will not be good for him, just as the experiences created by the experience machine are thought by some to be without value because they do not arise from one's encounter with the real world.

This aspect of his departure from experientialism, like his limited acceptance of posthumous goods, should not be of serious concern to an experientialist. For his thesis that one cannot have a good life unless one has the sophisticated intellectual virtue of practical wisdom is unattractive and should be rejected. It should be replaced by the thesis that the quality of one's life is unlikely to be high if one is guided in one's choices by badly mistaken assumptions about what has prudential value. Even so, some people are lucky. They just happen to have the right ideas about what well-being is, not having given the matter much thought. They do not have *phronêsis* as Aristotle understands that state of mind, but fortunately their assumptions about what to seek for their own good are correct. If their lives are filled with good experiences, they live well, even though they lack a philosophical understanding of well-being.

Aristotle's thinking about well-being is guided by assumptions about human development and about how humans differ from animals, and these sometimes serve him well and sometimes badly. His great insight is that we do well to develop our natural faculties, taking the rudimentary potentialities of infancy and childhood and training them so that they benefit us (and others) when we are adults. The times of our lives are not equal, if they are judged in terms of the value of what they can contain. Our lives go best for us when we move beyond the pleasures of childhood and develop our powers of reasoning and feeling in a way that makes us full participants in ethical relationships and other adult activities (such as philosophy, science, poetry, and theater). When that happens, human life is superior to the kinds of lives that other animals can have. They too can experience pleasure and some of them even have a small measure of virtue and intelligence. But some pleasures are immeasurably inferior to others—we would not and should not exchange a small amount of the higher pleasures for any amount of those that are inferior. What Aristotle gets wrong here is childhood, which he regards as a period that does not count in the assessment of total lifetime well-being.

His statement that well-being is not a matter of a day or a short time should be contrasted with the later view, shared by Epicurus, the Stoics and Plotinus, that it does not matter whether one has a smaller or a larger temporal dose of well-being. Surely there is more plausibility in his thesis than theirs. One of the features of well-being that makes it philosophically perplexing is that it has—or seems to have—a temporal dimension. How do we bring together its inevitable ups and downs into a single all-things-considered retrospective assessment of its quality? Is this a matter of mere addition and subtraction? Aristotle's approach to this subject is far more sensible than that of these later schools, but it is marred by his assumption that a well-lived life must be guided by a single goal throughout.

I have not adopted his view that one's own good, properly understood, never conflicts with that of others, nor his thesis that people who care little or not at all about acting rightly in ethical matters cannot have good lives because they are ethical failures. These aspects of his outlook on the human situation are too rosy. Even so, moral philosophy would be guilty of evasion if it neglected or refused to confront the question Aristotle faces—one he inherits from Plato's *Republic*: are there prudential reasons to be a good person and act as a good person acts? It would be bad news for us if there were none, or if such goods were not robust enough to constitute a flourishing life, apart from the social advantages that accompany a reputation for virtue, or the heavenly rewards bestowed in an afterlife. That issue properly belongs on the agenda of philosophical ethics.

An experientialist conception of well-being helps us see that the human situation is not as dark as we might have feared. What it is like to be a good person is an excellent reason to want to become one, or to be a better person. It is unique among prudential goods, because the moral realm is the sphere of everyday social interaction that every child must learn to participate in. It is good news that a high quality of life is available not only to those lucky enough to know the joys of intellectual inquiry, or to excel in the realms of athletics and dance, or to be transported by literature, music, and the other fine arts. It is available to any morally sensitive human being upon whom no lifelong and grave misfortune descends. If only one could protect oneself against such misfortune, and yet experience all the good that human life has to offer!—that is the aspiration that explains the appeal of an experience machine. To the fortunate, reality already is such a machine. They have need of no other.

Bibliography

Ancient Authors

Aristotle, *Nicomachean Ethics*, translated and edited by Roger Crisp (Cambridge: Cambridge University Press, 2000).

Cicero, *On Moral Ends* (*De Finibus*), translated by Raphael Woolf, edited by Julia Annas (Cambridge: Cambridge University Press, 2001).

Diogenes Laertius, *Lives of Eminent Philosophers*, The Loeb Classical Library, vol. 1 (Cambridge, MA: Harvard University Press, 1972).

Epicurus, *The Principal Doctrines*, translated and edited by Brad Inwood and L. P. Gerson, in *The Epicurus Reader: Selected Writings and Testimonia* (Indianapolis, IN: Hackett Publishing, 1994).

Marcus Aurelius, *Meditations*, translated by G. M. A. Grube (Indianapolis, IN: Hackett Publishing, 1983).

Plato, *Complete Works*, edited by John M. Cooper, associate editor D. S. Hutchinson (Indianapolis, IN: Hackett Publishing, 1997).

Plato, *Republic*, translated from the New Standard Greek Text, with Introduction by C. D. C. Reeve (Indianapolis, IN: Hackett Publishing, 2004).

Plotinus, *Enneads*, vol. 1, translated by A. H. Armstrong, Loeb Classical Library (Cambridge, MA: Harvard University Press, 1966).

Modern Authors

Annas, Julia, 'Virtue Ethics and the Charge of Egoism,' in Paul Bloomfield (ed.), *Morality and Self Interest*, 205–21 (Oxford: Oxford University Press, 2008).

Arrhenius, Gustaf and Wlodek Rabinowicz, 'Value Superiority,' in Iwao Hirose and Jonas Olson (eds.), *The Oxford Handbook of Value Theory*, 225–48 (Oxford: Oxford University Press, 2015).

Arrhenius, Gustaf, Jesper Ryberg, and Torbjörn Tännsiö, 'The Repugnant Conclusion,' in Edward N. Zalta (ed.), *The Stanford Encyclopedia of Philosophy*, <https://plato.stanford.edu/entries/repugnant-conclusion/>, January 2017.

Badhwar, Neera K., *Well-Being: Happiness in a Worthwhile Life* (Oxford: Oxford University Press, 2014).

Bloomfield, Paul, *The Virtues of Happiness: A Theory of the Good Life* (New York: Oxford University Press, 2014).

Bommarito, Nicolas, *Inner Virtue* (Oxford: Oxford University Press, 2018).

Bonds, Mark Evan, *Absolute Music: The History of an Idea* (New York: Oxford University Press, 2014).

Bradford, Gwen, 'Perfectionism,' in Guy Fletcher (ed.), *The Routledge Handbook of Philosophy of Well-Being*, 124–34 (London: Routledge, 2016).

Bradley, Ben, *Well-Being and Death* (Oxford: Clarendon Press, 2009).

Bradley, Ben, 'Objective Theories of Well-Being,' in Ben Eggleston and Dale E. Miller (eds.), *The Cambridge Companion to Utilitarianism*, 220–38 (Cambridge: Cambridge University Press, 2014).

Brandt, Richard, *A Theory of the Right and the Good* (Oxford: Clarendon Press, 1979).

Brink, David O., 'Self-Love and Altruism,' *Social Philosophy and Policy* 14 (1997), 122–57.

Brink, David O., 'Prospects for Temporal Neutrality,' in Craig Callender (ed.), *The Oxford Handbook of the Philosophy of Time*, 353–81 (Oxford: Oxford University Press, 2011).

Brink, David O., *Mill's Progressive Principles* (Oxford: Clarendon Press, 2013).

Broad, C. D., *Five Types of Ethical Theory* (London: Routledge & Kegan Paul, 1930).

Broome, John, *Weighing Lives* (Oxford: Oxford University Press, 2004).

Bykvist, Krister, 'Value and Time,' in Iwao Hirose and Jonas Olson (eds.), *The Oxford Handbook of Value Theory*, 117–35 (Oxford: Oxford University Press, 2015).

Campbell, Stephen M., 'The Concept of Well-Being,' in Guy Fletcher (ed.), *The Routledge Handbook of Philosophy of Well-Being*, 402–13 (London: Routledge, 2016).

Carlson, Erik, 'Organic Unities,' in Iwao Hirose and Jonas Olson (eds.), *The Oxford Handbook of Value Theory*, 285–99 (Oxford: Oxford University Press, 2015).

Caston, Victor, *The Stoics on Content and Mental Representation* (Cambridge: Cambridge University Press, forthcoming).

Chamovitz, Daniel, *What a Plant Knows* (New York: Farrar, Straus & Giroux, 2012).

Chang, Ruth, 'Value Incomparability and Incommensurability,' in Iwao Hirose and Jonas Olson (eds.), *The Oxford Handbook of Value Theory*, 205–24 (Oxford: Oxford University Press, 2015).

Chudnoff, Elijah, *Intuition* (Oxford: Oxford University Press, 2013).

Crisp, Roger, *Routledge Philosophy Guidebook to Mill on Utilitarianism* (London: Routledge, 1997).

Crisp, Roger, 'Hedonism Reconsidered,' *Philosophy and Phenomenological Research* 73 (2006), 619–45.

Crisp, Roger, *Reasons and the Good* (Oxford: Clarendon Press, 2006).

Crisp, Roger, 'Pleasure and Hedonism in Sidgwick,' in Thomas Hurka (ed.), *Underivative Duty: British Moral Philosophers from Sidgwick to Ewing*, 26–44 (Oxford: Oxford University Press, 2011).

Crisp, Roger, 'Well-Being,' in Edward N. Zalta (ed.), *The Stanford Encyclopedia of Philosophy*, <https://plato.stanford.edu/entries/well-being/>, May 2013.

Crisp, Roger, *The Cosmos of Duty: Henry Sidgwick's Methods of Ethics* (Oxford: Clarendon Press, 2015).

Dainton, Barry, 'Time Passage and Immediate Experience,' in Craig Callender (ed.), *The Oxford Handbook of Philosophy of Time*, 382–419 (Oxford: Oxford University Press, 2011).

Darwall, Stephen, *Welfare and Rational Care* (Princeton, NJ: Princeton University Press, 2002).

De Brigard, Felipe, 'If You Like It, Does It Matter If It's Real?,' *Philosophical Psychology* 23 (2010), 43–57.

Destrée, Pierre, 'Aristotle on The Paradox of Tragic Pleasure,' in Jerrold Levinson (ed.), *Suffering Art Gladly: The Paradox of Negative Emotion in Art*, 3–27 (New York: Palgrave Macmillan, 2014).

Emilsson, Eyjólfur K., 'On the Length of a Good Life,' in Steven Luper (ed.), *The Cambridge Companion to Life and Death*, 118–31 (Cambridge: Cambridge University Press, 2014).

Feldman, Fred, *Pleasure and the Good Life: Concerning the Nature, Varieties, and Plausibility of Hedonism* (Oxford: Clarendon Press, 2004).

Feldman, Fred, 'What We Learn From the Experience Machine,' in Ralf M. Bader and John Meadowcroft (eds.), *The Cambridge Companion to Nozick's Anarchy, State, and Utopia*, 59–86 (Cambridge: Cambridge University Press, 2011).

Fletcher, Guy, 'Objective List Theories,' in Guy Fletcher (ed.), *The Routledge Handbook of Philosophy of Well-Being*, 148–60 (London: Routledge, 2016).

Foot, Philippa, *Natural Goodness* (Oxford: Clarendon Press, 2001).

Frankfurt, Harry G., *On Inequality* (Princeton, NJ: Princeton University Press, 2015).

Gershwin, Lisa-ann, *Stung! On Jellyfish Blooms and the Future of the Ocean* (Chicago, IL: University of Chicago Press, 2016).

Glover, Jonathan, *What Sort of People Should There Be?* (Harmondsworth: Penguin Books, 1984).

Goethe, Johann Wolfgang, *Sämtliche Werke*, Band 7/1. *Faust*, Texte, herausgegeben von Albrecht Schöne (Frankfurt am Main: Deutscher Klassiker Verlag, 1994).

Goldie, Peter, *The Mess Inside: Narrative, Emotion, and the Mind* (Oxford: Oxford University Press, 2012).

Griffin, James, *Well-Being: Its Meaning, Measurement, and Moral Importance* (Oxford: Clarendon Press, 1986).

Hadot, Pierre, '"Only the Present is Our Happiness": The Value of the Present Instant in Goethe and in Ancient Philosophy,' in *Philosophy as a Way of Life*, edited with an introduction by Arnold I. Davidson, 217–37 (Oxford: Blackwell, 1995).

Hawkins, Jennifer, 'The Experience Machine and the Experience Requirement,' in Guy Fletcher (ed.), *The Routledge Handbook of Philosophy of Well-Being*, 355–65 (London: Routledge, 2016).

Haybron, Daniel M., *The Pursuit of Unhappiness: The Elusive Psychology of Well-Being* (Oxford: Oxford University Press, 2008).

Heathwood, Chris, 'Subjective Theories of Well-Being,' in Ben Eggleston and Dale E. Miller (eds.), *The Cambridge Companion to Utilitarianism*, 199–219 (Cambridge: Cambridge University Press, 2014).

Heathwood, Chris, 'Desire-Fulfillment Theory,' in Guy Fletcher (ed.), *The Routledge Handbook of Philosophy of Well-Being*, 135–47 (London: Routledge, 2016).

Hirose, Iwao, *Egalitarianism* (London: Routledge, 2015).

Hurka, Thomas, *Perfectionism* (New York: Oxford University Press, 1993).

Hurka, Thomas, *Virtue, Vice, and Value* (Oxford: Oxford University Press, 2001).

Hurka, Thomas, *The Best Things in Life: A Guide to What Really Matters* (Oxford: Oxford University Press, 2011).

Hurka, Thomas, 'The Well-Rounded Life,' in *Drawing Morals: Essays in Ethical Theory*, 37–54 (Oxford: Oxford University Press, 2011).

Hurka, Thomas, 'Two Kinds of Organic Unity,' in *Drawing Morals: Essays in Ethical Theory*, 94–112 (Oxford: Oxford University Press, 2011).

Hurka, Thomas, 'Aristotle on Virtue: Wrong, Wrong, and Wrong,' in Julia Peters (ed.), *Aristotelian Ethics in Contemporary Perspective*, 27–36 (New York: Routledge, 2013).

Hurka, Thomas, *British Ethical Theorists from Sidgwick to Ewing* (Oxford: Oxford University Press, 2014).

Hursthouse, Rosalind, *On Virtue Ethics* (Oxford: Oxford University Press, 1999).

Irwin, Terence, 'Conceptions of Happiness in the *Nicomachean Ethics*,' in Christopher Shields (ed.), *The Oxford Handbook of Aristotle*, 495–528 (Oxford: Oxford University Press, 2012).

Ismael, Jenann, 'Temporal Experience,' in Craig Callender (ed.), *The Oxford Handbook of Philosophy of Time*, 460–82 (Oxford: Oxford University Press, 2011).

Joyce, James, *Portrait of the Artist as a Young Man*, edited with an introduction and notes by Seamus Deane (New York: Penguin Random House, 2016). First published 1916.

Kagan, Shelly, 'The Limits of Well-Being,' *Social Philosophy and Policy* 9 (1992), 169–89.

Kagan, Shelly, 'Me and My Life,' *Proceedings of the Aristotelian Society* 94 (1994), 309–24.

Kagan, Shelly, *Death* (New Haven, CT: Yale University Press, 2012).

Kamm, F. M., *Morality, Mortality*, vol. 1 (New York: Oxford University Press, 1993).

Kant, Immanuel, *Foundations of the Metaphysics of Morals*, edited by Thomas Hill and translated by Arnulf Zweig (Oxford: Oxford University Press, 2003). First published 1785.

Keller, Simon, 'Posthumous Harm,' in Steven Luper (ed.), *The Cambridge Companion to Life and Death*, 181–97 (Cambridge: Cambridge University Press, 2014).

Kivy, Peter, *Music Alone: Philosophical Reflections on the Purely Musical Experience* (Ithaca, NY: Cornell University Press, 1990).

Kivy, Peter, *Introduction to a Philosophy of Music* (Oxford: Clarendon Press, 2002).

Kivy, Peter, *Antithetical Arts: On the Ancient Quarrel Between Literature and Music* (Oxford: Clarendon Press, 2009).

Kraut, Richard, 'Two Conceptions of Happiness,' *Philosophical Review* 88 (1979), 167–97.

Kraut, Richard, *Aristotle on the Human Good* (Princeton, NJ: Princeton University Press, 1989).

Kraut, Richard, *Aristotle Politics Books VII and VIII*, Translation and Commentary (Oxford: Clarendon Press, 1997).

Kraut, Richard, 'Aristotle's Method of Ethics,' in Richard Kraut (ed.), *The Blackwell Guide to Aristotle's Ethics*, 76–95 (Malden, MA: Blackwell, 2006).

Kraut, Richard, *What Is Good and Why: The Ethics of Well-Being* (Cambridge, MA: Harvard University Press, 2007).

Kraut, Richard, *Against Absolute Goodness* (New York: Oxford University Press, 2011).

Kraut, Richard, 'Human Diversity and the Nature of Well-Being: Reflections on Sumner's Methodology,' *Res Philosophica* 90 (2013), 307–22.

Kraut, Richard, 'Aristotle on Well-Being,' in Guy Fletcher (ed.), *The Routledge Handbook of Philosophy of Well-Being*, 20–9 (London: Routledge, 2015).

Kraut, Richard, 'Altruism,' in Edward N. Zalta (ed.), *The Stanford Encyclopedia of Philosophy*, <https://plato.stanford.edu/entries/altruism/>, August 2016.

Kraut, Richard, Review of Neera K. Badhwar, *Well-Being: Happiness in a Worthwhile Life*, *Philosophical Review* 126 (2017), 390–3.

Kraut, Richard, 'Oysters and Experience Machines: Two Puzzles in Value Theory,' *The Tanner Lectures on Human Values*, vol. 37, forthcoming, 2019.

Kriegel, Uriah, *The Varieties of Consciousness* (Oxford: Oxford University Press, 2015).

Larmore, Charles, *The Practices of the Self* (Chicago, IL: University of Chicago Press, 2010).

Lazari-Radek, Katarzyna de and Peter Singer, *The Point of View of the Universe: Sidgwick and Contemporary Ethics* (Oxford: Oxford University Press, 2014).

Lear, Gabriel Richardson, 'Aristotle on Happiness and Long Life,' in Øyvind Rabbås, Eyjólfur K. Emilsson, Hallvard Fossheim, and Miira Tuominen (eds.), *The Quest for the Good Life: Ancient Philosophers on Happiness*, 127–45 (Oxford: Oxford University Press, 2015).

LeBar, Mark, *The Value of Living Well* (New York: Oxford University Press, 2013).

Lippert-Rasmussen, Kasper, *Luck Egalitarianism* (London: Bloomsbury, 2016).

Long, A. A. and D. N. Sedley, *The Hellenistic Philosophers*, vol. 1 (Cambridge: Cambridge University Press, 1987).

MacIntyre, Alasdair, *Ethics in the Conflicts of Modernity: An Essay on Desire, Practical Reasoning, and Narrative* (Cambridge: Cambridge University Press, 2016).

McKerlie, Dennis, 'McTaggart on Love,' in Thomas Hurka (ed.), *Underivative Duty: British Moral Philosophers from Sidgwick to Ewing*, 66–86 (Oxford: Oxford University Press, 2011).

McMahan, Jeff, *The Ethics of Killing: Problems at the Margins of Life* (Oxford: Oxford University Press, 2002).

McTaggart, J. M. E., *The Nature of Existence*, vol. 2 (Cambridge: Cambridge University Press, 1927).

Maddy, Penelope, *What Do Philosophers Do? Skepticism and the Practice of Philosophy* (Oxford: Oxford University Press, 2017).

Maher, Chauncey, *Plant Minds: A Philosophical Defense* (New York: Routledge, 2017).

Moore, G. E., 'Mr. McTaggart's Ethics,' *International Journal of Ethics* 13 (1903), 341–70.

Moore, G. E., *Principia Ethica*, revised edition, edited by T. Baldwin (Cambridge: Cambridge University Press, 1993). First published 1903.

Nagel, Thomas, *The Possibility of Altruism* (Oxford: Oxford University Press, 1970).

Nagel, Thomas, 'Death,' in *Mortal Questions*, 1–10 (Cambridge: Cambridge University Press, 1979).

Nagel, Thomas, 'What is it like to be a bat?,' in *Mortal Questions*, 165–80 (Cambridge: Cambridge University Press, 1979).

Nietzsche, Friedrich, *Twilight of the Idols, or How to Philosophize with a Hammer*, Oxford's World's Classics (Oxford: Oxford University Press, 1998). First published 1889.

Nietzsche, Friedrich, *The Birth of Tragedy out of the Spirit of Music*, Oxford World's Classics (Oxford: Oxford University Press, 2000). First published 1872.

Nozick, Robert, *Anarchy, State, and Utopia* (New York: Basic Books, 1974).

Nozick, Robert, *The Examined Life: Philosophical Meditations* (New York: Simon & Schuster, 1989).

Parfit, Derek, *Reasons and Persons* (Oxford: Clarendon Press, 1984), reprinted 1987.

Parfit, Derek, 'Overpopulation and the Quality of Life,' in Peter Singer (ed.), *Applied Ethics*, 145–64 (Oxford: Oxford University Press, 1986).

Parfit, Derek, 'Equality or Priority?' in Matthew Clayton and Andrew Williams (eds.), *The Idea of Equality*, 81–125 (Basingstoke: Palgrave Macmillan, 2002).

Parfit, Derek, *On What Matters*, vol. 1 (Oxford: Oxford University Press, 2011).

Parfit, Derek, *On What Matters*, vol. 3 (Oxford: Oxford University Press, 2017).

Pater, Walter, *The Renaissance: Studies in Art and Poetry* (London: Macmillan and Co., 1888; Mineola, NY: Dover Publications, 2005).

Pettit, Philip, *The Robust Demands of the Good: Ethics with Attachment, Virtue, and Respect* (Oxford: Oxford University Press, 2015).

Prichard, H. A., 'Does Moral Philosophy Rest on a Mistake?' *Mind* 21 (1912), 21–37; reprinted in *Moral Writings*, 7–20 (Oxford: Clarendon Press, 2002).

Pritchard, Duncan, *Epistemic Angst: Radial Skepticism and the Groundlessness of Our Believing* (Princeton, NJ: Princeton University Press, 2016).

Proust, Marcel, *In Search of Lost Time*, vol. 6, *Time Regained*, translated by Andreas Mayor and Terence Kilmartin, revised by D. J. Enright (New York: Modern Library, 1999). First published 1927.

Proust, Marcel, *In Search of Lost Time*, vol. 6, *Finding Time Again*, translated with an Introduction and Notes by Ian Patterson (London: Penguin Books, Allen Lane, 2002).

Putnam, Hilary, *Reason, Truth and History* (Cambridge: Cambridge University Press, 1981).

Railton, Peter, 'Facts and Values,' in *Facts, Values, and Norms: Essays Toward a Morality of Consequence*, 43–68 (Cambridge: Cambridge University Press, 2003).

Rawls, John, *A Theory of Justice* (Cambridge, MA: Harvard University Press, 1971).

Raz, Joseph, 'The Central Conflict: Morality and Self-Interest,' in Roger Crisp and Brad Hooker (eds.), *Well-Being and Morality: Essays in Honour of James Griffin*, 209–38 (Oxford: Clarendon Press, 2000).

Ridley, Aaron, 'Nietzsche and the Arts of Life,' in Ken Gemes and John Richardson (eds.), *The Oxford Handbook of Nietzsche*, 415–31 (Oxford: Oxford University Press, 2013).

Ross, W. D., *The Right and the Good* (Oxford: Clarendon Press, 1930).

Roth, Philip, *The Human Stain* (Boston, MA: Houghton Mifflin, 2000).

Russell, Bertrand, *The Problems of Philosophy* (New York: Oxford University Press, 1997). First published 1912.

Russell, Daniel C., *Happiness for Humans* (Oxford: Oxford University Press, 2012).

Sainsbury, R. M., *Fiction and Fictionalism* (London: Routledge, 2010).

Schechtman, Marya, *Staying Alive: Personal Identity, Practical Concerns, and the Unity of a Life* (Oxford: Oxford University Press, 2014).

Scheffler Samuel, *Death and the Afterlife* (Oxford: Oxford University Press, 2013).

Schmidtz, David and Christopher Freiman, 'Nozick,' in David Estlund (ed.), *The Oxford Handbook of Political Philosophy*, 411–28 (Oxford: Oxford University Press, 2012).

Sen, Amartya, 'Utilitarianism and Welfarism,' *The Journal of Philosophy* 76 (1979), 463–88.

Sidgwick, Henry, *Methods of Ethics*, 7th edn. (Indianapolis, IN: Hackett Publishing, 1981). First published 1907.

Skorupski, John, *The Domain of Reasons* (New York: Oxford University Press, 2010).

Slote, Michael, *Goods and Virtues* (Oxford: Clarendon Press, 1983).

Sumner, L. W., *Welfare, Happiness, and Ethics* (Oxford: Clarendon Press, 1996).

Temkin, Larry S., *Inequality* (New York: Oxford University Press, 1993).

Temkin, Larry S., *Rethinking the Good: Moral Ideals and the Nature of Practical Reasoning* (New York: Oxford University Press, 2012).

Thomasson, Amie L., *Fiction and Metaphysics* (Cambridge: Cambridge University Press, 1999).

Thompson, Michael, *Life and Action* (Cambridge, MA: Harvard University Press, 2008).

Tolstoy, Leo, *Anna Karenina*, translated by Marian Schwartz (New Haven, CT: Yale University Press, 2014). First published 1878.

Velleman, J. David, 'Well-Being and Time,' in *The Possibility of Practical Reflection*, 56–84 (Oxford: Clarendon Press, 2000).

Weijers, Dan, 'Nozick's Experience Machine is Dead, Long Live the Experience Machine!,' *Philosophical Psychology* 27 (2014), 515–35.

Weinberg, Rivka, *The Risk of a Lifetime: How, When, and Why Procreation May Be Permissible* (Oxford: Oxford University Press, 2016).

Whiting, Jennifer, *First, Second, and Other Selves: Essays on Friendship and Personal Identity* (Oxford: Oxford University Press, 2016).

Williams, Bernard, 'The Makropulos Case: Reflections on the Tedium of Immortality,' in *Problems of the Self*, 82–100 (Cambridge: Cambridge University Press, 1973).

Wohlleben, Peter, *The Hidden Life of Trees: What They Feel, How They Communicate* (Vancouver: Greystone Books, 2015).

Wolf, Susan, *Meaning in Life and Why It Matters* (Princeton, NJ: Princeton University Press, 2012).

Index